OBJECT-ORIENTED PROGRAMMING WITH ACTIONSCRIPT 2.0

JEFF TAPPER,
JAMES TALBOT, AND
ROBIN HAFFNER

www.newriders.com

800 East 96th Street, Indianapolis, Indiana 46240

An Imprint of Pearson Education

Boston • Indianapolis • London • Munich • New York • San Francisco

Object-Oriented Programming with ActionScript 2.0

International Standard Book Number: 0-7357-1380-4

Library of Congress Catalog Card Number: 2003116668

Printed in the United States of America

First printing: Febrary, 2004

09 08 07 06 05 04   7 6 5 4 3 2 1

Interpretation of the printing code: The rightmost double-digit number is the year of the book's printing; the rightmost single-digit number is the number of the book's printing. For example, the printing code 04-1 shows that the first printing of the book occurred in 2004.

Trademarks

Warning and Disclaimer

PUBLISHER
Stephanie Wall

PRODUCTION MANAGER
Gina Kanouse

ACQUISITIONS EDITOR
Linda Bump Harrison

DEVELOPMENT EDITOR
Jill Batistick

SENIOR PROJECT EDITOR
Kristy Hart

INDEXER
Lisa Stumpf

COMPOSITION
Amy Hassos

PROOFREADERS
Sarah Kearns
Debbie Williams

MANUFACTURING COORDINATOR
Dan Uhrig

INTERIOR DESIGNER
Wil Cruz

COVER DESIGNER
Aren Howell

MEDIA DEVELOPER
Jay Payne

MARKETING
Scott Cowlin
Tammy Detrich

PUBLICITY MANAGER
Susan Nixon

FROM JEFF:

As always, to my wife, Lisa. Without your continued love, support, encouragement, and patience, I wouldn't be here today.

FROM JAMES:

I would like to dedicate my contributions to my wife, Sally, who has served as my inspiration for everything.

FROM ROBIN:

My contributions to this book are dedicated to my husband, Peter—my rock.

Contents at a Glance

Table of Contents

SECTION III DESIGNING, IMPLEMENTING, AND DEBUGGING THE APPLICATION

About the Authors

Jeff Tapper is the Chief Technologist for Tapper.net Consulting. He has been developing internet-based applications since 1995 for a myriad of clients, including Toys R Us, IBM, Allaire, Dow Jones, American Express, M&T Bank, Verizon, and Allied Office Supplies, among others. As a Macromedia instructor, he is currently certified to teach all of Macromedia's courses on ColdFusion and Flash development.

Jeff has worked as a contributing author on *The Allaire Spectra e-Business Construction Kit, Advanced Macromedia ColdFusion 5 Application Development, Dynamic Publishing with ColdFusion MX* (New Riders Publishing, 2002) and the recently released *Macromedia Flash MX 2004 ActionScript 2.0 Dictionary* (Macromedia Press, 2003). He was also one of the technical editors for the updated *Flash MX 2004 Training from the Source* (Macromedia Press, 2003) book. He is also a frequent speaker at Macromedia Development Conferences and user groups. Jeff formed Tapper.net Consulting to focus on developing Rich Internet Applications and empowering clients through mentoring.

James Talbot has been with Macromedia for four years. Before he came to Macromedia, he was a Project Manager in the e-learning space where he worked with Flash and Generator. James started out at Macromedia as a Sales Engineer, and he traveled around the world visiting customers and doing seminars. After the Allaire merger, he moved to New York City and worked for the Macromedia Educational Services team. He has put together the Flash training curriculum, including co-authoring the "Developing Rich Internet Applications" course and the "Advanced ActionScript for Applications" course.

James has also worked directly with the Flash engineers and provided guidance on future product direction. He develops curriculum, teaches courses, performs instructor certifications, and assists with consulting assignments. Most recently, he has worked on high-visibility, high-profile sites for AOL/Time Warner and TV Guide. He has also worked on many of the Macromedia certification exams, contributed to articles and tutorials on DevNet, and has spoken at numerous conferences and trade shows.

 **Robin Haffner** is an Enterprise Technologist with HaffnerGraphic, a company she founded in January of 2000. After earning a computer science degree at Roger Williams University, Robin pursued a technical career that revolved around education and consulting. As a perpetual student, a dedicated instructor, and a consultant, she has kept ahead of the technology curve. Over the years, Robin has had the opportunity to speak internationally on many topics, including venues such as Macromedia DevCon 2001, 2002, 2003, Sybase User Conference Vienna, Austria 1997, Los Angeles, CA 1998, Orlando, FL 1999. Currently, Robin is engaged in Flash consulting for large-scale applications in the New York City area. Robin fills her spare time with golfing and sailing. She lives in Rhode Island with her two sons, Jonathan and Christopher, and husband, Pete.

About the Technical Editors

Aria Danika is an interactive designer, a Senior Moderator at Flashkit.com, and a member of the Hypermedia Research Centre in London where she completed her graduate studies. She originally trained as a photographer but turned to interactive media while pursuing a B.A. in multimedia and photography at Westminster University in London.

Aria freelanced for various broadcasters in the UK, including TV3, VH-1, and Granada, and she later joined the BBC for five years where she designed and developed rich media applications and games.

Aria is the contributor to *Flash MX Magic* (New Riders Publishing, 2002) and *Flash MX 2004 Magic* (New Riders Publishing, 2004) and has written articles on experience design and design for interaction. She is currently based in Brooklyn, NYC, spending her free time skateboarding, testing games, shooting short films, and exploring interactivity across different platforms. This has resulted in a series of sound/video experiments, installations, and web toys designed in Director and Flash. See `www.openedsource.net`.

MD Dundon is the author of *Macromedia Flash MX Production Techniques* and the creator, with Magnet Media (`www.digital-mediatraining.com`), of the video training CD "Inside Flash MX: Production Essentials." She has exposed her Flash-geekdom at conferences such as FlashForward, DEVCON, and TechTV™ Screen Savers. She has created the curriculum for several Flash training programs, including her current courses at sfsuonline.org: "Flash Production" and "Flash ActionScripting."

As founder of her company, Flash411, she has explored issues of interactivity in documentary photography, psychobiology, film directing, screenwriting, art/video installations, interface design, and usability. As an "experience" designer, she has developed cutting edge prototypes and working applications for e-learning, virtual reality, interactive television, and walk-through and Web-based interactions.

 **William B. Sanders** is a professor in the Interactive Information Technology program at the University of Hartford. He has written over 40 computer-related books, ranging from assembly language programming to Flash ActionScript. His interests in Internet applications and programming focus on the use of the Internet for developing natural interactive environments for use in business, entertainment, and pure sociability. Flash, including Flash Communication Server, Communication ActionScript, and ActionScript 2.0, have proven to be the ideal tools for developing such rich interactive applications. Bill founded Sandlight Productions (www.sandlight.com) in 1984.

Acknowledgments

From Jeff Tapper: I would like to thank my co-authors, James Talbot and Robin Haffner. This book would never have been possible without them. Thanks are also due to Kevin Towes. Without his knowledge of Flash Communication Server and his unique demeanor in presenting that knowledge, the book would be incomplete. Thanks are also due to the editorial team at New Riders: Linda, Jill, Stephanie, and Angela. Your hard work and dedication shaped our raw ideas into a complete work.

Several others who didn't contribute specifically to the book were still integral to the process. Jon Briccetti, Ben Elmore, and George Jagodzinski acted as frequent sounding boards, helping me through specific issues along the way. Thanks also to Bryan Rice, as he was a tremendous help in building the application.

Of course, thanks are due to my family: Mom, Dad, Dan, Jon, and Gram. Your love and support has never faltered over the years. Lastly, none of this would be possible without my wife, Lisa.

From James Talbot: I would like to thank my co-authors Robin Haffner and Jeff Tapper who have made this book possible. I would also like to thank the Macromedia Educational Services team, including Matt Boles, Robert Crooks, Sue Hove, and Jeanette Stallons for all of their help and advice.

From Robin Haffner: In everyone's life there is usually a person that is a driving force and a mentor. I am fortunate to have had four very special mentors in my life. First—my mother, without whom I wouldn't have had the strength and perseverance to survive my 20s and 30s. Second—my grandmother who taught me compassion and faith, both of which have served me well in all facets of my life. Last—Ginny Cavallaro and Dr. Ruth Koelle for making me reach higher and expect more from life...and I haven't stopped yet.

I would also like to thank New Riders, Jeff Tapper, and James Talbot for making me a part of this project.

Tell Us What You Think

As the reader of this book, you are the most important critic and commentator. We value your opinion and want to know what we're doing right, what we could do better, what areas you'd like to see us publish in, and any other words of wisdom you're willing to pass our way.

As a Senior Acquisitions Editor for New Riders Publishing and Peachpit Press, I welcome your comments. You can fax, email, or write me directly to let me know what you did or didn't like about this book—as well as what we can do to make our books stronger. When you write, please be sure to include this book's title, ISBN, and author, as well as your name and phone or fax number. I will
carefully review your comments and share them with the author and editors who worked on the book.

Please note that I cannot help you with technical problems related to the topic of this book, and that due to the high volume of email I receive, I might not be able to reply to every message.

Fax: 317-581-4663

Email: linda.harrison@peachpit.com

Mail: Linda Bump Harrison
          Senior Acquisitions Editor
          New Riders Publishing/Peachpit Press
          800 East 96th Street, Third Floor
          Indianapolis, IN 46240 USA

INTRODUCTION

Thanks for buying our book. For those of you just browsing this on the shelves in the book store, I hope this introduction is compelling enough to entice you to buy. I'd like to think of this as a real page-turner, a who-done-it that will keep you up at night guessing what's going to come next. Of course, this book is really just an attempt to help bring about an understanding of object-oriented programming (OOP), ActionScript 2.0, and the interaction of the two.

Who Should Read This Book

There are a few audiences at which we are directing this book. One audience comprises existing Flash developers. These people are familiar with ActionScript (either the current version or previous versions), and they want to learn more about the benefits of OOP and how it is done in ActionScript 2.0. The second audience comprises programmers. These people are comfortable with OOP and want to learn how to apply the OOP principles they know from other languages in ActionScript 2.0.

Who Shouldn't Read This Book

It's hard for me to dissuade anyone from purchasing this book. However, the reality is that there are some audiences who will not benefit as much as others from it. This book is not an introduction to programming. Although it doesn't assume all readers have years of experience developing applications, it does assume a basic knowledge of programming terminology and constructs (for example, we don't explain what a conditional statement or loop is). A basic understanding of programming principles (variables, functions, conditions, and loops) will greatly aid the reader.

This book is also not intended as an introduction to the Macromedia Flash MX 2004 interface. There are several very good books that cover the topic in depth. We simply chose to focus on the fairly specialized topic of OOP with ActionScript 2.0.

Lastly, folks without a sense of humor may have trouble with this book. We have taken great pains to attempt to keep this text light-hearted and humorous. Please understand that we mean no offence by our attempts at levity. The material covered in this book is deep and detailed, and we make our best efforts to keep readers from becoming bored as they read and (hopefully) learn from it.

About This Book

Depending on the experience you bring with you as you read this book, you may want to approach it in different ways. Chapter 1, "What's New in ActionScript 2.0?", is applicable to anyone not yet familiar with the constructs of ActionScript 2.0, and it will be particularly meaningful to developers with experience using ActionScript 1.0. Chapter 2, "All the World Is an Object," focuses on the benefits of OOP. Developers already comfortable with the concepts of OOP and the reasons one would choose to build an application following OOP principles can safely skip Chapter 2. Chapters 3–9 look at specific OOP constructs and discuss their implementation in ActionScript 2.0.

This Book's Organization

Organizationally, this book is divided into three main sections:

    I. The Basics (using OOP with ActionScript 2.0)

    II. The Other Half of the Equation (using a server in Flash applications)

    III. Designing, Implementing, and Debugging the Application

Section I (Chapters 1–9) begins with an introduction to ActionScript 2.0 in Chapter 1. Chapters 2–4 take on the specifics of building classes in ActionScript 2.0, as well as adding properties and methods to those classes. Chapters 5 and 6, "The Meek Shall Inherit the Earth" and "Understanding Interfaces in ActionScript 2.0," respectively, address inheritance and interfaces. Chapter 7, "Are You Talking to Me," explains inter-object communications, and Chapter 8, "Object-Oriented Design," investigates the details and implications of object-oriented design as a process. Chapter 9, "Building and Using UI Components," looks at working with Flash UI components, as well as building custom components.

Section II (Chapters 10–15) investigates the server-side of applications. In the new Rich Internet Application (RIA) paradigm, Flash MX 2004 is used to build an Internet-based client-server application. Chapter 10, "To Protect and Serve," discusses why a server would be needed. Chapters 11–14 discuss specific methods to interact with different server-side technologies, including Web Services, extensible markup language (XML) files, and even simple text files. Chapter 15, "Flash Communication Server MX Applications," looks at the specific ramifications of working with this technology and many of the benefits we can see in applications making use of it.

Section III (Chapters 16–17) uses the principles discussed in all the previous chapters to build a single cohesive application. Chapter 16, "Pulling It All Together," walks through building an application, starting from the functional and business requirements straight through the implementation. Chapter 17, "Debugging and Tuning the Application," describes how to troubleshoot and optimize the application.

Planning, Designing, Building, and Testing the Application

Rather than building a single application throughout all the chapters in this book, we decided it would be better to let each chapter use whatever examples best fit. So, we've dedicated Section III to using the lessons from the book in a single application. By taking this approach, we enable readers to pick and choose which chapters they care to read, and we give everyone an equal opportunity to build the application, even though they may have skipped some chapters along the way.

The application we build in Section III is an intranet-based call center application. It is for a phone-based, magazine–subscription-selling company (XYZ Subscriptions). It describes the entire process in building their application, beginning with an investigation of what their current application is and why it needs to be replaced, moving through the requirements gathering phase, proceeding on to the technical design of the application, and finally moving on to the implementation.

Chapter 17 then takes this application and walks through the process of debugging and tuning it, pointing out several great tips along the way.

Why Do We Care About OOP?

This entire book focuses on developing object-oriented applications. This often brings out the question, "Why should I build this application using OOP, instead of the traditional way I've built applications for years?" Unfortunately, there is no one easy answer to this question, but like most business decisions, it becomes a matter of time and money.

An object-oriented system acts as a scale model of the business entity for which it was built. By designing the system this way, the system can be adaptive to the business it was built to serve.

Studies have repeatedly shown that 70–80 percent of all costs throughout the lifecycle of a software project come after the software has been launched. Specifically, these costs result from maintenance and changes to the software. Object-oriented systems by their nature are more adaptable to change and therefore can reduce these costs significantly.

The three key benefits of OOP are extensibility, reusability, and adaptability:

- **Extensibility.** An object designed with this in mind is more likely to be reusable in other applications for that business; for example, a product company with an object modeled around their products can likely use that object in all their applications. Additionally, these objects are more likely to be adaptable or extensible to other needs for that same business.
- **Reusability.** If an object can be reused from other projects, it doesn't need to be built or tested again. This saves time and money.
- **Adaptability.** An object that is easily adaptable in new and originally unforeseen situations mitigates the need for new development, also saving time and money.

The true differentiations between procedural programming and OOP are three key concepts known as encapsulation, inheritance, and delegation.

Encapsulation

The most basic concept of object-oriented design is encapsulation. Encapsulation is nothing more than designing a system with objects that contain all the data of an entity in the system (properties) as well as all the actions that can be done to or by the entity (methods). It is this encapsulation that is the core difference between OOP and procedural programming.

The procedural world uses a series of independent functions to achieve its goals, and each function requires that the data on which it operates be passed to it with each invocation. In a well-designed, object-oriented system, these functions are *encapsulated* into objects as methods. The objects with these methods are self-aware, meaning that the data of the object does not need to be passed into the method.

In Chapter 7, we examine the idea of messages, which is how objects talk to each other. You will see that in inter-object communication, data is still passed into the methods, but methods operating on the objects to which they belong have no such need.

Inheritance

As you model objects based on the real-world objects they mimic, you find relationships between objects that can be defined by the model "x is a y." One example of this is "a triangle is a shape." In the object-oriented world, you could implement this type of relationship with inheritance. Thus, any properties and methods of the Shape class would be inherited by the Triangle class.

Let's look deeper into this example. Triangles come in many varieties: isosceles (where two sides have equal lengths), equilateral (where all three sides have equal lengths), and right (where two sides meet at a 90-degree angle). Of course, there are also triangles that meet none of these conditions.

It is safe to say that all four types of triangles share the properties and methods of a triangle. What are the properties of a triangle? Every triangle has a number of sides (always three, by definition). They also have a height and width (often referred to as a "base" for triangles). How about methods? What can be done to, or with, a triangle? A simple method available for all triangles is the ability to calculate the area. Listing I.1 shows a simple Triangle class.

LISTING I.1   A Simple Triangle Class Definiti on

```
class Triangle{
      var sides:Number=3;
      var height:Number;
      var base:Number;
      function calculateArea():Number{
            return .5*height*base;
      }
}
```

> **NOTE**
>
> Don't worry about the specific syntax here; class definition is covered in detail in Chapter 2.

This code defines a `Triangle` class that has three properties (`sides`, `height`, and `base`) and one method (`calculateArea`). Using inheritance, you could build a *subclass* that takes this class as a foundation and builds on it. `Equilateral`, `Isosceles`, and `RightTriangle` classes could all be created as subclasses of `Triangle`. They would all have access to the properties and methods defined here for the `Triangle` class, without the need to cut and paste this definition into each of them.

> **NOTE**
>
> Inheritance is covered in detail in Chapter 5.

The ability to extend an existing class into a new class using inheritance is one of the key reasons object-oriented applications are as adaptable as they are. The core classes do not need to be redesigned to cover every possibility. Instead, they are designed to cover the details common across all instances, and sub-classes are used to cover the differences.

Polymorphism

Polymorphism is a way of describing something that can take many forms, meaning that it can react differently in different contexts. Chapter 5 delves into the concepts of polymorphism and how it applies to development.

In a polymorphic system, the same command can be interpreted by different objects independently. In the real-world example of driving a car, the driver sends a message to drive the car by putting the car in gear and pressing the gas pedal. How this message is interpreted by the car will vary greatly, based on whether it is a gas or electric engine and whether it is carbureted or fuel injected. However, the end result is always the same. The great benefit of polymorphism is that we need not understand how the object will interpret the command; we can simply tell the object what we want it to do and then let it be done.

In the object-oriented world, we can use polymorphism in a similar fashion. A subclass can use the methods of its parent class or override those methods in its own implementation. Therefore, it can always be known that the class will have a method with the same name as the method of the superclass, but we do not need to know specifically how that subclass will implement its method.

OOP Versus Object-Oriented Languages

Developing an application in an object-oriented language does not mean one is developing an object-oriented application. It is not only possible, but common, to find applications written in an object-oriented language, such as C++, Java, or even ActionScript 2.0, that follow none of the principles of OOP. An object-oriented language has the tools necessary for one to do OOP, although, as the cliché goes, "Owning a hammer won't make you a carpenter."

OOP involves more than the use of an object-oriented language; it requires planning, thought, and design. It also requires the will to implement the system using object-oriented principles. Implementing an application using OOP can seem a daunting task. Many newcomers will dip their toes in the proverbial OOP waters, but fall back on the familiar patterns of procedural programming. Nonetheless, with a bit of practice, newcomers will soon realize that building systems with OOP reaps many benefits.

> **NOTE**
>
> Object-oriented design is covered in detail in Chapter 8.

Conventions Used Within This Book

Understanding a few typographic conventions in this book will help you in your readings:

- New terms are set in *italics* the first time they are used.
- Objects, classes, properties, methods, and other "computer language" words are set in a fixed-pitch font, like so: `var me:Person = new Person("Jeff","Tapper","author");`.
- Any variables, objects, classes, and so on used within a paragraph are shown in code font, like this: `ASampleClassName`.
- Any text instance that you are asked to type are set in **boldface.**

Moving Forward

Clearly, OOP is a vast topic. In this introduction, the foundation was laid, giving quick definitions of the key concepts. Many more details will follow over the next several chapters. Chapters 2, 3, and 4 explore classes and the entities that comprise them (properties and methods). Chapter 5 explores inheritance. Chapter 6 explains a concept similar to inheritance—interfaces. Chapter 7 delves into communications between objects, and Chapter 8 gives a primer on the fundamentals of object-oriented design. Don't despair if this is all a bit overwhelming at the moment. The more you work with these in everyday development, the easier the concepts will become.

We hope reading this book brings you far more enjoyment than it brought those of us who wrote it (just kidding!). Actually, we sincerely hope you enjoy your explorations of the world of OOP with ActionScript 2.0 and that you find this book to be the perfect guide.

For the latest updates on code used in the book, errata, and other notes, please see our website at `www.oopas2.com`.

SECTION I
THE BASICS

CHAPTER 1

WHAT'S NEW IN ACTIONSCRIPT 2.0?

What Is ActionScript 2.0?

With each new version of ActionScript, Flash developers have pushed the ActionScript language to its limits. To compete in the world of Rich Internet Applications (RIAs), Macromedia has had to take ActionScript to the next level and provide a language that uses a model that enables seasoned application developers to embrace ActionScript. The model also had to provide enhanced functionality to Flash developers. To do this, the entire language has been restructured and new standards have been put in place. ActionScript 2.0 enables the development of more reusable, maintainable, and scaleable applications that appeal to both large and small development teams because it is now an object-oriented language.

Improvements in ActionScript

ActionScript 2.0 conforms to a familiar and more mainstream model for writing applications: the JavaScript 2.0 and ECMAScript Edition 4 proposal.

The ActionScript 2.0 constructs in the following list have been taken directly from the ECMAScript 4 proposal at `www.mozilla.org/js/language/es4/`:

- Variable typing
- Static members
- Public and private members
- Implicit getters/setters
- The Class construct
- Packages

The implementation of interfaces was taken directly from the JavaScript 2 proposal available at `www.mozilla.org/js/language/js20/index.html`.

The ActionScript 2.0 language is much easier to learn for anyone who has had experience with an object-oriented language, and many of the frustrations encountered with ActionScript 1.0 are no longer an issue.

The ActionScript editor itself has also been greatly improved. Normal mode has been eliminated and word wrap has finally been implemented in the editor. Scripts can now be imported as well as exported from the Actions panel. In the Professional edition, it is possible to edit ActionScript files (files with the extension .AS) directly, without seeing the timeline or any other tools.

Before and After in ActionScript

Much of the syntax in ActionScript 1.0 is strange and clunky even to experienced application developers. The language is loosely typed and does not provide an adequate level of error handling. As an example of the difficulty in learning ActionScript for a server-side person, imagine that a Java or C# developer was tasked with learning ActionScript 1.0 to add a front end to a server-side application. For most people familiar with the syntax of an object-oriented language, the weird prototype chaining of ActionScript 1.0 would seem strange and intimidating.

The process of creating classes in ActionScript 1.0 is an odd and convoluted process for those unfamiliar with ActionScript; it bears little resemblance to any other object-oriented language. Finally, the error handling inherent in

ActionScript 1.0 is enough to make someone pull out their hair in frustration! Simply spelling a method name or property incorrectly can result in huge frustrations because Macromedia Flash MX 2004 does not always tell the developer about these errors. It just sits there and does nothing!

The new standards of coding in ActionScript 2.0 remedy these problems and enable the user to specify a datatype when declaring variables, use a standard class construct when defining classes, and enable simple and intuitive organization of the application through packages. Best of all, it generates accurate and detailed compile-time errors, as seen in Figure 1.1.

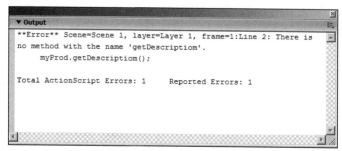

FIGURE 1.1   Flash now has an error-handling system to make the lives of developers much easier.

Using ActionScript 2.0 to Publish Flash Player 6 Applications

Although the language itself has been entirely restructured to follow uniform coding standards, it is possible to use ActionScript 2.0 to develop for Flash Player 6. The new functionality in ActionScript 2.0 runs on Flash Player 6 because the ActionScript 2.0 code is ultimately compiled to ActionScript 1.0 code. Figure 1.2 shows the interface, which can be used to publish ActionScript 2.0 movies for Flash Player 6. More information on publishing for Flash Player 6 is available in the product help files.

Behind the scenes, the new ActionScript 2.0 class construct is actually a formalization of the dreaded prototype chain; of course, all the prototyping is completely hidden from ActionScript 2.0 developers. The main disadvantage of the old prototyping was that it was difficult for developers to learn because it did not follow object-oriented standards. To add methods or to create inheritance, you had to use the prototype property of the class. Ultimately, ActionScript 2.0 is still compiled to ActionScript 1.0; however, it is now hidden and it follows standards.

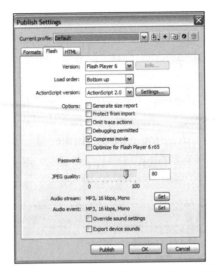

FIGURE 1.2   You can still target Flash Player 6 even when writing code in ActionScript 2.0.

An added benefit of restructuring the language is that Flash can extract more information about its own code and render practices such as using suffixes for objects (remember using _mc for the MovieClip object?) unnecessary. This is true because every object must be declared using variable typing. Even movie clips, components, and text fields can be formally declared in ActionScript 2.0 to take advantage of code hinting.

Whether you use ActionScript 1.0 or ActionScript 2.0, the performance of ActionScript is now blazingly fast. The compiler in Flash now performs enhanced optimizations to *all* ActionScript code that is compiled. These compiler optimizations greatly enhance the byte code that is generated from ActionScript. Variable-lookup function calls have all been greatly optimized. This results in impressive performance boosts for all ActionScript code, even if you are still writing your applications using ActionScript 1.0. In fact, just by republishing existing applications in Flash MX 2004 (even those that still use Flash Player 6), you can realize significant performance gains. The new ActionScript compiler alone justifies the upgrade to Flash MX 2004!

Basic Syntax

ActionScript 2.0 is a much more "strict" language than previous versions of ActionScript. As a best practice, you need to strictly type all your variables, although Flash will not fall over if you do not do this. However, Flash will provide better error handling and code hinting if you type all variables.

There are some situations where Flash will generate errors. For example, if you do not keep in mind that ActionScript is now a case-sensitive language or if you try to define classes on a timeline instead of in a separate file, Flash will have problems. We discuss each of these issues in turn.

Case Sensitivity

There are some changes Flash developers will have to get used to in ActionScript 2.0. First off, ActionScript 2.0 is a case-sensitive language. The following code displays as undefined because of the mixed case of the variable myProduct. In contrast to ActionScript 1.0, a variable must be referenced with the appropriate case.

```
var myProduct = "Call Center Server";
trace (myproduct);
```

Case sensitivity can be a big issue when using ActionScript 2.0 to develop for Flash Player 6 because case-sensitive variables can conflict. For example, Flash Player 7 would interpret the following code as two different variables, but Flash Player 6 would see these two as the same variable:

```
var myProduct = "Call Center Server";
var myproduct = "Call Center Client";
```

At its core, ActionScript is still interpreted by the Flash Player and this can cause conflicts at runtime (not compile time) when all the error checking occurs. In this situation, the Flash developer is responsible for debugging his or her own code; of course, this is not an issue if you use ActionScript 1.0, which is not a case-sensitive language (in most cases).

> **NOTE**
>
> The preceding ActionScript code is a definite bad practice; never use the same variable name and different case to create two different variables.

Typing Variables

Typing variables is purely a compile-time feature and it enables much more sophisticated error handling than any previous version of Flash. It is also how this version of Flash handles code hinting in the ActionScript editor.

Every class in ActionScript 2.0 has its own datatype, and each time that class is declared and instantiated, it should be preceded by the var keyword and its datatype. For example, if you created an object from the Object class, also known as instantiation, the following code would suffice:

```
myObject = new Object();
```

However, for code hinting and error handling, it would be a better practice to use the following code:

```
var myObject :Object = new Object();
```

Code Hinting

For code hinting to work with visual objects (such as the user interface [UI] components), you need to formally declare those objects in your ActionScript. Developers should always specify explicitly from what class a visual object is derived. At first, this might seem like a chore, but it is worth it. The following code shows variable typing for different types of objects, including strings, numbers, objects, and a visual object, ComboBox.

```
var productName:String = "Call Center Server"
var productNo:Number =2;
var myObject:Object = new Object();
var myCombo:mx.controls.ComboBox;
```

The following ActionScript code results in a syntax error because variable typing is not supported in this manner:

```
var myProduct:Object = new Object();
myProduct.prodName:String = "Call Center Server";
```

Flash does not support this syntax because it is usually much more effective to define the variable within a class, rather than as attached to an object. Only variables defined directly on a timeline or in a class can be typed. The following code would also result in an error:

```
_parent.myVariable :String = "Call Center Server";
```

Strict variable typing is in stark contrast to ActionScript 1.0 where loosely typed variables were the rule. It is something that all Flash developers should get used to because it greatly enhances the debugging capabilities in ActionScript. All variable types are checked at compile time, and if there is a type mismatch, for example, a number is assigned to a string, Flash generates an error message telling the developer what is wrong. Mismatches can occur during assignment operations, function calls, and class member dereferencing using the . operator. All classes used in ActionScript are valid as datatypes, including any custom classes that the developer has created.

NOTE

An error does not result if a datatype is not specified, but it is a best practice to always specify a datatype when defining a variable or creating an object.

Datatypes

Note these recognized datatypes. Every one, except for Void, is the name of a class in ActionScript and should be handled with care:

- Array
- Boolean
- Button
- Color
- CustomActions
- Date
- Function
- LoadVars
- LocalConnection
- Microphone
- MovieClip
- NetConnection
- NetStream
- Number
- Object
- SharedObject
- Sound
- String
- TextField
- TextFormat
- Video
- Void
- XML
- XMLNode
- XMLSocket

It is a best practice to always declare what type of variable a function is actually returning. This especially helps Flash display appropriate error messages; note, however, that it is not required.

```
function getProductName () :String {
      Return this.productName;
}
```

Note that the datatype Void does not exist as a class but just as a type. All functions that do not return any other datatype, such as a string or a number, should be declared as Void, as in the following example:

```
function setProductName (productName:String) :Void
{
      this.productName = productName;
}
```

As you continue to examine the new functionality of Flash MX 2004, you will see that the focus is on class-based development. As you will see, attaching code to timelines and object instances will result in less maintainable and less scaleable applications. Variable typing and building packages and classes will result in more manageable applications.

The ActionScript Editor

Flash MX Professional 2004 now has a built-in ActionScript editor that, when editing an ActionScript file, disables all panels, including the timeline, the tools, and the components. All the built-in error checking and auto-formatting functionality is built into the ActionScript editor. Every time an ActionScript file is opened in Professional, the ActionScript editor, as shown in Figure 1.3, opens.

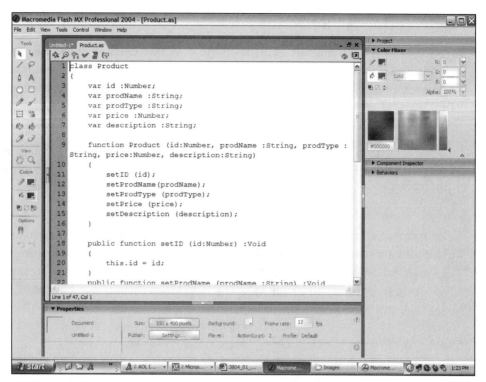

FIGURE 1.3   Note the integrated ActionScript editor in Flash MX Professional 2004.

ActionScript Classes

Class-based development in ActionScript enables development of maintainable and scaleable solutions while grouping code logically. ActionScript 2.0 has an entirely new approach to class-based development that encourages developers to use best practices.

In previous versions of Flash, it was considered good practice to define all classes in separate ActionScript files. Doing this facilitated the use of version control systems and made working in a team environment on a large Flash project that much easier and more organized. In ActionScript 2.0, all class definitions *must* be located in separate ActionScript files. In addition, it is not possible to define classes on a timeline (such as in Frame 1 of an Actions layer). All native classes in ActionScript (for example, the `MovieClip` class) are stored in separate ActionScript files.

Referencing ActionScript Files

Each external ActionScript file can define only one class, and the file must share the same name as the underlying class. For example, a class called `Product` must be located in a file called Product.as. If you are not using the Professional version of Flash, you will need a separate editor for your ActionScript files. Editors include Dreamweaver, SciteFlash, and Notepad.

To use a custom user-defined class, the ActionScript file can be located in the same folder as the SWF file referencing that class. It is possible to use folders and subfolders to store class definitions by using the import keyword or by referring to the class in the script.

The following code illustrates two ways to refer to the `Product` class located in a subfolder called `Data`. This subfolder is also known as a package and Flash automatically builds that object for us in relation to the directory structure. Note that in contrast to Flash MX, the developer cannot use #includes to reference classes.

```
var myProduct:Product = new Data.Product();
```

and

```
import Data.Product;
```

The *class* Keyword

The `class` keyword is a developer-friendly and intuitive way of doing the prototype chaining that you had to do in ActionScript 1.0; behind the scenes, the `class` keyword is building those prototype chains and registering your classes using `Object.registerClass()`, which makes it easier to use the class in component authoring.

A constructor function can be created in ActionScript 2.0 by defining a function with the same name as the class. However, if no constructor is defined, the `class` keyword automatically builds a constructor function. The class construct enables you to structure your code much more efficiently and in a way that is similar to other object-oriented languages, such as Java. It also provides you with the many debugging tools unavailable in Flash MX.

Examine a very simple class file located in the file Product.as:

```
class Product {

    var id:Number;
    var prodName:String;
    var description:String;

    function Product (id:Number, prodName:String, description:String)
    {
        this.id = id;
        this.prodName = prodName;
        this.description = description;
    }
}
```

The constructor function `Product` has the same name and case as the underlying class. If we do not specify a constructor, the class construct automatically creates that for us, but specifying a constructor can give us a lot more flexibility. In addition, note that the keyword `this` is no longer required when referring to properties; however, it still can be used in class definitions.

> **NOTE**
>
> The ActionScript 2.0 compiler generates accompanying files for every class that is created with the extension ".aso". These files contain the binary code that represents the class, and other scripts use these files for type checking. These files cannot be opened by Flash.

Public and Private Attributes

The use of the keyword `public` means that a method or property can be accessed outside a class; if public or private is not specified, ActionScript 2.0 assumes public. The keyword `private` indicates that the method or property can be referenced inside the class only.

> **NOTE**
>
> The `private` keyword in Flash MX 2004 works like the protected keyword in other languages because all methods and variables designated as private are accessible from any subclass of the class in which they were defined; this is not the case in other object-oriented languages.

Methods and properties can be designated as public and private; it is a best practice to always indicate whether a method or property is public or private.

Let's examine the Dump class, which you build later in this book. It serves to display complex data structures to assist in debugging. Note that only the dumpThis() method can be called outside the class; the dumpArray() and dumpObject() methods are called internally within the class by the public function dumpThis().

```
class Dump {

        function Dump() {}          //constructor

        public function dumpThis (theObject:Object):Void {
                if (theObject instanceof Array) {
                        dumpArray(theObject);
                }else if (theObject instanceof Object) {
                        dumpObject(theObject);
                }else {
                        trace (theObject);
                }
        }
        private function dumpObject (theObject:Object):Void {
                trace ("Object:");
                for (var prop in theObject) {
                            if (theObject[prop] instanceof Object) {
                                    dumpThis(theObject[prop])
                        }else{

                        trace (prop+":");
                        trace (theObject[prop]);
                }
        }
    }
  }
private function dumpArray (theArray:Object) :Void {
                trace ("Array:");
                var len = theArray.length;
                for (var i=0;i<len;i++) {
                        trace ("[" + i + "]");
                        dumpThis(theArray[i]);

        }
    }
  }
}
```

Static Attribute

Methods or properties designated in a class as static cannot be associated with an instance. The name of the class must be referenced directly, as in the following example:

```
classclass Product {
      static function getType():String {return "Product"};
}
Product.getType();
```

Only static properties can be accessed inside static methods; it is not possible to access class instance variables. The static attribute can be used *only* within a class definition. An example of a class in ActionScript that uses only static methods and constants is the Math class.

The *extends* Keyword

For classes to inherit from other classes, the extends keyword can be used. In the following example, the class Drag inherits all public and private methods and properties from the MovieClip class; in this case, the code is using onPress(), onRelease(), startDrag(), and stopDrag(), all from the MovieClip class. In ActionScript 2.0, a class cannot inherit from multiple classes.

```
classclass Drag extends MovieClip {

      function Drag () {
          onPress = doDrag();
          onRelease = doDrop();
      }
      private function doDrag(){
          this.startDrag();
      }


      private function doDrop(){
              this.stopDrag();
      }
}
```

Dynamic Attribute

Any class that is designated as dynamic might add or remove dynamic properties at runtime. For example, if you call a method that does not exist on a regular class, you get the "No method with the name..." error message. By defining that class as dynamic, you can call an undeclared method on the class in the instance, even if it is not in the class definition.

```
dynamic class Drag extends MovieClip {

    function Drag (){

            onPress = doDrag();
            onRelease = doDrop();
    }
    private function doDrag(){

            this.startDrag();
    }
    private function doDrop(){


            this.stopDrag();
    }
}
```

By using the `dynamic` keyword in the preceding ActionScript code, you can easily add methods to an instance of the class by using `createEmptyMovieClip()` or `createTextField()`, which are methods of the `MovieClip` class.

Visual Class Linkage

It is now possible to link a visual object with a class file without using `object.registerClass()`. For example, Figure 1.4 shows a movie clip, `mcBall`, being linked to the `Drag` class. This enables a class that implemented drag-and-drop functionality to be linked to any visual object or to an underlying class. The Export for ActionScript check box must be checked to enable this feature. Of course, if you create visual objects in code, you can still use the `object.registerClass()` technique.

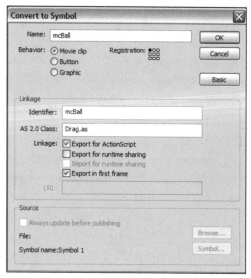

FIGURE 1.4   mcBall being linked to the Drag class.

Implicit Getters/Setters

In general, good object-oriented programming (OOP) practice dictates that functions methods are used to access and set properties. In Flash, you often had to access properties directly, as in the following examples:

```
my_mc._x = 100;
var xpos = my_mc._x;
```

This is considered bad OOP practice and it is almost always better practice to build getter and/or setter functions to set properties. Consider the Product class you were working with earlier:

```
class Product {

    var id:Number;
    var prodName:String;
    var description:String;

    function Product (id:Number, prodName:String, description:String)
    {
        this.id = id;
        this.prodName = prodName;
        this.description = description;
    }
}
```

It certainly would be possible to set the `prodName` property in the following manner:

```
var myProduct:Product = new Product();
myProduct.prodName = "Call Center Server";
```

However, this would be bad OOP practice and result in less maintainable applications. The established OOP way of doing this is to write getter and setter methods instead of accessing the properties directly. If the following class is used, there is no reason to ever have to access properties directly:

```
class Product {

        private var id:Number;
        private var prodName:String;
        private var description:String;

        function Product (id:Number, prodName:String,
description:String){

                setID(id);
                setProdName (prodName);
                setDescription(description);
        }
        public function getId() :Number{

                return this.id;
}
        public function setID (id:Number) :Void{

                this.id = id;
}
        public function getProdName () :String{

                return this.prodName;
}
        public function setProdName (prodName:String) :Void{

                this.prodName = prodName;
}
        public function getDescription () :String{

                return this.description;
```

```
        public function setDescription (description:String) :Void{
        this.description = description;
}
}
```

After this class has been defined in an ActionScrpt file, the following code (for example, on a frame script) can be used to get and set properties. This is done instead of accessing the properties directly:

```
var myProduct:Product = new Product();
myProduct.setID (1);
myProduct.setProdName ("Call Center Server");
myProduct.setDescription ("Allows any call center service center to
improve service");
```

Writing getter and setter methods manually can result in lots of extra code (and typing!), so Flash MX 2004 includes implicit getter and setter methods (these are syntactic shortcuts for the old Flash MX object, addProperty). All implicit getter and setter methods must be public, and they use the keywords get and set within a class definition block.

Getter and setter methods are actually two separate methods; one gets the value of the property and one sets the value. Note that the getter and setter methods generally have the same name.

When getter or setter methods are called, you do not include parenthesis at the end as you do with other methods; in fact, your code almost looks like you are referencing properties, but they are in fact methods. Note that getter and setter methods *cannot* have the same name as existing properties within a class.

Getter and setter methods should be called within the class constructor, if properties are set there. Implicit getter and setter methods can seem confusing at first because they look just like the old getter and setter properties in Flash MX. Examine the following best practices Product class:

```
class Product {

        private var id:Number;
        private var prodName:String;
        private var description:String;

        function Product (id:Number, prodName:String, description:String)
//constructor
        {
```

```
            idNo = id;
            productName = prodName;
            productDescription = description;
        }
        public function get idNo() :Number
{
            return this.id;
}
        public function set idNo (id:Number) :Void
{
            this.id = id;
}
        public function get productName () :String
{
            return this.prodName;
}
        public function set productName (prodName:String) :Void
{
            this.prodName = prodName;
}
        public function get productDescription () :String
{
            return this.description;
}
        public function set productDescription (description:String) :Void
{
        this.description = description;
}
}
```

Note that in the constructor, the setter methods are called to set the properties that are passed in. After getter and setter methods have been defined properly, you never need to set properties directly. The following code sets and gets the product id, product name, and product description, as shown in Figure 1.5:

```
var myProduct:Product = new Product();
myProduct.idNo = 1;
myProduct.productName = ""Call Center Server";
myProduct.productDescription = "Allows any call center to improve
service";

trace (myProduct.idNo);
trace (myProduct.productName);
trace (myProduct.productDescription);
```

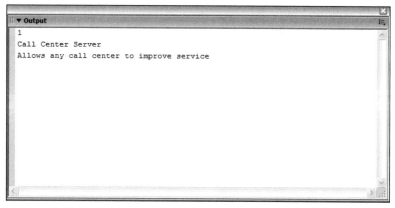

FIGURE 1.5   ActionScript is now "smart" enough to figure out whether you are setting or getting a property.

Interface and Implements Constructs

Interfaces are a compile-time functionality that enable the developer to specify certain methods that every class that implements the interface must have. Interfaces cannot contain properties, static methods, or private methods. Interfaces must be defined within their own package ActionScript file. Multiple inheritance can be simulated with interafaces as classes can implement more than one interface. Any class that uses the `implements` keyword to extend the `iproduct` interface will require a `getName` and a `getID` method.

```
interface iProduct
{
    function getName():String;
    function getID():Number;
}
```

Every class that implements this interface *must* have at least two methods entitled getName() and getID(), as in the following example:

```
class Product implements iProduct
{
        function getName():String {return name};
        function getID() :Number {return id};
}
```

The following example would return a "class must implement interface methods" error because no `getID()` method is defined:

```
class Product implements iProduct
{
    function getName():String {return name};
}
```

Objects in ActionScript 2.0 can implement multiple interfaces; however, they are limited to inheriting from only one class. This is the main advantage of interfaces over class inheritance.

Organizing Classes in Packages

In ActionScript 2.0, classes and interfaces can be organized using packages. This allows for cleaner organization and management of large-scale projects. Packages are used by ActionScript 2.0 at both compile time and at runtime. At compile time, packages are simply the hierarchy of folders that contain the class definitions. In the following code, at compile time, mx.data represents subfolders in a directory where the Product.as file is stored. At runtime, mx and data are objects that are created.

```
cClass mx.data.Product
{
//code
}
```

In the preceding example, the `Product` class (Product.as) would be located in the subfolder mx and then the subfolder data. Remember that class definitions must always be stored in a separate ActionScript file. Thus, for a frame script to reference this class, you would need to import the class or explicitly spell out the path somewhere in the code, as in the following example:

```
var myProduct:Product = new mx.data.Product();
```

It is also possible to explicitly import the class using the `import` keyword, as in the following example:

```
import mx.data.Product;
```

Importing a class *and* referencing the path is acceptable and does not generate any errors. You can also import classes, as shown in Figure 1.6.

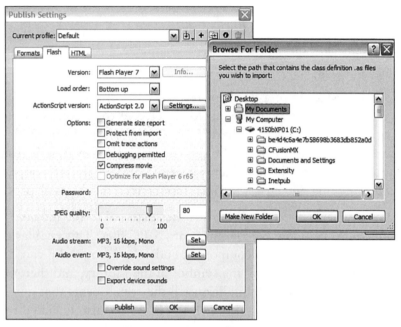

FIGURE 1.6   Using publish settings to allow easy importing of multiple classes from one package.

At runtime, packages exist as Object containers and can be referenced in that manner. For example, in the following code, `mx` and `data` are both objects:

```
class mx.data.Product
{
//code
}
```

V2 Components

All UI components that come with Flash MX 2004 have been rewritten in ActionScript 2.0. The components run faster and are lighter weight than the v1 components. The components use classes, the `extends` keyword, and the other techniques mentioned previously, including the getter and setter methods. For example, if you needed to populate a combo box with data, rather than using the setDataProvider method, you would use the dataProvider getter/setter method:

```
cbTypes.dataProvider = types_array;
```

V2 components are very different than v1 components, and the v2 components were built with OOP best practices in mind. V2 components will work only with Flash Player 7.

Note that Macromedia does not recommend combining v1 and v2 components in the same file. Of course, you can still target the Flash Player 6 using v1 components. V2 components inherit from specialized component classes (the UIcomponent and classUIobject classes), and they inherit from the MovieClip class. The new hierarchy of UIobject and UIcomponent classes makes building and customizing components a much easier process.

V2 components are located in FLA files external to the movie. However, v2 components can now be compiled into SWC files. This enables a faster compilation time and conceals component code. Any movie clip can be exported as a SWC file by right-clicking the symbol in the Library, and then making the appropriate selections. In addition, all the components that come with Flash MX 2004 use SWC files (although the FLAs are also included to enable developers to understand the component architecture).

> **NOTE**
>
> Component architecture is covered in detail in Chapter 9, "Building and Using UI Components."

V2 components use an event listener model syntax to handle events. For example, to set up an onChange handler on a combo box, which calls a function when the user makes a selection in the combo box, you would use the following code:

```
var  cbTypes:ComboBox;
var  eventObj = new Object();
eventObj.change = function(){

        trace ("combo box selected");
}
cbTypes.addEventListener("change", eventObj);
```

Connecting Flash MX 2004 Professional to an Application Server

Accessing server-side data in Flash MX 2004 Professional is divided into three areas: data connection, data management, and data binding. The following sections discuss each in turn.

Data Connection

Data connection involves making the connection to an external data source, such as a web service or an extensible markup language (XML) file, and then reading and writing data to and from that web service or XML file. Currently, the XML and Web Services connector facilitate this, but more connectors will be released.

The Data Management component (known as the dataset) enables manipulation of the server-side data on the client, and the dataset does much of the work for the developer by using a "database cursor" metaphor. Data binding simply links the data to a visual control, such as a combo box or a data grid. In Flash MX 2004, data binding can be done through a visual property inspector or through code. See Figure 1.7.

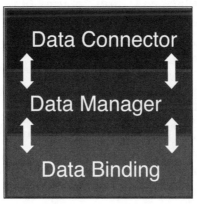

FIGURE 1.7   Data binding.

To create compelling RIAs, Flash MX 2004 must be able to connect to external data sources. Flash MX 2004 can exchange complex data structures with an application server through the Web Services component and/or the XML component. Of course, Flash Remoting is still available as well. Flash Remoting enables you to call server-side methods from the Flash player.

Note that the new Data Connection components benefit from the compiler optimizations in Flash MX 2004 and result in much faster accessing of data. They have also been written entirely in ActionScript 2.0 and are more scaleable and maintainable. Currently, there are two data connectors available (the XML connector and the Web Services connector), but there will be more connectors available soon.

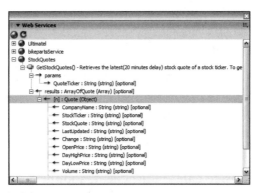

FIGURE 1.8   The Web Services panel tells you in plain English the parameters and results that the web service expects.

The new XML Connector component points to an XML file and automatically parses through that file and returns an array of objects that the developer can easily use. No more parsing and looping thorough every single node of an XML file, as you had to do in earlier versions of Flash! The XML Connector object is covered in detail later in this book.

Visual Data Binding

Visual data binding enables the developer to link the web service or XML data structure to a visual UI component. In fact, it is now possible not to write any ActionScript code and simply use the Component Inspector to do this, as shown in Figure 1.9.

FIGURE 1.9   Using the Component Inspector to link the results of a web service call to a visual combo box on the Stage.

Summary

ActionScript 2.0 moves Flash into the world of serious development tools. No longer will there be a huge learning curve in learning ActionScript. Developers will be able to create maintainable applications quickly because ActionScript 2.0 follows standard OOP practices.

ActionScript 2.0 requires you to perform certain best practices, like keeping all your classes in ActionScript files. ActionScript 2.0 is compiled to ActionScript 1.0, which means that you can use ActionScript 2.0 to create applications that run in Flash Player 6.

All classes must be defined in separate ActionScript files with the file extension .as. Packages are supported both at compile time (through folders) and at runtime by the creation of objects representing those folders. Organizing applications through packages and classes results in a much more maintainable application; it also is much more logical than hanging code off timelines.

You can simulate multiple inheritance by using interfaces in ActionScript 2.0; you can also protect your data by declaring methods and properties, either public or private. It's best practice to create getter and setter methods either manually or with the `get`/`set` keywords. All the components have been completely rewritten in ActionScript 2.0 and they incorporate all these best practices. One of the best ways to understand the new functionality is to delve into the component code.

ActionScript now supports XML, Remoting, and Web Services to connect to dynamic data. You can easily take the returned data from any of these and connect the data to visual UI components using either ActionScript or visual property inspectors. There is no better solution that lets you create rich Internet applications.

CHAPTER 2

ALL THE WORLD IS AN OBJECT

Over the past forty years, there has been an undercurrent in the programming world. That undercurrent is known as object-oriented programming (OOP). During its humble beginnings in 1962 with the introduction of SIMULA (arguably the world's first object-oriented language), the undercurrent was a whisper. For the past decade, the voices have risen, and that whisper has become a deafening roar. This chapter examines what all the fuss about OOP is and how it affects the world of ActionScript development. At the core of OOP is a fiendishly simply concept: the object.

What Is an Object?

An object is a conceptual representation of an entity within a system. In short, everything is an object. Within Macromedia Flash MX 2004, there are several familiar entities with which we deal; these entities are objects. Among these are movie clips, buttons, and components—in fact, everything that can be pro-grammatically interacted with in Flash is an object.

Objects consist of characteristics that describe them (properties) and behaviors that describe what they can do or what can be done to them (methods). A Flash `MovieClip` object has properties describing where it is on the Stage (`_x`, `_y`), its opacity (`_alpha`), the number of frames (`_totalframes`), and so on. There are also behaviors of movie clips in common usage, including `play()`, `stop()`, `goToAndStop()`, and so on.

NOTE

See Chapter 3, "We're All Described by Our Properties," for more details on properties, and Chapter 4, "Method to the Madness," for more details on methods.

Why Objects?

The idea behind OOP is that computer systems modeled after the real-world environment that they represent are more adaptable. What does this really mean? Well, each phrase taken independently is self-explanatory. Hopefully, the concepts of "computer systems," "real-world environment," and "adaptability" are easily understood, but what about the concept of "modeling"? This simply refers to how a computer system is designed. Thus, a computer system modeled on real-world entities refers to an application that is comprised of units with characteristics and behaviors similar to their real-world complements.

An example here might help. Imagine a human resources (HR) department. In that department, an HR employee is responsible for dealing with employees, jobs, benefits, and salaries. Therefore, an object-oriented system to support this HR department will have entities (known as objects) such as `Employee`, `Job`, and `Benefit`. The closer the characteristics and behaviors of an `Employee` entity in the system resemble those of a true employee, the easier it is to adapt the system to changes in the business.

OOP Versus Procedural

We've been discussing how OOP is a revolutionary approach to developing applications. To properly understand any change of this magnitude, it is best to begin with an understanding of what is being changed. The traditional programming style, known as procedural programming, is where the change begins.

Procedural programming takes the point of view that an application is a list of instructions that are executed in a particular order and that can usually be described accurately with a flow chart.

Consider an example of an e-commerce application. In a traditional procedural system, there would be multiple routines, including the following:

- Create products
- Categorize products
- Edit products
- Display products
- Add products to cart
- Ship products

In the equivalent object-oriented system, there could simply be a `Product` object. The `Product` object would be aware of its properties (`id`, `name`, `description`, `price`, and so on), and there would be methods for interacting with it. Note that there would be only one place in the system where each task would be performed.

One such task would be the `Retrieve` method. This method would take an argument determining the id of the `Product` to retrieve, and it would return the entire object. With this method in place, any other action that might affect a `Product` object would use this method. Therefore, the `Edit Product` method could call the `Retrieve Product` method to get the product so that its details could be edited. Equally, the `Display Product` method could call the same `Retrieve Product` method to get the product details so that they can be shown to a customer. Even the `Add Product to Cart` and `Ship Product` methods could make use of this method. In a procedural system, changes to the way a product is shown would need to be coded in several places. In the object-oriented system described here, only code in a single place needs to be modified, without the need to give thought to how it affects the rest of the system.

A well-designed object-oriented system should closely mirror the world in which it will work. For example, the following are types of objects one might find in an e-commerce system:

- `Product`
- `Customer`
- `Warehouse`

In the next few chapters, we discuss the details behind determining the properties and methods of an object and how they are implemented in ActionScript 2.0.

Understanding Classes

Objects begin as ideas or concepts that eventually become part of a solution. Think of the process as a puzzle, where each unique piece has a place in the final picture. For the puzzle to fit together, each piece must be carefully considered in regards to how it fits. This is accomplished with a *blueprint* methodology. Each object's defining characteristics are outlined in a blueprint or class definition.

A class definition is much like an architectural blueprint, which identifies what a house will look like and what amenities it will have. A blueprint can be used many times to create many houses. The blueprint guarantees some similarities in all houses built from the blueprint.

The blueprint might include details such as the following:

- Number of rooms
- Room dimensions
- Heating system
- Plumbing systems
- Electrical system
- Window frames
- Air conditioning

Each element describes what shape the final house takes and how it performs. You could say that these are the properties and functions of the house.

In OOP, the blueprint of an object is called a class definition. It defines what the object does and identifies its associated data. Therefore, a class definition is a blueprint for an object that defines its properties and functions (called methods in OOP).

What if an architect had to design every element of a new house? Finding an architect who is also a plumbing and heating expert might be a challenge. A better choice would be to have a heating expert design and build the heating system, a plumber to do the plumbing work, and so on.

Many of the components of the house can be prebuilt. Using prebuilt objects, the complexity of building a house is greatly reduced. Prebuilt objects are tested and guaranteed by experts in the problem domain. Individual objects can be replaced without rebuilding the entire system. For example, if you decide to upgrade your heating system to a more energy-efficient system, you don't have to build a new house from scratch. You can simply replace the existing system.

When we apply object-oriented principles to the problem of building a new house, we can say the following:

- A house is made up of objects interacting with each other. For instance, turning up the thermostat sends a message to the heating system to heat the house.
- Building a house involves many different systems that are brought together for a common goal—to provide shelter.
- Each object in the house has a well-defined role. The roles include heating, plumbing, and so on.

These same principles apply in object-oriented application development:

- An application is made of objects interacting with each other.
- Creating a program involves assembling objects and making them communicate.
- Each object has a well-defined role in the system.

Using these principles enables real-world concepts to be modeled in a computer program. In ActionScript 2.0, there are many new constructs to help us employ solid object-oriented techniques in Flash MX 2004.

Anatomy of a Class

A class is a collection of properties and methods. Properties define the data associated with a class, and methods operate on the data. Together they define the capabilities of the object instance that is generated by the class definition.

In ActionScript 2.0, a class is defined using the `class` keyword, a class name, and a code block defined by curly braces. For example, let's say you need to define a class that represents a loan. A loan could be used to represent a car loan, a student loan, or a home loan. In each case, the loan would be different based on the amount of the loan, the interest applied, and the term of the loan. Listing 2.1 defines the `Loan` class.

LISTING 2.1   Pseudocode for the Class Definition

```
class Loan {
        //properties
        principal; //loan amount
        rate; //loan loan interest rate
        term; //length of the loan

        //methods
        calculateMonthlyPayment(){
        }
}
```

The name of the class must be the same as the name of the external file that contains the class. Anything defined within the curly brackets is considered a *class member*.

> **NOTE**
>
> All classes are defined in files that are stored external to the Flash document. The files are named with the class name and have the extension ".as".

Properties

A class can contain properties. Properties are variables that are defined within the class block. They are used to hold data of a specific type used by the class instance. They are also called instance variables.

The syntax of a property definition is shown in Figure 2.1:

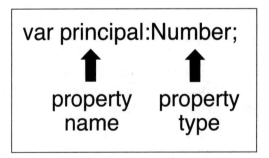

FIGURE 2.1   Class property declaration.

The var keyword indicates a variable definition and the : separates the variable name from its data type. In ActionScript 2.0, case sensitivity and strict data typing are implemented, as shown in Chapter 1, "What's New in ActionScript 2.0?" What this means to you is that "principal" is not the same as "Principal." ActionScript 2.0 also implements strict datatyping. In the following example, principal is defined as a Number; therefore, it cannot be assigned "5.0" because "5.0" is treated as a string.

```
var principal:Number = "5.0";
```

Note this valid assignment, however:

```
principal = 5.0;
```

Properties can also be declared and assigned a value in a single statement:

```
var principal:Number = 5.0;
```

> **NOTE**
>
> Another advantage of strict datatyping is that Flash automatically displays code hints for built-in objects when they are strictly typed.

Our Loan class needs several properties to hold the data that makes an individual loan unique. Listing 2.2 adds four class properties to the Loan class: principal, rate, term, and customerName.

LISTING 2.2   Class Definition with Properties

```
class Loan {
    //properties
    var principal:Number; //loan amount
    var rate:Number; //loan interest rate
    var term:Number; //length of the loan
    var customerName:String; //name of loan customer

    //methods

}
```

Variable Scope

By using the var keyword within the class block, you are defining the scope of the properties to be the class block. The class properties are available for the life of the instance; they are in scope when the instance is created and out of scope when the instance is destroyed. After the instance is created, class properties are called instance data.

Methods

Methods are operations that can be performed by an object. They are capable of taking data as arguments and returning data to the caller. Methods are also call functions. They define the operations that the instance can perform.

Figure 2.2 lists the components of a method declaration:

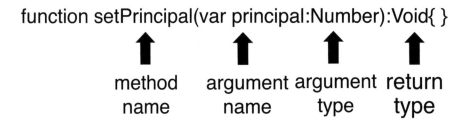

FIGURE 2.2   Class method declaration.

This method takes one argument and returns nothing. You can use this method to set the value of the `principal` property in the `Loan` class, as shown in Listing 2.3.

LISTING 2.3   Class Definition with Methods

```
class loan Loan {
      //properties
      var principal:Number; //loan amount
      var rate:Number; //loan interest rate
      var term:Number; //length of the loan
      var customerName:String; //name of loan customer

      //methods
      function setPrincipal(thePrincipal:Number):Void{
            this.principal = thePrincipal;
      }

}


setPrincipal(5.5);
```

This method is used to set the instance data for `principal` and requires no return statement.

How About this?

In ActionScript 2.0, this is a keyword that refers to the current executing scope, which is the container class instance. In the setPrincipal method, the keyword this referenced the class property, principal, from within the class. It enables you to use a relative path to reference class members.

Return Type

Listing 2.3 used the keyword Void to indicate that this method does not return any data to the caller. However, what if you wanted to return data to the calling code? For example, the Loan class needs a method to calculate a monthly payment. The method returns the value and it requires more information to do the calculation. In Listing 2.4, the getMonthlyPayment() method requires data to do the calculation. thePrincipal and theTerm are passed in as method arguments and have a return statement.

LISTING 2.4   Class Definition with Method Return Statement

```
class Loan {
      //properties
      var principal:Number; //loan amount
      var rate:Number; //loan interest rate
      var term:Number; //length of the loan
      var customerName:String; //name of loan customer

      //methods
      function setRate(theRate:Number):Void{
            this.rate = theRate;
      }
      function getMonthlyPayment(thePrincipal:Number,
theTerm:Number):Number{
            var monthlyPayment:Number;
            //calculate payment
            ...
            return monthlyPayment;
      }

}
```

The return type in the method signature is the datatype of the return value. The data returned must match the datatype declared in the return type of the method. Listing 2.5 defines the getNumber() method with a valid signature and return variable, as opposed to Listing 2.6, where the return type doesn't match the signature return type.

LISTING 2.5   Valid Signature and Return

```
function getNumber():Number{
      var num:Number;
      return num;
}
```

LISTING 2.6   Invalid Signature and Return

```
function getNumber():Number{
      //will generate a compiler error :
      //'The expression returned must match the
      // function's return type.'
      var numStr:String;
      return numStr;
}
```

If the method returns nothing, the return type is Void. Although you can omit the return type of a method, it is highly recommended as a best practice to always include the return type, even when there is nothing being returned.

Any valid datatype can be returned from a method. Number, String, and Boolean are all valid datatypes. A class is also considered a valid datatype, so it also can be returned by a method.

Method Name

The method name distinguishes one method from another in a class. In ActionScript, each method name must be unique.

> **NOTE**
>
> Some object-oriented languages, such as Java, permit method overloading, which means that you can have two methods named the same with different signatures. However, this is not the case in ActionScript 2.0. Each method name must be unique within one class.

The Constructor

Currently, you are missing a means to create an instance of the class. An instance is to a class what a house is to a blueprint. It is the physical manifestation of the object defined by the class. In ActionScript 2.0, you can create a special method to create an instance of a class. It is called a *constructor*.

A constructor is a special kind of method used to create an object instance. The constructor method is named the same as the class name (including the case). Listing 2.7 adds a constructor to the `Loan` class definition:

LISTING 2.7   Class Definition with Constructor

```
class Loan {
        //properties
        var principal:Number; //loan amount
        var rate:Number; //loan interest rate
        var term:Number; //length of the loan
        var customerName:String; //name of loan customer


        function Loan(){
                trace("in Loan constructor");
                //initialize the loan object
        }
        //methods


}
```

As stated, the constructor is a special kind of method that breaks many of the rules of a method. For example, a constructor doesn't require a return type. As a matter of fact, if it has one, it generates a compiler error.

The constructor is generally used to initialize an object. If the class has no constructor, the compiler adds a "no-argument" constructor. Thus, as long as your constructor doesn't require any arguments, you can omit the constructor and use the default, "no-argument" constructor.

What's in a Name?

There are different approaches to naming class members. On the one hand, verbose naming of class members makes your code easier to read and maintain. For example, a variable to hold an interest rate for a mortgage might be called `annualPercentageRate`. Although it is easy to read, it may be prone to typos because of its length. On the other hand, `apr` might not provide enough information to the programmer.

Whether you choose verbose or abbreviated or somewhere in between, it's a good idea to have some structure. The following subsections give guidelines you should follow when naming class member identifiers.

Naming Identifiers

An identifier is a name given to a property, variable, class, or method. Identifiers adhere to the following rules:

- They are case sensitive.
- They begin with a letter or underscore (_) and subsequent characters can be digits or letters.
- They have no maximum length.
- They cannot be a reserved word.

There are some words within ActionScript that are reserved words, which means that they have a specific use within the language. These words cannot be used as identifiers for properties/variables, methods, or class names. The following is a list of all ActionScript keywords:

break	case	class	continue
default	delete	dynamic	else
extends	for	function	get
if	implements	import	in
instanceof	interface	new	private
public	return	set	static
switch	this	typeof	var
Void	while	with	

Suggested Naming Conventions

You should have a naming convention when building any application, especially when you are using a well-formed language with conventions such as case sensitivity and strict datatyping. Now, more than ever, a naming convention in Flash saves you time and headaches. Table 2.1 has some suggested conventions.

TABLE 2.1   Naming Conventions

ITEM	DESCRIPTION	EXAMPLE
Class	A class name begins with a capital letter.	`Loan`
	If a class name is comprised of more than one word, capitalize the first letter of each word.	`Customer`
Variables and properties	Variables always begin with a lowercase letter.	`principal` `monthlyPayment`
	If a variable is comprised of more than one word, every word after the first begins with a capital letter.	
Methods	Methods typically begin with a word that is a verb whose first letter is lowercase.	`addItem( )` `getLastName( )`
	If a method is comprised of more than one word, every word after the first begins with a capital letter.	

The Objects Shall Inherit the Earth

Now that you know how to define a class, you have to learn how to use it. A class definition is used to create an object instance at runtime. Figure 2.3 shows the class definition and its transformation to instances.

Just as an architectural blueprint is used to create the actual physical house, so too is a class definition used to create an instance of a class.

Creating Objects from Classes

When you compile an FLA into an SWF, the ActionScript compiler adds all the class definitions needed to the SWF. This includes any built-in or core classes, such as `MovieClip`, as well as all your custom classes that have either been referenced or explicitly included. For the compiler to find the classes, however, you may have to take additional steps, such as modifying the class path or explicitly including the file containing the class definition.

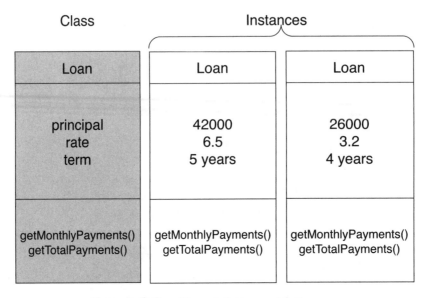

FIGURE 2.3   Class definition and instances.

include Versus *import*

To include a file containing ActionScript explicitly in a Flash document, you can use the #include directive. This includes the contents of the specified file, as if the commands in the file were part of the Flash document itself. The #include directive is invoked at compile time. Therefore, if you make any changes to an external file, you must recompile any FLA files and redeploy. In Listing 2.8, you can see how to access files from the current directory, as well as from other directories.

LISTING 2.8   *#include* Directive Variants

```
#include "utilityMethods.as"
#include "includeDir/utilityMethods.as"
#include "../includeDir/utilityMethods.as"
```

> **NOTE**
>
> Notice that there is no semicolon terminating the statements in Listing 2.8. If you include a semicolon, the compiler generates an error.

The `#include` directive is used to include ActionScript 2.0 code that exists in an external file—such as a set of utility methods or initialization variables. The `#include` directive can appear in a Flash document on the timeline or in an external ActionScript 2.0 file except when the external ActionScript 2.0 file is a class definition. The class file counterpart for `#include` is `import`.

The `import` directive enables you to import the definition of a class, thus making it available within the including class. `import` is an OOP standard for referencing classes within classes. Most OOP languages have this construct. The `import` directive tells the compiler to incorporate the imported class when building the .swf file.

You can use `#include` in FLAs to include unstructured code or class definitions. You can also use it in .as files that are not class definitions to include unstructured code or class definitions.

Note that `import` is an OOP construct that it is used in class files to include other class definitions.

Packages and the Classpath

We can import an entire group of classes. To do this, you organize your class files in packages. A package is a directory that contains one or more class files and that resides in a designated classpath directory. A package can, in turn, contain other packages, called *subpackages*, each with its own class files.

To locate the external ActionScript 2.0 files that contain the class definitions, Flash searches the classpath. Classes should be saved to one of the directories specified in the classpath, or a subdirectory therein. Otherwise, Flash cannot *resolve*, or locate, the class specified in the script. The subdirectories created within a classpath directory define the packages. You can change the classpath for all Flash files through the Preferences panel, as shown in Figure 2.4.

The classpath can also be set for a particular document through the Publish Settings panel, as shown in Figure 2.5.

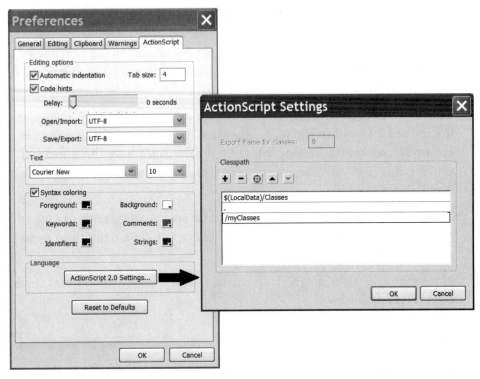

FIGURE 2.4   Modifying the global classpath for all Flash files.

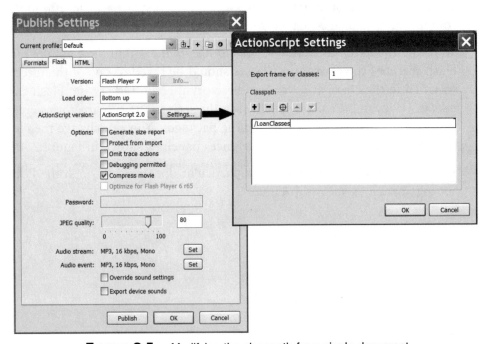

FIGURE 2.5   Modifying the classpath for a single document.

As mentioned, packages are commonly used to organize related classes. For example, you might have three related classes, Loan, Customer, and Calculator, that are defined in Loan.as, Customer.as, and Calculator.as, respectively. They are saved to a directory called LoanPackage.

There are two ways that you can reference the Customer class. If the calling file is in a different directory, you can use a qualified path, as in Listing 2.9. This allows the compiler to find the class at compile time regardless of where it is stored on the local file system.

LISTING 2.9   Using a Fully Qualified Classpath

```
class Loan(){
    ...
    var customer:LoanPackage.Customer;
    ...
}
```

The path uses dot notation just as you would use the "/" in a directory structure.

You can also import the entire package into the calling class and reference it directly, as in Listing 2.10. The wildcard * is used to include the entire contents of the directory.

LISTING 2.10   Using an Import Statement to Import an Entire Package

```
import LoanPackage.*;
class Loan(){
    ...
    var customer:Customer;
    ...
}
```

The import statement can import an entire directory, as shown in Listing 2.10, or you can specifically import only one class, as shown in Listing 2.11.

LISTING 2.11   Using an Import Statement to Import a Single Class

```
import LoanPackage.Customer;
class Loan(){
    ...
    var customer:Customer;
    ...
}
```

So far, you have managed to make the class definition accessible in your class, but you haven't created an instance. To create an instance, you have to introduce the new keyword. The new keyword is used to invoke the constructor of a class and create an instance in memory. If you recall, the constructor of a class always has the same name as the class. Listing 2.12 creates an instance of the Customer class as a class property within the Loan class.

LISTING 2.12   Creating an Instance of a Class by Calling the Constructor

```
import LoanPackage.Customer;
class Loan(){
    ...
    var customer:Customer = new Customer();
    ...
}
```

You can create an instance of the Loan class inside a user interface called loanCalc.fla. To create an instance of the Loan class, you use the following syntax with the new keyword to invoke the constructor:

```
var loanInstance:Loan;
loanInstance = new Loan();
```

The variable loanInstance now has a reference to the Loan object instance in memory, including all of its properties and methods. Figure 2.6 diagrams the process of generating an instance in memory at runtime.

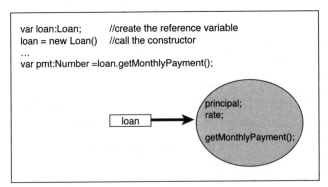

FIGURE 2.6   Generating an instance in memory at runtime.

In Flash, you can create class files in the same environment as you create FLA files. A class file has the same name as the class itself, and it has the extension .as. Thus, your `Loan` class will be in a file called Loan.as.

In Figure 2.7, the Loan.as file is in the same directory as LoanCalc.fla; therefore, you do not need an explicit `include` directive. The compiler finds the class file using the classpath. In Figure 2.4, you might have noticed a classpath entry of '.' (a single period). This tells the compiler to look in the current working directory.

Notice that in Figure 2.7 on line 3, we are creating the reference variable of type `Loan` called `loanInstance`, while on line 4, we are creating the instance in memory.

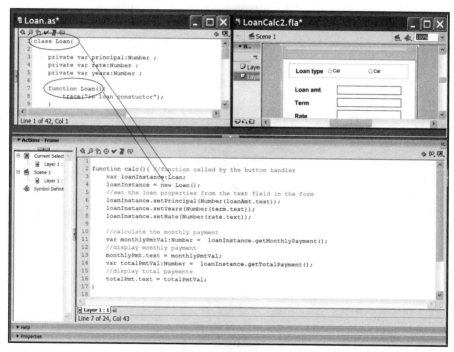

FIGURE 2.7   Using the `Loan` class from LoanCalc.fla within the development environment in Flash.

Built-In Classes

In ActionScript 2.0, as with other object-oriented languages, you have built-in classes available. In Flash, the most common built-in class (and a foundation object within Flash) is the `MovieClip` class.

In Flash, a `MovieClip` object has many predefined methods and properties that enable you to easily build rich user interfaces. Although this text does not cover many of the animation and user interface (UI) features of the movie clip, it is important to note that code often builds on the existing foundation of the `MovieClip` class. This is done using inheritance, as discussed in Chapter 5, "The Meek Shall Inherit the Earth."

Note that components are built-in classes with a specific purpose. They are easy to use in Flash because they have exposed properties and methods. By investigating the Components panel in Figure 2.8, you might notice the many common UI and data components that are often needed when building applications. The Component Inspector enables you to view exposed members.

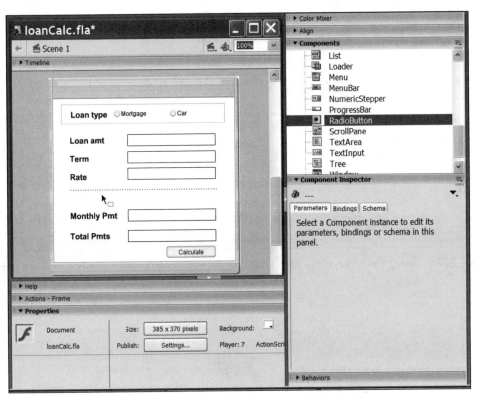

FIGURE 2.8   Available components in Flash.

> **NOTE**
>
> Components are covered in more detail in Chapter 9, "Building and Using UI Components."

You have many tools, such as components, at your disposal. In Flash, you can create your own custom solutions or build hybrid solutions using prebuilt and tested components to augment custom solutions. The following list identifies the benefits of using prebuilt components:

- **Abstraction and reduced complexity.** The assembler doesn't need to know how individual objects are built to be able to use them.
- **Flexibility and maintainability.** Individual objects can be replaced without rebuilding the entire system.
- **Quality and performance.** Objects are developed by domain experts.
- **Individual objects.** These are pretested for quality and performance.

Dynamic Classes

Throughout this chapter, you have learned about defining classes that have a fixed set of properties and methods. When you create instances of these classes, you expect the properties and methods to be available. The good news is that this is still true. All properties and methods in the class definition are in the instance.

However, what if you were using a class and you decided it needed a new property: For example, the `Loan` class could be used to calculate many different kinds of loans. To support different kinds of loans, you might have to add a fee specific to the loan type. Because these properties don't currently exist in the `Loan` class definition, you would have to go back to the Loan.as file, add the properties, and recompile it along with everything that uses the `Loan` class. You have to do this because an instance of a class can't create or access properties or methods that weren't originally declared or defined in the class. To do this, you would have to declare the class `dynamic` to add class members at runtime.

The `dynamic` class modifier lets you do just that. For example, Listing 2.13 adds the dynamic modifier to the `Loan` class.

LISTING 2.13   Using the dynamic Class Modifier

```
dynamic class Loan {
   var principal:Number;
   var rate:Number;
   var term:Number;
...
}
```

Now, at runtime, instances of the Loan class can add and access properties and methods that were not defined in the original class. Listing 2.14 adds a loan origination fee to the loan instance and assigns it a value.

LISTING 2.14   Adding an Instance Member to a Dynamic Class

```
var loan:Loan = new Loan();
loan.originationFee = 150; // no compiler error because class is
dynamic
```

In the Loan class, you can customize the data returned to the user by adding a message indicating the type of loan for which he or she is searching. Because this data has no impact on the output of the loan calculation, there is no reason to bog down the class definition with properties that are specific to this particular user interface. You need to add loanType as a dynamic property of the loan instance by first declaring the class as dynamic and then adding a dynamic property to hold the loan type. In Figure 2.9, you can see the dynamic property added to loanCalc.fla when the loan payments are calculated.

You then use this information to return a custom message. You could not do this in the earlier version of the Loan class. The code now has the dynamic modifier for the Loan.as file, as shown in Figure 2.10.

Type checking on dynamic classes is less strict than type checking on non-dynamic classes because members accessed inside the class definition and on class instances are not compared to those defined in the class. Class methods, however, are still type checked for return type and parameter types.

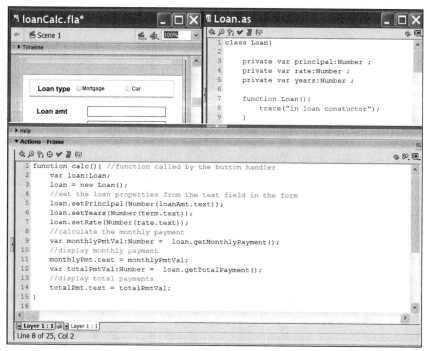

FIGURE 2.9   Adding a dynamic property to the Loan class instance.

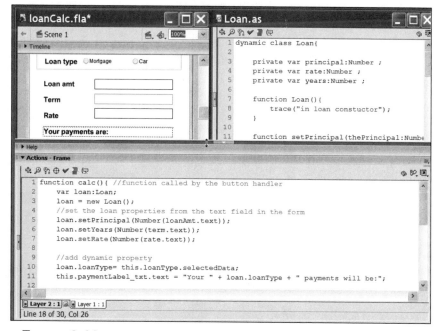

FIGURE 2.10   Outputting a dynamic class property by using loanType.

Summary

This chapter introduced the building blocks that are fundamental for OOP in Flash. With the introduction of objects and a diversion from procedural programming, OOP becomes possible. Class definitions formalize the conceptual object, thus allowing objects to be assembled into applications. Regardless of the level of complexity in an OOP, objects are the core.

Flash MX 2004 has full support for OOP concepts both syntactically at development time and performance-wise at runtime. But that doesn't preclude the development of bad applications. OOP is more that just syntax; it is an approach to programming. Think about objects as discrete, self-contained, mini programs that can work in harmony with other objects. This thinking is the first step in writing object-oriented programs.

The next four chapters build on the foundation provided in this chapter. We continue to expand on the class definition by looking at variations in property and method declarations. Terms like inheritance, encapsulation, and polymorphism might once have caused the hair on the back of your neck to raise, but they soon will become banter for your next visit to Starbucks.

Chapter 3

We're All Described by Our Properties

Objects are described by their properties, and a class of objects enables us to define how properties are assigned to new instances. In this chapter, you delve a bit deeper into the idea of properties. It will help you garner a deeper understanding of what a property is and how properties are used within the context of objects.

Variable-to-Property Analogy

In Chapter 2, "All the World Is an Object," the text looked at a class called Loan. The Loan class had several properties that described aspects of a loan, such as principal, rate, and term. These properties acted much like a variable within the loan instances. In reality, that's exactly what a property is: a variable belonging to an object. Properties can be used in exactly the same ways as a variable. That is, they can be passed to functions, compared with conditionals, and so on.

In reality, what we know of as a variable is actually a property; the movie clip or timeline on which it is coded is the object to which it belongs. Consider this example: In Frame 1 of the Actions layer on the main timeline, this code is entered:

```
var myName:String = "jeff";
```

> **NOTE**
>
> Just like we saw with other object types, adding a strong data type to the String declaration enables the code hinting for strings.
>
> Logically, we recognize that this is creating a variable, called myName, and assigning it a value of "jeff". In reality, as it is coded on the timeline of a movie clip, it is actually a property of that movie clip.

This can be demonstrated by tracing it in several different ways:

```
trace(myName);
trace(this.myName);
trace(_root.myName);
```

Each elicits exactly the same response. What this shows is that a simple variable within a movie clip can be referred to as a variable (shown with the first trace statement) or as a property of an object (shown in the second and third trace statements).

To refer to the variable as a property, it needs to be referenced using the object.property notation. It is a property of a movie clip on whose timeline it is coded, which we can refer to by its relative address this or its absolute address _root.

Properties in the Real World

A key goal of object-oriented programming (OOP) is to design the objects for the system to closely mirror the characteristics and behaviors of the real-world objects they represent. The Loan example shows this well; loans have three properties inherent to them: the amount being borrowed (principal), the interest (rate), and the time that will be taken to repay the loan (term). These are properties of a loan, and they describe a loan pretty thoroughly. Everywhere we look in the real world, the objects we interact with have properties. Even the book you are reading now has properties, as shown in Table 3.1.

TABLE 3.1   Properties of This Book

PROPERTY	VALUE
Authors	Tapper, Talbot, Haffner
Publisher	New Riders
Chapters	17

Hopefully, this illustrates that properties aren't really that foreign of a concept; everything has properties, even you!

Properties of Familiar Macromedia Flash MX 2004 Objects

Just as all real-world objects can be described by their properties, the same holds true for internal Flash objects. Figure 3.1 shows the properties for a movie clip.

FIGURE 3.1   The properties of a movie clip.

Some of these properties are familiar, indicating positioning on the Stage (_x, _y), size (_height, _width, _xscale, and _yscale), and information about frames (_totalFrames, _framesLoaded, and _currentFrame). Each property describes the unique characteristics of an instance of a movie clip.

We can also find similar information about the properties of any of the built-in objects in Flash. For example, an instance of the Array class has a property describing the number of elements within the array (length), a TextField instance has a property that describes the text currently within it (text), and an instance of the Sound class has a property to describe how long the sound lasts (duration).

Working with properties of an object is as simple as working with variables on the main timeline. Figure 3.2 shows a simple use of the properties of TextField instances to facilitate simple addition.

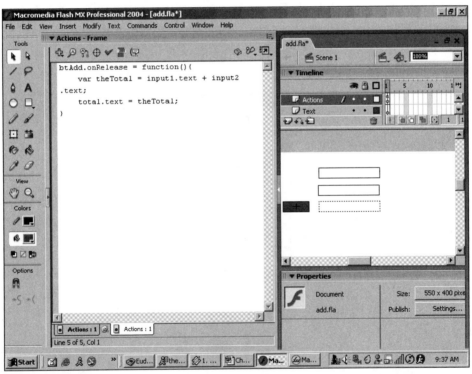

FIGURE 3.2   Using the text property of TextField instances enables you to read and write to them.

On the Stage are three text fields and a button. The top two text fields (`input1` and `input2`) are input text; the bottom is a dynamic text field (`total`). An `onRelease` event is added for the button instance (`btAdd`). When clicked and released, the text properties of the two input fields are added, and the results are shown in the total field. We can see that to read a user's input from a text field, we refer to the text property of that field. In addition, to assign text to a text field, we also use the same text property.

Note that this simple example of the use of properties within Flash is flawed. Figure 3.3 shows what happens if we run the file and attempt to use it to add 2 and 3.

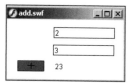

FIGURE 3.3   The Addition tool shows some unexpected results.

Strong Datatypes for Properties

The flaw we find in Figure 3.3 is that it is not adding the two numbers; instead, it is *concatenating* them. In ActionScript 2.0, as well as several other languages, the + operator is *overloaded*. This means it will perform different operations, based on the types of data on which it is acting; when acting on numbers, it will add them, when acting on strings, it will concatenate them.

NOTE

As is standard in programming parlance, *concatenating* is the act of joining two strings to make a new single string. For more details on operators in ActionScript, see *Macromedia Flash MX 2004 Advanced Training from the Source,* by Derek Franklin and Jobe Makar.

As we learned in Chapter 1, "What's New in ActionScript 2.0?," ActionScript 2.0 is a strongly typed language. This means that when Flash determines what type of data a variable (or property) will hold, it won't accept other types of data, unless specifically instructed to do so. The text property of a text field is typed as a `String` object. Therefore, when Flash was instructed to show the results of the following:

```
input1.text + input2.text;
```

it took the string entered in the first box and concatenated it with the string in the second. If we truly want Flash to add the numbers instead of concatenating them, we will need to cast them to the proper datatype. Casting is how we instruct Flash to change the datatype of an object. If we want to cast a string as a number, we use the built-in `Number()` function. Equally, if we wanted to cast a number as a String object, we could use the `String()` function. Listing 3.1 shows the `onRelease` handler for the button rewritten to properly add the numbers that have been input.

LISTING 3.1   The Addition Tool Now Shows the Expected Results

```
btAdd.onRelease = function(){
    var theTotal:Number = Number(input1.text)+Number(input2.text);
    total.text = String(theTotal);
}
```

Here, we can see that we are explicitly casting the input from the text fields to numbers so that Flash can add them properly. We also need to cast the resulting number back to a string, as the text property of a text field is built to accept only strings. Figure 3.4 shows the full code, Stage, and results with the proper casting.

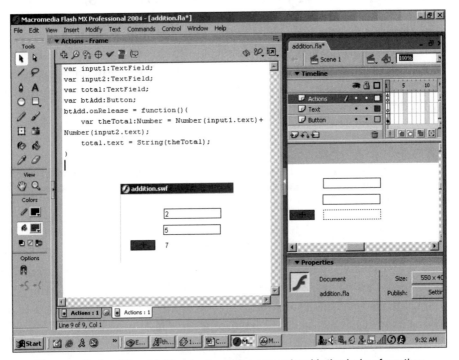

FIGURE 3.4   The Addition tool working properly with the help of casting.

> **NOTE**
>
> The first four lines of ActionScript 2.0 shown in Figure 3.4 are declaring the datatypes of the visual objects on the Stage. Although this is optional, it helps the Flash compiler force the datatype checking within the application, and it also enables code hinting.

Private Property

A new feature within ActionScript 2.0 gives us the ability to determine from where properties can be accessed. This is done with the keywords `public` and `private`.

Public Versus Private

Most object-oriented (as well as some procedural) languages share the ability to set the access rights to properties. Although other languages give many choices (public, protected, package, private, and so on) in setting access, ActionScript 2.0 gives us only two choices: `public` and `private`.

A private element of a class can be accessed only from within the same object. In the "Data Hiding" section that follows, we'll discuss why this would be done. For now, note that a public element is available from other objects, movie clip instances, and so on.

Listing 3.2 shows a modification on the `Loan` class from Chapter 2. This time, `class` is setting all the properties as `private`.

LISTING 3.2   Modifications to the *Loan* Class Show the Properties as Private Members

```
class Loan{

        private var principal:Number ;
        private var rate:Number ;
        private var years:Number ;
        ...
}
```

> **NOTE**
>
> Any property not specifically set as private is by default public. However, it remains a best practice to explicitly declare public properties with the `public` keyword.

Data Hiding

It is nice to know that we have the ability to declare properties as private or public, but the real question is why would we? The concept of data hiding exists across all object-oriented languages. With an effective use of data hiding, any object can have its data effectively encapsulated within it. This follows the same object-oriented principles implemented in Java and C++, in that the details of how an object is implemented do not need to be understood by those using the object.

For example, we do not need to know the implementation details of our car to be able to drive it. Regardless of whether a car has a carburetor or fuel injectors, whether the cams are overhead or not, we as users of the car do not change how we drive it. The properties of the car are hidden from us. Internally, the car knows about its properties and how to make use of them, but those details are not exposed to the driver behind the wheel.

The same is true of objects. By hiding the details (such as properties), we as developers can determine the way a movie clip and other objects can interact with ours. This grants many benefits to development, including less confusing code implementations, less chance of developer error from interacting with properties whose true use is not understood, and easier integration of development teams consisting of experienced and less experienced developers.

Frequently in OOP, we create methods to enable interactions with private properties. Figure 3.5 shows a failed attempt at directly interacting with a private property from an instance of the `Loan` class.

WARNING

Although the Flash compiler prevents direct access to private properties using the standard `object.property` syntax, a bug within the compiler's implementation enables private properties to be accessed using the `object["property"]` syntax. This can lead to unexpected results.

NOTE

Another construct exists within ActionScript to control how developers can interact with properties. `AsSetPropFlags` is a function that can hide and protect properties and methods at runtime. This is different from the `private` and `public` keywords, which are used for compile-time checks to enforce data integrity. For full details on the implementation of `AsSetPropFlags`, see the FlashGuru's Flash MX 101 page at `http://flashguru.co.uk/000037.php`.

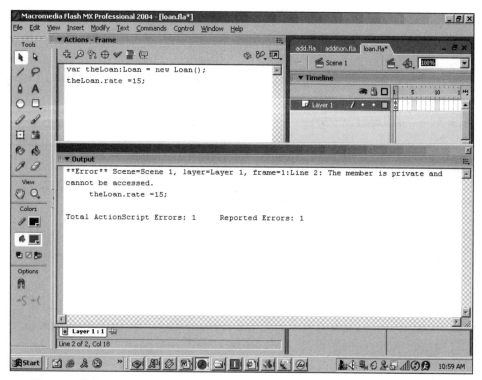

FIGURE 3.5 The compiler prevents us from directly accessing private elements.

Getters and Setters

Integral to the idea of data hiding is providing an interface to enable controlled access to properties. By limiting developers access to properties through the use of methods, we can shield developers from potential changes to the underlying data of an object. If the properties names or datatypes should change, developers will not need to change their interactions with the object, so long as the methods that they are using to access the data remain consistent. They can simply modify the workings of the interface to reflect the new structure. The signature will remain the same. This means that as far as the rest of the system is concerned, nothing has changed. These interfaces are traditionally built as methods, which enable modification and retrieval of data from the object. These types of methods are generally referred to as getter and setter methods.

Explicit Getters and Setters

Traditional getter and setter methods have explicitly declared method names, such as getName() or setPrice(). These are referred to as explicit getters and setters because using them requires explicitly invoking their names. Listing 3.3 shows the explicit getters and setters of the Loan class.

LISTING 3.3   Explicit Getters and Setters Are Added to the *Loan* Class to Facilitate Interaction with Their Private Properties

```
class Loan{

      private var principal:Number ;
      private var rate:Number ;
      private var years:Number ;

      function setPrincipal(thePrincipal:Number ) {
            if(thePrincipal > 0){
                  this.principal = thePrincipal;
            } else {
                  trace("error, principal must be greater than 0");
            }
      }

      function setRate(theRate:Number) {
            this.rate=theRate;
      }

      function setYears(theYears:Number ) {
      this.years=theYears;
      }

      function getYears( ):Number {
            return this.years;
      }

      function getRate( ):Number{
            return this.rate;
      }

      function getPrincipal( ):Number{
            return this.principal;
      }

}
```

There are two methods for each property, one named `get<propertyName>` and the other named `set<propertyName>`. Although the properties themselves are private, meaning that they are directly accessible only within the object, these methods enable the properties to be accessed externally. The `setPrincipal` method shows another benefit: data can be validated within the methods before it is added to the object.

> **NOTE**
>
> Getter and Setter methods are covered in more detail in Chapter 4, "Method to the Madness."

Implicit Getters and Setters

ActionScript 2.0 has implemented another style of getter and setter methods, which they refer to as *implicit getters and setters*. These implicit methods make use of the new keywords `get` and `set` within the method definition. This style of getter and setter methods is very similar to the constructs with the same names within C#. To declare an implicit getter method, the syntax is this:

```
function get methodName(){};
```

Note that implicit setter methods use the keyword `set` in place of `get`.

> **NOTE**
>
> Implicit getter and setter methods cannot have the same name as the properties they are getting or setting.

Listing 3.4 shows the `Loan` class modified using implicit getter and setter methods.

LISTING 3.4   C#-Style Implicit Getters and Setters Are Used in Place of the More Traditional Getter and Setter Methods That Were Used Earlier

```
class Loan{

    private var _principal:Number ;
    private var _rate:Number ;
    private var _years:Number ;

    function set principal(thePrincipal:Number ) {
        if(thePrincipal > 0){
            this._principal = thePrincipal;
        } else {
            trace("error, principal must be greater than 0");
        }
```

continues

LISTING 3.4 Continued

```
      }

      function set rate(theRate:Number) {
            this._rate=theRate;
      }

      function set years(theYears:Number ) {
            this._years=theYears;
      }

      function get years( ):Number {
            return this._years;
      }

      function get rate( ):Number{
            return this._rate;
      }

      function get principal( ):Number{
            return this._principal;
      }
}
```

A few changes were made structurally to accommodate the implicit getters and setters. To comply with the requirement that the method name not match the property names, the property names are modified and prefixed with an underscore (this is the same convention that the user interface [UI] components follow). Next, a series of functions are written using the get and set keywords. The internals of the methods are identical to the explicit methods we had before; the only difference is how they are defined.

The odd thing about this style of method is how it is invoked. To use an implicit getter or setter method, it is called just like a property of the object, like so:

```
var theLoan:Loan = new Loan();
theLoan.rate = 8;
```

It looks like we are setting a property called rate. In reality, however, the object no longer has a property called rate; instead, the property is named _rate.

To illustrate this point, we can try to trace the _rate property, as well as the results of the implicit rate getter, as shown in Figure 3.6.

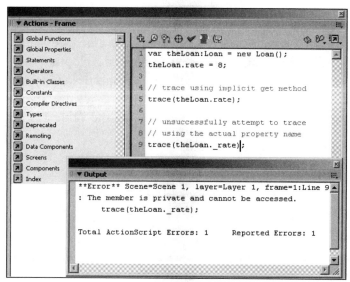

FIGURE 3.6   A compile-time error is thrown trying to access the private property _rate.

At first glance, the use of implicit getters and setters may seem preferable, as developers using them can continue to believe they are interacting with the properties directly. However, we do not consider their use a best practice. The reason for this is that developers new to OOP should learn that they should not build objects that enable direct access over the objects properties. The use of implicit getters and setters lets these new developers believe that experienced developers are building objects that allow for direct access to properties. This is likely to lead to new developers not using proper encapsulation and data hiding.

TIP

While implicit getters and setters are perfectly adequate for the job of data hiding and abstraction, they lack the clarity of an explicit getter and setter method. For this reason, we encourage developers to use explicit getter and setter methods, rather than their implicit counterparts.

Static Properties

One last addition in ActionScript 2.0 as it applies to properties is the addition of the keyword static. A static property is a property of the class, as opposed to a property of an instance of a class. This allows for an easy, non-redundant way for each member of a class to share a particular piece of data.

Built-In Objects with Static Properties

While the term *static property* may seem like a new concept, the reality is that we have dealt with static properties in Flash development for years. The properties of the Math class are all static properties. They are never invoked against an instance of the Math class; instead, they are invoked against the class itself. Consider the syntax we use to refer to the value PI:

```
var ecircumference = Math.PI * diameter;
```

Notice how PI is referred to as a property of the Math class, not as a property of an instance of the Math class.

> **NOTE**
>
> The reality is that the Math class is one of a special breed of classes, known as *singletons*, that can have only one instance, so there is no way to refer to PI as a property of an instance. While this is true of the Math class, it is not necessarily true for all classes with static properties.

Adding Static Properties to Custom Classes

In addition to built-in objects having static properties, it is also possible for us to add static properties to our own classes. To declare a property as static, we use the `static` keyword before the `var` declaration, but after the `public` or `private` declaration, if it exists. Listing 3.5 shows the declaration of a static property in an `Employee` class.

LISTING 3.5   A Newly Defined Employee Class Is Using a Static Property Describing the Company for which the Employee Is Working

```
class Employee {
    private var firstName:String;
    private var lastName:String;
    private static var company:String = "Tapper.net Consulting";

    function getCompany():String{
        return Employee.company;
    }
    function getFirstName():String{
        return this.firstName;
    }
}
```

In addition to instance properties `firstname` and `lastname` (an instance property is any property attached to an instance of a class), a static property is defined to hold the company name. This is a good fit for a static property, as any employee in the system is, by definition, an employee of this company.

It's important to notice the difference between the getter methods for the instance property (`getFirstName`) and the static property (`getCompany`). The `getFirstName()` method returns `this.firstName`. This works because the keyword `this` refers to an instance of the class, so when `getFirstName()` is invoked, it returns the `firstName` property of that instance. The `getCompany()` method returns `Employee.company` because `company` is a static property. Therefore, it belongs to the class `Employee`, rather than to any instance of the class. If this method was mistakenly coded as shown in the following code, the compile-time error shown in Figure 3.7 would be thrown.

```
function getCompany():String{
       return this.company;
}
```

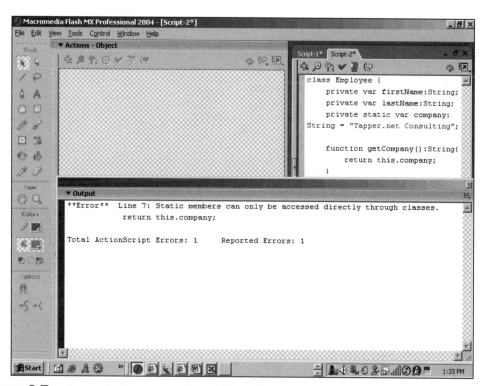

FIGURE 3.7   A compile-time error is thrown if a static property is referred to as an instance property.

> **NOTE**
>
> In Chapter 4, you learn that the `static` keyword can be used for methods as well as for properties.

Summary

Properties are an integral part of classes and OOP. In practice, they are no different than any other variable, except that they are specifically bound to a particular object (or class, in the case of static properties). Chapter 4 describes the behaviors of an object with methods.

METHOD TO THE MADNESS

In Chapter 3, "We're All Described by Our Properties," we covered how properties are important to the idea of a class definition. The Loan class in that chapter had variables attached to the class, including principal, rate, and years.

In this current chapter, we delve into the idea of attaching functions to the class. Just as a variable, when attached to a class, is known as a property, a function when attached to a class is known as a method. When a method is defined in a class definition, all these methods are available to any objects created from that class. For example, getURL() is a function that is defined by the MovieClip class. Every movie clip object that you create, whether with the drawing tools, the createEmptyMovieClip() method, or by subclassing the MovieClip class, will contain the getURL() method. See Figure 4.1.

FIGURE 4.1   The methods of the `MovieClip` class, as shown in the Actions panel.

As you go through this chapter, you will find that understanding methods and their benefits is essential to object-oriented programming (OOP).

Understanding the Role of Methods in ActionScript 2.0

ActionScript has had a very interesting and unique history. It started in Flash 4 as a procedural language with limited syntax and functionality. It is now an object-oriented language that is similar to Java and known as ActionScript 2.0.

> **NOTE**
>
> There are many functions and methods with the same name in ActionScript 2.0; for example, there is both a `gotoAndPlay` function in ActionScript 2.0 as well as a `gotoAndPlay` method of the `MovieClip` class. To maintain backward compatibility, Macromedia will usually not remove old functionality.

ActionScript 2.0 is utilized by both designers and developers and these two audiences have very different needs. For example, when a designer uses a `gotoAndPlay` method on the main timeline, there is no need to instantiate an object because the main timeline is always instantiated. A developer may also create a user-defined function in ActionScript 2.0 on the main timeline; this is really a method of the main timeline object. As we will see throughout this book, it can be inefficient to attach code to timelines, and in many cases, pure class-based development can make more sense because it makes sense to include methods as parts of classes.

Understanding Methods in Real-World Coding

A method is an action that can be performed on or by an object. For example, with a book, we could have methods on the object such as `read`, `write`, and `edit`. A method is aware of all the public and private properties of the object and because of this, can easily work with that object using a method. For example, a `read` method of a book object would know the properties `authors`, `chapters`, and `publisher`.

Assuming that we had a class of `Book`, and an object derived from that class called `oopAs` that contained properties of `publisher`, `totalChapter`, and `currentPage`, you could go to Table 4.1 for a list of the methods of that class.

TABLE 4.1   Methods of This Book

METHOD NAME	RETURNS
getPublisher()	New Riders
getTotalChapters()	17
gotoNextPage()	currentPage +1

In the following subsections, the text contains further details about methods.

ActionScript 2.0 Functions Versus ActionScript 2.0 Methods

All methods in ActionScript 2.0 are defined with the function keyword. However, there are very few real, free-standing functions in ActionScript 2.0. Most functions are methods of an object. For example, the getURL () function is actually a method of the MovieClip class. This function works fine if referenced from a MovieClip object (such as the main timeline), but will return an error of undefined if used within a class that has no relation to the MovieClip class, as shown in Listing 4.1:

LISTING 4.1   *getURL* Is Available to Use on the Timeline

```
function getHomeAdvisor() :Void
{
 this.getURL (http://www.homeadvisor.com, "_parent"); //opens up URL in
external browser window
}
this.getHomeAdvisor();
```

In Listing 4.2, the function from Listing 4.1 is used within the Loan class, which, in this case, has nothing to do with a movie clip. Flash states that getURL is undefined, as shown in Figure 4.2.

LISTING 4.2   The Function from Listing 4.1 Fails Here

```
class Loan {
     function Loan() {} //constructor

     function getHomeAdvisor(){
     this.getURL ("http://www.homeadvisor.com)", "_parent" )//results
in an undefined error
     }
}
```

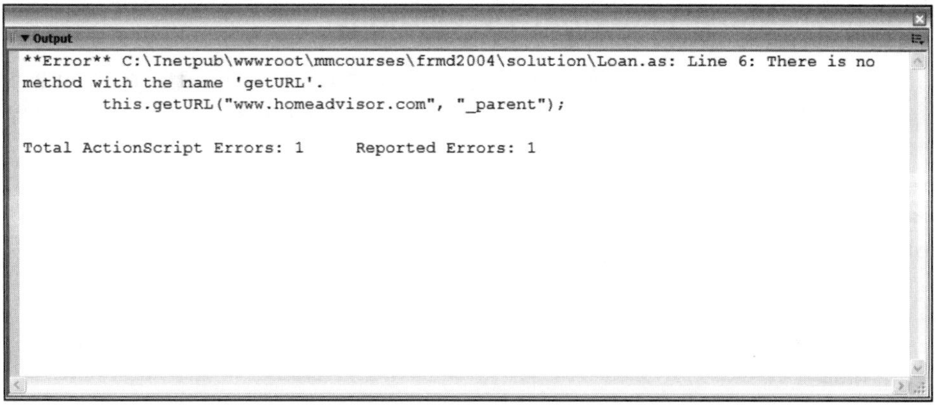

FIGURE 4.2   Undefined getURL.

There are some functions in Macromedia Flash MX 2004, however, that are truly global, stand-alone functions. Examples include getTimer() and setInterval(). These functions can be used anywhere and objects do not have to be instantiated to use them, as shown in the following code:

```
{
        function Loan () {} //constructor
        function getElaspedTime ()
{
        return getTimer() //returns the number of milliseconds elapsed
since the SWF was loaded
}
}
```

Here is a list of some true functions (not methods) within ActionScript 2.0:

- getTimer()
- setInterval()
- clearInterval()
- getVersion()
- isNan()
- MMexecute()
- Number()
- eval()
- escape()
- unescape()
- trace()

User-Defined Functions to Methods

Whenever you add a function to the main timeline, you are creating a method attached to that timeline. For example, consider the following code attached to the main timeline:

```
var name :String = "James";
this.getName = function ()
{
return this.name;
}
trace (getName());
```

The output of "James" would result from the preceding code. getName() is now a method that is attached to only one object, not a class. In this case, the object is referenced by the this keyword. When the preceding code is placed on the main timeline, the this keyword refers to the main timeline.

Note that the scope of a method is affected by the order of the code; for example, the following code would result in an error of undefined because getName() has not yet been defined:

```
var name :String = "James";
trace (getName());
this.getName = function ()
{
return this.name;
}
```

To avoid these errors of scope, you should define methods using the function keyword. Using the function keyword, scope is not an issue. The following code would return "James":

```
var name :String = "James";
trace (getName());
function getName ()
{
return this.name;
}
```

You should get in the habit of defining all methods using the `function` keyword. Reason? Doing it the other way is not permitted in a class definition. For example, the following class definition results in an error:

```
class Loan
{
        var interestRate = 5.1;
        function Loan () {} //constructor
        this.getInterestRate = function () {
                return interestRate;
        }
}
```

The preceding code would produce the error in Figure 4.3.

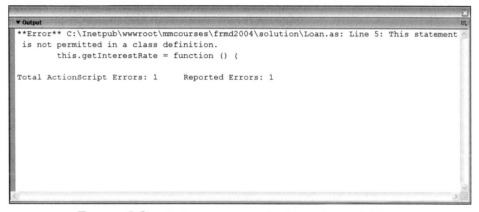

FIGURE 4.3   Statement not permitted in a class definition.

Functions within classes *must* be defined, as shown in the following code:

```
class Loan
{
        var interestRate = 5.1;
        function Loan () {} //constructor
        function getInterestRate () {
                return interestRate;
        }
}
```

> **NOTE**
>
> From this point on, all method definitions in this book will use the preceding notation.

Note that this book focuses on class-based development. In OOP, you should not assign functions to an individual object, but instead to a class. Generally, it is a bad practice to create methods that are attached to only one object. Following these best practices, this book attaches code directly to classes and uses only the timeline to instantiate those classes.

TIP

Understanding methods is integral to class based development. If we just create unique movie clips, as opposed to creating classes, distribution becomes difficult. It is much easier to distribute class files to other developers than it is to extract all the code from an individual movie clip in a FLA file. It also results in more maintainable and scaleable applications because it is much easier to make global changes in a movie clip.

Strong Datatypes for Methods

All methods (when they are declared) should specify the type of data they are returning. For example, in the following code, the getName() method is indicating that a string will be returned:

```
var name :String = "James";
trace (getName());
function getName () :String
{
return this.name;
}
```

Flash MX 2004 has added a new datatype/returntype of Void. When you have a method that does not return any data, it is a best practice to always specify that the method does not return anything by using the Void keyword, as shown in the following code:

```
class Loan {
var interestRate = 5.1;
function Loan (){}

function getInterestRate() :String {
        return interestRate;
}

function setInterestRate(interestRate:String) :Void {
        this.interestRate = interestRate;
}
}
```

Private Attribute for Methods

A new feature within ActionScript 2.0 gives us the ability to determine from where methods can be accessed. This is done with the keywords `public` and `private`. Methods that will not be used outside the class should be declared as `private`. In the following example, the methods `doDrag` and `doDrop` will be used only within the `Drag` class and therefore should be referenced as `private`:

```
class Drag extends MovieClip
{
function Drag ()
{
onPress = doDrag;
onRelease = doDrop;
}
private function doDrag () :Void
{
        this.startDrag();
}
private function doDrop () :Void
{
        this.stopDrag();
}
}

}
```

> **NOTE**
>
> The `extends` keyword means that we can use all the methods of the `MovieClip` class.

In Flash MX 2004, private methods are not truly private because they are inherited by any subclasses from that class. In the following example, the `RollEffect` class inherits all methods from the `Drag` class even though the methods have been assigned the `private` attribute in the `Drag` class:

```
class RollEffect extends Drag
{
        function RollEffect ()
        {
                onPress = doDrag;
                onRelease = doDrop;
                onRollOver = doAlpha;
        }
```

```
private function doAlpha () :Void
{
        this._alpha = 50;
}
}
```

In most OOP languages, inheriting from a method, but not being able to access it, is known as working with a protected method. However, in ActionScript 2.0, protected methods are referred to as private. There is no way in ActionScript 2.0 to build a class that does not inherit its private properties.

Of course, it is certainly possible in ActionScript 2.0 to access a property directly, as shown in the following code:

```
class Loan {
var interestRate
function Loan (latestRate :Number){
        this.interestRate = latestRate
        }
}
```

There is nothing wrong with this approach, but using methods will result in more maintainable and scaleable applications.

Data Hiding

As we saw in Chapter 3, it is a best practice to always access properties within a class through methods instead of directly accessing the property. When we use methods to access a property, we have more control over any changes that are made because the property itself is hidden and accessed only through external methods. Data hiding makes code more maintainable and scalable.

Let's take the TextField class in Flash MX 2004 as an example of data hiding. Throughout many applications, people have repeatedly accessed the .text property directly, as shown in Figure 4.4.

Setting a property directly could result in maintainability problems if Macromedia ever decided to change the name of the .text property to another name. We would have to go through every single line of code of every application built and change the property references to the new property name. However, if the text field had been built with getter/setter methods (discussed in the next section), all we would have to do is change the property name within the method and it would not affect the end application at all.

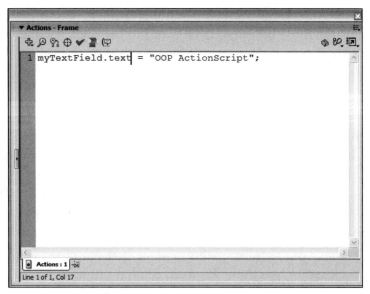

FIGURE 4.4   Setting the `.text` property directly.

> **NOTE**
>
> Of course, this is just an example. One of the top priorities of any Flash release is backward compatibility, so it is highly unlikely that the `.text` property will ever change; however, we are not always so lucky with custom classes because property names can change on a whim based on the customer.

Getters and Setters

To completely understand the importance of getter/setter methods, we are going to create a movie clip with a text field inside it. Instead of accessing the `.text` property directly, we are going to access the property through two new methods, `getText()` and `setText()`. The first step is to define a new class that extends the current text field class, as shown in the following code:

```
class TextControl extends TextField
{
      function TextControl () {}; //Constructor
}
```

> **NOTE**
>
> The `extends` keyword is covered in detail in Chapter 5. Used in the preceding code, it simply means that we can use all the methods of the `TextField` class.

In Chapter 3, we looked at two ways of creating getter/setter methods. We determined that the best practice was not to use the keywords `get` and `set`. Because we extended the `textField` class, the `.text` property is inherited by our new `TextControl` class. All we need to do is build getter/setter methods for that class.

For instance, in the `setText` method, we set the `autoSize` property of the `textField` to `true`, and we populate the text property to the value that is passed in from the method. The `getText` method returns the value of whatever is in the current `textField`. The advantage of this approach is that it separates the development of the class from the use of the class. No matter what happens, the `TextControl` class will use `getText()` and `setText()` even if other parts of the code change.

As an example of the functionality, assume that our client would now like all `textFields` to be one font. We could set that up in `setText()`:

```
class TextControl extends TextField
{
        function TextControl () {};

        public function setText(textToSet :String) :Void
        {
                trace (this.theText);
                this.theText.autoSize = true;
                this.theText.text = textToSet;
        }

        public function getText () :String
        {
                return this.theText.text;
        }
}
```

The final step in building a new `TextControl` class is to link a visual object, which, in this case, is a text field inside a movie clip, to the class we just built. You can do this with the following step sequence.

1. Save the class as TextControl.as.

2. Create a new FLA file and create a new movie clip by choosing Insert > New Symbol.

3. Name the symbol **TextControlSymbol**.

4. Click Advanced and in the class field, type **TextControl**.

5. Place a TextField object inside the movie clip.

6. Assign the text field an instance name of **theText**.

7. Drag an instance of the TextControlSymbol onto the Stage.

8. Assign the TextControlSymbol instance a name of **myText**.

9. Add the following code to populate the `textField` with a method:

```
myText.setText("OOP ActionScript");
```

Building Implicit Getters/Setters

Implicit getter/setter methods are one way to access properties in ActionScript 2.0. *Implicit* methods use the keywords `get` and `set`. The big difference between explicit and implicit getter/setter methods is how they are called. They are referenced by the end user as properties even though behind the scenes they are actually methods. For example, in v1 components, `setDataProvider()` was a method. In v2 components, it is now an implicit setter property (still really a method) and accessed as shown in the following code:

```
var myArray :Array = new Array();
myArray[0] ="US";
myArray[1] = "Canada";
var myCombo.dataProvider = myArray;
```

These getter/setter methods cannot share the same name as the underlying property. The following code would be a bad practice because `text` is an existing property of the `TextField` class:

```
class TextControl extends TextField
{
        function OOText () {};

        public function set text(textToSet :String) :Void
        {
                trace (this.theText);
                this.theText.autoSize = true;
                this.theText.text = textToSet;
        }

        public function get text () :String
        {
                return this.theText.text;
        }
}
```

If we wanted to use implicit getter/setters, we would need to change the name of the methods to something else, such as _text, as shown in the following code:

```
class TextControl extends TextField
{
        function TextControl () {};

        public function set _text(textToSet :String) :Void
        {
                trace (this.theText);
                this.theText.autoSize = true;
                this.theText.text = textToSet;
        }

        public function get _text () :String
        {
                return this.theText.text;
        }
}
```

The getter/setter methods would be invoked by simply referencing the _text method just like a property, as shown in the following code:

```
<instance>._text = "OOPActionScript";
<variable> = <instance>._text;
```

With implicit getters/setters, it is impossible for the end user to tell if a method or a property is being accessed and this is why we encourage the use of explicit getters/setters. Of course, by using implicit getter/setters, we still only have to make changes in the class, and not in the use of the class, so those advantages are retained.

Using Static Methods

It is possible to access class fields and class methods without creating an instance or an object of a class. You can do so by using the static key word. By declaring a method with the static key word, the method becomes associated with the class itself, not with instances of the class. In a sense, static or "class" fields and methods are global variables and methods that we can touch using the class name. The major advantage of static methods is that each object does not have to use memory in the Flash Player. A disadvantage is that static methods are not aware of properties in an object instance because they are only associated with a class. Static methods are not useful when you need to know about properties and methods in an object.

You call static methods by actually referencing the class name, as in the following example; there is no need to create an object instance from the class.

```
trace (Math.Random());
```

We can add custom static methods to our own classes. For example, in the Employee class, where employer is a static method, it makes sense to retrieve that information using a static method. If there are multiple employees, this will conserve memory because it will be stored with the class and not each object.

```
class Employee {
        private var firstName:String;
        private var lastName:String;
        private static var company:String = "Tapper.net Consulting";

        public static function getCompany():String{
                return Employee.company;
        }
        function getFirstName():String{
                return this.firstName;
        }
}
```

Summary

Methods, in practice, are no different than any other function, except that they are specifically bound to a particular object (or class, in the case of static methods). Methods are essential to performing an action on an object, and object methods are aware of the properties of that class.

ActionScript 2.0 is mostly composed of methods. If you place your code on the main timeline or on the timeline of a movie clip, you are basically attaching methods to a MovieClip object. This can be one of the most confusing concepts of ActionScript 2.0 because the main timeline is always instantiated. For example, getURL can be used on the main timeline but cannot be used within a class because it's a method of the MovieClip object. Whenever a function is defined on the main timeline, it's really a method of the main timeline MovieClip object. There are some freestanding built-in functions in ActionScript 2.0, such as getTimer(). These functions can be used anywhere.

If a method returns a datatype, it is a best practice to specify what datatype, such as String, Object or Array, is returned. If the method returns nothing, the datatype of Void should be specified.

The best practice in ActionScript 2.0 is to perform as much class-based development as possible. This means creating methods within classes, instead of creating methods attached to the timelines of objects. It is important to do this because it allows us to build much more scaleable and maintainable applications.

By creating methods within classes, we can specify whether they are public or private. If they are private, methods can be accessed only in the class (or any subclasses). In terms of OOP development, it is a best practice to always access variables through methods.

Note that static methods enable us to conserve resources and they cannot be data aware. In addition, methods are an integral part of classes and class-based development.

CHAPTER 5

THE MEEK SHALL INHERIT THE EARTH

In Flash, everything is an object. This chapter reveals the mechanics that support that statement—the mechanics of inheritance. The hierarchy of built-in objects in Flash will serve as a foundation for all custom objects created in a Flash application. Techniques (such as polymorphism), which are at the core of object-oriented programming, will be demonstrated and their benefits realized in this chapter.

Understanding Object Composition and Inheritance

So far, we have covered the mechanics of object composition. We saw the evolution of the class definition to an object instance, variations on method and property definitions, and encapsulation by restricting access to those class members. We saw that we can create a `Loan` class that has a property called `rate` and a method called `getPayment()`.

All this is known as object composition. In the coming sections of this chapter, we establish relationships between objects. We call this process inheritance. We also cover the importance of inheritance in an object-oriented language and the mechanics of implementing inheritance in ActionScript 2.0.

With inheritance, we want to establish an "is a" relationship. We can say a banana "is a" fruit or a garage "is a" building. In both cases, we have established a relationship that equates to inheritance. Throughout this chapter, we cover the mechanics of developing "is a" relationships, the importance of them, and how they facilitate polymorphism.

What Is Inheritance Exactly?

We can equate inheritance in object-oriented programming (OOP) to human inheritance. Just as our children can potentially inherit all our characteristics and capabilities, so too can one object inherit from another. In the human genetic code, mother nature randomly selects which characteristics our off-spring will have and which will be overridden.

In OOP we, as programmers, play mother nature. An object that is "a child" of another object has all the characteristics of the parent, unless we decide to replace or override the characteristic. We do not, however, use random logic to include or exclude a characteristic. Instead, we carefully plan our object hierarchy based on sound and proven patterns and methodology. A good object hierarchy is the foundation of a well-built, object-oriented application.

Where object-oriented inheritance differs from human inheritance is that in object-oriented inheritance, we can extend an object definition by adding methods and properties that don't exist in the ancestor. This enables us to start with a generalized set of characteristics in the ancestor and move to a more specialized set in the descendant.

Why Is Inheritance Important?

Reusability is one of the primary characteristics of OOP. Inheritance helps us to write application components that are efficient, compact, and reusable. Inheritance enables us to create new classes that are based on an existing class.

By creating a *subclass* of an existing class, the subclass contains, by virtue of inheritance, all the properties and methods of the *superclass*. The subclass typically defines additional methods and properties, which is also known as *extending* the superclass. Subclasses can also change an inherited behavior by *overriding* superclass methods.

For example, you might create a `Loan` class that defines certain properties and methods common to all loans. From the `Loan` class, you could then create a `CarLoan` class that extends the `Loan` class. This promotes code reuse. All loans have common elements, so instead of recreating all the code common to both classes, you can simply extend the `Loan` class. You can say a `CarLoan` *is a kind of* Loan. In Figure 5.1, you can say that an apple *is a kind of* fruit and fruit *is a kind of* food.

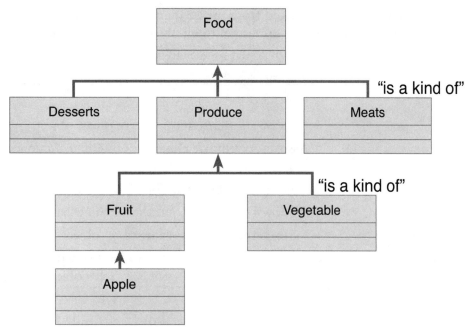

FIGURE 5.1   Fruit hierarchy.

In a complex application, the structure of the objects and their inheritance hierarchy is determined during the design process. But in many cases, inheritance is a natural progression during the development process where you find yourself writing the same code more than once. This is the first clue that you should consider an inheritance structure.

NOTE

Rule of inheritance: Create a superclass-subclass relationship when you can argue that the subclass can be viewed as an instance of itself as well as an instance of the ancestor. For example, an apple is a kind of fruit or a garage is a kind of building or a car loan is a kind of loan.

The Class Hierarchy of Built-In Objects

In Flash, there is a built-in object hierarchy that is used even without creating a single superclass or subclass. Each time you use a built-in object in Flash, you are using the object hierarchy.

Everything Is an Object

In Flash, everything is derived from the `Object` class. The `Object` class provides a set of methods that are useful to all objects, visual and nonvisual. Table 5.1 shows the methods in the `Object` class definition.

TABLE 5.1   Object Methods (from Flash Help Files)

METHOD	DESCRIPTION
`Object.addProperty()`	Creates a getter/setter property on an object
`Object.registerClass()`	Associates a movie clip symbol with an ActionScript 2.0 object class
`Object.toString()`	Converts the specified object to a string and returns it
`Object.unwatch()`	Removes the watchpoint that `Object.watch()` created
`Object.valueOf()`	Returns the primitive value of an object
`Object.watch()`	Registers an event handler to be invoked when a specified property of an ActionScript 2.0 object changes

Because every object in Flash inherits from the `Object` class, they all have the `Object` methods available. Of particular interest is the `Object.registerClass()` method. This method allows us to create a link or relationship between a visual Library entry and an object definition.

Visual and Nonvisual Objects

In ActionScript 2.0, as in other languages, we can classify our objects as visual or nonvisual. This is an important distinction and should be determined during the design phase of an application. There are many design patterns that strictly delineate between visual and nonvisual entities in a pattern. Chapter 8, "Object-Oriented Design," provides examples of design patterns.

We can also use this distinction for application partitioning. Classic partitioning uses a client/server model, where the client represents the visual or display components and the server represents the nonvisual or data components. In Flash, the `MovieClip` object is the most commonly used visual object. Nonvisual objects are created as classes to encapsulate data and business logic. Implicitly both the `MovieClip` object and all nonvisual classes share a common ancestor in Flash—the `Object` object.

For example, in our loan application, loanCalc.fla is the client or visual component and Loan.class is the nonvisual data component serving data to the client. See Figure 5.2.

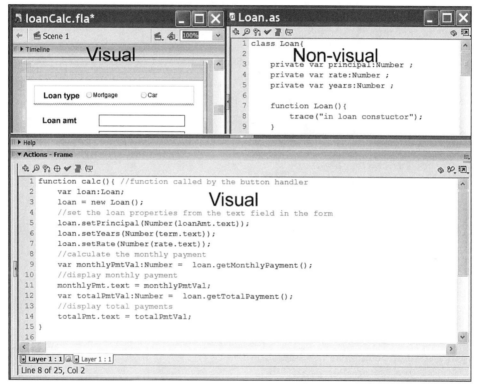

FIGURE 5.2   Loan hierarchy.

Where Do Our Classes Fit In?

As we start to create objects in an application, we categorize them as visual and nonvisual. After we have made the delineation between the two, we can use built-in Flash objects to get us started. All nonvisual objects implicitly inherit the properties of the `Object` class. Visual objects can inherit from the `MovieClip` class or any other class derived form the `MovieClip` class.

Implementing Inheritance

Before we can implement inheritance, we should understand the basic guidelines for architecting superclasses and subclasses. The basic guidelines are as follows:

- Common attributes and methods are *generalized* in the superclass.
- Specific attributes and methods are *specialized* in the subclass.

In the Loan class, we have methods and properties that are common to all types of loans. Listing 5.1 shows the Loan class.

LISTING 5.1   Revisiting the *Loan* Class

```
class Loan{
        private var principal:Number ;
        private var rate:Number ;
        private var years:Number ;

        public function Loan(){
                trace("in loan constuctor");
        }

        public function setPrincipal(thePrincipal:Number ) {
                principal = thePrincipal;
        }

        public function setRate(theRate:Number) {
                rate=theRate;
        }

        public function setYears(theYears:Number ) {
                years=theYears;
        }
        public function getYears( ):Number {
                return years;
        }

        public function  getMonthlyPayment( ):Number {
                var months:Number = this.getYears() *12;
                var monthlyRate:Number = this.rate /(12*100);
                var payment:Number = this.principal * (monthlyRate / (1 -
Math.pow(1 + monthlyRate,-months)));
                return payment;
        }
```

```
public function getTotalPayment( ):Number {
      var months:Number= this.getYears() * 12;
      return getMonthlyPayment() * months;
}

}
```

What if we wanted to specialize the Loan class for a car or a mortgage? We could add additional properties and methods to the Loan class for each type of loan or we could use inheritance to extend the loan definition for each new type of loan. In Figure 5.3, you can see the hierarchy we might use to solve the problem. Notice that the generalized properties and methods exist in the ancestor, Loan, while the properties and methods specific to cars or mortgages are in the descendants only. The descendants also have all the members of the ancestor.

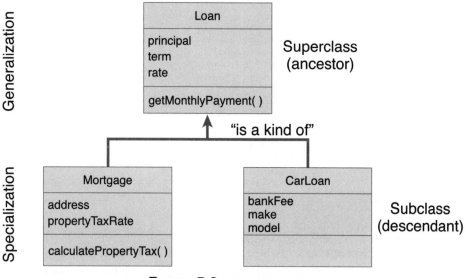

FIGURE 5.3   Loan hierarchy.

> **NOTE**
>
> Unified Modeling Language (UML) is the notation used in Figure 5.3. It is a standard used for describing object relationships and hierarchies.

extends Keyword

To implement the inheritance hierarchy for the loan solution in Figure 5.3, we can use the extends keyword, as seen in Listing 5.2.

LISTING 5.2   Subclassing the *Loan* Class

```
class CarLoan extends Loan{

    private var bankFee:Number ;

    public function  getBankFee( ):Number {
        return this.bankFee;
    }
    public function setBankFee( fee:Number):Void {
        this.bankFee = fee;
    }
}

class Mortgage extends Loan{

    private var insurancePremium:Number ;

    public function  getInsurancePremium( ):Number {
        return this.insurancePremium;
    }
    public function setInsurancePremium( fee:Number):Void {
        this.insurancePremium = fee;
    }
}
```

When a class is created using the extends keyword, the class inherits all the methods and properties of the ancestor class. In Listing 5.2, you can see that the CarLoan and Mortgage classes extend the Loan class. In both cases, we have added the members that are specific to the type of loan.

At this point, we have made each loan type unique by adding the attributes. To use the attributes, the implementing application, LoanCalc, has to be modified. Additional logic also has to be added to determine which type of loan is required.

If you recall, LoanCalc.fla has a method called calc(), as shown in Listing 5.3.

LISTING 5.3 *calc* Method in LoanCalc.fla

```
function calc(){ //function called by the button handler
      var loan:Loan = new Loan();

      //set the loan properties from the text field in the form
      loan.setPrincipal(Number(loanAmt.text));
      loan.setYears(Number(term.text));
      loan.setRate(Number(rate.text));

      //calculate the monthly payment
      var monthlyPmtVal:Number =  loan.getMonthlyPayment();

      //display monthly payment
      monthlyPmt.text = monthlyPmtVal;
      var totalPmtVal:Number =  loan.getTotalPayment();

      //display total payments
      totalPmt.text = totalPmtVal;
}
```

To determine the loan type, we have to add the selection capability to the user interface, as shown in Figure 5.4:

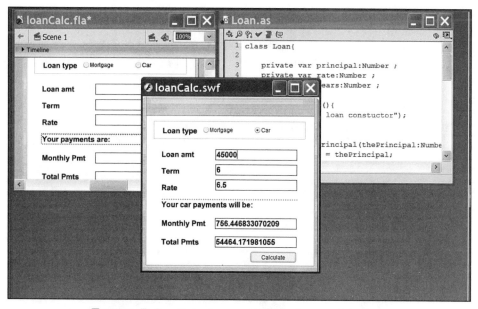

FIGURE 5.4 Selection capability in the user interface.

After the user has indicated a loan type, the selected value is used to determine which type of loan to instantiate. Listing 5.4 shows the additional logic needed to implement the correct type of loan object.

LISTING 5.4 *calc* Method in LoanCalc.fla

```
function calc(){ //function called by the button handler
        var loan;
        if (loanType.selectedData == "mortgage"){
                loan = new Mortgage();
                loan.setPropertyTaxRate(15);

                //set the loan properties from the text field in the form
                loan.setPrincipal(Number(loanAmt.text));
                loan.setYears(Number(term.text));
                loan.setRate(Number(rate.text));

                //calculate the monthly payment
                var monthlyPmtVal:Number =
loan.getMonthlyPayment()+loan.getPropertyTax();
                var totalPmtVal:Number =  loan.getTotalPayment();
        }else if(loanType.selectedData == "car"){
                loan = new CarLoan();
                loan.setBankFee(25);

                //set the loan properties from the text field in the form
                loan.setPrincipal(Number(loanAmt.text));
                loan.setYears(Number(term.text));
                loan.setRate(Number(rate.text));

                //calculate the monthly payment
                var monthlyPmtVal:Number =
loan.getMonthlyPayment()+loan.getBankFee();
                var totalPmtVal:Number =  loan.getTotalPayment();
        }


        //display monthly payment
        monthlyPmt.text = monthlyPmtVal;

        //display total payments
        totalPmt.text = totalPmtVal;
}
```

To calculate the car loan, add the bank fee to the monthly payment before displaying the results. In the case of a mortgage, add the `propertyTax` property to the monthly payment. The only problem with this approach is code redundancy. In both cases, we are calling all the same methods except those that make the loan unique.

A better solution would be to hide the complexity of the differences in the objects themselves. For example, we could apply the property tax and the bank fees in the individual classes. To do this, we can use a concept called *overriding*.

Method and Property Overriding

When we describe inheritance as extending a definition, in some cases, that might mean changing an original member. In the subclass, we have identified a need to hide the complexity of the new elements of the class within the subclass. Note that we can hide or limit access to class members using access modifiers such as private or protected. Table 5.2 shows the restrictions access modifiers place on objects as part of an inheritance hierarchy.

TABLE 5.2   Property and Method Accessibility

ACCESS MODIFIER	CLASS ITSELF	SAME PACKAGE	SUBCLASS	ANY CLASS
public	X	X	X	X
private	X		X	

In the subclass, we can make the new property private and limit access to it from within the containing class. Listing 5.5 shows the `CarLoan` class hiding the `bankFee` property and `getBankFee()` method by making them private. We can still set the property from another object, but the only place where we can read it is in the object itself.

LISTING 5.5   *CarLoan* Class in CarLoan.as

```
class CarLoan extends Loan{

    private var bankFee:Number ;

    public function setBankFee( fee:Number):Void {
         this.bankFee = fee;
    }

    public function  getMonthlyPayment( ):Number {
         var months:Number = years*12;
         var monthlyRate:Number = rate /(12*100);
```

continues

LISTING 5.5   Continued

```
            var payment:Number = principal * (monthlyRate /
            ➥(1 - Math.pow(1 + monthlyRate,-months))));
            return payment + this.bankFee;
    }

    public function getTotalPayment( ):Number {
            var months:Number= this.getYears() * 12;
            return (this.getMonthlyPayment()+this.bankFee)* months
;
    }
}
```

We can provide the same encapsulation for the Mortgage class, as shown in Listing 5.6.

LISTING 5.6   *Mortgage* Class in Mortgage.as

```
class Mortgage extends Loan{

    private var insurancePremium:Number ;

    public function setInsurancePremium( fee:Number):Void {
            this.insurancePremium = fee;
    }

    public function  getMonthlyPayment( ):Number {
            var months:Number = years*12;
            var monthlyRate:Number = rate /(12*100);
            var payment:Number = principal * (monthlyRate / (1 -
Math.pow(1 + monthlyRate,-months)));
            return payment + this.insurancePremium;
    }

    public function getTotalPayment( ):Number {
            var months:Number= this.getYears() * 12;
            return (getMonthlyPayment()+this.insurancePremium)
  * months;
    }
}
```

By doing this, we will have less redundancy in the client, LoanCalc. In Listing 5.7, we have eliminated the need for separating the calls that calculate monthly payment by loan type because we have moved the type-specific properties into the subclass.

LISTING 5.7   *calc* Method in LoanCalc.fla

```
function calc(){ //function called by the button handler
      var loan;
      if (loanType.selectedData == "m"){
            loan = new Mortgage();
            loan.setInsurancePremium(15);
      }else{
            loan = new CarLoan();
            loan.setBankFee(25);
      }
      //set the loan properties from the text field in the form
      loan.setPrincipal(Number(loanAmt.text));
      loan.setYears(Number(term.text));
      loan.setRate(Number(rate.text));

      //calculate the monthly payment
      var monthlyPmtVal:Number =  loan.getMonthlyPayment();

      //display monthly payment
      monthlyPmt.text = monthlyPmtVal;
      var totalPmtVal:Number =  loan.getTotalPayment();

      //display total payments
      totalPmt.text = totalPmtVal;
}
```

We are almost done implementing a sound inheritance structure. If you revisit Listings 5.5 and 5.6, you will notice that we still have a lot of redundancy. The code in getMonthlyPayments() and getTotalPayments() is almost identical to that of the code's ancestor, and it appears in both subclasses. Because a primary goal of OOP is to prevent coding redundancy, we need one more super object-oriented concept to get us there.

super—Thanks for Asking...

One more little thing to add to our inheritance model is the ability to refer to a superclass from a subclass. In Listing 5.8, we can see that the getMonthlyPayment() method has changed. It is now calling the method in its ancestor, Loan, rather than having the code itself. This truly centralizes the method code in one object, the ancestor, so that the only class members needed in the descendant object are the new members.

To call the ancestor method, we use the super keyword. super always refers to the direct ancestor of the calling object. In Listing 5.8, we are using the super keyword to call the Loan class method that returns the base amount. We can then add the bank fee and return the value to the client.

LISTING 5.8   *CarLoan* Extending *Loan*

```
class CarLoan extends Loan{
    private var bankFee:Number ;

    public function  getBankFee( ):Number {
        return this.bankFee;
    }
    public function setBankFee( fee:Number):Void {
        this.bankFee = fee;
    }
    public function  getMonthlyPayment( ):Number {
        var monthlyPayment:Number = super.getMonthlyPayment()
        ➥+ this.getBankFee();
        return monthlyPayment;
    }
    public function getTotalPayment( ):Number {
        var months:Number= super.getYears() * 12;
        var totalPayments:Number = super.getTotalPayment()
        ➥+ ( months *  this.getBankFee());
        return totalPayments;
    }

}
```

The Mortgage class can use the same construct and reduce redundancy, as we see in Listing 5.9.

LISTING 5.9   *Mortgage* Extending *Loan*

```
class Mortgage extends Loan{
    private var insurancePremium:Number ;

    public function  getInsurancePremium( ):Number {
        return this.insurancePremium;
    }
    public function setInsurancePremium( fee:Number):Void {
        this.insurancePremium = fee;
    }
    public function  getMonthlyPayment( ):Number {
        var monthlyPayment:Number = super.getMonthlyPayment()
        ➥+ this.getInsurancePremium();
```

```
            return monthlyPayment;
        }
    public function getTotalPayment( ):Number {
            var months:Number= super.getYears() * 12;
            var totalPayments:Number = super.getTotalPayment()
            ➥+ ( months *   this.getInsurancePremium());
            return totalPayments;
        }
}
```

super and Constructors

Constructors are special methods. They are used to initialize an object. If we don't explicitly create a constructor, one is created for us by the compiler at compile time. The implicit constructor is called a no-argument, default constructor. Just as the compiler creates this constructor for us, it will also implicitly call it for us when the object is instantiated at runtime.

This has an impact on our inheritance hierarchy because there will be times when we will have a constructor with arguments that will often need to call its ancestor. There are special rules that govern this process.

As with any object, if you don't place a call to super() in the constructor function of a subclass, the compiler automatically generates a call to the constructor of its immediate superclass with no parameters as the first statement of the function. If the superclass doesn't have a constructor, the compiler creates an empty constructor function and then generates a call to it from the subclass. The problem arises when the superclass constructor takes parameters in its definition. In Listing 5.10, we have modified the constructor to take the necessary arguments to initialize the Loan object.

LISTING 5.10   *Loan* Constructor Modified

```
class Loan{

        private var principal:Number ;
        private var rate:Number ;
        private var years:Number ;

        function Loan(principal:Number, rate:Number, years:Number){
                trace("in loan constuctor");
                this.setPrincipal(principal);
                this.setNumber(rate);
                this.setYears(years);
        }
.. ..
}
```

Because the superclass constructor now takes arguments, we must add a constructor to the subclass to pass in the required parameters. Remember that the compiler will add a call to the no-argument constructor implicitly if we do not have a constructor at all. In Listing 5.11, we have added a constructor to the subclass that calls the superclass constructor with the required parameters.

LISTING 5.11   Constructors Using *super()* in Subclasses

```
class CarLoan extends Loan{

    private var bankFee:Number ;
    function CarLoan(principal:Number, rate:Number, years:Number){
        super(principal, rate, years);
    }
.. ...
}
```

You might have noticed that the first line of the subclass constructor seems different than superclass method calls we saw earlier. This is a special syntax used only for superclass constructor calls. The superclass constructor call must always be the first call in a subclass constructor, as shown.

A Word on Multiple Inheritance

Many object-oriented languages support multiple inheritance. That is, they inherit from more than one class. In Listing 5.12, class C is trying to inherit from A and B. This is not allowed in ActionScript.

LISTING 5.12   Illegal Multiple Inheritance

```
// not allowed
class C extends A, B {}
```

In Flash 2004, multiple inheritance is not allowed. However, we can achieve a similar result using the inheritance chain shown in Listing 5.13.

LISTING 5.13   Pseudo Multiple Inheritance

```
// allowed
class B extends A {}
class C extends B {}
//c inherits from both a and b.
```

Will the Real Method Please Stand Up

At runtime, when a method is called, there is a particular look-up through the inheritance chain to determine which method to execute. For example, let's consider the object hierarchy in Figure 5.5. Consider an object structure within a retail business application for all persons. All objects are persons. Some are employees, some are customers, and some employees are managers. This also shows how we might implement human resource methods in this hierarchy to calculate salaries, vacations, and bonuses for employees.

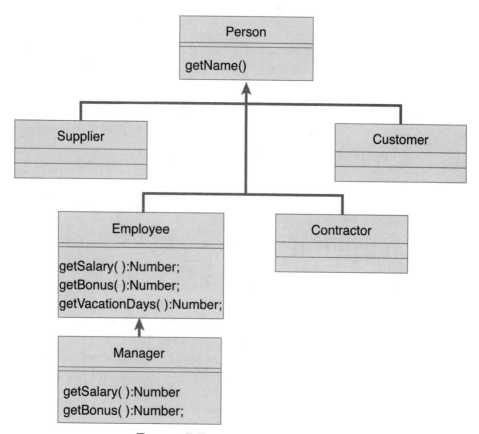

FIGURE 5.5   Person-object hierarchy.

At each level, methods are added or overridden as needed. It is important to understand how methods are executed at runtime. Figure 5.6 depicts the method lookup for methods when they are called from a `Manager` class instance.

Using the Manager instance:

    mgr:Manager = new Manager( );

mgr.getBonus( );	Calls the manager class method
mgr.getVacationDays( );	Calls the employee class method
mgr.getSalary( );	Calls the manager class methods
mgr.getName( );	Calls the person class method

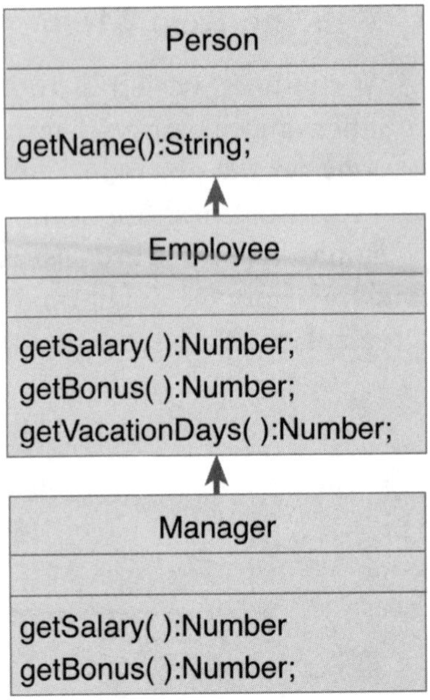

Person

getName():String;

Employee

getSalary( ):Number;
getBonus( ):Number;
getVacationDays( ):Number;

Manager

getSalary( ):Number
getBonus( ):Number;

FIGURE 5.6   Method Lookup for the `Manager` class.

Polymorphism

Let's say you have reserved a rental car for a trip to San Francisco. You have a confirmation for a car. A midsize car has been requested, but the exact make of the car won't be known until you get to the car rental counter and see what is actually available. But that doesn't preclude you from reserving the car. The actual make of the car will be known at runtime. This is polymorphism. In other words, polymorphism is the ability for objects to act like other objects in the inheritance hierarchy.

What Is It Again?

Polymorphism is an object-oriented mechanism that enables the method version executed to be determined at runtime based on the datatype of the object instance. It lets us use a superclass object datatype, knowing that at runtime, the object datatype will be of a subclass object datatype. We do this because the object datatype can be determined only at runtime.

In our loan calculator application, we use polymorphism. In Listing 5.14, you can see that depending on the user's selection at runtime, the type of loan could be car or mortgage. The `loan` instance variable has a static datatype of type `Loan`. However, at runtime, the loan instance could hold either a `Mortgage` instance or a `CarLoan` instance (called dynamic or actual datatype). In either case, the call to `getMonthlyPayment()` is identical.

LISTING 5.14 *Object Datatyping*

```
var loan:Loan; ←static datatype
if (loanType.selectedData == "m"){
      loan = new Mortgage(…)); ←datatype determined at run-time
}else{
        loan = new CarLoan(…); ←datatype determined at run-time
}
//calculate the monthly payment
var monthlyPmtVal:Number =  loan.getMonthlyPayment();
```

How Does It Work?

To better understand polymorphism, we can look at object datatyping and the superclass-subclass relationship. In the process, we will discover how casting, which is the changing of an object from one type to another, plays a key role in polymorphism.

Starting with object datatypes, Figure 5.7 shows a legal assignment with regard to the `Loan` class hierarchy. Notice that a variable of a superclass datatype can be used to reference an instance of a subclass.

When we create a variable of a particular type, the blueprint for that type is loaded and used to validate its usage. Because any subclass has everything its superclass has, there is no problem when a superclass blueprint is used to validate a subclass.

Although there will be many times when you will want to use the superclass datatype to point to a subclass instance, there is one limitation: Only the methods defined in the superclass can be invoked. In Figure 5.7, when we tried to execute a mortgage method, `calculatePropertyTax()`, the compiler generated an error. The method we want to execute would be that of the actual (dynamic) type of the object and not the method of the reference variable (static) type.

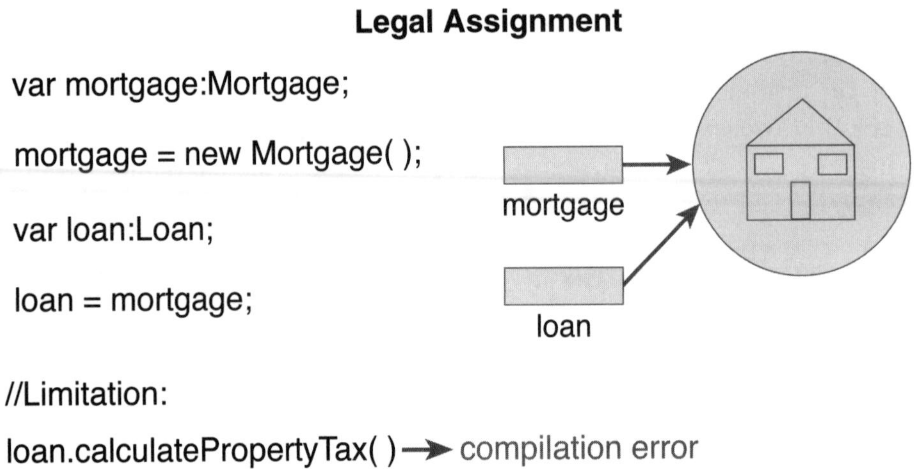

Legal Assignment
var mortgage:Mortgage;
mortgage = new Mortgage( );
var loan:Loan;
loan = mortgage;
mortgage
loan
//Limitation:
loan.calculatePropertyTax( ) → compilation error

FIGURE 5.7 Legal object assignment.

> **NOTE**
>
> In other object-oriented languages, such as Java, the datatype of the reference variable is called the static datatype and the datatype of the instance is called the dynamic datatype. In Figure 5.7, the static datatype is `Loan` and the dynamic datatype is `Mortgage`.

Because a subclass can have new members that are not in the superclass, the compiler will complain when we use a subclass reference variable to point to a superclass, as shown in Figure 5.8.

Illegal Assignment
var loan:Loan;
loan = new Loan( );
var mortgage:Mortgage;
mortgage = loan;
loan
mortgage

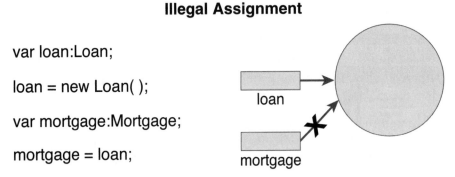

FIGURE 5.8 Illegal type assignment.

Casting

Another important concept for polymorphism is *casting*. ActionScript 2.0 lets you cast one datatype to another. The cast operator that Flash uses takes the form of a function. When you cast a variable from one type to another, you are telling the compiler that the actual type of the object will be different at run-time. The compiler treats the object as having a set of properties that its initial datatype does not contain. This can be useful, for example, when iterating over an array of objects that might be of differing types.

> **NOTE**
>
> Casting in ActionScript 2.0 is also referred to as "explicit coercion," as specified in the ECMA-262 Edition 4 proposal.

The syntax for casting is a function syntax, as seen in Figure 5.9. The function call is *newtype(instance)* where you want the compiler to behave as if the datatype of *instance* is *newtype*. Casting is used when the compatibility can be determined only at runtime.

1. var Mortgage mortgage1:Mortgage;

2. var Mortgage mortgage2:Mortgage;

3. mortgage1 = new Mortgage( );

4. var loan:Loan;

5. loan = mortgage1; ◄—Legal assignment

6. mortgage2 = loan; ◄—Compiler error

7. mortgage2 = Mortgage(loan); ◄— Casting, no compiler error

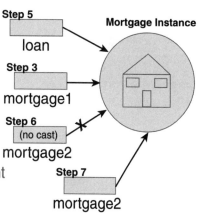

FIGURE 5.9   Casting example.

> **NOTE**
>
> The casting function call returns null if the cast fails. If the cast succeeds, the function call returns the original object. There is one caveat: The compiler doesn't generate type-mismatch errors when you cast items to datatypes that you have created in external class files, even if the cast will fail at runtime.

In Listing 5.15, we have used polymorphism to calculate and display the loan payments. Notice that this function takes an argument of type Loan.

LISTING 5.15   Polymorphism in the *calc* Method

```
function calc(loanInstance:Loan){ //function called by the button
handler

     //calculate and display the monthly payment
     //the actual run-time datatype could be CarLoan or Mortgage
     //regardless, getMonthlyPayment() will return the correct results
     var monthlyPmtVal:Number =  loanInstance.getMonthlyPayment();
     monthlyPmt.text = monthlyPmtVal;

     //calculate and display total payments
     var totalPmtVal:Number =  loanInstance.getTotalPayment();
     totalPmt.text = totalPmtVal;
}
```

Because we know that the Loan class defines the calculate methods, we can call the methods regardless of the actual datatypes of the class passed in. We know that the actual type of the argument can be either Mortgage or CarLoan, as shown in Listing 5.16.

LISTING 5.16   Passing *loan* to the *calc* Method

```
this.calc_btn.onPress = function(){
       var loanInstance:Loan;
       if (loanType.selectedData == "m"){
              loanInstance = new Mortgage(loanAmt, term, rate);
}else{
              loanInstance = new CarLoan(loanAmt, term, rate);
       }
       this._parent.calc(loanInstance);
}
```

Another example of polymorphism can be seen in Listing 5.17. The Employee and Manager classes both have methods for calculating bonuses. In an application used for handling bonus letters, each object, Employee and Manager, uses different algorithms to calculate bonuses. In Listing 5.17, the object of type Employee is passed and letters are printed. The runtime datatype of the object can be either Employee or Manager.

LISTING 5.17   *Polymorphism Example*

```
processBonusLetter(emp:Employee){
     var empName = emp.getName();
     var empBonus = emp.getBonus();←bonus calculate based on emp type
     print(empName, empBonus);
}
```

For programmers new to OOP, polymorphism can be a challenging concept to grasp. As you gain experience in OOP, polymorphism becomes clearer. In most cases, polymorphism opportunities have a way of exposing themselves rather than being planned into an application.

A Nod to the Past—Prototype-Based Objects

In ActionScript 1.0, objects in Flash were created using prototype-based language. In the previous version, class-based monikers, such as `class` and `extends`, were not part of the language. To define classes and achieve inheritance, a different syntax was required.

A class in ActionScript 1.0 was known as a prototype object. The Language used for prototyping is shown in Listing 5.18. This definition exists in an external file and is included, using the `#include` directive, on the timeline where it will be used. Notice that class members have no datatypes or access modifiers.

LISTING 5.18   *Prototype-Based Object Definition*

```
//Begin prototype definition for ancestor - Loan

     //Prototype properties - no datatyping
Loan.prototype.principal;
Loan.prototype.rate;
Loan.prototype.years;

     //Constructor
function Loan (){
}

     //Prototype Method
```

continues

LISTING 5.18   Continued

```
Loan.prototype.setPrincipal = function(thePrincipal){
     this.principal = thePrincipal;
}

//End prototype definition - Loan

//Begin prototype definition for descendant - CarLoan

     //Prototype properties - no datatypeing
CarLoan.prototype.model;

     //Constructor
function CarLoan (){
     super();
}

     //Inheritance/prototype chain
CarLoan.prototype = Loan;

//End prototype definition - CarLoan
```

Listing 5.19 shows the comparable, ActionScript 2.0, class-based syntax for the Loan-CarLoan class definitions in Listing 5.18.

LISTING 5.19   Class-Based Object Definition

```
class Loan{
     private var principal:Number ;
     private var rate:Number ;
     private var years:Number ;

     public function Loan(){
          trace("in loan constuctor");
     }

     public function setPrincipal(thePrincipal:Number ) {
          this.principal = thePrincipal;
     }
}

class CarLoan extends Loan{

     private var model:String;
```

```
function CarLoan (){
       super();
}

}
```

Another major difference in ActionScript 2.0 is the way visual objects in a Library are linked to a class definition. In ActionScript 1.0, a prototype object definition can be linked to a Library item by giving explicit instruction to the compiler. The Library item relationship is established by explicitly including the file on the first frame of the symbols timeline. This guarantees that the code is available to be compiled as part of the definition. In Flash, when a SWF is compiled, it contains anything on the timeline and only Library symbols that have been identified as required in the final SWF. The symbol must be marked for import as part of the Library symbol properties. The symbol linkage properties are set to export the symbol in the first frame. Figure 5.10 is the Linkage panel for Library symbols. It is accessed through the context menu on the Library item or in the Main Library menu at the top of the Library panel.

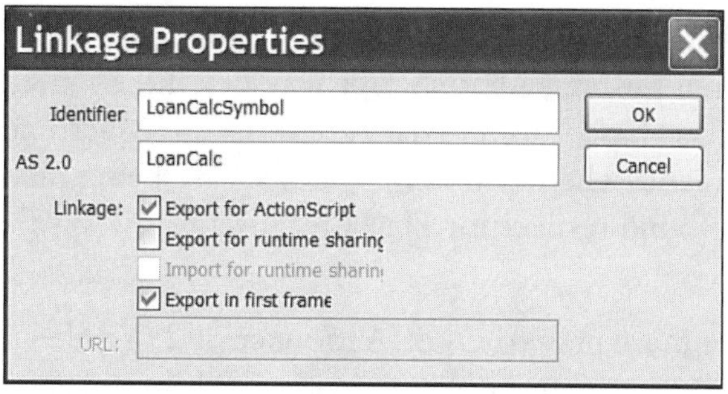

FIGURE 5.10   Library Symbol Linkage panel.

In Figure 5.10, the *Identifier* is the unique name associated with the symbol in the Library. In ActionScript 1.0, this was the key to associating an external prototype definition with a Library symbol. The unique identifier was used to create a relationship between the external definition and the symbol using the syntax shown in Listing 5.20.

LISTING 5.20   Prototype Object Linkage

```
// Linkage (associating a prototype definition  with a visual object)
Object.registerClass("LoanCalcSymbol", LoanCalc);
```

This works assuming the prototype object is named *LoanCalc* and that the file in which it is defined has been included in the first frame of the timeline for the Library symbol.

In ActionScript 2.0 the linkage is much simpler. In Figure 5.10, the *AS 2.0* property links the symbol to an external class file. There is no need to explicitly include the file. The external file is located by the compiler through the class-path. An advantage of this technique is that more that one symbol can use the same external class definition. In ActionScript 1.0, that is not possible. Library symbols and class definition have a one-to-one relationship.

Summary

For years, Flash developers have been finding innovative ways to mimic OOP in Flash, often pushing ActionScript way beyond its intended usage. By implementing a class-based object structure in Flash, Macromedia has guaranteed its place at the table when technology choices are being made. OOP developers have a new-found respect for Flash because it now speaks a language they understand.

For those who are new to OOP, ActionScript 2.0 makes it approachable. There are many advantages to OOP, many of which have been discussed in this chapter. The only way to get started is to dig right in.

CHAPTER 6

UNDERSTANDING INTERFACES IN ACTIONSCRIPT 2.0

In Chapter 5, "The Meek Shall Inherit the Earth," we talked about inheritance. If you recall, an object can inherit all the members of a class. The new class is called a subclass, or descendant, and the original class becomes a superclass, or ancestor. The relationship created between subclass and superclass is one-to-one. That is, a subclass can have one, and only one, ancestor. But what if you were trying to create a class that had the properties of two ancestors? Given the rules of inheritance and what we know at this point, we cannot have two direct ancestors.

This can be a problem.

Fortunately, in this chapter, we investigate an object-oriented concept called *interfaces*, which helps us implement multiple inheritance, but with a twist. We also see how interfaces can enhance what we already know about polymorphism.

Interfaces and Inheritance

So, what is an interface? To answer this question, let's take a look at an inheritance example: a class called `Apple` that is a direct descendant of the `Fruit` superclass. Figure 6.1 shows the `Apple-Fruit` inheritance hierarchy.

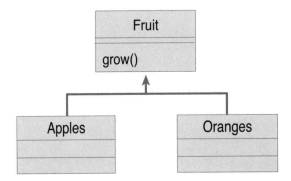

FIGURE 6.1   `Apple-Fruit` inheritance hierarchy.

What if we want apples to also have the capability of becoming a pie so that if apples are destined to become pies, they will have the `Pie` methods and attributes? If the desired outcome is to have the attributes of both classes in one, the class would have to inherit all the `Fruit` attributes as well as the `Pie` attributes, as shown in Figure 6.2. This is known as multiple inheritance.

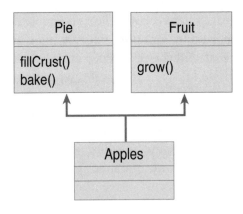

Multiple inheritance is not allowed.

FIGURE 6.2   `Apple-Fruit-Pie` multiple inheritance hierarchy.

Unfortunately, because multiple inheritance is not allowed, this is not a viable solution. We could, as suggested in Chapter 5, add the `Pie` class into the class hierarchy, as shown in Figure 6.3, but then we are assuming that all fruit types are pies.

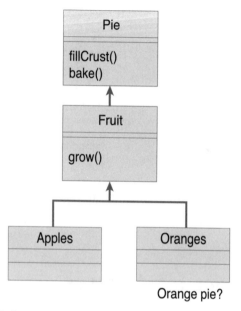

FIGURE 6.3   `Apple-Fruit-Pie` inheritance hierarchy.

In this case, the hierarchy forces a relationship between all fruit subclasses and the `Pie` class. Because not all fruit types are appropriate for pies, we would be forcing relationships that don't follow the "is a kind of" test. After all, apple may be a kind of fruit, but watermelon is not always a kind of pie.

NOTE

Rule of inheritance: Create a superclass-subclass relationship when you can argue that the subclass can be viewed as an instance of itself as well as an instance of the ancestor. For example: an apple "is a kind of" fruit or a garage "is a kind of" building or a car loan "is a kind of" loan.

Another solution is to implement the `Pie` methods only in the subclasses that will need the methods. Figure 6.4 illustrates this implementation.

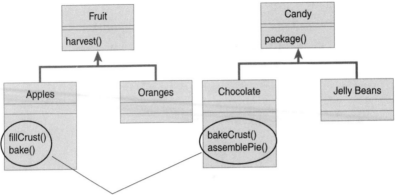

The end results are the same; you can eat pie, but the chocolate pie and the apple pie are prepared in very different ways.

FIGURE 6.4   `Pie` method implementation.

Notice that we have added an unrelated class hierarchy that may also benefit from having the `Pie` methods.

A Contract for Classes

In the preceding section, implementing the additional methods in the subclass provided a viable solution for making chocolate pies and apple pies. But what if you are a large baked-goods manufacturer? You might have one team that prepares crusts and fillings and another team that fills the crusts and bakes the pies. Yet, regardless of the filling, all crusts are filled and baked.

To guarantee consistency in pie preparation, it would be better to have a common nomenclature for these processes. The team could agree on using the nomenclature `prepare()` and `bake()`. Depending on the filling, the bake time might be longer and the crust treated differently, but in both cases, the pie is prepared and baked. If we say that all classes that can become pies will have methods called `prepare()` and `bake()`, we have established a relationship between classes that can become pies and a set of predetermined methods and attributes for the "pie-able" classes. This is often referred to as a contract.

In object-oriented programming (OOP), we can establish and enforce a contract using interfaces. We establish the contract using the `implements` keyword in the class definition. The compiler enforces the contract by requiring that the class contain an implementation for each method in the interface. In Figure 6.5, we can see that a contract has been established between `Apples` and `Pie` and between `Chocolate` and `Pie`. Both `Apples` and `Chocolate` have contracted with the same interface to provide method implementation for the `Pie` methods.

The contract exists between the `Apples` class and the `Pie` interface and the `Chocolate` class and the `Pie` interface. The contract ensures that for any class to become a pie or be called a pie, it must have certain methods. The interface itself has no implementation. The interface `Pie` is merely a specification, an empty set of methods. The implementation exists in the class, such as `Apples` or `Chocolate`, that implements the interface. In Figure 6.5, this is illustrated with the code block { ... } for the `Pie` class methods in the implementing class.

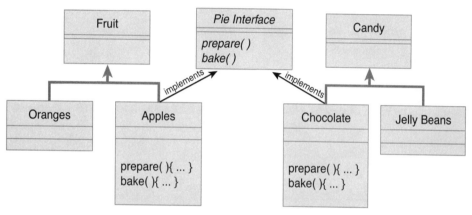

FIGURE 6.5   `Pie` interface relationship.

Why Use Interfaces?

There are two benefits to using an interface. The first is that there are consistent method and attribute names for all classes that have a contract with the interface. The second, and more important, benefit is that any class with a relationship to the interface can be referenced by the interface datatype.

Because an interface is much like a class, it can be used as an object datatype. Using an interface is much like using a superclass and inheritance; the relationship enables us to use the interface datatype to reference the object. This is often considered a side door to multiple inheritance.

As shown in Figure 6.5, our apple can be called a fruit or it can be called a pie. If we call it a fruit, we can use the method `grow()`. If we call it a pie, we can use the methods `prepare()` and `bake()`.

In Listing 6.1, the `preparePie()` method takes an argument of type `Pie`. `preparePie()` will take any object datatype that has implemented the `Pie` interface. The actual code that is executed is determined by the datatype of the object at runtime. If it is a chocolate pie, the methods `prepare()` and `bake()` will be called on the chocolate object instance; if it is an apple pie, the methods `prepare()` and `bake()` will be called on the apple object instance.

LISTING 6.1   Using the *Pie* Datatype

```
var apples =   new Apples( );
var chocolate = new Chocolate( );
preparePie(apples);
preparePie(chocolate);

function preparePie(thePie:Pie){        //this method doesn't have to
know
        thePie.prepare( );              //whether it is a chocolate pie
or an apple pie.
        thePie.bake( );
}
```

Creating Interfaces

Interfaces are created in much the same way as class definitions. They are defined in a text file. They are then compiled and used by any class that desires to conform to the contract. They are created in external files and follow the same accessibility rules as a class file.

To create an interface, we can use the `Interface` keyword, just as we would use the class keyword to create a class definition. An interface is similar to a class, with the following important differences:

- Interfaces contain only declarations of methods, not their implementation. That is, every class that implements an interface must provide an implementation for each method declared in the interface.
- Only public members are allowed in an interface definition. In addition, instance and class members are not permitted.
- Get and set statements are not allowed in interface definitions.

Listing 6.2 shows how to create the `Pie` interface. Notice that there is no code in either of the methods, not even an empty code block { }.

LISTING 6.2   Creating the *Pie* Interface

```
interface Pie {
function prepare( );
function bake( );
}
```

To use the `Pie` interface, all the methods must have implementations. Listing 6.3 shows the `Apple` class implementing the `Pie` interface.

LISTING 6.3   *Apple* Class Implementing the *Pie* Interface

```
class Apple implements Pie{
function prepare( ){//implement };
function bake( ){ //implement };
}
```

You may have noticed that there really isn't any more code in the `Apple` class than in the `Pie` class. However, there is a begin and end block for the `prepare` and `bake` methods. This satisfies the compiler as an implementation.

So how do we use the power of the interface, you ask? Well, let's say that we have a class called `Bakery`. In Listing 6.4, the `Bakery` class has a method called `bakePie` that takes one argument of type `Pie`. Regardless of whether we are baking an apple pie or a chocolate pie, the call is the same—`bake()`. This is an example of polymorphism using an interface.

LISTING 6.4   Polymorphic Use of the *Pie* Interface

```
public class Bakery {
      public bakePie (item:Pie){
            item.bake( );
}
}
```

For another example, examine Figure 6.6. In it, we have a hierarchy of different types of documents, some electronic and others that are on paper. By implementing the `Printable` interface at the `PaperDoc` class level, all descendants of the `PaperDoc` class will have the `print()` method. It's important to note that the `print()` method is overridden in the descendants. Even though `PaperDoc` satisfies the contract with the interface, the code to print is at the descendant level.

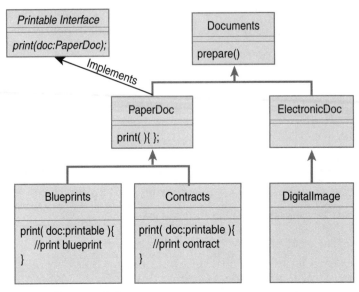

FIGURE 6.6   `Printable` interface example.

Implementing Interfaces

Using the concept of the interface to create a contract between certain documents and the `Printable` interface, we have a guarantee that if we have an instance of `PaperDoc`, it will have a method called `print()`. In addition, it will print correctly for that type of `PaperDoc`. Listing 6.5 shows a class called `PrintQue` that has a method `print()`. `PrintQue` is used by many different types of classes and regardless of the actual instance of the object, printing will take place based on the actual type of the class being printed.

LISTING 6.5   Using the *Printable* Interface

```
public class PrintQue {
      public print (item:Printable){
            item.print()
}
}
```

Let's take a look at the `LoanCalc` example using an interface to provide printing functionality, as shown in Listing 6.6.

LISTING 6.6   Using the *Printable* Interface with the *LoanCalc* Example

```
interface Printable{
      function print();

}class Loan implements Printable{

...

      function print( ) { // satisfy the contract by implementing
print()
            trace("Loan printing: "+this);
            //using the interface here
            //do some formatting and print
      }}function calc(loan:Loan){ //function called by the button
handler

      //calculate the monthly payment
      var monthlyPmtVal:Number =  loan.getMonthlyPayment();

      //display monthly payment
      monthlyPmt.text = monthlyPmtVal;
      var totalPmtVal:Number =  loan.getTotalPayment();

      //display total payments
      totalPmt.text = totalPmtVal;

      //print the loan
      this.print(loan); //call the print method passing in the loan
instance
}
function print(item:Printable){ // method argument is an interface
instance
trace ("in loancalc.print"); item.print();
}
```

Multiple Interfaces

Now let's consider adding more application functionality to the Loan class
hierarchy using multiple interfaces.

The loan calculator has basic functionality for giving customers estimates of
actual loan payments. It would also be helpful if a customer could complete a
loan application, print the application, and submit the application to the bank
using our code. To facilitate this, we can use our existing loan calculator

application and add the functionality using interfaces. Listing 6.7 shows the Printable interface and the application interface that can be used by the loan object hierarchy.

LISTING 6.7   Interfaces for the *LoanCalc* Example

```
interface Printable{
      function print();

}

interface Application{
      function fillOut();
      function sign();
      function submit();
}
```

The Loan class can implement both interfaces, as shown in Listing 6.8. By implementing this functionality in the Loan class, we ensure that all the Loan descendants have the printing and application functionality.

LISTING 6.8   Using Multiple Interfaces with the *LoanCalc* Example

```
class Loan implements Printable, Application{

      function print ( ) {
              trace("Loan printing: "+this);
              //using the interface here
              //do some formatting and print
      }
      function fillOut(){
              /*show a form and collect info*/
      }
      function sign(){
              /*sign (electronic) the form*/
      }
      function submit(){
              /*submit the form*/
      }
}


function calc(loan:Loan){ //function called by the button handler

      //calculate the monthly payment
      var monthlyPmtVal:Number =  loan.getMonthlyPayment();
```

```
        //display monthly payment
        monthlyPmt.text = monthlyPmtVal;
        var totalPmtVal:Number =  loan.getTotalPayment();

        //display total payments
        totalPmt.text = totalPmtVal;

        //print the loan
        this.print(loan);
        this.apply(loan);

}
function print(item:Printable){
        trace ("in loancalc.print");
        item.print();
}
function apply(item:Application){
        trace ("in loancalc.print");
        item.fillOut();
        item.sign();
        item.submit();
}
```

Extending Interfaces

Interfaces are similar to classes with respect to inheritance. An interface can extend an interface to add functionality. In our previous example, we used a print interface and an application interface. We could have extended the application interface to add the printing functionality. We would do this by extending the application interfaces, as shown in Listing 6.9.

LISTING 6.9   Extending Interfaces for the *LoanCalc* Example

```
interface Printable{
        function print();

}

interface Application extends Printable{
        function fillOut();
        function sign();
        function submit();
}
```

Summary

Interfaces can add a great deal of structure and uniformity to an application and, at the same time, allow us to use polymorphism, which is one of the great features of an OOP language. It does, however, require a great deal of forethought and application architecture before you even write one single line of code.

The benefits of interfaces can best be seen in a large application with many diverse elements. When you are analyzing a business problem and find yourself redefining that same functionality in many different places, you may want to consider an interface. Using an interface also allows you to abstract the details of an implementation so that you can complete one area of programming without knowing or caring about the others defined in the interface.

CHAPTER 7

ARE YOU TALKING TO ME?

Up to this point, we have discussed objects, how they are created, what they contain, and the principles of object-oriented programming (OOP). In this chapter, we explore how objects communicate with each other.

Effective Communications

Effective communication is a fundamental requirement for success. In the workplace, the required communications often take place between people: co-workers strategizing together, account managers working with clients, and so on. In these cases, a lack of communication can put a tremendous strain on the system (whether that system is an efficient office, vendor-client relations, or even software systems). In the object-oriented world, the entities that need to effectively communicate are the objects themselves.

Communications between objects in the object-oriented world can happen in one of two ways: with messages or with events.

Messages as Inter-Object Communications

Messages are a fancy way to refer to an object calling the method of another object. In Chapter 4, "Method to the Madness," we examined methods in depth. Methods of objects play an important role in inter-object communication because they are used as the receiver of messages within ActionScript 2.0. What this means is that for an object to send a message to another object, the sending object will invoke a method on the calling object.

To invoke a method, we simply write the object name, a dot, the method name, and a pair of parentheses that can contain any data to be passed as part of the message (referred to as the arguments of the message). A message in ActionScript 2.0 is nearly identical to the equivalent message in ActionScript 1.0, with the exception that strong datatyping is now available. A simple message might look like this:

```
var thePayment:Number = myCarLoan.getMonthlyPayment();
```

In this example, the object making the call (the sender) is calling an object named myCarLoan (the receiver) and is passing no specific data to it (hence the empty parentheses). The receiver of a message can respond through its return statement, and the results will be stored in the new variable thePayment. In Chapter 5, "The Meek Shall Inherit the Earth," the getMonthlyPayment() method was defined like so:

```
public function  getMonthlyPayment( ):Number {
        var monthlyPayment:Number = super.getMonthlyPayment() +
this.getBankFee();
        return monthlyPayment;
}
```

This method signature tells us that when called, it will always return a numeric value. In this case, the number is computed in the local variable monthlyPayment. By specifying a return type for methods, the calling objects can know what to expect when the receiver responds.

In the first example, a message is sent to the getMonthlyPayment() method of the myCarLoan object. The message is asking myCarLoan to respond with the monthly payment for that loan. When getMonthlyPayment() responds to the message with the requested data, it is assigned to a variable named thePayment, which is defined to hold only a number.

Having the ability for objects to call methods on other objects might not seem important initially; however, it is this simple concept that enables our systems to be as flexible and maintainable as they are. With the ability to define any functionality once, and only once, as a method of an object, and with the ability to interact with that method from any other object in the system, there is no need for redundant code. Each block of functionality exists in only one place, so if it needs to be enhanced or maintained, there is only a single block of code that will change. This greatly reduces the complexity (and therefore the cost) of maintaining and extending applications.

Events as Inter-Object Communications

The other type of communications that can occur between objects is the event. An event is any action that can be captured in code. Often times, these actions are driven by users who might, for example, be clicking a button. Other times, these actions, such as a screen being revealed, are driven by the system.

> **NOTE**
>
> Screens and the events related to them are not specifically addressed within this book; however, they are covered in depth in Chapter 6 of *Macromedia Flash MX Professional 2004: Application Development Training from the Source*, by Jeannette Stallons.

The prevalence of OOP has greatly increased in the past decade or so. This increase is directly related to the growth of the popularity of graphical user interfaces (GUIs) in modern applications. One key reason for this relationship is that object-oriented languages have a native ability to handle events. A GUI by its nature is a hot bed of events. Each time the user interacts with items on the screen (such as by clicking, dragging, typing, and so on), an event is fired. It is the event-handling nature of object-oriented languages that makes the GUIs possible.

There are two types of events that are encountered in OOP: events that occur as a result of a user's action, known as user events, and events based on actions within the application itself, known as system events.

User Events

The events most familiar to Flash developers and designers are driven by the end user. Each time a Flash application responds to the user's interaction, it is done through events.

Each class in Flash has events to which it can respond. Table 7.1 shows some user events and the classes to which they belong.

TABLE 7.1   User Events and the Classes to Which They Belong

EVENT	CLASS
onKeyDown	
onKeyUp	
onSetFocus	
onKillFocus	
onMouseDown	
onMouseMove	
onMouseUp	
onPress	
onRelease	
onRollover	
onRollOut	
onReleaseOutside	
onDragOut	
onDragOver	MovieClip
onChanged	
onSetFocus	
onKillFocus	TextField
onKeyDown	
onKeyUp	
onSetFocus	
onKillFocus	
onPress	
onRelease	
onRollover	
onRollOut	
onReleaseOutside	
onDragOut	
onDragOver	Button

Although this list is not comprehensive, it clearly shows that there are quite a few end-user actions that can drive events within applications.

NOTE

For more details on these specific events, refer to *Flash ActionScript 2: Advanced Training from the Source*, by Derek Franklin and Jobe Makar.

System Events

Although many events are driven by the end user, some events are purely system events. These events react to specific application functionality, such as an external file being loaded or an error being thrown. We will see an example of a system event being handled a bit later in the chapter, when we discuss callbacks. (In that section, Listing 7.2 shows the process of loading a file into Flash and responding to the system event, which fires when the file has completely loaded.) Table 7.2 shows system events for a few classes in Macromedia Flash MX 2004 Professional.

TABLE 7.2   System Events and the Classes to Which They Belong

EVENT	CLASS
onData	
onLoad	
onEnterFrame	
onUnload	MovieClip
onResult	
onFault	WebService
onData	
onLoad	XML

Again, although the list of classes with system events shown in Table 7.2 is not comprehensive, it is still important. For instance, consider the onResult event of the WebServices class. Often, data from a web service will be used to populate the interface of an application. There is no use in attempting to work with the data until it has completely arrived in the Flash Player. The onResult event is fired to indicate that the data has finished loading.

NOTE

For more information about Web Services and the onLoad event, refer to Chapter 13, "Web Services."

Handling Events

Any event triggered in an application, regardless of whether it comes from a user or the system, can be handled. Events are handled in one of two ways, either with *listeners* or with *callbacks*.

Handling Messages with Listeners

Listeners are a basic means for handling events in object-oriented languages. A listener is an object that is notified when an event occurs. To create a listener, the object on which an event will occur (such as an instance of the `WebServices` class) needs to be notified about which object will respond to its events. This is known as *adding a listener* to an object.

Listeners use a publisher-subscriber methodology, in that object A can *subscribe* to listen to object B. When object B broadcasts any messages, object A, as a listener, will be able to react to them. For a listener to react, it must have a method with the same name as the message being broadcast. Consider the example in Figure 7.1.

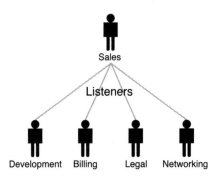

FIGURE 7.1   The various departments of a consulting organization are set as listeners to the sales department; they are waiting for a message that a client project has been sold.

In this example, four people are set to listen to a single person. The billing, development, legal, and networking people are listening to the salesperson. They are waiting for an indication that a sale has been closed. When the salesperson *broadcasts* that he or she has closed a sale, each of the four listening persons has a series of tasks that needs to be done. Legal will create the contracts, networking will prepare the servers, and so on.

As it turns out, the salesperson has lots of different messages that may be broadcast, but these four listeners are interested in only one particular message, gotJob. For them to respond to only that message, each needs to have a gotJob() method, which can fire when the salesperson broadcasts the gotJob event. Any messages that are broadcast to a listener, but to which the listener does not need to have a response, will be ignored as long as the listener does not have a method matching the name of the broadcast message. In the example from Figure 7.1, the four listeners will respond to the gotJob event because they each have a gotJob() method, but they will have no response to any other message broadcast by sales, so other communications, such as callingProspect, will be ignored by these listeners.

This same paradigm applies to objects. One object can be set to listen to another. Many built-in classes are designed with methods that enable other objects to listen to them. Any class with the methods addListener() and removeListener() are specifically built to enable external objects to listen for their events. Many of the native classes, such as Key, Mouse, and TextField, also have these methods.

To instruct one object to listen to an object that is broadcasting events, the broadcasting object's addListener() method is invoked. The addListener() method takes the listening objects as an argument. Listing 7.1 shows an example of an object listening to the Key class to capture any keys pressed by the user.

LISTING 7.1   An Object Is Assigned to Listen to the *Key* Class so That Any Key Pressed by a User Can Be Detected

```
var myListenerObject:Object = new Object();
myListenerObject.onKeyDown = function(){
      trace("The ASCII code for the key you pressed is: " +
Key.getAscii());
}

Key.addListener(myListenerObject);
```

Listing 7.1 begins by creating myListenerObject as a new instance of the Object class. Next, a method named onKeyDown is added to myListenerObject. This method has the same name as the event that is broadcast by the Key class each time a user presses a key. This method is defined to trace a message, showing the ASCII code for the key that was pressed. Lastly, myListenerObject is assigned as a listener to the Key class.

> **NOTE**
>
> As was mentioned in Chapter 4, certain classes, such as `Key` and `Mouse`, are known as singleton or top-level classes. These classes do not need to be instantiated; a single instance of them already exists. These singleton classes have their methods, including `addListener` and `remoteListener`, set as static methods, so they can be invoked directly against the class, as opposed to against instances of the class.

Although these classes have specific methods for adding and removing listeners, the "Using `AsBroadcaster` to Broadcast Custom Messages" section of this chapter will explore how any class or object in ActionScript can broadcast messages.

In addition to the ability of an object to listen to another object for messages, many internal objects are built to listen for specific events. For example, the `MovieClip` class is built to automatically listen for any of the events listed for it. This enables a `MovieClip` instance to react to its own events instead of relying on an external object to react to them.

An object handling its own events is fairly common in the object-oriented world. Often when a user interacts with an item on the Stage, the item is expected to have a reaction. For example, a `MovieClip` object might be built to change colors when the user puts the mouse over it. This type of interaction would not involve an external object acting as a listener, but would instead have the `MovieClip` instance listening for its own `onMouseOver` event.

Often, an object needs to respond to an event only under certain circumstances. Should an object no longer need to respond to events from another object, the `removeListener()` method can be invoked. After an object has been removed as a listener, it will no longer respond to any broadcast events.

We can keep an object listening to another object, but remove its ability to react to a particular event. By simply removing the method matching a particular event, an object will still be able to listen to the other events from the broadcasting object, but it will no longer respond to the event matching the deleted method, as shown in the following code:

```
this.onRelease = function(){
      this.changeColor(0xff0000);
      this.onRelease = null;
}
```

In the preceding code, an object is built to handle a user clicking and releasing it. When the object is clicked, its changeColor() method is invoked and the onRelease method is deleted. This happens because the method set the onRelease event handler equal to null. After the onRelease method has been set to null, it will no longer have a response to a user's click and release.

Handling Messages with Callbacks

The other way messages can be handled in ActionScript 2.0 code is through the use of callbacks. Callbacks exist to handle asynchronous method calls. They are frequently used when loading external data, as will be seen in Chapters 11–15. When a call is made from the Flash Player to a server, some amount of time will pass before the server responds to the call. This encompasses the time taken for the message to travel across the network from the Player to the server, for the server to receive the message and send a response, and for that response to travel across the network and be received again by the Player. Examine Figure 7.2.

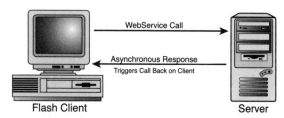

FIGURE 7.2   Asynchronous calls are handled with callbacks.

This process might take only a fraction of a second to occur, or it may take several minutes. For this reason, calls of this sort are handled *asynchronously*. This means that the Flash Player does not stop running the movie and wait for the data to arrive. Instead, it continues running and has the ability to react to the results, regardless of when they arrive.

The reaction to the result is handled by a *callback*, which is a special type of method automatically invoked when certain asynchronous operations, such as the Flash Player receiving data from the server, occur.

There are fundamental differences between listeners and callbacks:

- One message might have several listeners; a message is limited to a single callback.
- Listeners receive the message as soon as it is sent; callbacks are asynchronous and do not receive the message until the data is returned to it.

Listing 7.2 shows an example of a callback in action.

LISTING 7.2   Using a Callback Method with the *LoadVars* Object

```
var myLoadVars:LoadVars = new LoadVars();
myLoadVars.onLoad = function(){
        // call back only called when data loaded
        title.text = this.title;
        trace("Time when data is received: " + getTimer()+" ms");
}
myLoadVars.load("listing7_2.txt");
trace("Time when method was called: " +getTimer() +" ms");
```

> **NOTE**
>
> The nature of the `LoadVars` object is explained in depth in Chapter 12, "XML and Flash."

Listing 7.2 begins by creating `myLoadVars` as an instance of the `LoadVars` class. Next, the callback method `onLoad()` is defined, which, when invoked, will populate a text field named `title` with the `title` property loaded from the server. This method also fires a trace statement that will illustrate the time discrepancy between when the data is requested from the server and when it is received. Next, the `load()` method is invoked, requesting that the contents of a file named listing8_2.txt be read into the `myLoadVars` object. Last, a `trace` statement is used to output the amount of time that has elapsed at the point when the `load()` method is called.

It is important to note that the `onLoad` callback is never explicitly invoked (the code `myLoadVars.onLoad()` never explicitly appears). This method is invoked automatically as a callback, executing when the requested file has been loaded. Figure 7.3 shows the results when the code in Listing 7.2 is run. As can be seen, the dynamic text field `title` is populated with the title from the text file.

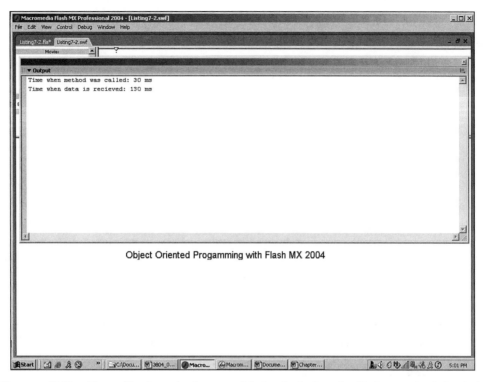

FIGURE 7.3 The callback method `onLoad` is invoked when the file is completely loaded, which is 100 milliseconds after the request is sent.

Callbacks are not needed every time an object passes a message to another; however, in the case of asynchronous operations, they are invaluable.

Handling Events from Flash User Interface (UI) Components

The components in Flash MX 2004 have their own broadcasting mechanism. Each Flash component has a method called `addEventListener()`, which behaves similarly to the `addListener()` method discussed earlier. Listing 7.3 shows a listener being added for an event of a combo box.

LISTING 7.3　Using *addEventListener* to Respond to Events from Components

```
var myResponder:Object = new Object();
var myCombo:mx.controls.ComboBox;
myResponder.change = function(){
        trace(myCombo.value);
}
myCombo.addEventListener("change",myResponder);
```

In Listing 7.3, the `addEventListener()` method of a combo box is used to broadcast any change events from the combo box to the `myResponder` object. This example shows how similar `addEventListener()` is to `addListener()`. However, as can be seen, there is one key difference between the two methods—`addEventListener` takes the name of the event as an argument in addition to the object name. This enables a single component to have different objects listening for individual events.

`addEventListener()` also has a few other ways it can be used. Rather than specifying an object as the event listener, the second argument passed to it can instead be a function located on the main timeline, as seen in Listing 7.4:

LISTING 7.4　*addEventListener* Can Specify a Function to Respond to Events from Components

```
var myCombo:mx.controls.ComboBox;
function showValue(){
        trace(myCombo.value);
}
myCombo.addEventListener("change",showValue);
```

Of course, in OOP, it is a best practice to avoid functions on the main timeline. Instead, you should create functions as methods on an object. Fortunately, `addEventListener()` also supports this construct, enabling a listener object to have any of its methods respond to an event instead of requiring the method to have the same name as the event. Although the usefulness of this might not be obvious, it can enable a single method to handle disparate events from multiple components.

Listing 7.5 shows `addEventListener()` being used to route the `change` event of a combo box to a method named `someMethod()` within the `myResponder` object:

LISTING 7.5   *addEventListener* is Flexible Enough to Enable Methods of Any Name to Respond to Any Component Event

```
var myResponder:Object = new Object();
var myCombo:mx.controls.ComboBox;
myResponder.someMethod = function(){
        trace(myCombo.value);
}
myCombo.addEventListener("change",myResponder.someMethod);
```

NOTE

Flash UI components, and the events involved with them, are covered in detail in Chapter 10, "To Protect and Serve."

TIP

There is a difference regarding the scope in which a responding method will fire. It is based on whether an object, method, or function is passed in. If the listener is specified as an object (not the method of an object), the responder will fire in the scope of the specified object. However, if a function on the timeline or a method of an object is specified as the listener when the listener is invoked, it will be in the scope of the component, rather than of the timeline or object to which the function/method belongs. When in doubt, add the statement `trace(this)` to the listener to find out the scope of it.

Using *AsBroadcaster* to Broadcast Custom Messages

As was mentioned, we are not limited to listening to built-in objects. Flash MX 2004 has a static class that we can use to allow any Flash object to have listeners subscribe to it. This class is named `AsBroadcaster`.

NOTE

At the time this book was published, `AsBroadcaster` was an undocumented feature of Flash MX 2004. It should be used cautiously; there is no guarantee that it will be implemented in future versions of Flash.

`AsBroadcaster` essentially has a single method, `initialize`. This method takes an object as an argument. It returns that object, with three new methods added to it. These new methods are `addListener`, `removeListener`, and `broadcastMessage`. The first two methods act just like the methods of the same names discussed earlier in the chapter. The third method added with

AsBroadcaster and broadcastMessage enables an object to send a message that will be captured by any objects listening to it. Listing 7.6 shows an object being created and initialized as a broadcaster.

LISTING 7.6   Initializing an Object as a Broadcaster

```
var myBroadcastingObject:Object=new Object();
AsBroadcaster.initialize(myBroadcastingObject);
```

After an object has been passed to the initialize method of AsBroadcaster, the three methods are automatically associated with it. This can be verified by running this trace statement:

```
trace(myBroadcastingObject.addListener);
```

When run, the code will output [type Function], confirming that addListener is now a method of myBroadcastingObject.

Let's consider a slightly more complicated example within the framework of an object-oriented application. Figure 7.4 shows the Stage for our example. On the Stage, there are four visual elements all contained within a single movie clip. The movie clip has a symbol name mcBroadcast in the Library, and it has an instance name of broadcast_mc. In the Linkage panel for the mcBroadcast clip, this clip is set to be exported for ActionScript, and it is set to implement the ActionScript 2.0 class BroadcastView.

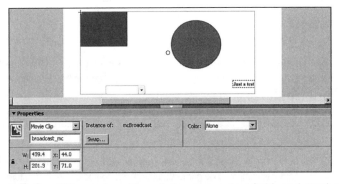

FIGURE 7.4   This movie, with a circle, square, text field, and combo box, serves as the framework to demonstrate AsBroadcaster.

Listing 7.7 shows the source code for BroadcastView.as. In the listing, all the code associated with the application is located in the class file; the code is neither on a frame of the timeline nor directly on the MovieClip object itself.

> **TIP**
>
> In Flash MX 2004, the use of suffixes such as "_mc" are no longer necessary to enable code hinting. However, as applications grow in complexity, it is always a good idea to have a naming convention in place to help developers quickly identify the types of any object by glancing at the name. There is no right or wrong naming convention, but we strongly recommend the use of a consistent naming convention throughout an application.

LISTING 7.7   *BroadcastView* Defines the Behaviors for Our Movie Clip

```
class BroadcastView extends MovieClip{
      // declare visual objects
      var combo:mx.controls.ComboBox;
      var rec_mc:MovieClip;
      var oval_mc:MovieClip;
      var text_mc:MovieClip;

      // declare properties of class
      var colorsArray:Array;
      var addListener:Function;
      var value:Number;

      // constructor
      public function BroadcastView (){
            colorsArray = this.buildArray();
      }

      function onEnterFrame(){
            this.postInit();
      }

      function postInit(){
            this.fillComboBox(this.colorsArray);
            this.combo.addEventListener("change",this.changeColor);
            AsBroadcaster.initialize(this);
            this.addListener(oval_mc);
            this.addListener(rec_mc);
            this.addListener(text_mc);
            this.onEnterFrame = null;
      }

      private function buildArray():Array{
            var theArray:Array= new Array();
            theArray.push(new TheColor("Red",0xff0000));
            theArray.push(new TheColor("Blue",0x0000ff));
            theArray.push(new TheColor("Green",0x00ff00));
```

continues

LISTING 7.7   Continued

```
            theArray.push(new TheColor("Yellow",0xffff00));
            theArray.push(new TheColor("Pink",0xff00ff));
            theArray.push(new TheColor("Cyan",0x00ffff));
            return theArray;
    }

    private function fillComboBox(colorsArray){
            for(var i:Number=0;i<colorsArray.length;i++){
                    this.combo.addItem(
                            colorsArray[i].colorName,
                            colorsArray[i].hexColor
                    );
            }
    }

    public function changeColor(){
            this._parent.broadcastMessage("changeColor",this.value);
    }
}
```

Listing 7.7 begins by declaring properties for the class. The first four properties represent the visual instances already on the Stage—three movie clips and a combo box. Next, colorsArray is defined as an array. The properties value and addListener are also defined; value represents the data associated with a selected item in the ComboBox component, and addListener represents the new methods that become available to the class by initializing it with AsBroadcaster. In reality, the only reason these need to be defined here is to escape compile-time errors. Writing this class file without those two definitions would cause Flash to throw an error because there is neither a property named value nor a function named addListener.

The class's constructor populates the colorsArray property using the buildArray() method (buildArray will be discussed shortly). Next, we define an onEnterFrame method. This method is actually a system event handler of the MovieClip class, which is invoked at the frame rate of the movie. It's being used here to enable a method to be invoked a few milliseconds after the rest of the clip has loaded.

The method we call next is named `postInit`. The `postInit` method works with the visual objects on the Stage. Due to synchronicity issues, it's necessary to wait until all the elements are drawn on the Stage before working with properties or methods of visual objects. Using the `onEnterFrame` event to invoke `postInit` enables the `postInit` method to be invoked 83 milliseconds after the stage is completely rendered (83 milliseconds is approximately 1/12 of a second, and the default frame rate is set at 12 frames per second). These 83 milliseconds are enough time for the synchronicity issues to be bypassed. Within `postInit`, the combo box is filled using the `fillComboBox` method.

Next, the `changeColor` method is assigned as the event handler for the change event of the combo box. This is done by using the `addEventListener` method discussed earlier. Then, we use `AsBroadcaster` to assign the movie clips on the Stage (`oval_mc`, `rec_mc`, and `text_mc`) as listeners to this class. Last, the `onEnterFrame` method is erased by setting it equal to `null`. This is done so that the method is called only once, shortly after initialization.

The `buildArray` method is defined next. It creates a new array and populates six elements as instances of the `TheColor` class. It then returns the array. Listing 7.8 shows the class definition of `TheColor`.

Next, the `fillComboBox` method is defined. It accepts an array of colors as an argument and uses the array to populate the combo box. The color's `colorName` property is used as the label, and its `hexColor` property is used as the underlying data.

Last, the `changeColor` method is defined. This is the method that is invoked when the value of the combo box is changed. The `changeColor()` method has a single line of code, which broadcasts the message `changeColor` and passes the value of the currently selected item in the combo box. Shortly, we will see how each of the listening movie clips will have a unique response to this one message.

NOTE

Notice that the `changeColor` method uses `this._parent` as the scope when it invokes the `broadcastMessage` method. It does this because a function or method acting as an event handler for a component is invoked within the scope of the component rather than the scope of the class, as was mentioned in a Tip earlier this chapter. This method broadcasts the selected color to all the listening objects.

LISTING 7.8   The Class File for *TheColor* Defines How Instances of *TheColor* Are Built

```
class TheColor{
      var colorName:String;
      var hexColor:Number;
      function TheColor(name,hex){
            this.setName(name);
            this.setHex(hex);
      }
      private function setName(name:String):Void{
            this.colorName = name;
      }
      private function setHex(hex:Number):Void{
            this.hexColor = hex;
      }
      public function getName():String{
      return this.colorName;
      }
      public function getHex():Number{
            return this.hexColor;
      }
}
```

This class is very simple. It has two properties, `colorName` and `hexColor`. The constructor sets the properties based on the values passed to it. A series of getter and setter functions complete the class. Instances of this class are used within the combo box to enable users to see the name of a color; the color's hexadecimal value will be available as the data.

The other visual objects on the Stage each have class files associated with them. These other classes simply define a `changeColor` method for the class, allowing them to respond to the `changeColor` message being broadcast.

Both `mcOval` and `mcRec` (the Library items associated with `oval_mc` and `rec_mc`) are defined through the Linkage panel as implementing the ActionScript 2.0 class `ColorChanger`. Listing 7.9 shows the implementation of the `ColorChanger` class.

LISTING 7.9   The *ColorChanger* Class Has a Single Method That Fires When the *changeColor* Message Is Broadcast to It

```
class ColorChanger extends MovieClip{
        function changeColor(color:Number):Void{
                var newColor = new Color(this);
                newColor.setRGB(color);
                delete newColor;
        }
}
```

The one method here accepts a numeric value, `color`. Next, it creates a new instance of the `Color` class, which will operate on it. The `Color` instance's `setRGB` method is used to assign the color to the instance. Last, the color instance is deleted because it is useful only until its `setRGB` method is invoked.

The `mcText` symbol (the Library item associated with `text_mc`) is defined through the Linkage panel as implementing the ActionScript 2.0 class `TextMovie`. Listing 7.10 shows the class definition for `TextMovie`.

LISTING 7.10   *TextMovie* Has a Single Method—*changeColor*—That Fires When the *changeColor* Message Is Broadcast to It

```
class TextMovie extends MovieClip{
        var dynTxt:TextField;

        public function changeColor(color:Number):Void{
                DynText.textColor=color;
        }
}
```

This class is aware of a single text field—with an instance name `dynText`—on its Stage. The `changeColor` method accepts a numeric color value and uses that value to change the color of the text within the `DynText` field.

With this example, we can see how custom messages can be broadcast with the use of `AsBroadcaster`. A single message is broadcast to three separate objects, implementing two independent classes. Each class has its own individual method for handling the message. Figure 7.5 shows the application running.

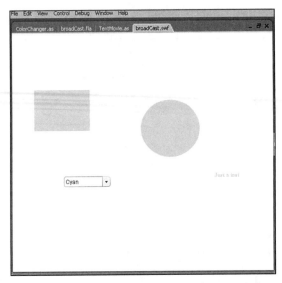

FIGURE 7.5   When the application is run, the text and two shapes change color to match the color chosen from the combo box.

Summary

Throughout this chapter, several examples of inter-object communication were examined, beginning with an example from the Loan class, where a message was explicitly passed from one object to another. Next, the topic of events was explored, and we were able to see how events and event handlers are essential to OOP.

Callbacks are another important means of inter-object communication, particularly when the messages are asynchronous.

The event handling framework of Flash components is another means for objects to communicate. In addition, the AsBroadcaster class can always be used to enable any object within Flash to broadcast its messages to any other object.

In much the same way that messages enabled the development of GUIs, the same style of message can ease the development of rich, intuitive, object-oriented Flash MX 2004 applications.

CHAPTER 8

OBJECT-ORIENTED DESIGN

The challenges faced by application architects and developers when designing object-oriented applications are the same challenges faced in the past decades, only at an accelerated pace. They are expected to design and build applications that are robust, responsive, and scalable. They are also expected to be able to quickly modify or enhance these applications as demands arise. Applications need to move quickly from prototype to production, and they need to evolve even after they are deployed.

In this chapter, we cover the characteristics that are commonly found in a good object-oriented design, as well as some proven techniques employed by designers in each phase of the project.

Characteristics of a Sound Object-Oriented Design

Based on a common set of characteristics, sound object-oriented designs enable developers to meet and surpass the expectations of the industry today. These characteristics support project success and should be adopted early on in the design phase of a development project. The characteristics include the following:

- Productivity
- Scalability
- Integration with existing systems
- Maintainability
- Less code and more planning

The following sections discuss each in turn.

Productivity

Given industry demands, productivity is a key to project success. An application architect can assure productivity by providing the development team with a solid application design. Using proven techniques, or models, the architect can map application data with interactions and usage scenarios. With object-oriented design, this is done using objects to model the real-life scenario that is being mimicked by the application. The scenario could be a person purchasing a product, an employee configuring a health care plan, or an assembly line team producing a car.

Scalability

Another key success factor is scalability. An application must be able to grow and change without having to be completely re-written. With a good object-oriented design, an individual object can be replaced without breaking down the stability of the entire application. In Chapter 2, "All the World Is an Object," we compared objects to a blueprint of a house showing that a house is best architected from separate components or objects that can be replaced without completely tearing down the house each time you want to upgrade your heating system or replace some windows. Now that we are ready to architect an object-oriented application, the blueprint model is emphasized.

Integration with Existing Systems

During the design phase of an application, integration with existing systems is a key factor. During this phase, existing systems should be fully understood and a determination made if they will be used as-is or if there will be a need to build a communication layer for the existing systems to work with your new architecture. This process can add a considerable amount of time and resource, requiring that multiple teams interface during development.

Maintainability

One more success factor that is often overlooked is maintainability. As we move into the deployment phase of an application, we are faced with maintaining the application. There are many things we can do in the design phase to promote ease of maintenance, even if we transfer that task to a different team. For starters, we can provide good documentation from the start. We can also conform to a design standard or pattern that will provide some conformity across the application, thus making it easier and more intuitive for new or different team members to pick up the work.

Less Code, More Planning

The task of building applications using an object-oriented design has many key considerations that drive the success of the design. Aside from satisfying the key success factors, the design will depend on many factors, including the type of application. Is it an intranet or Internet application? Does it interact with any legacy systems? Is the data dynamic and where does the data come from—Relational Database Management System (RDBMS), extensible markup language (XML), or Web Services? How many developers will be building the application? Answering these questions helps lay the foundation and determine what architectural approach to take because these factors will drive the complexity of the design.

Additionally, any successful object-oriented solution will have the following characteristics:

- **Use-case driven.** Being use-case driven means that business requirements for the project are captured through use cases. These use cases will be translated into objects that can be developed and tested.

- **Architecturally focused.** Applying an architectural focus to the development phases will highlight the division between the project's technical and business architectures and help ensure that the benefits can be realized.
- **Object-based.** During analysis and through development, all system entities are communicated using an object metaphor, even if they eventually become more than one object or are absorbed into other objects at development time.
- **Incremental and iterative.** A good design requires a step-by-step approach, often including several iterations over each step.

Phases of a Project

An object-oriented project has several phases, beginning with a design phase. The phases are iterative, so we may find ourselves going through the same process many times. As shown in Figure 8.1, we will repeat the same stage many times, through deployment and beyond.

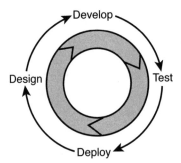

FIGURE 8.1   Iterative project cycle.

Before we can even begin the design phase of a project, a full analysis of the business requirements is required. This usually involves nontechnical representation from the business domain, often referred to as the business owners. The business owners are our customers. They provide us with information about the business problem as well as insight into how we will eventually solve the problem. This is the most important interaction or relationship that will exist in the project, as final acceptance of the application is dependent on how well we have communicated with the business owners.

Note that the business owner will have the final say as to whether we have successfully solved or satisfied the need of the business. This relationship will exist long after the application is deployed. This group will drive and support user acceptance as well as enhancements to the application.

For each phase, you will need to identify three components:

- **Roles and resources.** The people involved in that phase
- **Activities.** What those roles and resources will do during the phase
- **Deliverables.** What will be produced as a result of the phase

Identifying the Problem Domain

With a well-defined working relationship with the business owners, we can begin the process of clarifying the problem domain. By identifying the problem domain, we will uncover some fundamental requirements of the application. Some questions you should be asking at this point are as follows:

- Is this an Internet or intranet application?
- Will the application be directed to customers or business partners?
- Will there be dynamic data?
- Will the data source be RDBMS, XML, Web Services, or something else?
- Does this business logic already exist or is it new?
- Does the business require secure transactions?
- What are the profiles of the intended users?
- Will the application be delivered to multiple platforms?
- Will the look and feel of the application need to change?

Examine Figure 8.2.

Based on the results of this discovery, you can develop premises or assumptions about the application. These assumptions will carry through the development process and into deployment. Any changes in these assumptions can alter the development cycle and, in most cases, delay deployment.

After the assumptions have been gathered, you are ready to begin defining the solution.

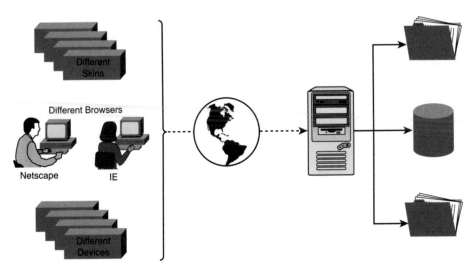

FIGURE 8.2 Possible application requirements.

Defining the Solution

There are many techniques available that aid in defining business solutions. In this section, we look at a specific use-case scenario and some sequence diagrams.

NOTE

Although we won't cover them in detail, there are other techniques from which to choose. These include flow charts, activity diagrams, and simulations, each with its own advantages and disadvantages.

A flow chart gives a pictorial, step-by-step presentation of a process or activity. It clarifies where key decisions are made and identifies the relationship between each element in the process. A flow chart looks not only at who, but also what, why, and how an activity or process is accomplished.

Activity diagrams focus on activities, chunks of process that might or might not correspond to methods or member functions of objects, and the sequencing of these activities. In this sense, it is like a flow chart supporting compound decisions. It differs from a flow chart, however, in that it explicitly supports parallel activities and their synchronization.

Simulation provides a means of measuring overall changes in the system caused by the specific changes you make to your processes. It identifies utilization rates of activities, revealing bottlenecks or underutilized activities.

Understanding how the user will interact with the application can help us design objects and object communication to support the usage. We start with a full analysis of how the application will be used by building use-case diagrams, which identify the objects of the system and system behaviors. Use-case diagrams are used for documenting existing process, analyzing new processes, identifying points of integration and repurposing opportunities, and addressing the nontechnical requirements for some scenarios.

Use-Case Diagrams

A use case describes the way in which a real world actor—a person, organization, or external system—interacts with an organization. They provide a high-level view of the intended functionality of the application that is understandable by business owners and developers alike.

A use case is a generic description of an entire application involving many objects. It can also describe the behavior of a set of objects. A use-case model thus presents a collection of use cases and is typically used to specify or characterize the behavior of a whole application or a part of a system, together with one or more actors or users that interact with that application. An individual use case is usually named and often written as an informal text description of the users and the sequences of events between objects that make up the interaction. Instances of this behavior might be formally specified using scenarios, but iteration and conditionality within scenarios is usually best expressed as informal text.

Each use case describes the sequence of events of an actor (user) using the system to complete a process. This description views the system as a black box. That is, the internal design and functionality of the software are not captured. As a result, use cases typically represent business processes. They capture key uses of the application and are an excellent means of communicating requirements.

An actor is a role a user plays with respect to a system, but a user can be a human being or another part of the system. If there is more than one user of the same type, all are represented as a single user. The standard icon for an actor is the stick man figure with the name of the actor below the figure, as shown in Figure 8.3.

Customer

FIGURE 8.3   Standard icon for an actor in a use case.

A use case is a collection of possible sequences of interactions between the application under discussion and its users (or actors) that relate to a particular goal. The collection of use cases should define all system behaviors relevant to the actors to assure them that their goals will be carried out properly. Any system behavior that is irrelevant to the actors should not be included in the use cases. Interactions are represented by ellipses with actions written inside.

A concrete use case is one that describes a fundamental process performed by the system. An actor of the system always invokes a concrete use case to achieve the requested result. Abstract use cases describe functionality common to two or more concrete use cases. Unlike concrete use cases, abstract use cases are not invoked directly by an actor, but are invoked only by other use cases.

Defining Use-Case Relationships

Use-case relationships can be categorized in the following ways:

- **Communicates.** The participation of an actor in a use case is shown by connecting the actor symbol to the use-case symbol by a solid path. When this is done, the actor is said to communicate with the use case. This is the relation between the actor and the use case.
- **Extends.** This shows the relationships between use cases. Relationship between use case A and use case B indicates that an instance of use case B might include (subject to specific conditions specified in the extension) the behavior specified by A. An extends relationship between use cases is shown by a generalization arrow from the use case providing the extension to the base use case. The arrow is labeled with "extends."
- **Uses.** A "uses" relationship from use case A to use case B indicates that an instance of the use case A will also include the behavior as specified by B. A uses relationship between use cases is shown by a generalization arrow from the use case doing the using to the use case being used. The arrow is labeled with "uses."

Figure 8.4 shows a use case for the online loan application scenario.

Normally, at least one scenario should be prepared for each significantly different kind of use-case instance. Each scenario shows a sequence of interactions between the actors and the system, with all decisions being definite.

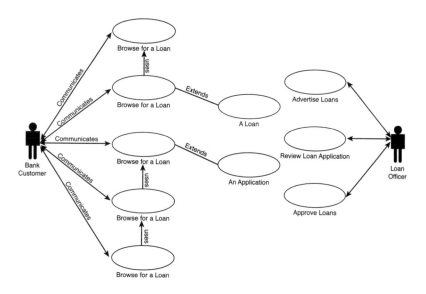

FIGURE 8.4   Use case for the loan application.

Sequence Diagrams

In the use-case scenarios, you will develop sequence diagrams. A sequence diagram maps the flow of the application, identifying points of interaction and uncovering entities that were missed in the use-case scenarios.

Sequence diagrams are models that describe how a group of objects collaborate in some behavior—typically a single use case. An interaction diagram shows a number of example objects and the messages that are passed between these objects within the use case. In sequence diagrams, objects are shown as vertical lines with the messages presented as horizontal lines between them.

A sequence diagram has two dimensions: the vertical dimension represents time and the horizontal dimension represents different objects. Normally, time proceeds down the page. (The dimensions can be reversed, if desired.) Usually, only time sequences are important, but in real-time applications, the time axis could be an actual metric. There is no significance to the horizontal ordering of the objects. Figure 8.5 shows the sequence diagram for the loan application.

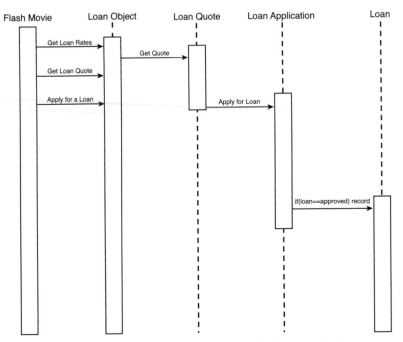

FIGURE 8.5   Sequence diagram for the loan application.

The Design

With the sequence diagram and the use-case scenarios defined, we can now begin to derive the class structures. First we will take a look at design patterns and determine which pattern will suit the application.

An object-oriented design builds an application out of a set of objects. Now that you have analyzed the usage scenarios of the application, you can begin to map the application needs to a design. Starting with a known design pattern can be very helpful. Design patterns are application patterns that have been designed and tested. They support the notion that one should not reinvent the wheel.

Of course, there are many patterns that have been used in object-oriented design and new patterns arise occasionally. This book uses one pattern that is particularly useful for Flash, Model-View-Controller (MVC), but there are many others. For more on Flash patterns, search for articles at www.macromedia.com.

The MVC pattern works well for an application with a clearly defined visual layer and a language that supports object-oriented development. Traditionally, we think of Flash as a presentation tool, but with the introduction of ActionScript 2.0 and the ability to create objects (both visual and nonvisual), partitioning an application using a pattern such as MVC becomes easy.

To fully understand MVC, let's consider the loan application. Each object has a very clear set of responsibilities. One of the tenets of object-oriented design is that the same job should not be done by two different types (or classes) of objects. One way to ensure uniqueness is to partition the behaviors. The application can be partitioned into three types of services:

- **User interface logic.** Defines how information is presented to the user and how the user interacts with the application
- **Business or application logic.** Includes business objects and defines the business rules and the data access logic in the application
- **System logic.** Includes utility objects, such as access to external resources, data conversions, and so on, that support the system

A class should belong to one and only one partition. In other words, a class should have a well-defined role related to user interface logic, business/problem domain logic, or system management logic. As shown in Figure 8.6, each partition maps to Model, View, or Controller.

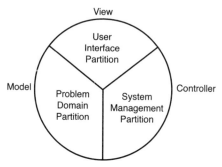

FIGURE 8.6   Application partitions mapped to MVC.

Working with the Model

The model of an application is responsible for data access and management. Experience tells us that data can come in many forms and from many sources. The more you can hide the complexity of the data from the rest of the application, the better off you will be in regards to scalability and modification. If, for example, the application data source changes from a static text file to a dynamic Web Services call, the user interface will never know the difference as long as the model can still make the data available. Depending on the complexity of the application, you might have many data objects partitioned by a problem domain.

In our application, the data access is done in the Flash file. To implement the MVC pattern, move the data access into its own object, thus creating a model object for the application. The model object will acquire the data, parse the data, and store the data, making it accessible to the application through accessor methods.

Working with the View

The view is often a set of objects that represents the visual part of the application. Each member of the view partition will probably have a class definition in an ActionScript 2.0 file as well as a Library entry in a FLA file. Using good object-oriented practice and encapsulation, each view object should have all the methods it needs to display itself. There will also be a messaging schema defined whereby the controller will notify the view to display itself. This might happen when some condition, such as the arrival of new data or user navigation, has been met that warrants a repaint.

Working with the Controller

The controller acts as the ringmaster for the entire application. The controller instantiates the objects just as the ringmaster introduces the acts. The controller handles application initiation. The controller also handles communication between the view and the model, notifying the view when data is available or has changed. The controller might also notify the model when new data is required.

The following is an example of controller communication:

- The controller initiates data access on the model.
- The model notifies the controller when data arrives.
- The controller notifies view that the model has new data.
- The view requests data from the model and displays the data.

Figure 8.7 illustrates the communication that takes place between the model, view, and controller.

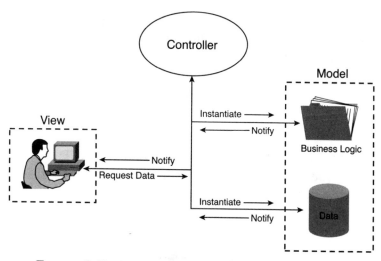

FIGURE 8.7   Model, view, and controller communication.

Identify Classes (and Inheritance)

As we begin to derive the classes, we will find that some classes are more obvious than others. In the Loan application, we will need a `Loan` class and a `Customer` class. With further investigation, it becomes obvious that there can be multiple kinds of loans and therefore we will need a loan ancestor with some descendants to represent the specialized loans, cars, and mortgages. Figure 8.8 shows the `Loan` object hierarchy that we created in Chapter 5, "The Meek Shall Inherit the Earth."

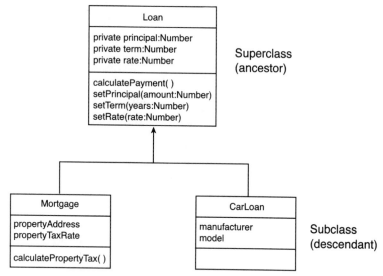

FIGURE 8.8   `Loan` object hierarchy.

Customers might also require a generalized and specialized definition. All customers have basic information, but some specialized customers might have requirements that are unique. For example, there might be a category for business customers that might carry additional fees or require a tax id number. By defining a customer ancestor and subclassing for the specialized case, we build a flexible hierarchy that enables us to add new customer types without reinventing the customer.

Figure 8.9 shows the customer hierarchy that enables commercial customers to be distinguished from noncommercial customers while both still have all the properties and methods of the customer ancestor.

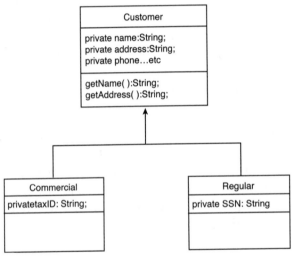

FIGURE 8.9   Customer object hierarchy.

Other objects that can be derived from our use-case diagram are the bank objects. The bank object would be responsible for publishing or advertising loans. The bank will need objects that manage loans and billing. A series of use cases for the banking side will flesh out the requirements.

Identifying class hierarchies in the design phase is not an easy task. Often we find ourselves in the midst of development when we realize that we missed something. We might need to alter the design to include an unforeseen inheritance hierarchy, or we might have overlooked a unique class structure. That is why we refer to this process as an iterative process. In a perfect world, we would begin development with a complete design that considers every possible scenario and defines every object. However, it is more often the case that we are back to the drawing board—so to speak—periodically during the development of the objects.

Identify Packages of Classes

Classes often form groups with a common theme. An example might be shipping, where the group would include all objects needed to perform and support the shipping process. To group classes with a common theme, we use a package concept. A package is equivalent to a folder, but it is used to group classes that are related, usually through inheritance. A package might include files that are not related if they are needed by the other classes in the package.

As an example of creating a package, the Loan class and all its descendants will be located in a package called loan. This package can then be used by other applications by importing the package. Because the loan calculation logic is encapsulated in these objects with a well-published application program interface (API), they can be reused by other applications.

Identify Interfaces

If you recall from Chapter 6, "Understanding Interfaces in ActionScript 2.0," interfaces provide a type of multiple inheritance. Interfaces solve the problem when two different types of classes require the same functionality but there is no common ancestor between them. In a sense, we want each object to inherit from a new class outside its hierarchy. Because classes can have only one direct ancestor, we can't add an ancestor to each hierarchy, so we will have to use an interface. Interfaces provide a structure for each class hierarchy that contains the additional functionality required.

Using Inter-Object Communication

Referring back to the sequence diagram in Figure 8.5 reveals the inter-object communication. The sequence diagram tells us which objects need to communicate. It also reveals bi-direction communication and the need for call-back functions.

In Figure 8.10, we can see how the Loan object will communicate with the controller and in turn notify the client. Figure 8.10 also identifies some of the inter-object communication needed for the Loan application.

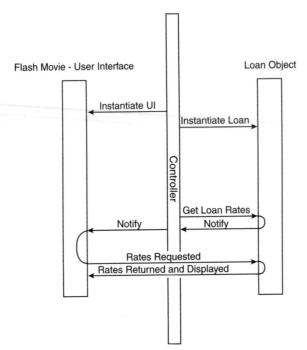

FIGURE 8.10   Inter-object communication sequence diagram.

Implementation (Iterative and Incremental Development)

Now it's time to implement. Using the road map created in the design phase, objects can be created. Each object hierarchy is defined using the interface specified in the design. In object-oriented programming (OOP), each object hierarchy can be built in isolation, tested, and then integrated. Given the conceptual plug-and-play model of OOP, each well-defined object can be plugged into the application as it is implemented.

Testing

Testing occurs at the unit level as well as at the system level. Unit level testing identifies the performance of a part of the application in isolation while system testing reveals the application as a whole with all units working together. Each object of the application is tested thoroughly in isolation and then again as part of the application after it is implemented. There are many other levels of testing that occur beyond implementation. They include load testing, stress testing, and fringe testing. Each reveals application strengths and weaknesses.

Again, new classes might be discovered in the coding process. This means further modeling activities are required. It's imperative that developers understand that they shouldn't explore these new classes in the code. Instead, they should allow them to be modeled first.

In this methodology, as in all others, testing verifies technical and business functionality. As the lifecycle's components differ, so too do their validation and verification. The goals are the same, but the verification focus is different.

There are four unique types of testing associated with object-oriented applications:

- **Class testing.** Test each class independently.
- **Scenario testing.** Test application using pre-defined scenarios or scripts to test assumptions and validate target users.
- **Use-case testing.** With the use cases defined early in design, test the application and validate that it meets the requirements outlined in the use cases.
- **System testing.** Overall application testing that usually leads to acceptance by the business owners.

Deployment

During deployment, the team must address appropriate platforms for specific functionality. For example, the presentation logic or user interface will be built into the Flash application, while some of the business objects reside on a mid-tier server or database tier. The technical architecture defined in the early stages of design takes into account the chosen infrastructure technologies to support intelligent object communication.

Note that data access requests and validation will more than likely live in the client, but much of the business logic will reside on a server in the form of Web Services, .NET, ColdFusion, Java, or some other server-side technology. During deployment, the Flash application as well as any server-side support objects must be deployed together.

Adapting to Change

Maintenance in an object-oriented solution is the reapplication of the lifecycle. Its primary concern is identifying when modification and enhancement requests suggest another development effort. The best course is to map those requests to use cases and assess the level of effort. Although the planning of changes to the application will follow the same best practices by using the lifecycle methodology, development and implementation should take considerably less time.

Summary

In this chapter, we discussed the development cycle of an object-oriented application. Even though this chapter covered various techniques for architecting an application and designing objects, consider this as an approach rather than a hard-and-fast formula.

Regardless of the language used, applications can be object-oriented or procedural. It is the style employed that distinguishes one from the other. Actionscript 2.0 has all the elements necessary to write truly object-oriented applications, but there is no object-oriented police preventing you from going astray.

This chapter provided you with tools that will help get the job done, but it is up to you to keep the following in mind:

- Object-oriented classes tend to have simple, singular responsibilities. Keep in mind that a good class does one thing and does it well.
- In OOP, you are thinking more about how classes interact than how to code them.
- Object-oriented development is architecture driven.
- The amount of time you spend coding is dramatically less than in procedural programming. A rule of thumb is 1/3 in analysis, 1/3 in design, 1/6 in coding, and 1/6 in testing.
- Object-oriented systems tend to be well organized, but procedural systems often end up as spaghetti code.
- In OOP, it's important to use abstractions, allowing the system to closely represent the real world.
- You know you are an object-oriented programmer when you don't have VB on your machine and you think Cobol is a shade of blue.

CHAPTER 9

BUILDING AND USING UI COMPONENTS

Before components, Flash developers had to build scroll bars, combo boxes, and so on from scratch, which often became complex and tedious. However, components were first introduced to the Flash community in Macromedia Flash MX and quickly became ubiquitous in Flash applications.

Components have fundamentally changed user interface (UI) design in Flash MX 2004. At their most basic level, Flash UI components speed up the development process by making life easier for Flash developers; they are the building blocks for applications.

Components in Flash can be divided into three different areas:

- **Data components.** These enable the developer to load and manipulate information from external data sources. Current data components include extensible markup language (XML) and Web Services. Future data components might include Flash Remoting Services, Oracle databases, SQL Server databases, and others. These components are available in Flash MX Professional 2004.

- **Media components.** These enable the developer to play back and control streaming media. These include the MediaController, the MediaPlayback component, and the MediaDisplay component. These components are available in Flash MX Professional 2004.
- **UI components.** These enable users to interact with an application. The RadioButton, CheckBox, and TextInput components are UI components. The DataGrid component is available in Flash MX Professional 2004.

We are going to focus on building and using UI components in this chapter. The data components are covered in Chapter 12, "XML and Flash," Chapter 13, "Web Services," and Chapter 14, "Using Client-Side Data Integration."

Where to Get UI Components

Flash comes with many prebuilt components and these can be found in the Components panel. Components are also available at the Developer Center Exchange, which is located at www.macromedia.com/exchange. In addition, each quarter, Macromedia releases new components in Developer Resource Kits, which are great resources for obtaining the latest components.

What's New in Version 2 Components?

The version 2 components are very different than the version 1 components available in Flash MX. As you will see, the application program interfaces (APIs) have been completely rewritten and the performance of the version 2 components has been greatly improved. In addition, all the new visual components have a new interface and a new look and feel; they also support data binding, which makes it possible to build applications without writing any ActionScript 2.0 code at all.

Of course, components do add a certain amount of file size to your Flash application because they use a component framework. Once this framework has been added to your application, however, there is very little additional file size cost for other components.

> **NOTE**
>
> Because version 2 components are so different than version 1 components, it is not recommended that version 1 components and version 2 components be combined in the same file. A great benefit of the version 2 component architecture is that they can be backward compatible with Flash Player 6.

Usability and Accessibility

In Flash, components are now accessible and screen readers can interpret their content. When a user tabs to a component, the Focus Manager enables the developer to set up logical behavior; in version 1 components, the user would just be stuck if he or she tried to tab to a component.

SWC Files

Components included with Flash are SWC files. SWC is the Macromedia file format for exported components. It is a compiled clip that has been exported for distribution. A compiled clip is basically just a compressed movie clip, very similar to an SWF file. When you add a component to the Stage from the Components panel, a compiled clip symbol is added to the Library, as shown in Figure 9.1:

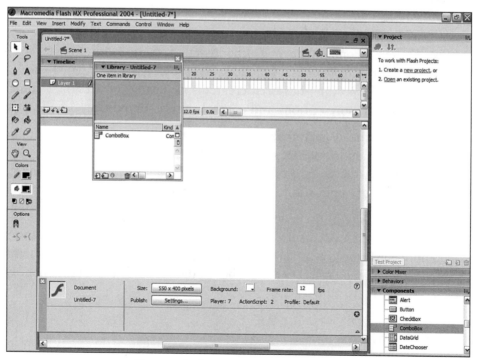

FIGURE 9.1 A compiled clip symbol.

The first step in creating an SWC file is to create a compiled clip. A compiled clip is an SWF file that resides in the Library of your application. Be sure your component is ready for production before you actually compile the clip, which is done through a menu setting in the Library. You cannot change a compiled clip; you must recompile it.

Note that SWCs are where components are stored and they are actually separate files. An SWC file is a compiled component in a separate file.

To create a compiled clip and publish it as an SWC file, do the following:

1. Right-click the movie clip symbol in the Library.
2. Choose Convert To Compiled Clip from the contextual menu.
3. Right-click the compiled clip.
4. Choose Export to SWC file from the contextual menu.
5. Restart Flash and you will see the component in the Components panel.

The Visual Interface for Components

The visual component interface comprises many elements. Each is discussed in turn in the following subsections.

The Component Inspector

Like version 1 components and other assets, version 2 components still use the Property Inspector for basic functionality. However, a new panel—the Component Inspector—has been created specifically for version 2 components and it gives us more options and control over a component visually.

The Component Inspector, as shown in Figure 9.2, is used to fill out component information properties manually. The Component Inspector is also used to set up bindings between the component and a data source, which enables the development of applications without typing any ActionScript 2.0 code at all.

The simplest way to use a component is to drag it on to the Stage from the Components panel and fill out the label and data information using the Component Inspector or the Property Inspector. Figure 9.3 is the interface that appears when the user clicks the label or data field of the Component Inspector.

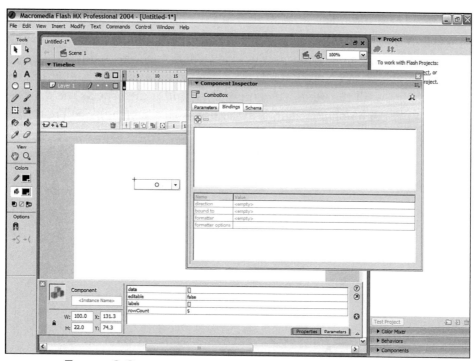

FIGURE 9.2 The new Component Inspector gives us a lot more visual options in setting up components.

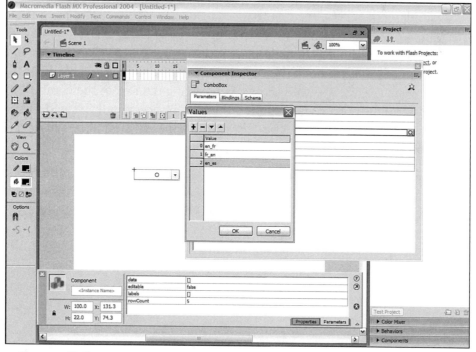

FIGURE 9.3 Using the Component Inspector to populate a combo box manually.

Visual Data Binding

Flash has made it easy to link components with data sources without writing any ActionScript 2.0 code. In the Component Inspector window, you can use the Bindings tab to access the Data Binding window. The add binding command shows all the bindable components, and it introspects the data associated with each component (which is also known as a schema). See Figure 9.4.

FIGURE 9.4   Adding a data binding to a component.

In Figure 9.5, the out field indicates the direction that the data is flowing. For example, in this case, the Component Inspector was accessed from the ComboBox component, and the combo box is passing a string (as a parameter) to the Babel Fish web service, so we indicate out. If the Component Inspector were accessed from the Web Service component, we would specify in for a parameter because the web service is receiving data from the combo box. If this combo box were receiving results from a web service call (instead of specifying a parameter for the web service), we would specify in if accessing it from the combo box.

The bound to field indicates the component to which this combo box component is bound. In this case, it is bound to a component that calls a web service (see Chapter 13 for more information on the web service connector).

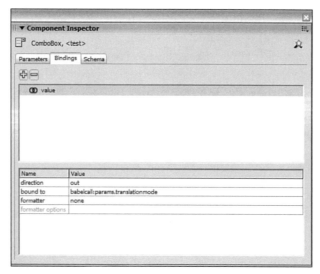

FIGURE 9.5   The Data Bindings window linking a ComboBox
component to a Web Service component with no ActionScript 2.0 code at all.

The Schema Tab

The Schema tab of the Component Inspector tells us exactly the type of data
structure that this component is expecting. For example, if we look at the
schema for a combo box, we can see that the component has a `dataProvider`.
A `dataProvider` can be an array, or just a plain value that is a string as well
as a `selectedIndex` and `selectedItem`. The Schema tab also works with
non-UI components. For example, by looking at the Schema tab of a web service, we can see exactly the data structures that are returned.

Creating a Simple Application with Components and Visual Data Binding

We are going to build a simple application that will use data binding and components. This application will accept input from a user in English and translate
that text to French by calling the Babel Fish web service.

1. Open Flash and create a new FLA file.
2. Open the Web Services panel (Window > Development Panels > Web
    Services) and enter the following URL:

    `www.xmethods.net/sd/2001/BabelFishService.wsdl.`

3. Examine the data structures that the web service requires and returns. Notice that it expects two String parameters, the translation mode, and the actual text to be translated. Notice the web service is returning a string as well. This will work perfectly with the text components because they are built for dealing with simple strings.

4. Find the `BabelFish()` method, right-click it, and choose Add Method Call, as shown in Figure 9.6.

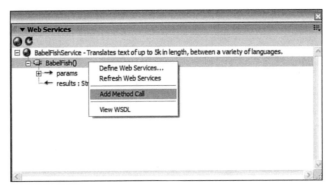

FIGURE 9.6   By choosing Add Method Call, an instance of the Web Services Connector component is automatically placed on the Stage from the Library.

5. Assign the Web Services Connector component an instance name of **babelCall.**

6. Drag three Text Area components (from the Components panel) and a Button component and arrange them as shown in Figure 9.7.

7. Assign the top-right text component an instance name of **language,** and using the Component Inspector or Property Inspector, be sure the text reads en_fr. This will be the translation mode parameter sent to the web service, meaning the service will translate from English to French.

8. Assign the top-left text area an instance name of **babelInput.** This will be the actual text the user can type in and send to the web service.

9. Assign the bottom text area component an instance name of **babelOutput.** This will receive and display the translated text from the web service and display it to the user.

10. Assign the button component a name of **babelCall.**

11. Select the Web Services component and open the Bindings tab in the Component Inspector.

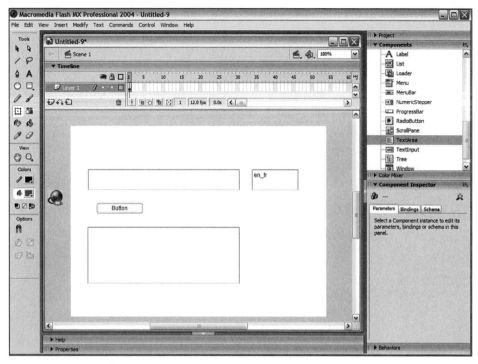

FIGURE 9.7   Dragging the needed components.

12. Add a new binding to the `translationmode` parameter, as shown in Figure 9.8. This links the web service parameter to the language text box.

FIGURE 9.8   Binding the `translationmode` parameter to the text area component.

13. Bind the `translationmode` parameter to the text area component you added earlier, as shown in Figure 9.9:

FIGURE 9.9   Binding the `translationmode` parameter to the text field.

14. Bind the `sourcedata` parameter of the Web Services component to the babelInput Text Area component. This will link the babelInput text field to the text that is to be the translated parameter of the web service.

15. Bind the results of the Web Services component to the babelOutput Text Area component. This will display the string sent back from the web service in the babelOutput text field.

16. Select the button and using the Component Inspector, change the label of the button to **translate**.

17. With the button still selected, open the Behaviors panel and add a web service call to the button. It is located in the data behaviors of the Behaviors pane.

The Version 2 Component APIs

Visual data binding is powerful, but ultimately, there is no substitute for being able to delve into ActionScript to control components. APIs enable the developer to have complete control over components. For example, it would be difficult with visual data binding to apply conditional logic to components if we wanted a combo box to affect a list box component. However, with APIs, the developer can have complete control over the component at runtime.

Component Classes

Each component is its own class with its own set of properties and methods. The class is instantiated by dragging a component from the Components panel (really a separate external SWC file) and assigning it an instance name.

The component packages are located in the classes directory, in the mx folder. The UI components are in the controls folder and the data components are in the data folder. The classes that components can inherit from are in the core folder.

To use code hinting in the version 2 components, you must explicitly declare and type the component at the top of your ActionScript 2.0 code, as shown in the following code:

```
var myCombo :mx.controls.ComboBox
```

The suffixes required for code hinting in Flash MX (such as _cb, _lb, and so on) are no longer required in Flash MX 2004, but they will still work.

All the components inherit from the `MovieClip` class, which means that *all* movie clip properties and methods can be used with any component. For example, `attachMovie()`, `_x`, and `_y` can be used with any component. Figure 9.10 is a diagram that explains the inheritance chain of components in Flash.

Flash MX 2004, like Flash MX, offers only single inheritance, so the actual ActionScript 2.0 code looks something like this:

```
class UIObject extends MovieClip
{
//class code
}

class UIComponent extends UIObject
{
//class code
}

class List extends UIComponent TYPO- no space between ui and component
{
//class code
}
```

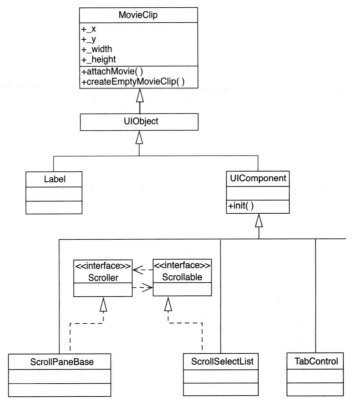

FIGURE 9.10   Inheritance chain of components.

The base UIObject class offers common behavior among components and all components are descended from this class. The UIComponent class is the base class for all components that have some type of user interaction. The ActionScript developer should never need to use these classes except when building components. The main advantage is that after you learn how to use the API of one component, it becomes very easy to learn how to use all other components. The base classes, UIObject and UIComponent, provide common APIs among all components.

Implicit Getter and Setter Methods in Components

Many methods in the version 2 components now use implicit getters and setters and are referenced like properties. For example, in the version 1 components, the setDataProvider() method took a complex data structure and populated the component, as shown in the following code (in ActionScript 1.0):

```
var myArray = new Array ('NewsWeek', 'The New Yorker', 'Time');
myCombo_cb.setDataProvider (myArray);
```

The setDataProvider() method is now a property in the version 2.0 components (built behind the scenes with the implicit getter/setter method):

```
var myCombo :mx.controls.ComboBox
var myArray :Array = new Array('NewsWeek', 'The New Yorker', 'Time');
myCombo.dataProvider = myArray;
```

Not all version 2 component methods are implicit getter/setters. The addItem() method remains pretty much in its original form, as does the getItemAt() method. The documentation that comes with Flash is the best source for figuring out what has and has not changed regarding component APIs.

The New Component Event Model

All components now generate and listen to different types of events that apply to that component. The developer can create one object and link the appropriate event to that object. This provides code reusability and scalability. It also enables us to handle events in a more object-oriented way, which will lead to easier and more effective class based development.

Examine the following code:

```
var myCombo :mx.controls.ComboBox;
var eventObj :Object = new Object();
eventObj.change = function ()
{
trace ("called")
}
myCombo.addEventListener ("change", eventObj);
```

The code is a version 2 replacement for the old setChangeHandler() method, which is no longer available. The function is called every time the user makes a change to the combo box. The combo box is now "listening" for the change event to occur. When the event occurs, it calls the method attached to the object specified in the addEventListener() method. The Flash documentation provides the most complete list of all available events, which vary by component and depend on functionality.

All UI components broadcast the following events, because these events are attached to the `UIComponent` class from which they all inherit:

- **Resize.** The component has been resized.
- **Move.** The component has been moved.
- **Load.** The component is loading its subobjects.
- **UnLoad.** The component is unloading its subobjects.
- **Focus.** The component now has the input focus.
- **Blur.** The component has lost the input focus.

Building a Simple Application with Version 2 Components

One of the most practical uses of Flash is to have two components link to each other. For instance, we are going to have a combo box with different types of magazines; the user will be able to select one magazine and have a list display only magazines that match that type. Doing this with any other technology is cumbersome at best. If we used a server-side solution, such as Macromedia Cold Fusion, a page refresh would be needed for every selection of the combo box. To use another client-side solution, such as Dynamic Hypertext Markup Language (DHTML) or JavaScript, would surely involve cross-browser issues and much more complicated code.

We are going to use the combo box, list box, and text components for our call center application. The user will be able to select a magazine type (such as news and technology) from a combo box, and a list box will populate based on that selection. The text components will then display the details of the selected magazine (the magazine id and the sales description). We are going to use static data in this case, but of course, in real life, this complex data would be obtained from a database through Web Services or XML.

1. To begin the application, drag a ComboBox component onto the Stage and assign it an instance name of **magTypes**.

2. Open the Actions panel and add the following code:

```
var magTypesArray :Array = new Array ();
magTypesArray[0] = "News";
magTypesArray[1] = "Technology";
magTypes.dataProvider = magTypesArray;
```

This populates the component labels with news and technology.

3. Suppose we wanted to add a setting of "All" to the combo box but not the underlying data structure so that the rep would have the option of seeing all magazines available. The `addItemAt()` method would seem to be perfect because we could make "All" the first selection on the combo box. Toward this end, add the following code, which specifies that we want to add the string All to the first (0) element of the combo box array:

```
magTypes.addItemAt(0, "All");
```

4. At first glance, this appears to work perfectly. Test the movie. The combo box now contains the selection "All," just as we expected. However, the underlying array now also has the value of "All" at index 0 (`magTypes_array`). Enter the following code to verify this:

```
trace (magTypesArray);
```

The data and component being linked is in stark contrast to the version 1 components where using `addItem()` did not affect the underlying data structure. This two-way communication enables us to easily divide our application into user interface and data layers. However, we can no longer store complex data structures inside a UI component; components are now only for visual displays, providing a much better separation between the presentation and data layers in Flash.

5. Drag a List component onto the Stage and assign it an instance name of **magList.**

6. Be sure the following class is in the same directory as your FLA file. Examine the class; the class is included with your files for this book.

```
class Product {

    var id:Number;
    var prodType:String
    var prodName:String;
    var description:String;

    function Product (id:Number, prodType:String, prodName:String,
    description:String)
    {
            idNo = id;
            prodType = prodType;
            productName = prodName;
            productDescription = description;
```

continues

```
    }
    public function get idNo() :Number
{
        return this.id;
}
    public function set idNo (id:Number) :Void
{
        this.id = id;
}
    public function get productType() :String
{
        return this.prodType;
}
    public function set productType(prodType:String) :Void
{
        this.prodType = prodType;
}

    public function get productName () :String
{
        return this.prodName;
}
    public function set productName (prodName:String) :Void
{
        this.prodName = prodName;
}
    public function get productDescription () :String
{
        return this.description;
}
    public function set productDescription (description:String) :Void
{
    this.description = description;
}
}
```

In most real-world scenarios, we deal with complex data structures, not just one-dimensional arrays. Our magazine application is no different. We have an array of magazines that includes important information about each magazine, such as the magazine id, the magazine name, the type of magazine it is, and a description of the magazine.

7. Add the following code to build and array of objects using the `Product` class:

```
var newsWeek :Product = new Product();
newsWeek.idNo =  1;
newsWeek.productName = "Newsweek";
newsWeek.productType = "News";
newsWeek.productDescription = "America's source for current events and
the latest in what's happening around the globe";

var time :Product = new Product();
time.idNo = 2;
time.productName = "Time";
time.productType = "News";
time.productDescription = "Insightful commentary and the latest in-
depth news articles";

var pcWorld = new Product();
pcWorld.idNo =3;
pcWorld.productName = "PC World";
pcWorld.productType = "Technology";
pcWorld.productDescription = "Get up to date on the latest trends in
the PC industry";

var macWorld = new Product();
macWorld.idNo = 4;
macWorld.productName = "Mac World";
macWorld.productType = "Technology";
macWorld.productDescription = "Get up to data on the latest trends in
the Macintosh World";

var magazine_array :Array = new Array();
magazine_array [0] = newsWeek;
magazine_array [1] = time;
magazine_array [2] = pcWorld;
magazine_array [3] = macWorld;
```

The next step is to populate the list box with the information.

8. Add this code to the Actions layer of the FLA:

```
magList.dataProvider = magazine_array;
```

This populates the list box with all the information, including id, type, name, and description. Of course, this is not the desired result; we want only the name of the magazine displayed to the user. To do that, you would specify the field that you want to be used as the label for the list.

9. Add the following code to the Actions layer after you set the `dataProvider` getter/setter method:

```
magList.labelField = "productName";
```

Now that we have both components populated with data, we need to link them together, which is not possible to do with visual data binding because we need to add if/else logic, which is possible only with ActionScript 2.0 code. When the user selects a magazine type such as news, we want Flash to filter the list to show only those magazines whose type is news.

10. Add a change event listener to the combo box by using the following code:

```
var myObject :Object = new Object();
myObject.change = function ()
{
        trace ("called");
}
magTypes.addEventListener("change", myObject);
```

11. Test the movie and you will see the change function is called each time you click the combo box component.

Our next step is to figure out which item the user selected and populate the list box based on that selection.

12. Add the following code within the change method, and delete the trace statement:

```
myObject.change = function ()
{
var selectedType = magTypes.selectedItem;
if (selectedType == "All")
{
        magList.dataProvider = magazine_array;
}
```

If the user selects "All," the dataProvider of the combo box will be the `magazine_array`. Now we need to add an else statement and test if the user has selected the type of news or technology. We need to build a new array with the appropriate magazines that meet the criteria. We then use that new array as the data provider for the combo box.

13. Create a new array outside the `if` conditional logic, but still in the change function, as shown in the following code:

```
myObject.change = function ()
{
var result_array:Array = new Array();
if (selectedType == "All")
{
        magList.dataProvider = magazine_array;
}
}
```

The most efficient way to accomplish the comparison would be to loop through the existing array that is used as the data provider for the list component, which is the magazine array. We would then compare any of the product types in that list array to the items that the user has selected using `if` logic. For example, if the user selects the type of news, we want to show only those products that have the `productType` (tracked as an object property) of news.

14. Add the following code within the else statement.

```
if (selectedType == "All")
{
magList.dataProvider = magazine_array;
}else{
var len = magazine_array.length;
for (var i=0; i<len; i++)
{
                if (magazine_array[i].productType == selectedType)
                {
                //do something
                }
        }
}
}
```

If the magazine array product type is equal to the product type that the user has selected, we will push that object at that index of the `magazine_array` into the `result_array`. We then use the `result_array` as the `dataProvider` for the list.

15. Be sure that your final change handler looks like the following:

```
myObject.change = function ()
{
var result_array:Array = new Array();
var selectedType = magTypes.selectedItem;

if (selectedType == "All")
{
magList.dataProvider = magazine_array;
}else{
var len = magazine_array.length;
for (var i=0; i<len; i++)
{
            if (magazine_array[i].productType == selectedType)
            {
            result_array.push (magazine_array[i]);
            magList.dataProvider = result_array;
            }
        }
}
}
```

16. Our combo box is almost finished, but there is one small problem: the combo box defaults to the "news" selection. We want the combo box to default to the "All" selection so that the rep immediately sees all the magazines available. To do that, we use the `selectedIndex` setter method; the "All" selection is located at index 0, so we can just add the following code:

```
magTypes.selectedIndex = 0;
```

The preceding code will not work unless the data has already been loaded into the component. The component does not have an index until the data is loaded in.

17. Add a load event to the magList component, and in the load event itself, set the selected index to 0, as shown in the following code:

```
var loadObject :Object = new Object;
loadObject.load = function ()
{
        magTypes.selectedIndex = 0;
}

magList.addEventListener ("load", loadObject);
```

You have now created a slick application that has no cross-browser issues and that saves on database calls by handling manipulation of the data on the client.

Examining Component Architecture

To get a better sense of the component architecture and best practices, we are going to look at how the CheckBox component is built. Before we actually start building a component, we need to think about the following issues:

- **Visual look and feel.** All components are based on movie clips and in almost all cases, begin their life as a movie clip by using Convert to Symbol. This is where the drawing tools, ActionScript 2.0 code, and other elements of Flash enable us to create the look and feel of the component.

- **Class hierarchy.** From what classes does this component need to inherit? All components, of course, inherit from the `MovieClip` class and the `UIObject` class, but there might be other classes that provide useful properties and methods. It is essential that a component developer understand all the prebuilt classes available for inheritance. It has the potential to save a lot of work! For example, the `View` class enables components to inherit methods that help manage the creation of child objects. The `View` class automatically handles all the code associated with the creation and destruction of child objects. Last, the Accordion component utilizes the `View` class and is a good component to examine to understand how the `View` class works.

  The `UIComponent` class is essential for those components that interact with users. The superclass of the `UIComponent` class is the `UIObject` class. The superclass of the `UIObject` class is the `MovieClip` class. The `UIObject` class offers a draw method that greatly helps with the initial component layout of subobjects. It also helps with end-user interactions, such as focus, clicking, and dragging. It can be important to consider if we need to build any custom classes that might be useful for other components.

  The version 2 component architecture also offers classes useful for specific tasks. One such class is the `Focus Manager`, which keeps track of where the focus of the user is. The `Depth Manager` automatically handles component depth. These classes are available in the package mx.managers.

- **API definition.** We need to consider the properties, events, and methods that will be unique to the component that we are building.

- **Skinning and style.** It is a best practice to divide all the visual aspects of a component into visual movie clips that can be attached at runtime. This enables the user of the component to easily go in and make changes to the appropriate clip.

Creating the Visual Look and Feel of a Component

All components are stored in FLA files in a separate Library. It is now possible to "hide" the FLA file from the Flash developer by using SWC files or compiled clips. Luckily, Macromedia has included all the FLA files for each component so that we can see how they were built.

Under the hood, the Components panel in Flash is really a separate FLA file. When a developer drags a component from the Components panel to the Stage, in reality, it is the same action as dragging a component from the Library of another FLA file.

Work through the following step sequence:

1. Open the file StandardsComponents.fla in C:\Program Files\
   Macromedia\Flash MX 2004\en\First Run\ComponentFLA\
   StandardComponents.fla. Then open the Library and the Library folder
   "Flash UI Components 2," as shown in Figure 9.11:

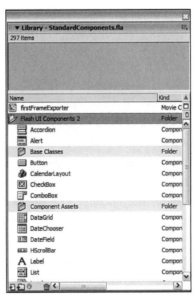

FIGURE 9.11   The visual component symbols available in StandardComponents.fla.

2. Open the CheckBox symbol in the Library and move the playhead to Frame 2. You will see all the different possible states of the check box represented visually, as shown in Figure 9.12:

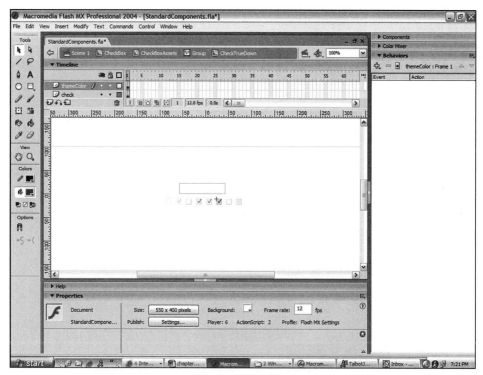

FIGURE 9.12 All the visual components of the CheckBox component are located in the CheckBox symbol.

In Flash, it is now possible to associate a class directly with a visual control by using the Class field in the Convert to Symbol dialog box.

3. Right-click the CheckBox component in the Library, and choose Properties. Click the Advanced button and your screen should resemble Figure 9.13:

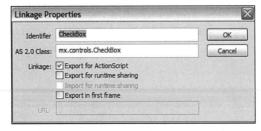

FIGURE 9.13   Notice that the `CheckBox` class is being imported from mx.controls.CheckBox.

4. Be sure the Library is open. Right-click the Checkbox component, and choose Component Definition. Here you see the visual controls, or parameters, of the component that are available in the Component Inspector and/or Property Inspector. You can also specify a custom UI for your component, indicate whether this component appears in the Components panel and/or the Actions panel, and set up the help for the component. See Figure 9.14:

FIGURE 9.14   The Component Definition panel.

Component parameters can also now be defined directly in class files, and Flash will use the class file to populate the parameters file.

5. Open the CheckBox symbol in the Library and move the playhead to Frame 2. Note the stop action on Frame 1. You will see a simple button on the Stage, right above all the Checkbox assets. All the CheckBox assets are assembled dynamically using the Draw method.

The Button component has been physically dragged onto the Stage because the Checkbox component needs to use the `Button` class. This is a common technique in component development. It is even possible to drag classes (such as `UIObject`) onto the Stage, which ensures that all base classes are imported.

The only reason that we need to use the symbols you saw in the previous step sequence is that they need to be exported for ActionScript. Thus, for example, we could use `attachMovie()` to bring them in dynamically (in the version 2 component architecture there are other ways to achieve this as well). It is a best practice to place them in Frame 2 (with a stop action on Frame 1) so that they are still exported but not physically rendered until we need them. This makes the application initialize faster because the components are not rendered until they are needed, thus saving processing power and CPU resources. See Figure 9.15.

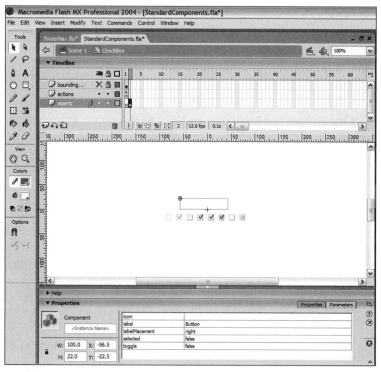

FIGURE 9.15　A simple Button component on Frame 2 of the Checkbox component.

Examining the Class Files of a Component

Now that we have examined the visual creation of the Checkbox component, we need to examine the class files that define the APIs of the component. In this section, we walk through the CheckBox class as an example of a component created with best practices in mind.

1. Let's start by examining the CheckBox class. Open c:\Program Files\Macromedia\Flash MX 2004\en\first run\classes\mx\controls\ CheckBox.as. The class definition of the component is extending the Button component, as shown in the following code:

```
class mx.controls.CheckBox extends Button{

    function CheckBox ()
    {
    }
}
```

2. Open c:\Program Files\Macromedia\Flash MX 2004\en\first run\ classes\mx\controls\Button.as and examine its inheritance structure. We can see all properties and methods of the Button class are inherited from the Simple Button class:

```
class mx.controls.Button extends SimpleButton {
}
```

3. Open the Simple Button class (c:\Program Files\Macromedia\Flash MX 2004\en\first run\classes\mx\controls\SimpleButton.as) and examine its inheritance structure. We can see that the simple button inherits from the UIComponent class:

```
class mx.controls.SimpleButton extends UIComponent{
}
Remember that the UIComponent class extends the UIObject class:
class mx.core.UIComponent extends UIObject{
}
```

Note that the UIObject class extends the MovieClip class:

```
class mx.core.UIObject extends MovieClip {
}
```

While every component can define unique events, events are inherited along the prototype chain. Because the Checkbox component was subclassed from the `UIObject` and `UIComponent` classes, typical events are available. They include `load`, `change`, `move`, and `draw`.

4. Move back to the CheckBox.as file, and you will see the following code:

```
static var symbolName:String = "CheckBox";
static var symbolOwner:Object = mx.controls.CheckBox;
```

The preceding code enables developers to use `createClassObject` to create instances of this component dynamically through this new method. It is a best practice to define these static variables at the beginning of every component class definition so that advanced developers will be able to use this method.

After this code, you will see all the private properties in use. It is essential to declare these properties before they are used. The following are examples of the properties declared. Note the __ denotes that they can be accessed only from within the class:

```
var __selected:Boolean = false;
var __labelPlacement:String = "right";
```

5. It is also important to declare all movie clips used within the component (if any). The next step is to define all of the getter/setter methods that will be used with the component. Within the `CheckBox` class, you will see getter/setter methods such as `toggle`, which indicates whether the check box functions like a toggle switch (`true`) or a push button (`false`).

```
function set toggle(v)
{

}

function get toggle()
{

}
```

You will also see metatags being used within the class definition. Metatags give Flash more information about the code you write. For example, the following code is used by the Component Inspector to display the component parameters:

```
[Inspectable(defaultValue="CheckBox")]
```

Another common metatag is bindable, which indicates that this component can be used with the new visual databindings, as shown in the following code:

```
[Bindable("writeonly")]
```

Almost all components will extend the UIObject or UIComponent classes. This provides a common framework that developers can use to create components.

Note that we must build the class file with certain methods: init, createChildren, draw, and size. These methods are called automatically by the component framework and ensure that components behave in a consistent manner. We also do not have to worry about any synchronicity issues if we use this framework.

The order in which the methods are called is shown in Figure 9.16:

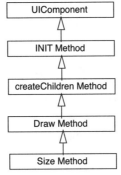

FIGURE 9.16   The method load order in the component framework.

All components should have an init method, which sets all the initial values for the properties and calls the init method of the superclass, as shown in the following code:

```
function init ()
    {
            super.init();
    }
```

The `createChildren` method is called after the `init` method by the component framework and this is where all objects should be created from classes. We can use movie clip methods to do this or we can use the new `createClassObject` method available in the component framework:

```
function createChildren ()
        {
                this.createTextField ("fontText", 1, 20, 20, 20, 20);
                this.createClassObject ("comboBox", "chooser_cb", 1);
        }
```

The draw method is where all components and text fields should be populated. The component framework includes a new drawing API that makes drawing easier. See the following code:

```
function draw ()
        {
                this.beginFill (0x000000);
                this.drawRect (0,0, height, width);
                this.endFill();
        }
```

Finally it's a best practice to create a size method that will redraw the component in case the component is resized. This functionality is automatically handled by the superclass simply by calling the invalidate method:

```
function size ()
        {
                super.invalidate();
        }
```

Components enable easy encapsulation, reuse of code, and control of visual elements. It can be very efficient to build custom components that you can use across different applications.

Consider the following step sequence:

1. The first step in component development is to decide what class our component will actually extend. The `UIObject` class is the base class for all graphical components. It can have shape, draw itself, and be invisible. `UIObject` handles most of the component events, such as `load` and `change`. `UIObject` provides alternate read-only variables for determining the position and size of a movie clip. You can use the `move()` and `setSize()` methods to alter the position and size of an object.

   The `UIComponent` class extends the `UIObject` class and is the base for all components that have user interaction. For example, the `UIComponent` class controls all interaction with the keyboard and mouse.

   Other components can be extended as well. For example, if we need a component that has all the same functionality of an alert but does more, we can extend the alert component rather than building that functionality ourselves.

2. The second step in component development is to define a class in an external ActionScript file. The external ActionScript class extends another class, adds methods, adds getters and setters, and defines events and event handlers for the component.

3. The next step is to define the `symbolName` property, which preserves the component's naming structure. This property is always static and a type of `String`. It is simply the name of the ActionScript class.

4. The next step is to define the symbol owner, which is the fully qualified package name of the class and is used in the `createChildren()` method of the component. This property is static as well but has a data type of `Object`.

5. The next step is to define the class name of the component in a `String` data type. A class constructor needs to be defined as well.

   So far the class structure of our component should look as follows:

```
//declare the class and identify parent class

class myPackage.MyComponent extends UIObject {

//identify the symbol name that this class is bound to

static var symbolName:String = "MyComponent";
```

```
//identify the fully-qual'd package name of the symbol owner

static var symbolOwner:Object = Object(myPackage.MyComponent);

//provide the className variable

var className:String = "MyComponent";

function MyComponent() {}

}
```

6. The next step is to define an `init` method for the component. This method is executed as soon as the class is instantiated and is usually called by the superclass. By calling this method, the `width`, `height`, and `clip` parameters are all defined. Usually the `init` method on the superclass, which is, in this example, `UIObject`, is called as shown in the following code:

```
function init(Void):Void {
super.init();
}
```

7. The next step is to define any objects that the component will use. For example, your component would likely contain text boxes. These can be defined in the physical asset of the component or in `createChildren()`. This method enables us to use methods of the `UIObject` class that will automatically bring assets from the Library into our component. These could include text boxes, other components, movie clips, and so on. These methods of the `UIOBject` class are fully described in the Flash documentation and it is much better to use these rather than the traditional `attachMovie()` or `createTextField()`.

An example `createChildren()` method that creates a text field might look like this:

```
function createChidren() :Void {
componentLabel = createLabel("textBoxLabel", 10);
}
```

The UIObject class also offers drawing capabilities similar to the drawing API of a movie clip, but it is much easier to implement. This is defined in a draw method. An example is the drawRect method, which will draw a rectangle for us:

```
function draw () :Void
beginFill(bgColor);
      drawRect(0,0,width,height);
endFill();
}
```

It also makes sense to set up the physical layout of your component interface in the draw method. For example, if you created a text field or a combo box, or a movie clip in the createChildren method, it would make sense to define the physical look and feel in the draw method, like so:

```
function draw () :Void {
      textBoxLabel.text = myText;
      textBoxLabel.setSize (textBoxLabel.textWidth + 1,
textBoxLabel.textHeight +1
}
```

8. The next step is to set a size method of the component. This is automatically called whenever the component is resized, and if you use the invalidate() method, this will automatically call the draw method.

```
function size () :Void {
      invalidate();
}
```

After the method creation has been completed, you define your getter/setters that retrieve the component properties. If you designate that the property is Inspectable, as shown in the following code, it will appear in the Property Inspector:

```
[Inspectable]
      function set text(newText:String):Void
      {
        _text = newText;
        invalidate();
      };
```

```
function get text():String
{
   return _text;
}
```

9. Next, you need to create a visual movie clip symbol with any physical assets the component will use, and to link that physical movie clip with the class that you created. Remember that the physical assets should be placed on Frame 2 of the movie clip with a stop action in Frame 1 of the clip.

    To define the physical area of the component on the Stage, you can create a movie clip on a layer in Frame 1 and assign the movie clip an instance name of boundingBox_mc. This will define the physical boundaries of the component. After the physical look and feel of the component has been set up, you need to link the class to the physical movie clip in the Component Definition menu.

10. Right-click the component and choose Component Definition. In the Class field, enter the name of your class. The component will read the class and pull out all the parameters that you specified. To easily distribute the component, you can export all assets into an SWC file, which is basically a file in pkzip format.

Summary

Components are a powerful object-oriented feature of Flash MX 2004. The new version 2 component model is completely different from the version 1 components, but it provides a much more efficient and object-oriented way of dealing with reusable code and assets.

All components are stored as separate class files and these class files inherit from the MovieClip object and also from specialized component classes, such as UIObject and UIComponent. This provides a much greater separation of visual and code elements.

The UIObject and UIComponent classes contain prebuilt functionality that greatly helps in the development of our own components. During this chapter, we worked in-depth with new component functionality, such as data binding, the component event model, and methods such as dataProvider, `selectedItem`, and `addItem`. All this functionality is built into the component classes from which our custom components can inherit, which helps make custom component development a snap.

Components greatly simplify development because they provide reusable functionality across different applications. By changing the structure of components and the inheritance model, Macromedia has made component development simpler and more powerful.

SECTION II
THE OTHER HALF OF THE EQUATION

CHAPTER 10

TO PROTECT AND SERVE

Throughout the previous section of this book, several aspects of object-oriented programming (OOP) were examined, and all the aspects focused on the client side of the development process. Because it is a client-side development language, this focus on the client makes sense. However, as Flash continues its transition from movie making to creating application user interfaces, chances are that Flash will not encompass the entire application.

To properly understand the new direction of Flash, it helps to see where it fits within the history of computer applications. Although many Flash developers began programming only since the introduction of the World Wide Web, computer applications actually predate that event by several decades. After examining the history of applications, we discuss the two types of data and hybrid applications.

A Brief History of Computer Applications

Computers have been playing a role in the business environment for more than four decades. Since the beginning of that time, server-side processing has played a major role in the majority of business applications. Let's take a look at how those four decades have played out.

Mainframe Computers

In the early 1960s, mainframe computers began to find their way into large enterprises. These mainframes consisted of extremely large computers that were responsible for all logic, storage, and processing of data. "Dumb-terminals" allowed various users to interact with the mainframe.

These systems continued in widespread use for more than 30 years, and to some degree, continue to exist today. Architecturally, these were designed at a time when processing power was scarce and expensive; therefore, it was cost effective to centralize all the power onto the server. The clients for the mainframe systems contained virtually no logic because they relied on the server for everything, including the display logic.

The Age of Microcomputers

As memory and processing power became cheaper, the microcomputer (also known as the personal computer) began to find its way into businesses. Originally, these were used to run stand-alone applications, where everything needed by the application resided directly on the terminal at which the end user worked. These terminals were often easier to use because the user interface had improved. It was during this time that graphical user interfaces (GUIs) became available, further increasing the ease of use of the systems. However, as stand-alone systems, there was still no effective way to centralize data or business rules.

Client/Server Computing

With the migration from mainframe to microcomputer, the pendulum swung from one extreme (having all logic on the server) to the other extreme (having all logic on the client). Sensing the imbalance in this, several vendors began to develop a system that could encapsulate all the benefits of the microcomputer as well as those of the mainframe systems. This led to the birth of client/server applications.

Client/server applications were frequently written in languages such as Visual Basic or PowerBuilder, and they offered a lot of flexibility to application developers. Interfaces that were very interactive and intuitive could be created and maintained independent of the logic that drove the application functionality. This separation allowed modifications to be made to the user interface (the place in an application where changes are most frequent), without the need to impact business rules or data access. Additionally, by connecting the client to a remote server, it became possible to build systems in which multiple users could share data and application functionality. With business and data access logic centrally located, any changes to these could be made in a single place.

Although traditional client/server applications offered tremendous advantages over stand-alone and mainframe applications, they all lacked a distributed client. This meant that for each change that needed to be made to the user interface, the files comprising the client needed to be reinstalled at each workstation, often requiring dynamic link libraries (DLL) files to be updated. The phrase "DLL hell" aptly captured the frustration of many IT professionals whose job it was to keep the client applications current within a business.

The Internet

During the days of the client/server dominance, the U.S. government project ARPANet was renamed "Internet" and started becoming available to businesses as a means to share files across a distributed network. Most of the early protocols of the Internet, such as File Transfer Protocol (FTP) and Gopher, were specifically related to file sharing. The Hypertext Transfer Protocol (HTTP) followed these and introduced the concept of "hyperlinking" between networked documents. The Internet, in many ways, is like the mainframe systems that predate it, in that an ultra thin client (the browser) is used to display information retrieved by the server. The documents on the server contain all the information to determine how the page will be displayed in the client.

Businesses began to embrace the Internet as a means to share documents, and in time, many realized that the distributed nature of the Internet could free them from the DLL hell of their client/server applications. This new-found freedom led to the introduction of the Internet as more than a document-sharing system and introduced the concept of the web-based application. Of course, these web-based applications lacked the richness and usability that was taken for granted in the client/server days.

Establishing the Need for Rich Internet Applications (RIAs)

Through the transition from client/server applications to web-based applications, businesses were able to save a tremendous amount of money on the costs of desktop support for applications. No longer was it necessary to move from one desk to the next to reinstall the latest version of the application client with each change. Instead, each time the application was used, the latest client logic was downloaded from the server.

Of course, within a few years, many businesses realized that there was a downside to this model. Although they were indeed saving money on the distribution costs, they also lost money, largely due to the productivity losses of their employees. The richness of the client in client/server applications allowed end users to achieve their goals quickly and efficiently. However, the page-based nature of web-based applications mandated that for each action they took, the data needed to be sent back to the server, and a new page needed to be retrieved. Although this often was a matter of only seconds per page, over the course of an eight-hour work day, those seconds quickly added up to several minutes per day. Many businesses found that over the course of a work week, employees heavily involved in data entry operations were losing as many as 3–5 hours a week in productive time, as compared to doing the same tasks in their earlier client/server applications.

Looking to regain the lost productivity, several variations of rich clients for Internet applications were attempted. One of the early attempts was Java applets, but these often failed because the file size was too large and there were many issues with platform independence.

Fortunately, with the release of Macromedia Flash MX in 2002, a new tool to solve the problem was introduced. With Flash as a client, it was again possible to have all the richness and benefits of a traditional client/server application along with the distributed nature of a web-based system. The end result was that the productivity of the client/server days was restored, without the added expense of keeping the user base up-to-date.

However, to begin using Flash in this way, Flash developers had to make a logic leap. Traditionally, Flash was used to build stand-alone applications, often in the form of animations or movies. These would most often use local data to run. To fully leverage the benefits of the client/server model, developers needed to understand the benefits of connecting to a server, and the proper delegation between local and remote processing of data.

Local Data

A local data application is one in which all the data needed to run the application is contained locally within the application. Developers can still create local data applications within Flash MX 2004, and there are times when this model makes perfect sense. Of course, there are times when it does not make sense. In the following sections, we discuss both.

Benefits

One main reason developers choose to build an application with local data is that it can run without an Internet connection. It is not uncommon for Flash applications to be distributed on CD, and to this day, many computers do not have a dedicated connection to the Internet. For this reason, there will always be a place for these local data applications.

Liabilities

The liability of local data is fairly obvious, in that the application can use only the data coded within it. This is analogous to the days of microcomputers before client/server applications became dominant. Should the underlying data need to change, the source code would need to be modified and the Flash movie republished.

Another place in which local data applications have a shortcoming is the area of security. Sadly, a series of Flash decompilers have existed for years. They allow their users access to all the variables within a Flash application. If any sensitive data is used, this can be exposed through the use of these decompilers.

Remote Data

To overcome the shortcomings of local data applications, we can introduce remote data into Flash. As we will see over the next five chapters, Flash can integrate external data and send data to a remote server. Such use of remote data overcomes both of the liabilities of local data applications. To change the underlying data in a remote data application, the data can be modified at its source (database, text files, extensible markup language [XML] documents, and so on) instead of being copied into the FLA source code. Additionally, should a remote dynamic data application be decompiled, the underlying data will not be exposed.

Additionally, this remote data can come in two forms, static data, which is read from text files (such as XML or delimited text), and dynamic data, which is tailored for each specific request to the server. Over the next several chapters, we examine how Flash can work with both static and dynamic remote data.

Of course, a remote data application lacks the one benefit of local data applications—the ability to operate in a stand-alone manner when it is not connected to the Internet. To truly benefit from both local and remote architectures, a hybrid application is needed.

Local/Remote Hybrid Applications

In Flash MX, local shared objects were introduced. Developers could store data in these shared objects between sessions of a Flash application. Through a creative architecture, in which a Flash application has some initial static data *and* the ability to connect to the Internet and work with dynamic data, a hybrid local/remote application can be constructed. With this architecture, if the application is run in a non-networked environment, it will operate off the static local data; however, when connected to the Internet, the data can be updated and stored in a local shared object. This way, each subsequent time the application is run without an Internet connection, the data loaded into the local shared object can be used by the Flash application. Figure 10.1 shows a flow chart detailing how such a system might be architected.

> **NOTE**
>
> For more information on local shared objects, see Chapter 11, "Reading Data Files."

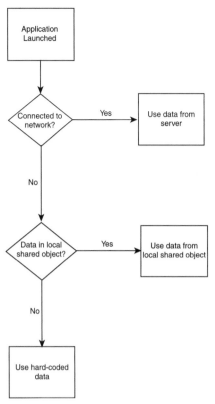

FIGURE 10.1   This flow chart details the decisions that determine where a hybrid application will get the data it uses.

Looking Ahead

Now that you understand why developers might want to connect Flash applications to a server, the next step is to understand how it is done. Toward that understanding, we have organized the subsequent chapters as follows:

- Chapter 11, "Reading Data Files," examines various aspects of reading data in from files. This could involve using name value pairs of data from text files; it also explores the use of local shared objects.

- Chapter 12, "XML and Flash," examines reading data in from XML, which can include static XML files, dynamically generated XML files, and dynamic XML sockets.

- Chapter 13, "Web Services," explores a new feature of Flash MX Professional 2004—the ability to consume Web Services within Flash.

- Chapter 14, "Using Client-Side Data Integration," explores the DataSet, DataBinding, and Flash Remoting features within Flash MX Professional 2004, explaining how they can be used for easing the process of building data-driven applications.
- Chapter 15, "Flash Communication Server MX Applications," examines the Flash Communications Server, which allows for true bidirectional communications with a server.

Summary

With a solid understanding of the various ways in which data can be exchanged between Flash and a server, developers have a very powerful tool added to their application construction toolbox. With its combined abilities of exchanging dynamic data with a server, building intuitive interfaces, and using a fully distributed architecture, Flash can rightfully take its place as the heir apparent to client-side development for modern business applications.

CHAPTER 11

READING DATA FILES

Quite often, when you are developing an application, the need arises to access data from an external source. In this chapter, we cover the input of text into Flash from many sources, including text files, Hypertext Markup Language (HTML) parameters, the local `SharedObject` object, and the `LocalConnection` object.

The fundamental differences between them are as follows:

- When the data is loaded
- Whether the data will be persistent
- Where the data is stored and maintained

For each external data source, we cover the mechanics as well as the justification for using one over the other. Table 11.1 enumerates the different types of data exchanges that might be required by a Flash application.

TABLE 11.1   Objects and Methods in Flash Used to Exchange Data

	FLASH MOVIE	LOCAL	SERVER
Flash Movie	`LocalConnection` object	`SharedObject` object (similar to cookies)	`LoadVars` object
	`SharedObject` object (similar to cookies)		`LoadVariables()` method
	`LoadVars` object		`XML` object
			URL query string
			FlashVars

> **NOTE**
>
> The XML object will not be covered in this chapter. See Chapter 12, "XML and Flash," for more information.

In this chapter, we cover the following:

- `loadVariables()` method
- `LoadVars` object
- FlashVars
- `SharedObject` object
- `LocalConnection` object

Each provides its own advantages and disadvantages, as we will see in the following sections.

loadVariables() and *LoadVars*

External data from text files can provide an easy way to externalize application data that doesn't change very often. For example, you might have style information for how text should display in your application or schedule data that is published monthly or quarterly.

In the Flash application, we can request the file containing the text using its URL. The URL can be to a server-side application that generates the text file or a static text file stored on the server. When the call is returned to the Flash application, a special storage object grabs and retains the data in the application as long as the application is running. This model offers a suitable solution for small datasets when the data is maintained separately from the application.

First we will look at the data and then we will use the built-in Flash objects to access the data. There are three key elements for externalizing data in text files:

- The format of text in the file
- The file location
- The reading of data from the text file

Proper Format for the Text File

Text files loaded into a Flash application have to be created using a special syntax. The syntax is called *name-value pairs*. This means that each entry in the file will have a variable *name* and a variable *value*. The text must also be URL encoded. Multiple pairs are separated by &.

Listing 11.1 shows a sample from a text file where name, age, and color are the variable names, while Hank, 42, and red are the values, respectively.

LISTING 11.1   Name-Value Pairs

```
name=Hank&age=42&colors=red
```

The name-value pairs can include arrays of data. The data would be formatted as a set of comma delimited strings. Listing 11.2 shows an example of array data for the colors variable.

LISTING 11.2   Name-Value Pairs with Array Data

```
name=Hank&age=42&colors=red,blue,green
```

> **NOTE**
>
> URL encoding is a replacement process for non-alphanumeric characters. For example, when a string is encoded, the spaces are replaced with a plus sign (+) and an exclamation point(!) and is encoded as %21. Most server-side applications, such as ColdFusion and Active Server Pages (ASP), have methods to encode text. For more information on URL encoding, see www.macromedia.com/support/flash/ts/documents/url_encoding.htm.

Where Can the File Be Located?

The Flash Player has a security model that is consistent with browser security models. That is, a movie running within a browser can access only external resources that are served from the same domain. Before Flash Player 7, accessing resources from a different domain required developers to use workarounds. With the new security model in Flash Player 7, the user decides to allow or deny data resources at runtime. For example, if a Flash movie is trying to access a text file from a different domain, the Flash Player will pop up a dialog box informing the user that the movie is trying to access data from a different domain. The user can choose to allow or deny the data access, as shown in Figure 11.1. Figure 11.1 shows two different dialog boxes. The first is showing a request to load data from a different domain. The second is requesting to load data from the same domain, but using a secure protocol.

FIGURE 11.1   Allow/Deny dialog box.

Reading Text Files

In Flash, there are built-in methods and objects that enable us to request and read external text files. There is an object called LoadVars and a method called loadVariables(). The LoadVars object has several methods for requesting and managing the data from text files while loadVariables() can be used globally or as a method of a movie clip. The LoadVars object offers a more robust solution because it has methods and event handlers for managing the loading process as well as the data after it is loaded.

> **NOTE**
>
> The loadVariables() method is not the preferred method for reading data from a text file. It is mentioned here because many legacy Flash applications were written using this method. The preferred solution uses an object, such as the LoadVars object (covered in this chapter) or the XML object (covered in Chapter 12), for loading data.

The loadVariables() *Method*

The `loadVariables()` method reads data from an external file and sets the values for variables in the receiving movie clip. This method assumes that all the data in the text file is URL encoded.

There are two ways to use the `loadVariables()` method:

- **Global function.** Your code should look like the following:
  ```
  loadVariables ("url" , target [, variables]).
  ```
- **Movie clip method.** Your code should look like the following:
  ```
  movieclip.loadVariables ("url" [, variables]).
  ```

Listing 11.3 shows an example of their usages.

LISTING 11.3   loadVariables() Method Invocation

```
//global function loading into the current timeline
loadVariables("http://www.myDomain.com/bankRates.txt", "");


or


//global function loading into the movieclip - rates
this.createEmptyMovieClip("rates",10)
loadVariables("http://www.myDomain.com/bankRates.txt", "rates");


or


//movieclip method
this.createEmptyMovieClip("rates",10)
rates.loadVariables("http://www.myDomain.com/bankRates.txt");
```

There are some shortcomings when using `loadVariables()`. If you are loading a text file that is more than a few data elements, you might need to wait until all the data is loaded to actually use the data. There is no mechanism to determine when the data has completely loaded into the application. The `LoadVars` object addresses this shortcoming. We discuss it next.

LoadVars *Object*

The `LoadVars` object is an alternative to the `loadVariables()` function for reading data from a server. The `LoadVars` object is also more object-oriented because `LoadVars` can be subclassed and the applications data access logic can be added and encapsulated in the subclasses object.

You can use the `LoadVars` object to obtain the following:

- Verification when data loading is complete
- Loading progress

The `LoadVars` object uses the methods `load()`, `send()`, and `sendAndLoad()` to access data from a server, as shown in Table 11.2 from the Flash 2004 Help Files. The `LoadVars` object expects data in the form of name-value pairs.

TABLE 11.2   Method Summary for the *LoadVars* Object from Flash 2004 Help Files

METHOD	DESCRIPTION
`LoadVars.load()`	Downloads variables from a specified URL
`LoadVars.getBytesLoaded()`	Returns the number of bytes loaded from a `load()` or `sendAndLoad()` method
`LoadVars.getBytesTotal()`	Returns the total number of bytes that will be downloaded by a `load()` or `sendAndLoad()` method
`LoadVars.send()`	Posts variables from a `LoadVars` object to a URL
`LoadVars.sendAndLoad()`	Posts variables from a `LoadVars` object to a URL and downloads the server's response to a target object
`LoadVars.toString()`	Returns a URL encoded string that contains all the enumerable variables in the `LoadVars` object

You must use the constructor `new LoadVars()` to create an instance of the `LoadVars` object before calling its methods. Listing 11.4 shows the creating of a `LoadVars` object and the calling of the `load()` method.

LISTING 11.4   Create a *LoadVars* Object

```
var rateObject = new LoadVars();
rateObject.load("http://www.myDomain.com/bankRates.txt");
```

We mentioned earlier that the `LoadVars` object has methods that help us determine when the loading is complete. There is also an event that is triggered when the loading has finished. The event is called the `onLoad` event. We can use this event to manipulate the data after it is loaded. Listing 11.5 shows that when the data has loaded completely, it is used to populate a combo box in the loan calculator application.

LISTING 11.5   *onLoad()* Used to Populate a Combo Box

```
var rateObject:LoadVars = new LoadVars();
rateObject.load("http://www.haffnergraphic.com/bankRates.txt");

rateObject.onLoad = function(){
        trace("number of bytes loaded = "+ this.getBytesLoaded());
        populateBankList(rateObject);
}
populateBankList = function(bankData){
        var bankArray:Array = bankData.banks.split(",");
        var ratesArray:Array = bankData.rates.split(",");
        for (var i =0; i<bankArray.length; i++){
                var label = bankArray[i]+": "+ ratesArray[i]+"%";
                var value = ratesArray[i];
                this.bankList_cbx.addItem(label, value);
        }
}
```

> **NOTE**
>
> The LoadVars object can be used to send data as well as to receive data. This chapter covers reading data into an application using LoadVars. The XML object is a better choice for sending data to a server. For more information on sending data from a Flash application using XML, see Chapter 12.

FlashVars and the Query String

We have talked about using text files as a source for application data in a Flash application, but sometimes if the dataset is small, you might want to use basic HTML mechanisms for passing data into an application.

There are two simple paradigms that enable us to pass data into the application through the HTML page:

- FlashVars
- Query string

The following subsections discuss each in turn.

> **NOTE**
>
> There is one other HTML-based method that isn't covered in this chapter but it's worth noting: FSCommand. It enables you to communicate from the HTML page using JavaScript to the Flash application on the page. This method has cross-browser issues and JavaScript dependencies. For more on FSCommand, see www.macromedia.com/support/flash/ts/documents/mozilla_fscommand.htm.

FlashVars

Using FlashVars, we can directly attach the variables as parameters in the object and embed tags in the HTML page. When the application launches in the browser, it reads the `param` tags attributes set in the object or embed tag. These parameters are used to initialize the application. The parameter FlashVars is used to pass in any number of variables. The format for the data is *name-value* pairs, the same as the format we saw earlier in `LoadVars` and `loadVariables()`. Note that the data must be URL-encoded as well.

On startup, the Flash application checks whether the variables exist. If they do, the values passed are assigned to the existing variables. If they don't, new variables with the given name are created and their values set. Listing 11.6 shows the object tag with the FlashVars param tag.

LISTING 11.6   Object Tag with the FlashVars Param Tag

```
<object classid="clsid:d27cdb6e-ae6d-11cf-96b8-444553540000"
codebase="http://download.macromedia.com/pub/shockwave/cabs/flash/
swflash.cab#version=7,0,0,0" width="385" height="370" id="loanCalc"
align="middle">
<param name="movie" value="loanCalc.swf" />
<param name="flashVars"
value="banks=Fleet,Citibank,BankOne&rates=6,5,7" />
<embed src="loanCalc.swf" quality="high" bgcolor="#ffffff" width="385"
height="370" name="loanCalc" align="middle" allowScriptAccess="sameDomain"
type="application/x-shockwave-flash" pluginspage="http://www.macrome-
dia.com/go/getflashplayer" />
</object>
```

Listing 11.7 shows how we would use the variables passed in through the object tag. In the application, we will take each set of data and stuff it into an object to be handled by the `populateBankList()` method.

LISTING 11.7   Variables Passed to a Flash Application from FlashVars

```
var banks:Array; ←populated by FlashVars at startup
var rates:Array; ←populated by FlashVars at startup
var ratesObject:Object = new Object();
ratesObject.banks = banks;
ratesObject.rates = rates;

populateBankList(ratesObject);
```

FlashVar string sizes of up to 64KB (65535 bytes) in length are supported by all browsers.

Query String

The variable information can also be passed to the main timeline of the Flash application passed in through the query string. In Listing 11.8, we have modified the object tag so that the variable data is appended to the SWF name. The application will behave the same as if we were using FlashVars.

LISTING 11.8   Variables Passed to a Flash Application from a Query String

```
<object classid="clsid:d27cdb6e-ae6d-11cf-96b8-444553540000"
codebase="http://download.macromedia.com/pub/shockwave/cabs/flash/
swflash.cab#version=7,0,0,0"" width="385" height="370" id="loanCalc"
align="middle">
<param name="movie"
value="loanCalc.swf?banks=Fleet,Citibank,BankOne&rates=6,5,7"/>
<embed src="loanCalc.swf?banks=Fleet,Citibank,BankOne&rates=6,5,7"
quality="high" bgcolor="#ffffff" width="385" height="370"
name="loanCalc" align="middle" allowScriptAccess="sameDomain"
type="application/x-shockwave-flash"
pluginspage="http://www.macromedia.com/go/getflashplayer" />
</object>
```

> **NOTE**
>
> The value must be assigned in both the object and embed tags for this method to work in all browsers.

Shared Object

Up to this point, we have discussed how to get data into our application from a server. This section covers a cookie-like Flash object called a `SharedObject` that enables us to write data from our application and to persist the data on the client machine—much in the same way as a cookie behaves.

Cookies are small bits of data stored in files on the client machine. They help an application or website remember information about you or how you used the website. The cookie can hold anything from your name to the contents of your last shopping cart. Quite often cookies are used to remember your prefer-ences or state. For example, you might visit a retailer's site and they have an option to view content as HTML or in Flash. Your choice is a likely candidate for a cookie so that the next time you visit the site, you are served the correct version without being asked.

Cookies are stored in a specific location on the client machine. The directory is based on which browser the client is using. SharedObject data is also stored on the client machine in a specific directory based on the domain from which the Flash application is loaded.

Creating and Populating a *SharedObject*

SharedObjects behave a bit differently than most other objects in Flash. To create a SharedObject, we do not call the constructor of the object. Instead we call the getLocal() static method. The getLocal() method determines if an object exists and if it does, opens it for reading; if it doesn't exist, it creates a new one. As shown in Table 11.3, the getLocal() method returns a SharedObject instance. This table is a method summary for the SharedObject.

TABLE 11.3 *SharedObject* Methods from Flash 2004 Help Files

METHOD	DESCRIPTION
SharedObject.clear()	Purges all of the data from the shared object and deletes the shared object from the disk
SharedObject.flush()	Immediately writes a locally persistent shared object to a local file
SharedObject.getLocal()	Returns a reference to a locally persistent shared object that is available only to the current client
SharedObject.getSize()	Gets the current size of the shared object, in bytes

If you recall, our loan calculator application uses several pieces of data to calculate monthly payments. It would be useful to save the last calculated loan so that when the user wants to calculate another loan, he or she is reminded of the previous use. We might also add a name to personalize the application.

Listing 11.9 shows an example of creating a SharedObject to maintain the state of our loan calculator application.

LISTING 11.9   Create a *SharedObject* to Maintain Loan Calculator State

```
//create LSO or open if it already exists
var loanCalcLso = SharedObject.getLocal("loanCalc");
```

After you have created a `SharedObject` in the application, it is ready for writing. All `SharedObjects` have a property called `data`. This property is itself an object and is used to store user data. In Listing 11.10, the variables that we want to save for our loan application are added as properties of the `SharedObject`'s data container.

LISTING 11.10   Writing Data to a Shared Object

```
//write to LSO
    loanCalcLso.data.lastLoanAmount=loanAmt.text;
    loanCalcLso.data.lastLoanTerm=term.text;
    loanCalcLso.data.lastLoanTerm=name.text;
```

We have chosen to save simple text as strings to the `SharedObject`. We could, however, save any ActionScript 2.0 variable to the `SharedObject`. We would do this if we were saving an array or an object with multiple properties.

Saving a *SharedObject*

Although the `SharedObject` has been created in the application, it hasn't yet been saved to the local storage. Saving the `SharedObject` to disk will happen automatically when the movie is closed. It will also happen when the `SharedObject` is deleted or garbage collected. You can, however, explicitly choose to save the `SharedObject` to disk using the `flush()` method.

There are different methods available to help us manage the process of writing to the disk. In Table 11.3, the two methods that will help us manage this process are `clear()` and `flush()`. By calling `SharedObject.flush()`, the entire contents of the object are written to the local disk. This method is preferred over passive saving because it provides you the opportunity to prompt the user with storage size requirements.

By default, the Flash Player accepts shared objects up to 100k. This is also a configurable attribute of the Player. If you right-click a Flash movie in the browser and select Settings, you will be able to modify the Player settings. Figure 11.2 shows the dialog box that enables you to increase the local storage size for shared objects.

FIGURE 11.2   Player settings for local storage.

If the application has minimum data requirements and the user tries to set the local storage value below the minimum, a warning dialog will be displayed, as in Figure 11.3.

FIGURE 11.3   Player settings warning.

NOTE

For more information on Player settings, see `www.macromedia.com/support/flashplayer/help/settings/`.

It's a good idea to know where the data is actually stored on the client. The file locations depend on what operating systems you are using. All local shared object files will have the extension .sol. In Windows XP for example, the shared object for the loan calculator would be stored as follows:

```
C:\Documents and Settings\userName\Application Data\Macromedia\Flash
Player\localhost\LoanCalculator\loanCalc.swf\loanCalc.sol
Host\directoryName\applicationName\solName.sol
```

Notice that the directory structure contains a reference to `Host\directoryName\applicationName\solName.sol`. By using the host name in the directory structure, Flash can guarantee uniqueness from other applications with the same name storing data in local shared objects.

There might be times when you will want to delete all the data from a local shared object. The method `clear()` will remove any existing data from the shared object. This is a good practice for keeping the size of the shared object down. We can also determine the size of the data in a shared object using the `getSize()` method. This will return the size in bytes. This can help us determine if we have exceeded the local storage threshold and need to respond accordingly.

NOTE

When using local `SharedObjects`, we are depending on the user to allow local storage. For this reason, it is a good idea to have some error checking to determine if the data was actually stored. The `flush()` method returns true/false, indicating whether the `SharedObject` was successfully written to the disk. You can use this value to inform the user to check the local storage settings.

LocalConnection Object

In this chapter, we have covered a variety of ways to get data into a Flash movie from servers and local storage. In this section, we talk about how to get data from one Flash movie into another.

To communicate between two movies, both should be running on the same system. Each movie will be running in a separate instance of the Flash Player and can be running in different applications. For example, one movie can be running in Netscape while the other is running in Internet Explorer or a standalone Player.

NOTE

Movie-to-movie communication on different systems (across a network) can be achieved using the XML object or Flash Communication Server (Comm Server). For more information on XML, see Chapter 12, and see Chapter 14, "Using Client-Side Data Integration," for more on the Flash Communications Server.

To implement movie-to-movie communication, the `LocalConnection` object is used. For communication to take place, there will be at least two instances of the `LocalConnection` object, one in the sender (the movie to send the data) and one in the receiver (the movie receiving the data). Table 11.4 shows the first line of code in each movie.

TABLE 11.4   Create a *LocalConnection*

SENDER	RECEIVER
`sender = new LocalConnection();`	`receiver = new LocalConnection();`

For one movie to communicate with the other, a connection name must be established and agreed upon. Table 11.5 shows how the movies will find each other. The receiver will listen for data from a given sender using the `connect()`

method of the `LocalConnection` object. The sender will send the data using the `send()` method of the `LocalConnection` object. Notice that the receiver is listening for a connection using the named connection `myData` and the sender is sending the data using the same named connection. Many different movies can tie into the same named connection.

TABLE 11.5   Connect to a *LocalConnection* Object

SENDER	RECEIVER
`sender = new LocalConnection();`	`receiver = new LocalConnection();`
	`receiver.connect("myData")`
`sender.send("myData","methodName",`	
`data);`	

Security on the Receiving Movie

By default, data can be sent between movies loaded from the same domain. To exchange data between movies of different domains, we can use the event, `allowDomain()`, to specifically allow a domain. `allowDomain()` is triggered when data is received from a movie though a `LocalConnection` object.

Listing 11.11 shows the `allowDomain()` event used to allow data from `www.myDomain.com` to be read into a movie loaded from `www.anotherDomain.com`.

LISTING 11.11   *AllowDomain() Example*

```
domain: www.myDomain.com
sendObject = new LocalConnection();

var rateObject:LoadVars = new LoadVars();
rateObject.load("bankRates.txt");

rateObject.onLoad = function(){
   sendObject.send("LoanData", "populateBankList", rateObject);

}
domain: www.anotherDomain.com
receiveObject = new LocalConnection();

receiveObject.allowDomain = function(domain){
      if(domain == "www.myDomain.com"){
            return true;
}else{
return false;
}
```

```
}

receiveObject.populateBankList = function(bankData, rateData){
    //do work here
}
receiveObject.connect("LoanData")  //Open for communication
```

If the movie is hosted at a domain using a secure protocol (Hypertext Transfer Protocol Secure [HTTPS]), it can be accessed only by other SWF files hosted using the same protocol (HTTPS). This implementation maintains the integrity provided by the HTTPS protocol.

Using the `allowInsecureDomain()` method, you can override the default behavior. This is not recommended, however, because it compromises HTTPS security by allowing any domain without exclusion. A better choice would be to enumerate the allowed domains instead of allowing all domains.

When you are done with a connection object, you can close the connection using `LocalConnection.close()`. Because an application can maintain only one local connection at a time, it is not necessary to name the connection when closing.

Security on the Sending Movie

We saw that `allowDomain()` protects a receiving movie when receiving data from another movie. We might also want to receive status as to whether the sent message was received. The `onStatus()` event can be used to determine if a message was received. `onStatus()` is triggered whenever `LocalConnection.onStatus()` is called. When the event is triggered, an object is available with the status of the operation. The object has a property called `level`. It can have one of two possible values: "status" if the connection was found and "error" if the connection was not found. Listing 11.12 shows an example of the `onStatus()` event.

LISTING 11.12 Using Local*Connection.onStatus()*

```
var sendObject:LocalConnection = new LocalConnection();

var rateObject:LoadVars = new LoadVars();
rateObject.load("bankRates.txt");

rateObject.onLoad = function(){ ← triggers onStatus()
    sendObject.send("LoanData", "populateBankList", rateObject);
}
```

continues

LISTING 11.12   Continued

```
sendObject.onStatus = function(infoObject:object){
if (infoObject.level == "error"){
      //try again
}else (infoObject.level == "error"){
      //connection found
}
}
```

Summary

In this chapter, we covered some of the methods for getting data into a Flash application. The importance of choosing the best data access solution in Flash is based on when the data is loaded, if the data will be persistent and if so, where the data is stored and maintained. Several solutions were presented to load external data. They include the loadVariables() method, the LoadVars object, and FlashVars and query string. SharedObject object and LocalConnection object enable us to store data locally and share data across Flash movies.

You might have noticed that we covered only those solutions that had no server-side dependencies. Additional topics related to data access in Flash with related server-side solutions will be covered in Chapters 12–15.

CHAPTER 12

XML AND FLASH

In Chapter 11, "Reading Data Files," we explored a few options for reading external data (text) into a Flash movie. `LoadVars` and URL or query strings were discussed, each revealing their strengths and weaknesses. You may recall that data was read into the applications as name-value pairs, as shown in Listing 12.1.

LISTING 12.1   Name-Value Pairs

```
myFlashMovie.swf?color=blue&fontsize=large
```

It's easy to see that by using these techniques, data can get complicated rather quickly, as shown in Listing 12.2. There are also size limitations inherent in this kind of implementation.

LISTING 12.2   Complex Name-Value Pairs

```
myFlashMovie.swf?color=blue&fontsize=large&menuFontColor=white&
stae=3&name=James&filter=true&prod1=872635&prod2=87411...
```

In this chapter, extensible markup language (XML) will be introduced. XML can be used for reading and writing data to and from a server, providing an alternative to the limitations of techniques previously discussed. XML has been approved as a standard by the World Wide Web Consortium (W3C) and been adopted by many companies including Microsoft, Netscape, and Macromedia.

This chapter will focus on XML support in Flash, starting with a brief introduction to general XML concepts. For a more detailed discussion of general XML concepts, see the *Real World XML*, published by New Riders Press.

What Is XML?

XML is a markup language much like Hypertext Markup Language (HTML); they are both derived from the Standard Generalized Markup Language (SGML). XML is used to describe data. The goals of XML are different than the goals of HTML. One fundamental difference between HTML and XML is that XML tags are not predefined. XML was designed to describe data and to focus on the information contained in the data. HTML was designed to display data and to focus on how it looks.

We could say XML is about describing information. To describe this information, XML uses a Document Type Definition (DTD) or an XML schema. XML with a DTD or XML schema is self-descriptive, meaning that if you have an XML document and you have its DTD, you can interpret the data. The DTD is like a road map for the data. XML is used to store and send information while the DTD reveals the structure.

Listing 12.3 shows an HTML segment that displays a peach cobbler recipe. Notice that HTML is used to display the content using header tags and a table structure.

LISTING 12.3   HTML Version of Recipe

```
<h1>Peach Cobbler</h1>
<h2> Sam Smyth </h2>

<P>Peach cobbler is made with bananas as the main sweetener.
It was delicious.</P>

   <table>
   <tr><td> 2 1/2 cups</td> <td> diced Peach</td></tr>
   <tr><td> 2 tablespoons</td>  <td> sugar</td></tr>
   <tr><td> 2 </td> <td> fairly ripe bananas</td></tr>
   <tr><td> 1/4 teaspoon</td> <td> cinnamon</td></tr>
   <tr><td> dash of</td>  <td> nutmeg</td></tr>
   </table>

Combine all and use as cobbler, pie, or crisp.
```

With XML, we can define our own "recipe markup language," where the markup tags directly correspond to entities, such as ingredients and amount, in the world of recipes. In Listing 12.4, we have translated the HTML recipe from Listing 12.3. Notice that there are no markup tags for display in the XML.

LISTING 12.4   XML Version of Recipe

```
<recipe id="117" category="dessert">
  <title>Peach Cobbler</title>
  <author>Sam Smyth </author>
  <description>
    Peach Cobbler made with bananas as the main sweetener.
    It was delicious.
  </description>

  <ingredients>
    <item><amount>2 1/2 cups</amount><type>diced Peach </type></item>
    <item><amount>2 tablespoons</amount><type>sugar</type></item>
    <item><amount>2</amount><type>fairly ripe bananas</type></item>
    <item><amount>1/4 teaspoon</amount><type>cinnamon</type></item>
    <item><amount>dash of</amount><type>nutmeg</type></item>
  </ingredients>

  <preparation>
    Combine all and use as cobbler, pie, or crisp.
  </preparation>
</recipe>
```

An XML document is an ordered, labeled tree. Text nodes contain the actual data (text strings), which are usually character data nodes and must not be empty.

Element nodes are each labeled with a name (often called the element *type*) and a set of attributes, each consisting of a name and value. These nodes can have child nodes.

In Figure 12.1, the recipe tree is detailed where the root node is a collection of "Recipes," and each subsequent recipe node contains a series of element and text nodes that comprise the recipe. Sticking to the tree metaphor, an XML document can be traversed recursively, allowing us to read data without knowing if it even exists. Each tree node has reference to its children (or branches), and those children to their children, and so on.

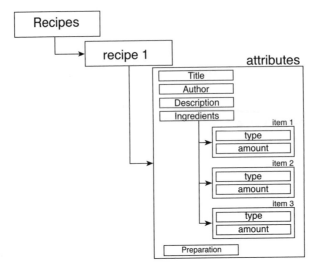

FIGURE 12.1   XML list of recipes.

Figure 12.2 shows a browser interpretation of an XML file. Note the expandable list icons, indicating that the tree can be expanded and collapsed, revealing the structure.

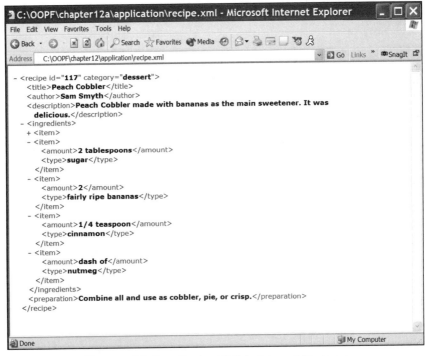

FIGURE 12.2   Recipe XML in Internet Explorer.

The recipe XML is an example of XML data represented as text nodes, where the data is text between an opening XML tag and a closing XML tag, as in `<author>Sam Smyth </author>`. Data can also be represented in XML using tag attributes. Using tag attributes can make the final XML file smaller and therefore more efficient. Listing 12.5 demonstrates an XML file using tag attributes.

LISTING 12.5   XML Using Attributes

```
<billingData>
    <row act="10" custId="0" date="05/12/2002" billable="true" />
    <row act="9" custId="0" date="05/13/2002" billable="true"  />
    <row act="8" custId="0" date="05/14/2002" billable="false" />
</billingData>
```

Notice that each of the row tags contains attributes in name-value pairs. Listing 12.6 shows a single row node from Listing 12.5 using the text node XML model. The size of a single row is greater when using text nodes. If the XML contained many rows, the file would be large. In this case, using attributes would be a better choice.

LISTING 12.6   XML Using Attributes

```
<row>
    <act>10</act>
    <custId>0</custId>
    <date>05/12/2002</date>
    <billable>true</billable>
</row>
```

The examples throughout this chapter will use tag attributes to contain the data in XML files.

Write Once, Read Anywhere

XML has many uses, as we will soon see. But one major strength for XML is that it transcends proprietary data structures across vendors and platforms. XML is platform and language independent, which makes it great for exchanging data between business domains. For example, if we look at a large e-commerce site, such as Amazon.com, and consider that many different products are sold there, we know that Amazon doesn't manufacture and stock all those products. They rely on business relationships with vendors. Amazon receives product information from a vendor's database in the form of an XML document, and because they have an established DTD (XML schema) for these documents, they can display and sell products from many vendors.

XML Object

Flash support for XML is manifested through several objects and methods, primarily the XML object. This object loads XML, transforms XML to an ActionScript datatype, and provides methods to manipulate the data. The XML object also provides the ability to send XML to a server. This is particularly useful when submitting data to the server requires secure transmission, as in passwords, or when a server-side script is expecting XML. XML enables us to read and write to a server without any additional data access components (see Chapter 14, "Using Client-Side Data Integration," for more information).

Reading an XML Document

XML provides a structured view of data that can be read by a Flash application on the Internet. The XML object has a method to load XML documents from a server. The Flash Player supports standard XML and has built-in parsing capability. Note that the XML document has to be well-formed for accurate data parsing.

In this part of the chapter, we build a Flash navigation system for a web application using an XML file to provide us with the menu item names and links. In this simple example, we do the following:

- Load an XML file
- Parse the XML
- Use the data to populate attributes of a Flash menu

The menu will consist of a movie clip that exists in the Library, a custom XML object that will load and parse the data, and a method to populate the menu. Figure 12.3 shows the final menu. The menu is created based on the number of elements in the XML document.

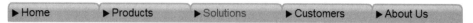

FIGURE 12.3   XML-driven menu.

The XML document used to create this menu is shown in Listing 12.7. The document root is the first node of the XML content. Notice the attributes of each root-child node. Each node contains a "name" and an "action" attribute. These will be used to populate menu items as they are created.

LISTING 12.7   Contents of XMLMenu.xml

```
<menu>// document root
     <item name="Home" action="/home.htm"/>// child node with
     attributes
     <item name="Products" action=http://www.amazon.com/
     product.htm&id=87/>

     <item name="Solutions" action="/solution.htm"/>

     <item name="Customers" action="/customers.htm"/>

     <item name="About Us" action="/aboutUs.htm"/>

</menu>
```

Loading XML Data

The first step to creating our XML-driven menu is to load the XML document into Flash. Using the XML Object constructor, create an instance of the XML object. Listing 12.8 shows the correct syntax for creating an instance of the XML class.

LISTING 12.8   Creating an Instance of the XML Class

```
var xmlInstance = new XML();
xmlInstance.load("http://www.mySite.com/XMLMenu.xml");
```

A better choice would be to create a custom class that inherits from the XML object. This enables us to encapsulate the file loading, parsing, and data manipulation in one class. Listing 12.9 creates a custom class named XMLMenu. This class is a subclass of the XML object. Notice that the constructor calls super(). In Chapter 5, "The Meek Shall Inherit the Earth," we learned that calling super() in the constructor of a class will call the constructor of its direct ancestor. In this case, it is equivalent to new XML().

LISTING 12.9   Creating a Custom XML Class

```
class XMLMenu extends XML{

public function XMLMenu(XMLFileName:String) {
        super();
        this.load(XMLFileName);
    }

}
```

The custom class constructor will load the XML file when the instance is created and passed a file name. Remember that when a subclass is created, the new class inherits all the properties and methods of the ancestor, in this case, the XML object. Therefore, we can call the load method of our custom class just as we would with the native XML class shown in Listing 12.8.

The instance is created in the host file that uses the XML content. In the case of the XML menu, that will be the host FLA file, XMLMenu.fla. Figure 12.4 shows the new instantiation code in the first frame of the main timeline of XMLMenu.fla.

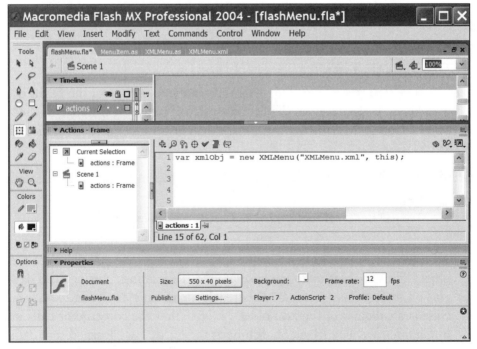

FIGURE 12.4   Creating an instance of a custom XML class.

The next step is to parse the data. Because there might be some latency between the file request and the file load, the XML object has an event that is fired when the file has finished loading. onLoad() is a method added to the custom class to capture file load completion. Listing 12.10 includes the onLoad() method that is executed when the file has been completely loaded into the object. In this method, we can parse the data and notify any interested objects when the data is loaded. This is also referred to as a callback method. Notice that the onLoad method contains a Boolean argument. If the file loaded successfully, the argument is true; otherwise, it is false. This allows for file access error handling.

LISTING 12.10   Adding the *onLoad()* Method to the Custom XML Class

```
class XMLMenu extends XML{

public function XMLMenu(XMLFileName:String) {
      super();
      this.load(XMLFileName);
}
=
public function onLoad(success:Boolean){
      if (success) {
             trace("file loaded");
             //parse data if needed
             //notify display objects that data has loaded
      }else{
             trace("FILE NOT LOADED");
             //handle file load error
      }
}

}
```

Parsing the Data

How you parse the data is dependent on what you are going to do with the data. In the case of the Flash menu, the attributes needed to build the menu are the name and action for each menu item. As we traverse the XML document, an array can be built and passed to the main timeline to build the menu.

> **NOTE**
>
> In Macromedia Flash MX 2004, there are components that can bind directly to an ActionScript XML instance. Chapter 13, "Web Services," covers direct data binding. In the example in this chapter, we manually parse the XML data.

In Flash, XML objects have a hierarchical tree structure. There are many methods and properties we can use to traverse the tree structure and extract the data. All XML objects begin with a root node. The root node can contain information called metadata, which describes the contents of the XML document. Each node has a reference to its data as child nodes. Child nodes are accessed using the `childNodes` property that returns a collection of nodes, as shown in Figures 12.5 and 12.6. Note that XML trees can be very deep. Each node can have children, and these child nodes can have children, and so on.

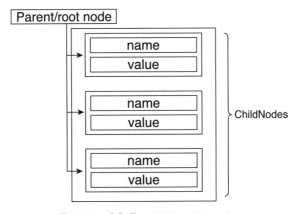

FIGURE 12.5   XML child nodes.

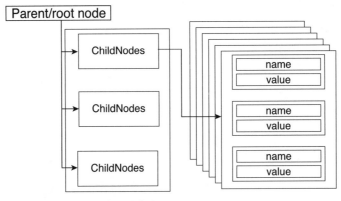

FIGURE 12.6   XML tree nodes.

The XML class provides methods and properties to facilitate traversing data both up and down the XML tree. It does this by providing both built-in references to neighboring elements and general tree structures. Table 12.1 enumerates the properties and methods that can be used while parsing the XML object.

TABLE 12.1   Properties, Methods, and Return Types of the XML Object

Property and Methods	Return Types
Attributes	Returns an associative array containing all of the attributes of the specified node
ChildNodes	Read-only; returns an array containing references to the child nodes of the specified node
FirstChild	Read-only; references the first child in the list for the specified node
hasChildNodes()	Returns true if the specified node has child nodes; otherwise, returns false
LastChild	References the last child in the list for the specified node
nextSibling	Read-only; references the next sibling in the parent node's child list
NodeName	The node name of an XML object
NodeType	The type of the specified node (XML element –type = 1, text node –type = 3)
NodeValue	The text of the specified node if the node is a text node
ParentNode	Read-only; references the parent node of the specified node
previousSibling	Read-only; references the previous sibling in the parent node's child list
RemoveNode()	Removes the specified node from its parent
toString()	Converts the specified node and any children to XML text

Listing 12.11 demonstrates the onLoad() method parsing the XML content. The onLoad() method employs XML properties and methods to parse the data. Notice that in the onLoad() method, the childNodes property is accessed twice. The first access points to the first node in the object. In this case, the first node is the root of the document labeled "menu," as seen in Listing 12.8.

LISTING 12.11   *onLoad()* Method Parsing the XML Content

```
class XMLMenu extends XML{
    public var menuItems:Array//;//create array to pass back
    public var parent:Object//;// create reference to calling object

    public function XMLMenu(XMLFileName:String, parent:Object) {
super();
        this.parent = parent;
```

continues

LISTING 12.11   Continued

```
            this.menuItems = new Array();//// instantiate menu array
            this.load(XMLFileName);


      }

   public function onLoad(success){
      if (success) {
            var rootList:Object = this.childNodes//;//access root nodes
            var itemList:Object = rootList.childNodes//;//access child
            nodes
            var itemListLen:Number = itemList.length;
            for (var i = 0; i < itemListLen; i++) {
               var itemObj:Object = {};
               itemObj.name = itemList[i].attributes.name;////
               attributes
               itemObj.action = itemList[i].attributes.action; ////
               attributes
               this.menuItems.push(itemObj); //// populate menu array
            }
            //send menu array back to the calling fla
      } else {
            trace("Menu content failed to load");
      }
   }
}
}
```

Populating the Menu with the Parsed XML Data

After the data is parsed into suitable ActionScript datatypes (which, in this
case, is an array), the menu can be populated. The calling script in the Flash file
will be notified when the data has been parsed. To facilitate communication
from the host to the XML object, a reference to the parent object was passed in
at the time of instantiation. This enables us to call back to the parent when the
data is ready.

In Listing 12.12, the callback to the Flash file is included. Using the parent reference, a callback to the parent's loadMenu() method is made, passing back
the menu items derived from the XML content.

LISTING 12.12   *onLoad()* Method Returning Data to Parent

```
class XMLMenu extends XML{
      public var menuItems:Array;// create array to pass back
      public var parent:Object;// create reference to calling object

      public function XMLMenu(XMLFileName:String, parent:Object) {
            super();
            this.parent = parent;
            this.menuItems = new Array();// instantiate menu array
            this.load(XMLFileName);
      }

   public function onLoad(success){
      if (success) {
            var rootList:Object = this.childNodes;//access root nodes
            var itemList:Object = rootList.childNodes;//child nodes
            var itemListLen:Number = itemList.length;
            for (var i = 0; i < itemListLen; i++) {
                var itemObj:Object = {};
                itemObj.name = itemList[i].attributes.name;//
                attributes
                itemObj.action = itemList[i].attributes.action;//
                attributes
                this.menuItems.push(itemObj); // populate menu array
            }
            parent.loadMenu(this.menuItems);
      } else {
            trace("Menu content failed to load");
      }
   }
}
```

In the parent object, flashMenu.fla, the loadMenu() method exists and accepts the menuItems array from the custom XML object. Figure 12.7 shows the loadMenu() method that dynamically attaches menu items and populates their values based on the menuItems array.

The menu we have built so far has a flat hierarchy, but most menus require additional level of depth, in the form of submenus. Because the structure of XML documents is hierarchical, or tree-like, it is suited for multi-level menus. To add submenus to our XML menu, we will add additional entries in the XMLMenu.xml file. Listing 12.13 shows the new XML that we will use to populate the menu.

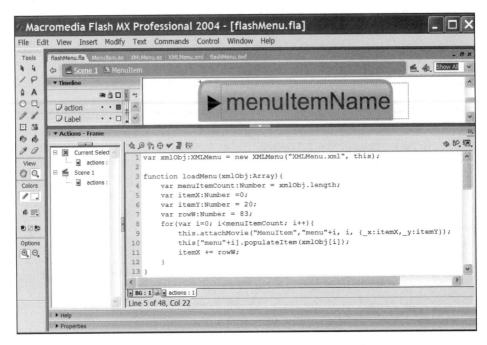

FIGURE 12.7   `loadMenu()` building first-level menu.

LISTING 12.13   XMLMenu.as with Submenu Entries

```
<menu >
      <item name="Home" action="/home.htm">
      </item>
      <item name="Products" action="none">
          <item name="Toys" action="/toys.htm"></item>←sub menu
          <item name="Electronics"
action="/electronics.htm"></item>←sub menu
          <item name="Books" action="/books.htm"></item>←sub menu
      <item name="Pets" action="/pets.htm"></item>←sub menu
      </item>
      <item name="Solutions" action="/solution.htm">
      </item>
      <item name="Customers" action="/customers.htm">
          <item name="FAO Schwarz" action="/toys.htm"></item>
          <item name="Best Buy" action="/electronics.htm"></item>
          <item name="Home Depot" action="/books.htm"></item>
          <item name="PetCo" action="/pets.htm"></item>
          <item name="TVGuide" action="/pets.htm"></item>
          <item name="Macromedia" action="/pets.htm"></item>
      </item>
      <item name="About Us" action="/aboutUs.htm">
```

```
        <item name="Corporate" action="/Corporate.htm"></item>
        <item name="Opportunities" action="/Opportunities.htm">
        </item>
        <item name="Contact Us" action="/Contact.htm"></item>
    </item>
</menu>
```

Using what we already know about traversing an XML document, we will load and parse the document by stepping down into the submenu level of the XML. Listing 12.14 shows the new onLoad() method of the XMLMenu.as. The onLoad() method will now build an array called sub[] that will hold the attributes of the submenus, if they exist.

LISTING 12.14   *onLoad()* Method Parsing Submenu Items

```
public function onLoad(success){
    if (success) {
        var itemList:Object = this.childNodes[0].childNodes;
    var itemListLen:Number = itemList.length;
        for (var i = 0; i < itemListLen; i++) {
            var subList:Object = itemList[i].childNodes;
            var subItemLen:Number = subList.length;
            var itemObj:Object = {};
            itemObj.sub = []; // create sub menu array
            itemObj.name = itemList[i].attributes.name;
            itemObj.action = itemList[i].attributes.action;
            //iterate through current items child nodes
            for (var j = 0; j < subItemLen; j++) {
                var subItemObj:Object = {};// create sub menu object
                subItemObj.name = subList[j].attributes.name;
                subItemObj.action = subList[j].attributes.action;
                itemObj.sub.push(subItemObj); // populate sub menu
                array
            }
                this.menuItems.push(itemObj);
        }
            parent.loadMenu(this.menuItems);
    } else {
            trace("Menu content failed to load");
    }
}
```

We will also have to modify the menuItem.as file to paint the submenu when it exists. Listing 12.15 show the new populateMenu() method. If the sub[] is populated, the menu item will create a submenu. Note that this could also be done using a recursive function, allowing a menu to be of any depth, but for the sake of clarity, we have chosen a more verbose coding style, thus limiting the menu to two levels.

LISTING 12.15   *populateMenuItem()* Creating a Submenu

```
public function populateItem(menuItem:Object) {
      if (menuItem.sub.length > 0){ //sub menu exists?
            this.subMenuItems = menuItem.sub;
            this.subMenu = true;
            this.createEmptyMovieClip("sub_mc", 100,{_x:0,_y:0});
            var xmlObj = this.subMenuItems;
            var subMenuItemCount:Number = xmlObj.length;
            var itemX:Number =0;
            var itemY:Number = this._height;
            var rowH:Number = this._height;
            for(var i=0; i<subMenuItemCount; i++){ // populate sub
            menu
                  this.sub_mc.attachMovie("MenuItem","subMenu"+i, I);
                  this.sub_mc["subMenu"+I]._x = itemX;
                  this.sub_mc["subMenu"+I]._y = itemY;
                  this.sub_mc["subMenu"+i].populateItem(xmlObj[i]);
                  itemY += rowH;
            }
            this.sub_mc._visible = false;
      }
      this.menuItem = menuItem;
      this.label_txt.text = menuItem.name;
      this.link_str =  menuItem.action;
}
```

The new menu now has submenus, and the menu content can be changed at any time without changing the Flash files. By simply changing the XML files, a completely different menu can be generated. Figure 12.8 shows the new menu with the expanded submenu.

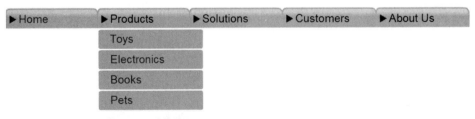

FIGURE 12.8   XML-driven menu with submenu.

Sending an XML Document

There are several ways to send data from a Flash movie to a server, and each has advantages and disadvantages. Using the `getURL()` method of the `MovieClip` object, we can append data to the URL. Using the query string on the end of the URL has length limitations and can become very unruly with large datasets. It also has security limitations.

Flash Remoting and Web Services also enable us to pass data back to a server from Flash. However, these involve server-side technologies and require an investment in software and resources. Using XML documents to pass data from Flash to a server is cheap and can provide a level of data security with minimal investment in software and IT resources. Most application servers, such as ASP.NET and ColdFusion, can parse XML on the server. Many databases can also parse and insert XML data directly into tables.

The `XML` object has methods to support the creation and packaging of XML data to be sent to a server. Table 12.2 enumerates the methods available to create and manipulate an `XML` object for sending data to a server.

TABLE 12.2   XML Methods for Creating and Sending Data

METHOD	DESCRIPTION
`XML.addRequestHeader()`	Adds or changes Hypertext Transfer Protocol (HTTP) headers for power-on self test (`POST`) operations
`XML.appendChild()`	Appends a node to the end of the specified object's child list
`XML.cneNode()`	Clones the specified node and, optionally, recursively clones all children
`XML.createElement()`	Creates a new XML element
`XML.createTextNode()`	Creates a new XML text node
`XML.getBytesLoaded()`	Returns the number of bytes loaded for the specified XML document
`XML.getBytesTotal()`	Returns the size of the XML document, in bytes
`XML.insertBefore()`	Inserts a node in front of an existing node in the specified node's child list
`XML.load()`	Loads a document (specified by the XML object) from a URL
`XML.removeNode()`	Removes the specified node from its parent
`XML.send()`	Sends the specified XML object to a URL
`XML.sendAndLoad()`	Sends the specified XML object to a URL and loads the server response into another XML object

send() *Method*

The send() method enables us to send XML data to a URL. It is a method of the XML object and takes a single argument, a URL. Listing 12.16 shows an example of the send() method in action. This method is used when no return response is required. For example, a site that is doing a public poll or a survey might want the user to answer a few questions and submit the answers. A simple way to do this in Flash is to create an XML object to hold the answers and then submit them to a server using the XML.send() method. Listing 12.16 lists an example of building the XML object and calling the send method.

LISTING 12.16   *XMLSendSurvey—an XML Subclass*

```
class XMLSendSurvey extends XML{

    public function XMLSendSurvey() {
        super();
    }

    public function sendSurveyResults(surveyAnswers:Array){
        for (var i=0; i<surveyAnswers.length; i++){
            //Create elements for each question
            var newElement = this.createElement("item");
            newElement.attributes.answer =
            surveyAnswers[i].answer;
            newElement.attributes.question =
            surveyAnswers[i].question;
            //append element for each question
            this.appendChild(newElement);
        }
        //send the XML
        this.send("http://www.mySite.com/survey.cfm" );
    }

}
```

The XML being sent to the server would contain questions and answers similar to Listing 12.17.

LISTING 12.17   Survey Data XML

```
<survey>
    <item question="1" answer="yes" />
    <item question="2" answer="no" />
    <item question="3" answer="maybe" />
</survey>
```

sendAndLoad() *Method*

The sendAndLoad() method enables us to send XML data to a URL. It also enables us to identify a client XML object that will receive any returning data. The object receiving the data is an XML object created through the XML constructor method. Listing 12.18 is an example of a sendAndLoad() method call for a registration system that returns confirmation to the client. Notice that we are using the same XML object to send the registration as we are to receive the response from the server.

LISTING 12.18   *sendAndLoad() for the Registration System*

```
class XMLRegistration extends XML{

    public function XMLRegistration() {
        super();
    }

    public function sendRegistration(formData:Array){
        for (var i=0; i<surveyAnswers.length; i++){
            var newElement = this.createElement("question"+i);
            newElement.attributes.label = formData[i].label;
            newElement.attributes.value = formData[i].value;
            this.appendChild(newElement);
        }
        //Send the registration to the server,
        //pass a reference to 'this'. this.onLoad()-receives the
        reply
        this.sendAndLoad("http://www.mySite.com/registration.cfm",
        this);
    }

    function onLoad(success){
        if (success){
            //parse the reply and notify the user
        }
    }

}
```

The sendAndLoad() method encodes the specified XML object into an XML document, sends it to the specified URL using the POST method, downloads the server's response, and then loads that response into the targetXMLobject specified in the parameters. The server response is loaded in the same manner used by the load() method.

When sendAndLoad() is executed, the XML object property loaded is set to false. When the XML data finishes downloading, the loaded property is set to true, and the onLoad() method is invoked. The XML data is not parsed until it is completely downloaded. If the receiving XML object previously contained any XML trees, they are discarded.

Sandbox Restrictions

For SWF files running in a version of the Player earlier than Flash Player 7, the receiving URL must be in the same superdomain as the SWF file that is issuing this call. For example, an SWF file at www.Yahoo.com can load variables from an SWF file at products.Yahoo.com because both files are in the same super-domain of Yahoo.com.

If the SWF is running in Flash Player 7 or later, the receiving URL must be in exactly the same domain. For example, an SWF file at www.Yahoo.com can load variables only from SWF files that are located at www.Yahoo.com. If you want to load variables from a different domain, you can place a *cross-domain policy file* on the server hosting the SWF file that is being accessed. For more information, see Chapter 13.

XMLSocket **Class**

The XMLSocket class enables you to open a continuous connection with a server. A socket connection enables the server to publish (or "push") information to the client as soon as that information becomes available. Without a continuous connection, the server must wait for an HTTP request. This open connection removes latency issues, and it is commonly used for real-time applications such as mail, stock tickers, and news feeds. The data is sent over the socket connection as a single string and should be in XML format. The XML class is used to structure the data for all communication.

There are server-side requirements for using XML sockets in Flash. The server must have a listening application that is waiting for the Flash application to notify or register as interested in receiving data. After initial contact has been made between the Flash movie and the server, the server application can send messages to the movie. There are many different server-side technologies that can support socket communication. For instance, Java is a common programming language used for server-side sockets.

How to Use a Socket

You can use the `connect()` and `send()` methods of the `XMLSocket` class to transfer XML to and from a server over a socket connection. The `connect()` method establishes a socket connection to a web server port. The `send()` method passes an XML object to the server specified in the socket connection.

Listing 12.19 is an example of creating a socket class named `XMLComm`. Note that we have subclassed the `XMLSocket` class to create the socket. The custom socket class opens a connection in the constructor. When the connection has been successfully established, data can be transmitted to the server. By implementing the `onXML()` method, the object is capable of receiving messages from the server.

LISTING 12.19   Custom *XMLSocket* Class

```
class XMLComm extends XMLSocket{
      var serverName:String;
      var port:Number;

      public function XMLComm(serverName, port) {
            super();
            this.serverName = serverName;
            this.connect(serverName, port);
      }

      // Define onConnect() method  that handles
      // the server's response. If the connection succeeds, send the
      // XMLData object. If it fails, provide an error message
      private function onConnect(success){
        if (success){
            this.send(XMLData);
        } else {
            trace("There has been an error connecting to
            "+this.serverName);
        }
      }

      private function onXML(XMLObj){
        //This is invoked when XML has been received from the server
        //parse the data and display in the client
      }



}
```

When you invoke the `connect()` method, Flash Player opens a TCP/IP connection to the server and keeps that connection open until one of the following happens:

- The `close()` method of the `XMLSocket` class is called.
- No more references to the `XMLSocket` object exist.
- Flash Player exits.
- The connection is broken (the network fails).

Socket Security

The `XMLSocket.connect()` method can connect only to TCP port numbers greater than or equal to 1024. One consequence of this restriction is that the servers that communicate with the `XMLSocket` object must also be assigned to port numbers greater than or equal to 1024. Port numbers below 1024 are often used by system services such as FTP, Telnet, and HTTP; thus, the `XMLSocket` object is barred from these ports for security reasons. The port number restriction limits the possibility that these resources will be inappropriately accessed and abused.

XML Connector

So far in this chapter, we have manually processed XML data. Although it is important to fully understand how to do this, there are shortcuts that will automatically parse the XML and convert it to ActionScript objects for you. This process is especially useful when the data in the XML is used to populate a Flash MX 2004 component. These components are designed to employ automatic databinding, which means that the data from an XML file will automatically display in a component, such as a list box, without having to parse the data. The remainder of this chapter takes a look at the XML Connector component.

NOTE

Databinding is covered in greater detail in Chapter 14.

XML Communications Simplified

You can use the XMLConnector component to connect to an external XML document. After the XML is available in the Flash document, it can directly bind to properties within the document. The XMLConnector can communicate with components in your application using data binding features of the authoring tool (on the Stage), or components can be associated with the XMLConnector data through ActionScript code.

The first step to binding visual elements with XML data is to specify a *schema*, which is the structure of the XML document that identifies the data elements in the document to which you can bind. The schema appears in the Schema tab in the Component Inspector panel. The schema identifies the fields in the XML document that are bound to user interface component properties in your application. You can manually create the schema through the Component Inspector or use the authoring environment to create one automatically.

The authoring environment will accept a copy of the external XML document to which you are connecting as a model for the schema.

Although the XMLConnector component has properties and events like other components, it has no runtime visual appearance. Figure 12.9 shows an example of using an external XML file to build a schema within the authoring environment.

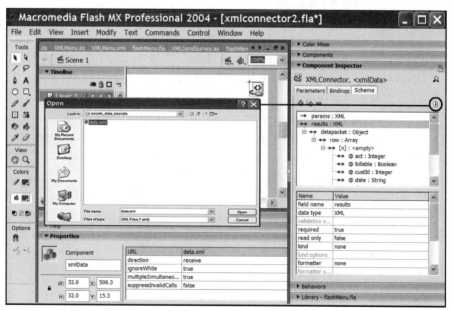

FIGURE 12.9   Establishing the schema for an XMLConnector component.

Binding XML Data

After the XML is available in the Flash document, it can directly bind to properties in the document. Databinding with components is covered in greater detail in Chapter 14.

Summary

In many cases, XML provides a viable solution for data access in a Flash document. Other options include Web Services and Flash Remoting, both covered in Chapter 13. Here are a few guidelines that will help you decide whether using XML to format data is the right choice for your application:

- **Performance and data load time.** To use an XML document in Flash, the document has to first be downloaded and then parsed before any of the data can be used. Large XML documents can cause latency in the application. Loading the same information from a text file will be faster because little or no parsing is required. After the text file loads, the data is available. Another option is to break the XML into smaller files and load them incrementally. The XML file will be smaller if you use attributes as opposed to plain text nodes.

- **Loading XML data created for other applications.** If the XML data is created for other applications, trying to merge it with Flash can cause undue parsing complexity. If possible, use XML data specifically designed for the Flash application. This will avoid any parsing problems.

- **Server and database load.** Is the data required to be realtime? If so, the XML would need to be generated for each request. How do the database and server respond under heavy traffic? If generating live data for each request causes server load issues, consider generating the XML periodically (hourly or twice a day) based on the nature of the data. You can then cache it on the server.

- **Alternate solutions.** Web Services and Flash Remoting are alternate solutions for loading data into a Flash application. Both require server-side applications to respond to data requests. For more on these alternate solutions, see Chapter 13.

WEB SERVICES

Web Services are one of the most talked about and hyped features of the Internet. In fact some people are saying that Web Services are one of the few, revolutionary ideas currently within the IT industry and that Web Services have the potential to change the world as we know it.

Web Services expose server-side objects and methods that expose application functionality across the Web. Web Services themselves are actually written on the server-side in a language such as ColdFusion, Microsoft .NET, or J2EE. For example, we could write a web service that would check our inventory from a database by accessing this information across the Web as well as from other applications.

There are public Web Services available that do everything from translating text to checking the latest traffic conditions in southern California. The most revolutionary part of Web Services is that other applications can call web service methods to extend their own functionality and not be concerned about the language in which the web service was written or on what platform it runs.

Web Services send information by means of extensible markup language (XML) packets, which means they can handle complex data structures. The beauty of XML is that it is completely platform independent. Server-side solutions, client-side solutions, and even desktop suites (such as Microsoft Office) can consume XML. When we consume Web Services in Flash, we do not need to know in what language the web service was written; we only need to know the data structures that the method returns by means of XML.

Before the advent of Web Services, the only way to expose methods to applications was through the use of a proprietary protocol, such as Remote Procedure Call (RPC), Remote Method Invocation (RMI), or Common Object Request Broker Architecture (CORBA). Developers had to choose a protocol and manually expose each method. Web Services are revolutionary because they make it easy to connect applications to other applications in a platform-independent way.

The key to Web Services is that they provide a uniform way for applications to communicate with one another using the Web Services Description Language (WSDL), which is just a special type of XML. Communication is achieved through the Simple Object Access Protocol (SOAP), which virtually all platforms can consume and generate. The WSDL description language, SOAP, and the Universal Description, Discovery and Integration (UDDI) standards provide a uniform, standard method of communication, which means Flash can easily work with any server-side solution. You'll learn about all this and more in the coming sections of this chapter.

Web Services Standards

The large players involved in Web Services include Microsoft, IBM, and SUN. They have all agreed to uphold certain conventions when using Web Services. The two key standards are WSDL and SOAP. In addition, UDDI provides a marketplace for all Web Services, which enables developers to easily find the appropriate Web Services. These standards are the key to creating cross-platform, XML-compliant Web Services.

WSDL

WSDL is language designed to describe the content of Web Services. A WSDL file is simply an XML file that is very similar to a data schema in Macromedia Flash MX 2004 Professional. The WSDL language description lists all the server-side methods that can be called; it also lists the parameters that must be passed to the server-side method. For example, the stock service WSDL shown in Figure 13.1 is expecting a company symbol (such as MACR or AAPL) to be passed to it, and this is indicated in the WSDL file. The WSDL file also describes the type of data that will be returned; this is known as the results of the web service. The WSDL also gives a description of what the web service does and its location.

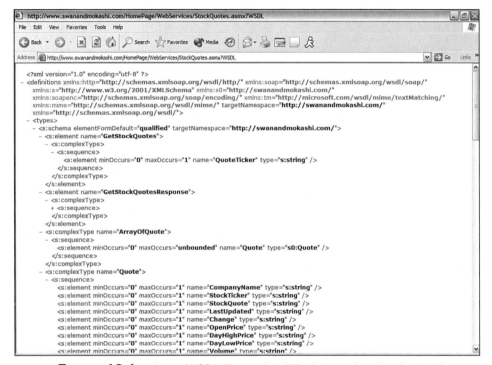

FIGURE 13.1   A raw WSDL file can be difficult to read and understand.

Figure 13.1 shows a raw WSDL file viewed in a browser; as you can see, it is not exactly very easy to read and understand. For more information on WSDL, you can find the full specification at www.w3.org/TR/wsdl.

Flash MX 2004 Professional has a new Web Services panel that takes the URL of any WSDL and translates it into plain English. The Web Services panel, for example, shows us exactly the method names of the stock services website and what parameters it requires. From the Web Services panel, we can see that only one parameter, a string, needs to be passed to the server-side method, and we can see that an array of objects will be returned from the web service. All we need to do to use the panel is to enter the URL of the WSDL in the Web Services panel. The Web Services panel makes learning about and using WSDL files easy.

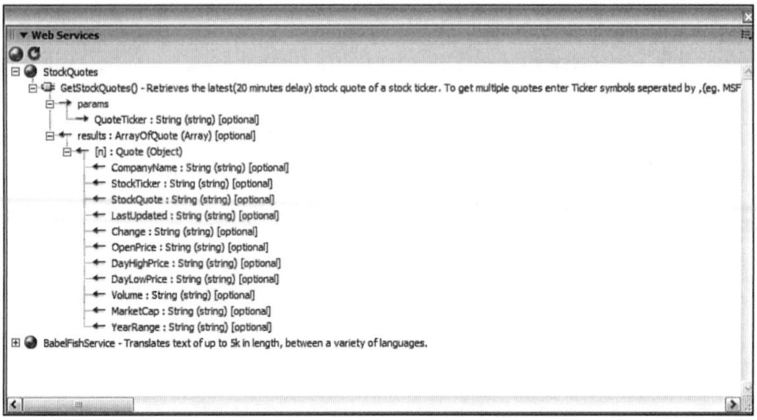

FIGURE 13.2   The Web Services panel translates a raw WSDL file into plain English that can be understood.

SOAP

SOAP is the protocol used to send information between applications through Web Services. It is the envelope that encapsulates the messaging to and from the Flash client and a web service. SOAP works in conjunction with WSDL. The data that is sent by means of SOAP is just raw textual data in an XML format, which is in contrast to other protocols that send information in a binary format. Protocols that use a binary format tend to consume less bandwidth because the data that is being sent is more compressed.

Macromedia has a propriety protocol that is used exclusively with Flash Remoting. It is known as ActionScript Messaging Format (AMF). The AMF format consumes much less bandwidth than SOAP because it is binary. The advantage of using Web Services and SOAP over AMF is that SOAP is a standard, it is not proprietary, and it is widely available across the Internet.

The SOAP protocol contains the name of the server-side object and method to be called. SOAP also contains the XML packets that contain the parameters to be passed to the server-side method. This information is all encapsulated within a SOAP envelope, as shown in the following code:

```
<soap:Envelope xmlns:soap="http://schemas.xmlsoap.org/soap/envelope">
<soap:Body>
<!—actual SOAP XML content here —>
</soap:Body>
</soap:Envelope>
```

The important fact to remember is that SOAP content is just XML data in a textual form with which we are used to dealing. The Web Services classes in Flash MX 2004 will automatically convert this XML data into useable data structures for ActionScript 2.0.

The SOAP protocol, like the AMF protocol, is specifically designed to work over the Hypertext Transfer Protocol (HTTP), which, of course, is an Internet standard. This is a big advantage that AMF and SOAP have over other protocols that do not work with web standards and all platforms.

SOAP has a big advantage over other protocols, such as the Component Object Model (COM) and CORBA, because it is platform independent and works with web standards. When we work with SOAP in Flash, all the complexity of the protocol is hidden from us and handled by the built-in Web Services classes.

UDDI

A third standard that helps make Web Services possible is UDDI, which is simply a directory of available Web Services. It gives developers a place to market the Web Services that have been created. It also gives customers, or consumers of Web Services, a place to search for Web Services that might meet their needs. A web service consumer can generate a query at these sites, and a list of available Web Services will be returned.

A number of UDDIs are maintained on the Internet; two of the largest public ones are run by Microsoft and IBM and are available at:

```
http://uddi.microsoft.com
```
and
```
https://www-3.ibm.com/services/uddi/protect/registry.html
```

Current State of Web Services Technology

Although Web Services offer a tremendous future for Internet applications, its critics rightly charge that its technology is not yet fully baked. The largest shortcomings of Web Services today are the issues surrounding security. For Web Services intended for free and open access to the world, the SOAP and WSDL standards offer a great framework. However, the issues surrounding security, specifically encrypting access to Web Services and guaranteeing the integrity of messages sent to and from them, are still being worked out.

To help solve these issues, IBM and Microsoft proposed an initial specification for the WS-Security standard. The initial specification addresses three key aspects of securing SOAP requests: authentication, encryption, and message integrity. The road map proposes to build on this foundation with additional specifications for configuring trust relationships and for handling complex security situations.[1]

Of course, on an intranet, where many Web Services are commonly used, security is not an issue because Web Services are secured like all intranet applications.

Note that the group currently controlling the Web Services security spec is the Organization for the Advancement of Structured Information Standards (OASIS). They can be reached at:

`www.oasis-open.org/committees/tc_home.php?wg_abbrev=wss`

Web Services in Flash

Flash MX 2004 Professional now has the ability to consume Web Services without the use of any other technology. The Web Services classes can create a schema directly from a WSDL file and automatically convert the XML data structures into native Flash data structures.

Flash cannot do anything with WSDL documents. Remember that a web service is really returning a specially formatted XML document by means of SOAP. To process XML, we usually have to write a series of complex looping structures to "walk through the XML tree" to convert the XML nodes into native Flash data structures. More information on how to do this manually can be found in Chapter 12, "XML and Flash." The Web Service classes in ActionScript as well as the Web Services Connector component will automatically convert the SOAP XML into native Flash data structures.

The XML object first appeared in Flash 5, but was written entirely in ActionScript and was really too slow to use for any practical purposes. The object became much more useable in Flash MX because the Flash engineering team converted the XML object into a native C++ object, which is the language in which Flash itself is written. This conversion vastly sped up the XML processing. However, we still had to write the complex code that would loop through the XML object and convert the XML into native ActionScript objects.

---

1 *"Secure Web Services: WS-Security is a Formidable Proposal," Randy Heffner, Giga Information Group 4/15/2002.*

The issue of having to write the complex code to loop through the XML data structures was solved in Flash MX 2004 Professional. ActionScript 2.0, through the use of a schema, will automatically convert the XML into native ActionScript 2.0 objects. After the data is in the schema, we can use visual data binding or ActionScript to link the data to a dataset or directly to user interface (UI) controls. The Web Services classes in ActionScript have schemas that are set up to work with SOAP XML data returned from Web Services. The XML connector in Flash is designed to work with straight XML (not SOAP XML); you can find more information about the connector in Chapter 12. See Figure 13.3.

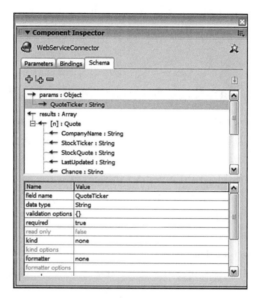

FIGURE 13.3   The schema converts the raw XML into native Flash data structures.

Lazy Decoding

As we have seen, all the web service parsing occurs in the Flash Player in Flash MX 2004 Professional. Because all the translation happens on the client, parsing the XML from the web service can be very resource intensive, even with all the performance improvements. The easiest way to deal with this is to parse the data in small chunks of XML data. Of course, this is not always possible, so ActionScript supports "lazy decoding," which defers the translation from XML to ActionScript until it is actually requested.

Within the process of lazy decoding, arrays are replaced with a new type of ActionScript object that acts similarly to an array, but that defers the processing. Lazy decoding takes this heavy client-side processing and spreads it out over a longer period of time to improve performance. Lazy decoding can be turned on and off by accessing the SOAP `Call` class.

Lazy decoding is always on and it works as follows: Whenever an array is received in the `results` property of the Web Services Connector component, the translation into an ActionScript array is deferred. The `results` property passed to the developer looks and acts like an array, but translates the XML data only when it is requested.

You request the data from the array by simply referencing the array by the index, as follows:

```
myArray[index];
```

It is not possible to use a for-in loop to loop over the array because the for-in loop begins at the last index of the array, and lazy decoding defers the request for this item.

Web Services Sandbox Security in the Flash Player

All XML that is loaded into the Flash Player (including the web service XML) is subject to the security sandbox restriction. This feature prevents the Flash Player from accessing any data that falls outside the domain of the SWF. For example, if you publish an SWF to www.bostons.com, you will be able to access Web Services only from www.bostons.com. It is important to note that subdomains are *not* included, as was the case in Flash Player 6; in Flash Player 7, the domains must match exactly. This restriction is not in effect when you test an application in the authoring environment (or when you publish an SWF as an .exe file), but it is in effect when you deploy the SWF to a web server.

You can access data from a different domain, as long as that domain contains a policy file that says it can accept data requests from your domain. The policy file must be in XML format, in the web root, and look like this:

```
<?XML version="1.0"?>
<!DOCTYPE cross-domain-policy
  SYSTEM "http://www.macromedia.com/xml/dtds/cross-domain-policy.dtd">
<cross-domain-policy>
  <allow-access-from domain="*" />
</cross-domain-policy>
```

Note the asterisk in line 5; this indicates that any Flash movie from any domain can access the data in this domain. We could just as easily change the policy file to indicate that data can be received only from certain domains; in the following code, Bostons.com and Macromedia.com could access data only from this domain:

```xml
<?xml version="1.0"?>
<!DOCTYPE cross-domain-policy
  SYSTEM "http://www.macromedia.com/xml/dtds/cross-domain-policy.dtd">
<cross-domain-policy>
  <allow-access-from domain="www.bostons.com" />
  <allow-access-from domain="www.macromedia.com" />
</cross-domain-policy>
```

> **NOTE**
>
> If you use Flash Remoting to connect to Web Services, there are no security sandbox issues because everything happens on the server and not in the Flash Player.

Connecting to Web Services in Flash

There are three ways of connecting to Web Services in Flash MX 2004 Professional:

- Call Web Services from Flash Remoting
- Use the Web Services Connector component
- Use the Web Services classes

Flash Remoting enables us to connect to Web Services on the server-side so larger chunks of data can be retrieved; note that the AMF format is used and conversion into ActionScript 2.0 objects happens on the server side. If we decide to connect to Web Services using the client-side classes in Flash, we have the option of using the Web Services Connector component or the Web Services classes. The advantage of using the connector is it is possible to connect to a web service without writing any ActionScript 2.0 code at all using visual data binding. If you do decide to use ActionScript 2.0 with the connector, it is a bit simpler than using the Web Services classes. The Web Services classes give the developer much more control over the code because everything can be controlled in ActionScript 2.0; in addition, there are more debugging capabilities in case something goes wrong.

The following sections discuss each method of connecting to Web Services in turn.

Connecting to Web Services with Flash Remoting

You can use Flash Remoting to connect to a web service on the server and then pass the resulting ActionScript objects back to Flash.

There are two advantages to using Flash Remoting to connect to Web Services. The first advantage is that connecting to the web service occurs on the server, so there are no security issues involved (such as requiring a policy file). The second advantage is that using Flash Remoting can be much faster than using the Web Services classes or the connector because all the data translation occurs on the server side. If we use the Web Services Connector component or the Web Services classes instead of Flash Remoting, there is a large amount of client-side processing of the XML that must occur, which can slow down performance if we are dealing with large chunks of XML.

The only disadvantage of using Flash Remoting is that you must have a server-side component, which is an additional cost for J2EE and .NET. If you are using Cold Fusion MX on the server, Flash Remoting is installed by default and is no additional cost.

To use Flash Remoting, we use the `getService` method to point to the WSDL file instead of a server-side object, and we call the server-side method as shown in the following code. Flash Remoting is covered in depth in Chapter 14, "Using Client-Side Data Integration."

```
var songs=
my_conn.getService("http://radio.tapper.net/artist.cfc?wsdl ");
songs.getArtistCount(responderObject, "Beatles");
```

NOTE

To use Flash Remoting with Web Services, we need to create a server-side proxy object. Cold Fusion MX automatically creates a server-side proxy when a web service is called. You will need to refer to documentation in .NET and J2EE to create a server-side proxy object using those technologies.

Web Services Connector Component

The Web Services Connector component is a quick and easy way to call Web Services from within a Flash movie, and it enables easy use of data binding. When we right-click a method of a web service from the Web Services panel, an instance of the Web Services Connector component is automatically added to the Stage. However, no component is visible when the actual SWF file is published.

It is simple to add a web service to the Stage by right-clicking from the Web Services window, as shown in Figure 13.4.

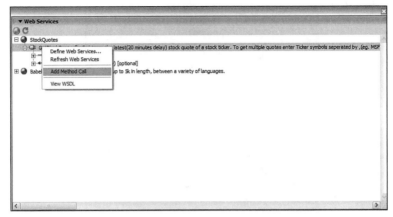

FIGURE 13.4   When a method is right-clicked, an instance of the Web Services Connector component is automatically added to the Stage.

When you click a web service method from the Web Services panel, the URL of the WSDL is automatically filled in. This can be populated by ActionScript or by the Property Inspector. ActionScript will override all other settings and can be done as follows:

```
<webServiceConnector>.WSDLURL =
"http://radio.tapper.net/artist.cfc?wsdl";
```

When we specify the WSDL URL for the web service, the Web Services Connector component goes out and defines (or reads) the web service WSDL and creates a data schema. From the Schema tab of the Web Services Connector component, we can modify this data by formatting, for example, a number to two decimal places, as shown in Figure 13.5.

The only way to have a connector actually execute is to use the trigger method. You must have this ActionScript 2.0 code in your application, even if you are using visual data binding. The syntax is as follows:

```
<connector_instance>.trigger();
```

Many Web Services require parameters to be passed to them; for example, the stock service requires a company symbol. We can pass this information either through the Property Inspector or through ActionScript 2.0 code. This can be in ActionScript by specifying the connector instance name and using the params property, which must be an array. The following ActionScript 2.0 code will pass the contents of a text field to a web service as a parameter:

```
<connector_instance>.params = new Array ("company_txt.text");
```

FIGURE 13.5   Modifying a schema for the Web Services Connector component.

Part of the appeal of the connector components is the ability to use visual data bindings; we can bind another UI component, such as a combo box or text component, directly to the parameters of the Web Services Connector component. In addition, we can connect a web service parameter directly to a text field, as shown in Figure 13.6:

FIGURE 13.6   Using data binding to connect the parameters of a web service to a text field.

After the web service has been called and executed, we need to access the results. If we do this with ActionScript 2.0 code, we need to use the new event listener syntax to listen for when the last byte of data has been received from the web service. The name of the event is `result`; the actual results are sent back from the web service as a property called `results`. The syntax is shown in the following code:

```
var resultObject:Object = new Object();
resultObject.result = function () {
trace (<connector instance>.results);
}
<connector_instance>.addEventListener ("result", resultObject);
```

Doing this by means of visual data binding is simple; all we have to do is bind the `results` property of the web service to the appropriate component. The data schema of the web service tells what type of data is being returned and we can then link that data to the right type of component. For example, the songsweb service will return a string, which could be connected to a text component. The stock service described earlier will return an Array of Objects, so it would make sense to bind the `results` property of that component to the `dataProvider` property of a list box, as shown in Figure 13.7:

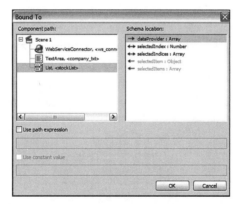

FIGURE 13.7   Binding the results of a web service that returns an Array of Objects to the `dataProvider` property of a list component.

If the server produces an error while connecting to the web service, the Web Services Connector component will return a status object with properties of `code`, `faultcode`, and `faultstring`, as shown in the following code. Status errors can be trapped and printed using the status event.

```
var statusObject :Object  = new Object();
statusObject.status = function () {
trace(stat.code);
trace(stat.data.faultcode);
trace(stat.data.faultstring);
};
<connector_instance>.addEventListener("status", statusObject);
```

The Web Services Connector component is a powerful way to easily connect to Web Services. If we want even more flexibility and power with ActionScript 2.0, we can use the Web Services classes.

Web Services Classes

The Web Services classes are a powerful way of connecting to Web Services. The main advantage that the classes offer is that they give the developer more control of the web service process. They include a logging functionality that tells, step-by-step, exactly what is happening; this, of course, makes debugging much easier as well. When we are dealing with a complex web service, it becomes essential to be able to follow the interactions that occur.

Let's explore how to connect to the song web service using the Web Services classes.

1. The Web Services classes are a compiled clip in SWC format that must be included in the Library of the finished application. Whenever we use the Web Services classes, we must include the classes in the Library of the SWF, as shown in Figure 13.8. The classes are accessible from Window > Other Panels > Common Libraries > Classes > Web Services classes.

FIGURE 13.8   All SWF files that use the Web Services classes must have the compiled clip included in their Library.

2. Everything else we do will now be in ActionScript 2.0. The first step is to create an instance of the class, as shown in the following code:

```
var songService = new
mx.services.WebService("http://radio.tapper.net/artist.cfc?wsdl";
```

3. The next step is to call the method, in this case, getSongs, which we can see from the Web Services panel. See Figure 13.9. We can also see that the method is expecting one parameter, the name of the artist, as a string.

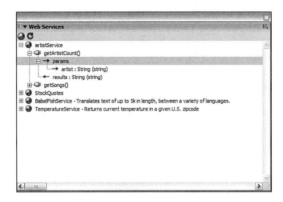

FIGURE 13.9   The Web Services panel reads a web service and tells us the methods available as well as the parameters and results for the service.

4. Now we can add the following ActionScript 2.0 code to call the method and pass the parameters:

```
var songResultObj :Object = new Object();
    songResultObj = songService.getArtistCoun("beatles");
```

5. The next step is to build an onResult method that will execute when Flash has received the last byte of data from the web service. The class also has an onLoad method that executes while the data is being sent, which we will add here as well:

```
songService.onLoad = function () {
trace ("Getting Songs");
}

songService.onResult = function(results) {
    trace (results);
}
```

6. You have now connected to a web service completely with ActionScript 2.0 code. One of the advantages of doing this is the improved error handling; an onFault event is generated that can give us crucial debugging information. If any part of the service is not working, the onFault event will be called. To show this, change the method call from getArtistCount to getArtistCounts, and then add the following code:

```
songResultObj.onFault = function(error) {
        trace(error.faultCode + "," + error.faultstring);
}
```

When this is run, the error message in Figure 13.10 is displayed:

FIGURE 13.10   The error message generated by the onFault event of the Web Services class.

7. Even better error handling can be added by using the Log class. If we add the following code to our file, we will see an exact description of everything that occurs. It can help us figure out exactly what is going wrong.

```
var songLog :mx.services.Log = new mx.services.Log(Log.VERBOSE);
songLog.onLog = function (logHistory) {
        trace (logHistory);
}
```

8. For the log to work, you now have to specify the name of the Log object after you specify the URL of the WSDL; you will need to modify the code as shown in the following code. See Figure 13.11.

```
var songService = new
mx.services.WebService("http://radio.tapper.net/artist.cfc?wsdl",
songLog);
```

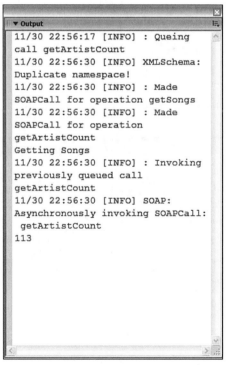

FIGURE 13.11   A detailed logging history of everything that happened with our web service call.

> **NOTE**
>
> The `Log` class has three settings:
>
> - **BRIEF.** Least-detailed error information
> - **VERBOSE.** More-detailed error information
> - **DEBUG.** Most-detailed error information
>
> The class is set as follows:
>
> ```
> var songLog :mx.services.Log = new mx.services.Log(Log.VERBOSE);
> ```

The SOAP protocol contains the data being sent between the web service itself and the Flash Player. It can be useful to actually see the raw XML that is passed back and forth between the client and server if, for example, the data translation is not occurring as expected. The raw XML will show exactly how the SOAP packets are being put together. To have your code do this, you can just reference the `request` and `response` objects in the `onResult` event, as shown in the following code:

```
Obj.onResult = function(results) {
trace (songResultObj.request);
trace (songResultObj.response);
    }
```

The raw XML will display in the output window, as shown in Figure 13.12:

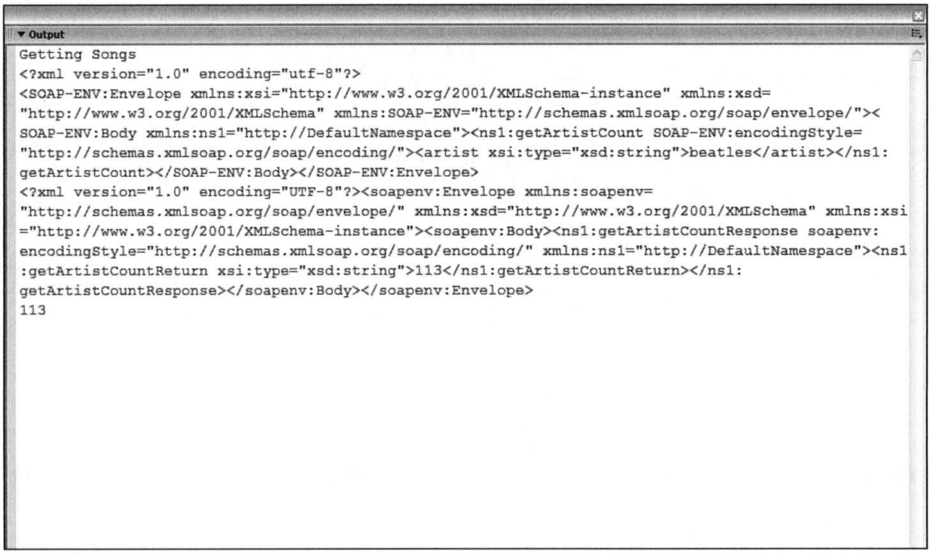

FIGURE 13.12 The raw SOAP XML data that is sent to Flash and parsed within the Player.

The *DataAccess* Class with Web Services

To create a more object-oriented way of dealing with Web Services, it makes sense to use a generalized `DataAccess` class. This class is ideal for class-based development, and it will enable us to easily access the results of a web service within a class. The class is effective because it encapsulates the creation of the Web Services objects, which use calls to the `onResult` and `onFault` events. We will use the `DataAccess` class to call the web service, send the results back to a method of our choosing, and send any errors back to a status method of our choosing. All we will have to do is pass the WSDL to the object, and we can pass functions that we want called to handle each event.

1. The first step in defining the class is to declare the private variable, which will hold the Web Services address, and the constructor; we also will instantiate the Web Services class. To use this class, the Web Services classes must be available either by dragging them from the Library to the Stage or by having an instance of the Web Services Connector component on the Stage. You can create a class with the name of `DataAccess` with the following code:

```
class DataAccess
{
        private var webService;
        public var callBack:Object = new Object();
        //Constructor
        public function DataAccess(address:String)
        {
                this.webService = new mx.services.WebService(address);
                this.webService.WSDLURL = address;
        }
}
```

2. We will now create a `remoteAccess` method that will actually call the web service and pass any parameters to it. We will also specify the names of the functions that we want called when the result event is executed or when an error occurs. Ensure that the `DataAccess` class looks like the following code:

```
class DataAccess
{
        private var webService;
        public var callBack:Object = new Object();
        //Constructor
```

```
    public function DataAccess(address:String)
    {
        this.webService = new mx.services.WebService(address);
        this.webService.WSDLURL = address;
    }
    public function accessRemote(methodName:String, object:Object,
resultFunction:Function, statusFunction:Function)
    {
        trace("accessRemote called: this.webService[\"" +
methodName + "\"](" + object + ");");
        this.callBack = this.webService[methodName](object);
        //
        //
        this.callBack.resultFunction = resultFunction;
        this.callBack.statusFunction = statusFunction;
        //
        this.callBack.onResult = function(result)
        {
            trace("Passing results to handler");
            resultFunction(result);
        };
        this.callBack.onFault = function(status)
        {
            trace("Passing status to handler");
            statusFunction(status);
        };
    }
}
```

3. To show how to use the DataAccess class, we will call a publicly available web service that will return the weather for any zip code in the United States. The first step is to figure out the parameters and results that the Web Services needs and returns. The easiest way to do this in Flash is to type the address of the WSDL into the Web Services panel. When that has been done, the content of Figure 13.13 is displayed.

We can see that the method name of the web service is GetTempgetTemp() and that it is expecting a zip code parameter. The service will return a number indicating the current temperature.

4. We now need to ensure that the Web Services classes are available; we can either drag them from the common Libraries or place an instance of the Web Services Connector component on the Stage.

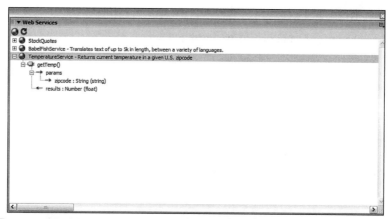

FIGURE 13.13   The parameters needed for the temperature web service.

5. Now we can instantiate the `DataAccess` object and pass the URL of the WSDL file to it. Create a new FLA file in the same directory as the `DataAccess` class and add the following code: `var myTemp :DataAccess = new DataAccess("http://www.xmethods.net/sd/2001/Temperature Service.wsdl");.`

6. Now we need to call the `accessRemote` method and pass the name of the method, any parameters that the method requires, the result function we want called, and the name of the status function, as shown in the following code:

```
myTemp.accessRemote ("getTemp", "94103", tempResult, tempStatus);
```

7. Our final step is to build the `result` function and the `status` function that will display the results of the web service call, as shown in the following code:

```
function tempResult (temperature) {
     trace (temperature);
}

function tempStatus (error) {
     trace (tempStatus);
}
```

8. When the movie is tested, we see the current temperature in the trace statement, as shown in Figure 13.14:

FIGURE 13.14   The data returned by the temperature web service.

The web service returns a current temperature of 70 degrees at Macromedia in San Francisco.

Summary

Web Services are a great way to access server application functionality within Flash. The primary advantage of Web Services is that they utilize accepted standards valid across the Internet. Web Services return structured data in such a way that it does not matter in what language the web service was written or on which platform the web service runs. There are multiple public Web Services available on the Internet, and of course, it is possible to build Web Services to create our own application functionality.

The two standards that make Web Services possible are WSDL and SOAP. The WSDL standard is a description of the web service that shows the developer the methods that can be called as well as any parameters that these methods may require. The second standard is the SOAP protocol. The SOAP protocol is just raw XML text that is sent down to the Flash player; the XML text contains unique SOAP formatting. The Flash Player is responsible for decoding this XML and converting it into useable ActionScript 2.0 objects.

Developers do not have to write code to parse the XML themselves in Flash MX 2004. There are two components created for this task: the Web Services Connector component and the Web Services classes.

The Web Services Connector component offers a way to process the XML data without having to use any ActionScript 2.0 code at all. The connector enables easy connection to other components through visual data binding.

The Web Services classes enables us to access all web-based services in code, which lends itself to more efficient coding practices.

Web Services is a very viable option, especially for smaller chunks of data. However, because all the XML is converted to ActionScript objects within the Flash Player, it can slow down performance, especially when dealing with larger chunks of data. In addition, when accessing XML data in the Flash Player, we are subject to the security sandbox restriction.

XML is the root of the host web server. For these reasons, in some cases, Flash Remoting may be a viable alternative to using the Web Services classes. Flash Remoting does the actual XML translation on the server, and then sends the native ActionScript object to the Flash Player. Therefore, with Flash Remoting, there are minimal performance issues and no security issues.

CHAPTER 14

USING CLIENT-SIDE DATA INTEGRATION

Macromedia Flash MX Professional 2004 provides new data components to connect with datasources as well as manage that data in the Flash Player. This data management enables the creation of true client/server systems with a significant client-side data layer. Because we are using the Flash Player, we still have all the advantages of the Internet. The best part is that Flash developers no longer have to build their own data management tools to manage data in the Flash Player.

Specifically, Flash MX Professional 2004 provides tools that manage the following:

- Connecting to data sources
- Translating external data into Flash data
- Editing data
- Sorting data
- Filtering data
- Saving changes to data

Flash MX Professional 2004 provides a robust model for creating client/server systems. One of the main advantages is that using the Flash Player to manage data enables a clean separation between the client and the server sides. If we use this effectively, we can greatly reduce the server load by performing many functions on the client side. In other versions of Flash, developers had to hard-wire all this functionality themselves. In Flash MX Professional 2004, Macromedia has built all this data management directly into the authoring tool, allowing for the best possible performance.

There are two ways of linking the different pieces of a Flash application together: Visual data binding and ActionScript 2.0. This chapter will cover both ways of linking components, but will focus on using ActionScript 2.0 because ActionScript 2.0 will ultimately result in a more maintainable system that will be easier to customize and manage. Using data binding does not enable access to the actual code generated; it can be changed only in the Visual Properties Inspector.

Understanding the Data Management Process

The first step in creating a dynamic application is to define and build the external datasource. Flash MX Professional 2004 can currently connect to Web Services or extensible markup language (XML) files by using the connector components or by using the XML or Web Services classes directly. Macromedia is planning the release of a remoting connector component; currently the only way to use Flash Remoting is to use the remoting classes directly. Remember that Flash is a client-side technology and it cannot build Web Services on the server (or return XML from the server). We use the connector components to connect to the server. Creating server-side logic that returns the appropriate data structure to Flash is the job of the ColdFusion, J2EE, or .NET developer.

The entire structure of the data integration process in Flash looks as shown in Figure 14.1.

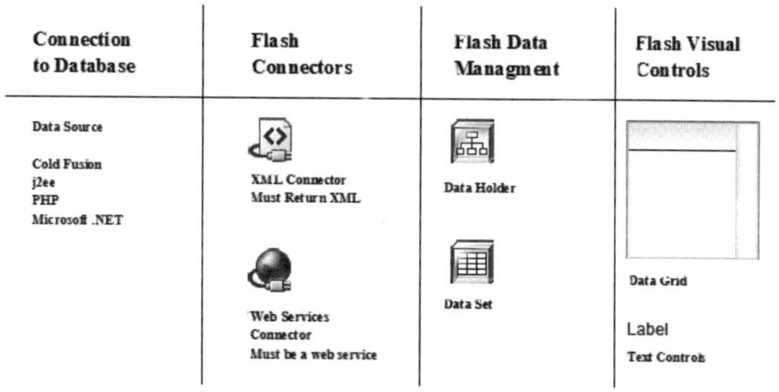

Connection to Database	Flash Connectors	Flash Data Managment	Flash Visual Controls
Data Source Cold Fusion J2ee PHP Microsoft .NET	XML Connector Must Return XML Web Services Connector Must be a web service	Data Holder Data Set	Data Grid Label Text Controls

FIGURE 14.1 The connector components connect to a server, and that data can be managed in the Flash client using the dataset.

In terms of application architecture, the connector components enable Flash to actually connect to a server, regardless of whether we use Web Services or XML. This can also be done completely in ActionScript 2.0 using the Web Services or XML classes. If Flash Remoting is used, you must connect to the server using the `NetServices` class. After the data has been loaded into the Flash Player, it is possible to link this data directly to user interface (UI) controls. However, in most applications, we have to manipulate the data before the user sees it. This is done through the data management components.

You will need to make a choice in the development of your application: do you use code or the visual data binding? The process described in Figure 14.2 can be performed with the Visual Component Inspector, using data binding, or directly with ActionScript 2.0 code. For example, assume that a connector needs to reference a data management component to transfer the data structures. This can be done with ActionScript 2.0 code or this can be done with the Visual Component Inspector using the Bindings tab. Using ActionScript will ultimately give us more flexibility, but using visual data bindings is useful for quickly getting an application developed.

The data management components, such as the dataset, have an underlying array with the names of items that are used to handle the data. A Web Services Connector component can retrieve an array from the server; this array can be referenced through the `results` property.

FIGURE 14.2   Linking a connector to a data management layer using the Visual Component Inspector.

Linking a dataset and a connector in code is as simple as pointing the array returned from the web service to the array used by the connector, as shown in the following samples:

```
var myResult :Object = new Object();
myResult.result = function () {
product_ds.items = product_ws.results;
}
product_ws.addEventListener ("result", myResult);
```

In this chapter, we focus on using Flash Remoting to return data from a server. Flash Remoting enables calling a server-side method directly from ColdFusion, .NET, or J2EE, and will result in the consumption of less bandwidth than Web Services or XML because it uses the ActionScript Messaging Format (AMF) protocol. This protocol is more efficient than XML or Simple Object Access Protocol (SOAP). AMF is a binary protocol; SOAP and XML are both basically just plain text.

Connector Components

The connector components are used to translate the results of method calls to server-side datasources. The connector components provide a more visual and user-friendly way to deal with the XML and Web Services classes. For example, if a ColdFusion web service returns an array of objects, the Web Services

Connector component will translate that data into an array of objects that Flash can use. Unlike Flash Remoting, this translation actually happens in the Flash Player at runtime. After you have your connector in place, you can link the results of connectors directly to visual UI controls, such as a list or a data grid. Even better, you can link the results to a data management component, which allows manipulation of the data.

Connectors are used not only to retrieve the results from the server, but also to send the results back to the server. A Flash application can have different instances of connector components: one to retrieve the data and one to save the data. You can call multiple Web Services in one Flash document, so this means that you can have many instances of connectors on the Stage. This is one advantage of not using the connector components and using the intrinsic Web Services or XML classes; we can make multiple calls to Web Services or XML documents without having multiple instances of the connectors on the Stage. The visual display for the connectors is used only in the authoring environment and isn't included with the published SWF. In addition, the connector components add more file size to your application if you are not using the component framework.

It is possible to link a connector directly to a UI control and bypass the data management layer where the dataset and `DataHolder` are used. However, this means that if you need to manage any changes, you will be responsible for handling them yourself. This might involve creating many loops, conditional logic sequence, additional arrays, and data structures—depending on the complexity of the application. The dataset and `DataHolder` make handling this data much easier because the data is presented in an intuitive way. For applications of any complexity, it is recommended to use the Flash data components to manage the data rather than linking a component directly to a UI control. After all, Macromedia has already built this sophisticated architecture for us; there is no reason why we should have to build it again.

The XML and Web Services Connector components have both parameters and results. The parameters are required by the server to execute. Examine Figure 14.3.

The web service requires a stock symbol as a parameter and will return an Array of Objects as the result. The Web Services panel tells us all this and more. In Flash MX Professional 2004, you have the option of binding connector objects to visual controls (or other data management components) using either the Visual Property Inspectors or ActionScript 2.0 code.

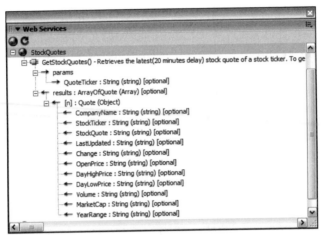

FIGURE 14.3   Viewing a web service in the Web Services panel.

Using Connector Components with Visual Data Binding

In a simple application, it can make sense to use visual data binding to link connector components directly to UI controls, bypassing the data management layer. Visual data binding is simply one way of connecting components to each other.

In many cases, visual data binding can be combined with ActionScript 2.0 code. In some cases, it is much easier to use the Component Inspector rather than ActionScript 2.0. For example, it is much easier to use the XML connector with data binding and a schema to convert XML objects into arrays. The ActionScript 2.0 code required to do this is long and complex. However, in some cases, data binding can fall short. For example, it is usually much more flexible to specify a label field through ActionScript 2.0 code instead of through a formatter on visual data binding. The formatters are available in the Bindings tab of the Component Inspector and are designed for people who would not code any ActionScript 2.0 code at all.

Components can be bound together without using any connector objects at all. For example, if you wanted to create a master detail view, which populates text fields when an item in a list box is selected, text components could display the details of the selected item on the list box using data binding. Visual data binding can be used only with version 2 components. Actually using visual data binding will give you a better idea of the process.

> **NOTE**
>
> If you copy and paste components with data binding set up, or if you place the components within a symbol, you will need to redo all the data bindings.

The following exercise builds an interface to a stock quote web service. The end user will pass parameters (stock quotes) to the web service. The components will also display the results of the web service in a list component.

1. Open the Web Services panel and type the following URL:
   `http://www.swanandmokashi.com/HomePage/WebServices/Stock Quotes.asmx?WSDL`

2. Right-click (or Ctrl-click) the `getStockQuotes()` method. This automatically adds an instance of the connector to the Stage. Assign the connector an instance name of **stockService**.

3. Drag a `textInput` component to the Stage and assign it an instance name of **tickerName**. Place a `pushButton` component next to the `textInput` component and assign it an instance name of **stock_pb**.

4. Drag a list component to the Stage and name it **stockResults**. For the web service to accept parameters and display the results, you will use the Component Inspector. Your controls should look like Figure 14.4:

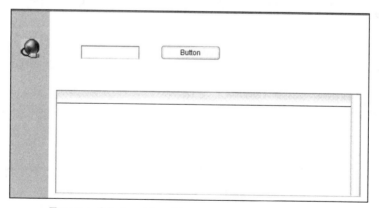

FIGURE 14.4   Visual layout of the stock application.

5. Select the component on the Stage and open the Component Inspector. Select Bindings on the Component Inspector.

6. Click the + sign and bind the `params.quoteTicker` to the `tickerName` text field, as shown in Figure 14.5:

FIGURE 14.5   Binding `params.quoteTicker`.

7. Select the list component and bind `dataProvider` (an array) to the array received from the web service (results :Array).

8. In the Component Inspector, select the `formatter` field and select Rearrange Fields.

9. Type **label=StockQuote** in the formatter options field.

10. Create an Actions layer and type the following ActionScript 2.0 code:

```
stock_pb.onRelease = function() :Void {
      stockService.trigger();
}
```

11. Test the movie and enter multiple ticker symbols in the text field. Your screen should resemble Figure 14.6.

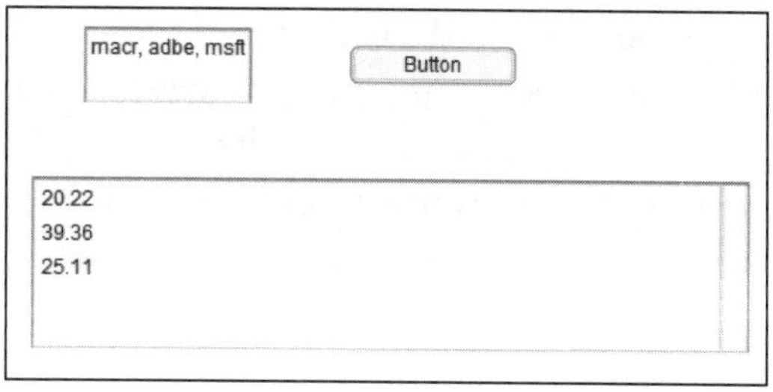

FIGURE 14.6 The finished stock quote application.

Using ActionScript 2.0 with Connector Components

The ActionScript 2.0 code for the same application as presented previously would follow the same process, but it would not use any of the visual inspectors at all. Ultimately, by using ActionScript 2.0 code, however, we will have more control over the application.

1. Right-click (or Ctrl-click) the getStockQuotes() method in the Web Services panel. Assign the web service connector an instance name of **stockService**.

2. Drag a textInput component to the Stage and assign it an instance name of **tickerName**. Place a pushbutton component next to the textInput component and assign it an instance name of **stock_pb**.

3. Now you need to set up the parameters for the web service within the button event, as shown in the following code. All parameters for a web service *must* take the form of an ActionScript array or ActionScript object.

```
stock_pb.onRelease = function() :Void {
    stockService.params = new Array ([tickerName.text]);
    stockService.trigger();
}
```

4. The next step is to have the web service listen for the result event, which occurs when the data is sent back from the web service to the connector, as shown in the following code:

```
var stockListener :Object = new Object();
stockListener.result = function () {}
stockService.addEventListener ("result", stockListener);
```

5. Finally, all you have to do is link the `dataProvider` of the list to the array being sent back from the web service. The array being sent back from the server is known as "results", and it is a property of the web service connector. This must be done in the `result` event; finally you can specify the `labelField` for the `stockResults` list component.

```
var stockListener :Object = new Object();
stockListener.result = function () :Void{
stockResults.dataProvider = stockListener.results;
stockResults.labelField = "StockQuote";
}
stockService.addEventListener ("result", stockListener);
```

Using Schemas

A schema is simply a graphical representation of a data structure. It could represent an array of objects, XML data, or even the properties of a UI component. As you may have noticed, all version 2 components have a tab called Schema on the Component Inspector. The Schema tab shows only those properties of the component that commonly contain data, such as the results and parameters of a web service.

Schemas are similar to document type definitions (DTDs) in XML. Just as a DTD defines the legal structure of an XML document, a schema defines the underlying data structure of a Flash component.

In many cases, the schema is automatically defined, such as when a web service is interpreted by the built-in Web Services Description Language (WSDL) parser; in such a situation, Flash MX Professional 2004 pulls out the appropriate data structures for the schema. With other components, the schema is predefined within the component. For example, with a text area component, the only bindable property by default is the `text` property. If, for example, you wanted to give the user the ability to turn a password field on or off, you could add the `password` property to the schema of the component object instance. Examine Figure 14.7.

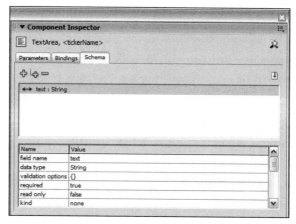

FIGURE 14.7   Content of the Schema tab.

1. Drag a TextInput component (instance name: `pass_txt`) and a CheckBox component (instance name: `pass_ch`) to the Stage.
2. Select the TextInput component and open the Component Inspector.
3. Select Add Property from the context menu; this defines a new schema value for the component. See Figure 14.8.

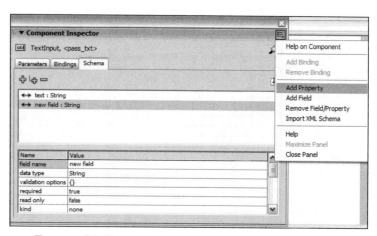

FIGURE 14.8   Defining a schema value for a component.

4. Set the field name to password and the datatype to Boolean.
5. Select the Bindings tab and a new binding for the `password` property.
6. Select the `Bound to` property and bind the TextInput component to the CheckBox component.

7. Select the check box, and set the default selected value to true.

8. Set the default password value of the TextInput component to true.

9. Run the application; you should have the ability to make the field a password or not, depending on your preferences.

In other cases, you need to define the schema for the component instance; it is not predefined in the class of component as with a text component. A good example of this is when using the XML Connector component. The schema can be loaded in from an external XML file, and it shows the Flash data structures to which the XML translates. The XML elements are interpreted into ActionScript data structures using the schema. Each child element of the XML is examined and the type of data of its contents is also documented. The schema is in addition to the loaded XML itself.

The XML in Figure 14.9 has attributes of name, which translate to a string, and individual nodes indicating description, which also translate to a string. These are stored as objects within an array and are perfect for binding to UI components. The `DataBinding` class, using the schema you define, is responsible for actually performing the translation of the XML to ActionScript data structures.

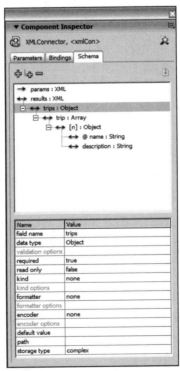

FIGURE 14.9   Viewing the attributes.

Even though the datatype of the results property is XML, the `DataBinding` class will perform the translation for us into ActionScript objects and arrays as long as the schema is defined.

Managing Data Using The Flash MX Professional 2004 Architecture

Flash MX Professional 2004 comes with multiple tools for managing the manipulation of client-side data in the Flash Player. As you have seen in Chapter 9, "Building and Using UI Components," using data in the Flash Player can require the building of complicated data structures on the client. However, Flash MX Professional 2004 has a built-in framework that lets us manipulate and handle data efficiently in the Player. You can perform various advanced operations on data within the Flash Player, including the following:

- Multiple sorts
- Offline caching
- Finding data
- Filtering data
- Linking data to UI controls
- Keeping track of all changes in delta packets

You have been working with data, but have not used any data management tools; you have simply used data binding to bind the data directly to UI controls. You have had to handle everything manually; as your applications get more complex, you will crave tools that will make your life easier. When we linked two components together in Chapter 9, we had to build all the arrays and data structures by hand. In effect, we built our own data management tools. This is where the dataset and/or the `DataHolder` component enters in. Let's review the entire process in the following subsections. See Figure 14.10.

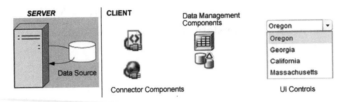

FIGURE 14.10   An overview of the data management process.

Moving Data from the Connector to the Dataset

The first part of working with data in Flash is using the connector components to connect to a datasource. You can use the Web Services connector, the XML connector, or the Remoting connector (not yet released), depending on the datasource to which you need to connect. It is possible to not use a connector component and just use the XML, Web Services, or Remoting classes directly to connect to a datasource. In either case, you need to be aware of the type of data being returned from the server; the XML and Web Services connectors will usually work best with an Array of Objects, but Flash Remoting works equally well with an Array of Objects, a `RecordSet` object, or many other datatypes.

The second part of working with data involves linking the connector to the dataset or the `DataHolder` component. One way of doing this is to use visual data binding, as shown in Figure 14.11:

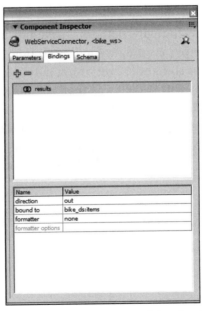

FIGURE 14.11   Linking a connector to a dataset using data binding.

Another way of doing this is through ActionScript 2.0 code. All you need to do is set up a `result` event and then bind the object directly to the dataset. The object that is bound to the dataset can implement a `dataProvider` interface, such as a `RecordSet`. You can also use an Array of Objects returned from an XML connector or a Web Services connector. If you are linking an Array of Objects from the server to the dataset, you can use the `items.array` property; if you are using an implementation of the `dataProvider` class, such as a record set, you use the `dataProvider` property. The ActionScript 2.0 code to link a `dataProvider` is remarkably simple; all you have to do is link the object from the results to the `dataProvider` of the dataset, as shown in the following code:

```
employeeObject :Object = new Object();
employeeObject.result = function() :Void{
        employee_ds.dataProvider = employee_ws.results;
}
employee_ws.addEventListener("result", employeeObject);
```

If you are using the XML connector or the Web Services connector, or are accessing an Array of Objects from the server using Remoting, you will be returning an Array of Objects. The best practice is to link that Array of Objects directly to the items array of the dataset, as shown in the following code:

```
employeeObject :Object = new Object();
employeeObject.result = function() :Void {
        employee_ds.items = employee_ws.results;
}
employee_ws.addEventListener("result", employeeObject);
```

That's it! You have now added data to the DataSet component.

Using the DataSet Component

The DataSet component enables you to manage your client-side data by creating and loading the data into anonymous objects that are accessed and controlled by a cursor. The cursor in the dataset can be moved from record to record and the appropriate information can be obtained by accessing properties within the record.

In the following step sequence, you will add the data from the stock quote web service to a dataset, and you will do it in ActionScript 2.0 code so that you have complete control over the data that is coming in.

NOTE

You are hard-coding the web service parameters here and not using the text field to pass the stock quote parameters.

---

1. Create a new FLA file and drag a web service connector from the Library to the Stage. Assign the connector an instance name of `stockService`.

2. Drag a DataSet component from the Components panel to the Stage and assign it an instance name of **stock_ds**.

3. Create an Actions layer and type the following code:

```
stockService.WSDLURL =
"http://www.swanandmokashi.com/HomePage/WebServices/StockQuotes.asmx?
WSDL";
stockService.params = new Array (["macr aapl adbe msft orcl sunw"]);
stockService.trigger();
var stockListener :Object = new Object();
stockListener.result = function () {
        stock_ds.items = stockService.results;
}
stockService.addEventListener ("result", stockListener);
```

The preceding code sets the URL for the web service connector and passes it parameters. When the results are received from the web service, it links the data from the web service to the dataset.

4. Add the trace statement after the data from the connector is linked to the dataset data, as shown in the following code:

```
stockListener.result = function () {
        stock_ds.items = stockService.results;
        trace (stock_ds.CompanyName);
}
```

To access records from the dataset, reference the property name that is coming back from the server, in the `result` event. The code will return MACROMEDIA, INC because this is what the web service returns based on the first parameter that you sent.

5. So how is the next record in the dataset, in this case `Apple`, accessed? Add the following ActionScript 2.0 code:

```
stockListener.result = function () {
      stock_ds.items = stockService.results;
      trace (stock_ds.CompanyName);
      stock_ds.next();
      trace (stock_ds.CompanyName);
}
```

6. Move the dataset cursor to the next record. The result of the second trace is `Apple` because that is the second parameter that you passed to the dataset.

Other methods can be used to facilitate navigation within the dataset. The `first()` method will move the data cursor to the first record in the dataset while the `last()` method will move the data cursor to the last record. A do-while loop is perfect for looping over a dataset; there is a method with the name of `hasNext()` that tests to see if the dataset does in fact have a record after the one the cursor is currently on. To loop through an entire dataset and retrieve the data, do the following:

1. Move the data cursor to the first record in the dataset with the first method of the dataset, using the following code:

```
stockListener.result = function () {
stock_ds.items = stockService.results;
stock_ds.first();
}
```

2. Set up a while condition using the `hasNext()` method of the dataset, as shown in the following code:

```
stockListener.result = function () {
      stock_ds.items = stockService.results;
      stock_ds.first();
      while (stock_ds.hasNext()) {}
}
```

3. After executing the code on the appropriate record, move the data cursor to the next record while still in the loop, as shown in the following code:

```
stockListener.result = function () {
      stock_ds.items = stockService.results;
      stock_ds.first();
      while (stock_ds.hasNext()) {
            trace (stock_ds.CompanyName)
            stock_ds.next();
}
}
```

That's pretty straightforward. Looping can also be used for searching for a particular record, such as companies that have a stock price of greater than 20. This is part of the reason it is more efficient to use ActionScript 2.0 for binding; adding this type of logic is difficult using the Component Inspector. To do so, you could add the following logic to the stock quotes application:

```
while (stock_ds.hasNext)) {
      if (stock_ds.StockQuote >20) {
            trace (stock_ds.CompanyName);
      }
      stock_ds.next();
}
```

The real power of a dataset comes into play when other components are synchronized to the cursor of the dataset. This makes it very easy to create dependent components. Note that the same choices of using the Data Bindings panel or using ActionScript 2.0 code still apply. To do this, make the selectedIndex of the component the same as the selectedIndex of the dataset. The beauty of this approach is that the dataset will automatically move the cursor from record to record in the dataset when the user moves the record in the UI control.

1. Add a list component to the Stage of the stock quote example with which we have been working. Assign the component an instance name of **stock results**.

2. Select the DataSet component on the Stage and open the Component Inspector. Bind the selectedIndex property of the dataset to the selectedIndex of the list component on the Stage (instance name of stockResults), as shown in Figure 14.12:

Figure 14.12 Linking the dataset to a list component using the Component Inspector.

3. Add a `TextArea` component to the Stage and assign it an instance name of **stockQuote**.

4. Remove the visual binding between the dataset and the `stockResults` list. Add the following ActionScript 2.0 code:

```
var changeList :Object = new Object();
changeList.change = function () {
       stock_ds.selectedIndex = stockResults.selectedIndex;
       stockQuote.text = stock_ds.StockQuote;
}
stockResults.addEventListener ("change", changeList);
```

Flash will manage everything automatically through the data cursor. When the user selects a company from the list, Flash will manage which company was selected and display the appropriate related information in the text fields. This makes it easy on the developer because the dataset handles all this interaction.

At first glance, it may seem like more work to use ActionScript 2.0 rather than the Component Inspector, but ActionScript does give us much more flexibility. It would be simple to apply conditional logic, for example, to affect other UI controls. Applying logic or modifying the data that already exists is cumbersome at best when using the Visual Data Binding Inspector. Certainly using a dataset here is saving lots of time; there is no need to loop through any data based on the user's selections because the two `selectedIndex` properties are bound together.

So far, the objects used within the dataset represent just a single record of data. The objects have properties that you have been calling that represent each field of data. The `DataSet` object also has the ability to create its own application program interface (API), which is a collection of methods on the client side. These methods can mirror the structure of a server-side object and even be sent back to the server for processing using the resolver components.

Note that the dataset is a collection of "transfer objects" modeled on the J2EE transfer object pattern. This server-side object exposes data with public attributes and has getter/setter methods to access and write that data. The transfer object is known as a pattern and more information about it is available from Sun at `http://java.sun.com/blueprints/corej2eepatterns/Patterns/TransferObject.html`.

It's important for Flash developers to understand the transfer object pattern because the dataset is a client-side implementation of this pattern. It enables developers to work with sophisticated client-side objects that are exactly the same as their server-side counterparts. It's also extremely easy and efficient to send data back and forth between the client-side object and the server-side object using delta packets.

Examine the following code:

```
interface mx.data.to.TransferObject {
   function clone():Object;
   function getPropertyData():Object;
   function setPropertyData(propData:Object):Void;
}
```

You use the `itemClassName` parameter of the dataset to specify the name of the class you create in ActionScript that implements the `TransferObject` interface, as shown in the following code:

```
mydata set.itemClassName = myClass;
```

The dataset will then automatically create instances of the object from the class upon the initial load of the data into the dataset as well as whenever the addItem method is used. You also must specify a fully qualified reference to the class somewhere within your SWF, as shown in the following code:

```
var myItem:my.package.myItem;
```

If you call server-side methods, they will be stored in the Flash Player until the object is sent to the server through Web Services or Flash Remoting using the resolver component. Another option is to use Flash Remoting or Web Services actually within the class; you then call the server-side method as soon as it is called on the client.

The Delta Packet Classes

Delta packets are one of the most powerful new features of Flash. Each dataset has an underlying delta packet that is changed whenever a user updates the dataset.

A lot of time was spent in the past section connecting a dataset to a UI control. Because of that hard work, the rest of the job becomes much easier. The ActionScript takes the results from a web service call, places the results into a dataset, and links that dataset to a data grid control. Whenever an end user moves to another record in the data grid, the data cursor in the dataset is moved automatically. The trace that is included in the change handler proves this.

The following code uses the stock quotes web service as an example, but the list has been replaced with a data grid that has an instance name of stockResults. Review the code and note the only difference is that the horizontal scrolling of the grid has been turned on:

```
stockService.WSDLURL
="http://www.swanandmokashi.com/HomePage/WebServices/StockQuotes.asmx?
WSDL";
stockResults.hScrollPolicy = "On"
stockService.params = ["macr aapl adbe msft orcl
sunw"];stockService.trigger();
var stockListener :Object = new Object();
stockListener.result = function () {
      stock_ds.items = stockService.results;
      stockResults.dataProvider = stock_ds.dataProvider;
      stockResults.labelField = "CompanyName";
}
```

```
var changeList :Object = new Object();
changeList.change = function () {
      stock_ds.selectedIndex = stockResults.selectedIndex;
      stockQuote.text = stock_ds.StockQuote;
}
stockResults.addEventListener ("change", changeList);

stockService.addEventListener ("result", stockListener);
```

Adding the following line of code makes the `DataGrid` UI control editable:

```
stockResults.editable = true;
```

You can change any one of the fields on the grid. The beautiful part of this is that by changing the field in the grid, the dataset is automatically updated as well. The dataset is managing all the data, and any changes that are made are captured inside the delta packet. The Delta Packet classes and interfaces enable viewing of the information being sent to the server, and they also enable the dataset to receive errors and make updates.

The delta packet consists of the following:

- **Delta Packet interface**. Allows developers to access the modified data, known as delta, from the dataset.
- **Delta interface**. The actual changed and unchanged values from the dataset.
- **DeltaItem**. Informs the developer about the particular type of change that was made, and whether it was made to a property of the transfer object in the dataset or to a method.
- **Delta PacketConsts**. Provides static variables indicating whether the information in the dataset was added, modified, or removed.

Resolvers

Now that the delta packet has been generated, it needs to be sent back to the server. The delta packet is accessible as a property of the DataSet component. However, it is not created until the `applyUpdates` method is called. The following code displays the delta packet of the `employee_ds` dataset, assuming a button, `stock_ds`, was on the Stage.

```
pusher_pb.onRelease = function () {
     stock_ds.applyUpdates();
     trace (stock_ds.deltapacket);
}
```

This returns an object that has these properties:

- _confInfo
- _timestamp
- _log
- _transId
- _keyInfo
- _source
- _optimized
- _Delta Packet

Examining the object shows that the delta packet consists of many objects not suitable for a server to easily use. This is where the resolver comes in. The resolver takes a delta packet that has been bound to it and generates an updatePacket containing the changes in the delta packet. This is in an XML format and can easily be consumed by a server using a web service or Flash Remoting to pass the XML back.

The following code sets up a binding between the Delta Packet property of the resolver and the Delta Packet property of the dataset. This can also be done with visual data bindings to bind the Delta Packet property of the dataset to the Delta Packet property of the Resolver. Once bound, the resolver automatically creates the updatePacket property, which is an XML document. It also assumes a resolver component with the instance name of stock_resolve is on the Stage. When the push button is pressed, a delta packed is generated from the dataset that shows the data that was changed. A trace is then added to display the XML delta packet.

```
pusher_pb.onRelease = function () {
     stock_ds.applyUpdates();
     stock_resolve.deltapacket = stock_ds.deltapacket;
     trace (stock_resolve.updatePacket);
}
```

For example, if we change the prices of the stocks in the grid, the resolvers will grab the delta packet from the dataset and generate an XML packet to update the content. We would need a server-side piece to grab the XML packet and it is unlikely that this web service would appreciate us updating the price of Macromedia to 200 and downgrading Adobe to 1, as shown in the following code:

```xml
<?xml version="1.0" ?>
 <update_packet tableName="" nullValue="{_NULL_}"
transID="IID17802395625:Thu Oct 16 20:15:55 GMT-0700 2003">
 <update id="IID26029991731">
  <field name="STOCKQUOTE" type="Number" oldValue=39.33  newValue=1
key="false" />
  </update>
 <update id="IID61346959788">
  <field name="STOCKQUOTE" type="Number" oldValue=20.23 newValue=200
key="false" />
  </update>


</update_packet>
```

Notice that `updatePacket` is not sending all the data in the dataset; it sends only the data that has changed, which results in a very efficient and powerful solution.

This update packet is generated through the resolver components. The resolver will take a delta packet from a `DataSet` object and create an `updatePacket` that is suitable for consumption by a server-side solution.

DataHolder Component

The DataHolder component is a simple component especially useful with visual data binding. Unlike the DataSet component, it does not have any tools for managing, tracking, or updating data. It is useful when you cannot directly bind components together. For example, if you write ActionScript code and need to link this code to a component, you could use the DataHolder component to store the information and data binding to bind it to the appropriate UI control.

Flash Remoting

Flash Remoting enables invocation of server-side methods from a client-side ActionScript object, also known as a proxy object. Using Flash Remoting, methods within a Cold Fusion component, .NET, or a J2EE class can be called.

Flash Remoting uses the Hypertext Transfer Protocol (HTTP) and AMF. Flash Remoting can be a more efficient solution for transferring large amounts of data because AMF is a binary protocol that consumes much less bandwidth than SOAP. In addition, much of the transformation from XML to Flash objects occurs on the server rather than the client, which frees up client-side resources.

Flash Remoting consists of a server-side element that runs on ColdFusion, the Microsoft .NET framework, or a J2EE server. This server-side component does the data translation. For example, it will take a query in ColdFusion, a dataset in .NET, or a ResultSet in Java and translate it into a Flash data structure called a `RecordSet` object. The server-side component will also take an array, which is a string from any of those languages, and translate this server-side data structure into a native Flash object of approximately the same type. Flash Remoting also consists of a client-side piece that can be downloaded from Macromedia at `www.macromedia.com/software/flashRemoting/downloads/components/`.

The client-side piece of Flash Remoting enables the creation of a proxy server-side object within the Flash Player (located within the NetServices.as class).

> **NOTE**
>
> At the time this book published, the Flash Remoting components had not yet been updated for ActionScript 2.0. Therefore, you must include the old ActionScript 1.0 class at the top of your FLA file, as in ActionScript 1.0. Macromedia is planning to rewrite the Flash Remoting components in ActionScript 2.0.

In addition, the client-side download also provides tools for debugging within the `NetBug` class and managing data within the Flash Player through the `RecordSet` class.

An overview of the entire process is shown in Figure 14.13.

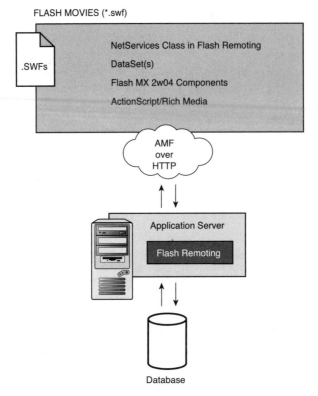

FIGURE 14.13   Flash Remoting enables the creation of client/server solutions where some processing is done on the server and some is done on the client.

Benefits of Flash Remoting

What advantages does Flash Remoting offer over Web Services and XML? The biggest advantage that Flash Remoting offers is performance. Whenever you use Web Services and XML, the Flash Player has to parse the XML and validate the XML against the schema. This takes time. Flash Remoting sends binary data down the wire and this data not only consumes less bandwidth (XML data or WSDL data is basically raw text data), but also is easier for the Flash Player to handle.

Flash Remoting exposes server-side methods and represents a clear delineation between server development and Flash development. With Flash Remoting, it is very easy to divide up teams of programmers. It also is generally easier on the server-side to build methods and objects instead of having to build Web Services.

Using Flash Remoting

As of the publishing of this book, the Flash Remoting classes have been written in ActionScript 1.0. Macromedia is planning to completely rewrite all the classes to follow best practices in ActionScript 2.0 as well as build a Remoting Connector component that will work with visual data bindings.

For now, we will be discussing the version 1 remoting components, which can be installed in Flash MX 2004. To use Flash Remoting is to include the appropriate remoting files at the top of your ActionScript code. This can be done using the Actions panel after the remoting components have been installed. The `NetServices` class contains the core remoting functionality and also includes the `RecordSet` class, which helps manage data. All FLAs that implement Flash Remoting should have the following included:

```
#include NetServices.as
```

CAUTION

If you include the `NetBug` class, which enables the built-in Remoting debugger, it is essential that this class be removed from any production server as there is an inherent security risk because it exposes data.

Examine Figure 14.14.

FIGURE 14.14   The Actions panel after the remoting components have been installed.

Creating a Gateway Connection

To use Flash Remoting, you must connect to the server-side piece. This is done by creating a gateway connection to the application server using the static method `createGatewayConnection` of the `NetServices` class. This object establishes the bidirectional connection between the Flash Player and the Flash Remoting service at the server. Note that the connection is not made until the server-side method is actually called.

To establish a connection with both Cold Fusion and Java application servers, you would use the following code:

```
#include "NetServices.as"
var myCon :Object = createGatewayConnection
("http://localhost}/flashservices/gateway");
```

To establish a connection using Microsoft .NET, you would use the following code:

```
#include "NetServices.as"
var myCon :Object = createGateWayConnection
("http://localhost/flashRemoting/gateway.aspx");
```

Creating a Responder Object

To catch the data from the server, it is a best practice to create a responder object, as shown in the following code:

```
var myResponder :Object = new Object();
```

It is possible to send the results of the server-side call to a movie clip, including the main timeline, but this can result in less maintainable code. Note that it is possible to send the results to any object in Flash, and it can be useful to build custom responder classes.

Building a Client-Side Proxy Object

The server-side object will need to be referenced in the Flash Player. This is done by creating an ActionScript proxy object; this is a client-side representation of the server-side object whose methods you are going to call. This object will have all the server-side methods of the object on the server, but Flash will be able to reference the proxy object. After you have created the proxy object in Flash, you can use this object to invoke server-side methods.

Creating the proxy object is done through the getService method of the NetServices class; this method requires one parameter, which is the package name on the server. The following code shows how a Cold Fusion object is referenced by the getService () method. "oopAS.examples" is the path or package to the Cold Fusion object with the name of myServerObject.

```
var proxyObject :Object = myCon.getService
("oopAS.examples.myServerObject");
```

Calling the Server-Side Method from ActionScript

After the proxy object has been set up using the getService method, you can call methods of that object just as you call methods on a regular Flash object. To do this, you just specify the name of the proxy object and the name of the server-side method you want to call. You also need to specify the name of the object where the results will be returned as the first parameter of the method call. Any additional parameters that the server-side method needs can be sent after the first method call. In the following code, the results of the method call will be sent to the myResponder object, and the contents of the id text field will be sent to the server-side object as a method parameter:

```
proxyObject.myServerMethod (myResponder, id.text);
```

Dealing with the Results from the Server-Side Call

After the method has been called and the last byte of data has been received from the server, the Flash Player automatically calls the onResult event, which is similar to the result event/listener you have worked with in Web Services and XML.

NOTE

Remoting can also call responder methods on the Flash side with the same name as the server-side method, but with the _Result suffix. These methods are called when the last byte of data bas been received from the server, as shown in the following code:

```
myServerMethod_Result = function (serverData) {
//code

}
```

However, these responder methods *must* be attached to MovieClip objects; you have already looked at the disadvantages of hanging code off movie clip timelines rather than using class-based development.

The object returned from the server will be passed as a parameter to the onResult event, as shown in the following code:

```
myResponder.onResult = function (serverData) {
//code
}
```

You can manipulate the server-side object that is returned, just as you could with any other ActionScript object. If you are using remoting with version 2 components, you could easily link the returned item with a DataSet object. Remember that a Cold Fusion query, a .NET dataset, or a Java ResultSet is automatically translated by Flash Remoting into a RecordSet object. The RecordSet object implements the dataProvider API, which means you can link the recordSet to the dataProvider of the version 2 dataset, as shown in the following code:

```
myResponder.onResult = function (serverData) {
      mydataset.dataProvider = serverData;
}
```

If you are returning an Array of Objects from the Remoting service, you would link the items property of the dataset.

Data Translation in Flash Remoting

The data translation in Flash Remoting varies by platform. As discussed, queries returned will translate into a recordSet in Flash. A recordSet appears as shown in Figure 14.15.

The RecordSet object is useful because it implements the dataProvider API, which means that you can use methods like addItem(), removeItem(), getLength(), and more. These methods work just like the component methods we have worked with before.

However, using a RecordSet object tends to have a higher overhead (both in terms of bandwidth consumed and client-side/server-side processing) than using an array of objects or other data structures. Thus, it is recommended to use native ActionScript data structures whenever possible.

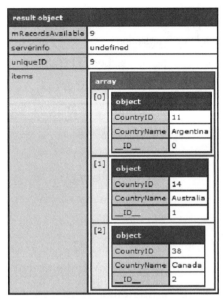

FIGURE 14.15 A visual representation of the Flash `RecordSet` object.

Table 14.1 lists Flash Remoting data translation from ActionScript to Cold Fusion:

TABLE 14.1 ActionScript-to-Cold-Fusion Data Translation

ACTIONSCRIPT DATATYPE	COLD FUSION DATATYPE
Number	Number
Boolean	Boolean
String	String
Ordered array	Array
Named array	Structure
Array of Objects	Array of structures
Date	Date
Ordinary object	CFC arguments structures
XML object	XML document

Table 14.2 lists Flash Remoting data translation from ActionScript to Java.

TABLE 14.2   ActionScript-to-Java Data Translation

ACTIONSCRIPT DATATYPE	JAVA DATATYPE
Number	Number
Boolean	Boolean
String	String
Ordered array	Array
Named array	Object
Array of objects	Array of objects
Date	Date
Ordinary object	Object
XML object	XML document object

Table 14.3 lists Flash Remoting data translation from ActionScript to .NET.

TABLE 14.3   ActionScript-to-.NET Data Translation

ACTIONSCRIPT DATATYPE	COLD FUSION DATATYPE
Number	Number
Boolean	Boolean
String	String
Ordered array	Array
Named array	Object
Array of objects	Array of objects
Date	Date
Ordinary object	Object
XML object	XML document object

Handling Flash Remoting Errors

The onStatus event is called whenever a server-side error is thrown. It is a good idea to always build an onStatus event, attached to the responder object, to catch any errors that may be thrown by the server, as shown in the following code:

```
myResponder.onStatus = function (statusObject){
//code to handle errors
}
```

The `statusObject` returned by Flash Remoting in the event of a server-side error contains these properties that describe the exact error:

- `level`
- `description`
- `code`
- `details`

The following code will loop through the returned `status` object and populate a text field with the string "Connecting to Server Error" so that the user knows something went wrong:

```
myResponder.onStatus = function (statusObject) {

for (var i:String in statusObject){
trace (i + "-" + statusObject[i]);

}
```

Summary

Flash MX 2004 provides multiple ways of creating a client-side data tier, which effectively enables us to manage data in the Flash Player. This changes the whole development dynamic because you can now manage data much like a client/server system and offload some server-side processing to the client. Flash MX Professional 2004 provides multiple tools to make this easier for us.

You can use the connector components to connect to Web Services or XML datasources. The connector components are extensible and more datasources will appear soon. One of the advantages of using the connector components is that they integrate well with the new visual data binding functionality in Flash MX Professional 2004. In addition, the connector components save us a lot of time, as compared to using the regular Web Services object or the XML object. For example, the XML connector automatically will convert an XML document into a native Flash object using a data schema, which means you don't have to build multiple loops to traverse through the XML tree.

If bandwidth is a concern or Web Services are not an option, Flash Remoting is an excellent alternative. At the current time, there is no Flash Remoting Connector component, but Macromedia plans to release one by the time this book is published. Flash Remoting enables you to call methods directly on the server through the creation of a client-side proxy object. The AMF protocol is used to send and receive data and this is a lot more compact than the textual data sent by Web Services and XML.

Whether you decide to use a connector component or Flash Remoting, you have to deal with the results returned from the server. The first step is to set up a `result` event for the connectors or to write an `onResult` event for Flash Remoting. The next step is to either connect the results of the connector/ Remoting call to a dataset or directly to a UI component.

By connecting the results to a dataset, Flash provides a developer-friendly interface for handling data. The dataset implements a data cursor metaphor, which can be connected to a UI component. This cursor can be linked to a visual components `selectedIndex`, making data management trivial because the cursor is moved from record to record whenever the user selects the appropriate index in the dataset. The developer does not have to worry about tracking the data or implementing multiple change events.

Whenever a user makes a change to a dataset, this is captured as a delta packet and you can use a resolver to pick up this information. The resolver will send the update packet to the appropriate server-side method to process it.

The tools provided by Flash MX 2004 Professional make creating complex, sophisticated Internet applications a reality.

CHAPTER 15

FLASH COMMUNICATION SERVER MX APPLICATIONS

I guess you thought you knew everything that Macromedia Flash MX 2004 has to offer. You've learned about ActionScript 2.0, building and extending classes, consuming Web Services, interacting with remote servers using Remoting, and building powerful reuseable user interface (UI) components. What's next?

Flash is a complex machine that offers a lot of opportunities. Understanding all that it can do gives you a powerful weapon for delivering business, e-learning, and entertainment solutions. You can now handle data more efficiently and connect to almost anything. The only problem is Hypertext Transfer Protocol (HTTP); it just keeps hanging up, just when the party gets started.

Enter the server component of Flash Player 7: Flash Communication Server MX. Flash Communication Server MX offers an always-connected solution for Flash applications and an instant-on solution for stream applications. This persistent communication is the next piece to your powerful Flash puzzle.

This chapter introduces you to sharing data, streaming data, and connecting Flash players together for a powerful collaborative experience.

Understanding the Flash Communication Server MX

Flash Communication Server MX is a powerful streaming solution for live and pre-recorded video and audio. However, its real power is in data management and messaging.

It's Not Just a Lean, Mean Streaming Machine

The first thing people consider when they hear "Flash Communication Server MX" is its ability to stream video and MP3 audio. It's true; Flash Communication Server MX makes the Flash Player the most widely distributed streaming-media player on the planet. It beats out Real Media, Apple QuickTime, and Windows Media Player. With the upgraded video codecs inside Flash Player 7, the story will get even better.

Flash MX 2004 and Flash Player 7 introduced the ability to play *Flash Video (FLV)* dynamically through a progressive download. This method uses the HTTP protocol, and while it is effective, there are advantages to the management and control of video streaming over a persistent connection. Streaming supports bandwidth negotiation, a variable bit rate, messaging, recording, and the best feature of all—using the Flash Player as a video transmitter. These features are available only with Flash Communication Server MX.

Note that video streaming is not what this chapter is about; if you are looking for a good primer, check out the definitive book on the topic: *Macromedia Flash Communication Server MX*. It was written by Kevin Towes and published by Macromedia Press.

It's About Sharing (and a Little Streaming)

Flash Communication Server MX has a powerful communication programming architecture called *SharedObject*. *Local SharedObjects (LSO)* can store persistent information on a client's hard disk. The *Remote SharedObject (RSO)* can store information on the server's hard disk and allow other connected users to access and change it. Data is always synchronized, and it can be as open or locked down as you need it to be. The best feature of the SharedObject is that, like Flash Remoting, you don't need to worry about transforming your ActionScript data and messaging objects to transport between the Flash Player 7 and the Flash Communication Server MX. All ActionScript remains in its native format!

Messaging is another key element to sharing data and creating collaborative experiences. A Flash Player connected to a SharedObject can broadcast messages to the server or other Flash Players. Messaging also provides the opportunity to call ActionScript functions remotely. For example: A Flash application can invoke functions that are defined on a remote server, similar to *Flash Remoting*. What is different is that the same Flash application can call functions defined in other remotely connected Flash applications. If that weren't enough, Flash Communication Server MX can also remotely call functions on any Flash Player or server connected to it.

Streaming will be touched on in this discussion, but not in a way you might imagine. In the spirit of this book, you will be introduced to recording a data stream using a technique of streaming and messaging. It's a great tool for creating log files or recording closed captioning, presentations, or anything else to add that live element.

NOTE

After all, it isn't like we're talking through tin cans any more; things do progress.

For What Is Flash Communication Server MX Used?

When Flash Communication Server MX was first introduced, developers had a tough time really understanding the power they were just given. Flash Communication Server MX is not only a new technology, but also a new way of thinking about Internet applications.

Flash Communication Server MX takes care of all the communication plumbing, and Flash provides a great development environment for the designer and developer. Let's look at some applications for which Flash Communication Server MX is being used:

- **Online gaming.** Multiplayer games using Flash Communication Server MX have become a hit among game developers. Because Flash Communication Server MX applications use the Flash Player, gamers don't have to download custom Java applications that eat away at a system's resources. Flash Communication Server MX games load fast, are visually rich, and are entertaining. Ohayo players (`faces.bascule.co.jp/ohayo/`) use Flash Communication Server MX and the Camera object's motion sensor abilities to move a player around a virtual forest.

- **Video streaming.** CBC Home Delivery in Canada (`www.CBCHomeDelivery.com`) and SBC Yahoo are using the streaming ability and instant-on functionality that Flash Communication Server MX offers. The video encoder and decoder in Flash Player 7 has increased the quality and stability of video playback to astonishing new levels. Video support in the Flash Player is only in its second version; already, it is proving a serious competitor to traditional online streaming clients.

- **Online collaboration and instant messaging.** Providing online presentations, online meetings, and instant live support, and connecting users directly with other users—these are some of the ways Flash Communication Server MX facilitates online collaboration. Macromedia Breeze Live is a product that leverages Flash Communication Server MX data sharing and collaborative environment. DateCam (`www.datecam.com`) uses these features for online dating. A user can record a video message and make it available to potential suitors.

- **The possibilities of e-learning.** Online learning is growing in popularity. More and more courses are delivered online each year. Flash Communication Server MX is playing a key role in some learning institutions for delivering online training from key experts in the field. For instance, Hong Kong Baptist University used Flash Communication Server MX to create a live virtual classroom when Hong Kong was struck with the SARS outbreak in early 2003.

Macromedia has a listing of companies that are building unique solutions using Flash Communication Server MX. For more ideas on how Flash Communication Server MX is used, check out `www.macromedia.com/software/flashcom/special/inspiration/`.

How Does Flash Communication Server MX Work?

Flash Communication Server MX maintains a *persistent connection* between the client and the server. Unlike HTTP, which is connected only when a request is made, Flash Communication Server MX is continually connected after a connection is established. Flash Communication Server MX works because of its unique connectivity, its streaming ability, and its powerful programming model, ActionScript.

Connectivity

Flash Communication Server MX operates like a hub that facilitates connections. Flash Players connect to the Flash Communication Server MX hub using a special always-on communication protocol called *Real-Time Messaging Protocol (RTMP)*. Just like a network hub, Flash Communication Server MX can connect to other communication server hubs to increase user and bandwidth capacity in licensing and hardware.

Flash Communication Server MX can also connect to J2EE, Web Services, and ASP.NET application servers to extend applications with database connectivity and other server resources using Flash Remoting. Examples of this connectivity are sending an email or authenticating connections using a Lightweight Directory Access Protocol (LDAP) server.

Streaming

Flash Communication Server MX's unique instant-on approach lets you instantly stream video or sound to or from your website with no additional plug-ins or downloads for your user. Flash Player 7 does support a "progressive streaming" solution for video without using Flash Communication Server MX; however, this solution has limits. When connected to Flash Communication Server MX, you can create play lists, have more control over the playback with specific starting points and duration parameters, and have options to mute the audio or video tracks to conserve bandwidth. Flash Communication Server MX will also let you send or receive live video or audio, and it provides the options for recording streams.

Programming

Flash Communication Server MX has a powerful programming model called Remote `SharedObjects`. `SharedObjects` synchronizes complex data and supports sending one-way messages between other Flash Players connected to the server.

Regular ActionScript objects are transported across network connections using the *Action Message Format (AMF)*. This format is used over a nonpersistent HTTP or secure HTTP (HTTPS) connection when exchanging data with application servers. The format is also used over the persistent RTMP when exchanging communication data between the Flash Player and the server. AMF is a binary format that is handled transparently by the server and Flash Player.

Developing Flash Communication Server MX Applications in Flash

Flash MX Professional 2004 is the complete authoring environment for developing applications that communicate with Flash Communication Server MX. You must download and install the *Flash Communication Server MX 2004 authoring components* from Macromedia.com to begin creating *communication applications*. After they are installed, Flash will be outfitted with a new Communications component Library, additional ActionScript objects, and some tools to help you develop your application.

The Integrated ActionScript window built into Flash MX Professional 2004 improves the efficiency of developing communication applications from previous versions of Flash. Figure 15.1 shows the new panel configuration for creating ServerSide ActionScript (SSAS). Flash MX Professional 2004 is the only authoring environment needed to develop communication applications because SSAS can be developed directly within Flash. This lets you easily switch between your Flash document and your SSAS.

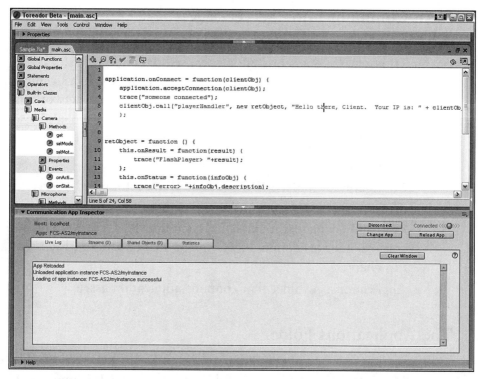

FIGURE 15.1   The authoring environment setup for developing SSAS.

Flash movies traditionally use SWF files and Hypertext Markup Language
(HTML) container files to deliver an application by means of a web browser.
Flash movies that use Flash Communication Server MX have significantly more
pieces working together to develop and deliver the application, including the
following:

- Flash Communication Server MX
- Applications folder
- Flash video and MP3 sound files
- ActionScript (Flash and server-side)
- Debugging tools
- An HTML container file
- A web server

Let's look at these seven key pieces in more detail to understand how they all
come together.

Flash Communication Server MX

Flash Communication Server MX is a server usually installed on a dedicated machine running Windows or Linux. It is used to connect Flash Players and other servers running Flash Communication Server MX. Flash Communication Server MX facilitates persistent communications over an IP network using a dedicated port number (the default port is 1935). When installed, Flash Communication Server MX creates folders on the server for the following:

- **Server files:** The core server service.
- **Configuration folders:** XML files used to customize the server and to manage server resources and connections.
- **Help and debugging tools:** HTML support files, the Administration console, and the Communication App Inspector tool (discussed later in this chapter).
- **Applications:** A folder that contains application assets.

The Applications Folder

An application that uses Flash Communication Server MX is defined by creating a folder within the applications folder on the server. It is important to know where your folder, `flashcom\applications`, is located because that is where you will set up applications and store its assets (video, MP3, and SSAS). If you installed Flash Communication Server MX on a Windows machine with a web server previously installed, its default install folder is as follows and is shown in Figure 15.2:

`C:\inetpub\wwwroot\flashcom\applications\`

FIGURE 15.2   The directory path showing a single application folder ready for use with Flash Communication Server MX.

If you installed Flash Communication Server MX without a web server installed or installed the Developer edition, the applications folder will be placed as shown in the following code:

```
C:\program files\macromedia\flash communication server
mx\flashcom\applications\
```

A communication application will be defined after a folder with the name of your application is placed within the applications folder.

If you use SSAS, this folder will contain the SSAS stored within a file called `main.asc`. The folder will also store streams and Remote `SharedObjects` that are persistent.

Flash Video and MP3 Sound Assets

FLV files and MP3 sound files that are streamed using Flash Communication Server MX are stored within the application folder. You can use Flash MX Professional 2004 to convert many popular digital video formats, including Windows Media (AVI and WMV), QuickTime (MOV), or Digital Video (DV), into the FLV format.

Any MP3 file can be streamed from Flash Communication Server MX. Song information such as artist, song name, and album title embedded within MP3 files can be accessed and displayed to the user. MP3 files are prerecorded and cannot be created from a live source.

FLV files can also be created from a live video source using Flash Communication Server MX or Sorenson Squeeze, a third-party tool developed by Sorenson Media (`www.sorenson.com`).

These media files are stored within a streams folder of the application. You must create the streams folder, plus a folder for each instance of the application. Application instances will be discussed later in this chapter. Figure 15.3 shows a typical directory structure that contains a streams folder for an application called "FCS-AS2."

Flash Communication Server MX also supports *virtual folders* that can be used to map streams folders available across all applications. Virtual folders are defined in the vHost.xml file located in the conf folder in your Flash Communication Server MX install folder.

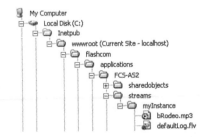

FIGURE 15.3   The directory path showing a streams folder for
the instance `myInstance` within the application "FCS-AS2."

ActionScript

Flash Communication Server MX applications are built using Flash MX and
therefore ActionScript 2.0 is used as the programming model. ActionScript is
used in two places when developing communication applications:

- On the Flash Player (ActionScript 2.0)
- On the server (SSAS 1.0)

SSAS is used to control and manage server connections and connected Flash
Players. It exists in a file called main.asc located within the application folder.
When the authoring components for Flash Communication Server MX are
installed into Flash MX Professional 2004, some ActionScript 2.0 objects definitions will be extended. These extensions will provide code hinting and support for Flash Communication Server MX-specific operations in SSAS and
Flash ActionScript 2.0.

Debugging Tools

There are two tools that are installed with Flash Communication Server MX:
the Communication App Inspector and the Communication Admin Console.
These tools let you interact with the server's operation and monitor activity
across all applications.

Here are the debugging options available in Flash MX Professional 2004 for
building applications that use Flash Communication Server MX:

- **Communication App Inspector.** Used to load and reload application
  instances after SSAS changes have been made. The tool also acts as a
  server output (trace) window, and it lets you monitor streams, messages,
  and other application-specific information.

- **Communication Admin Console.** This console lets you manage the server operation, including user accounts and licensing.
- **NetConnection Debugger.** This tool is installed with the Flash Remoting components. The debugger monitors AMF activity, which is the format used by Flash Remoting over HTTP. You can also monitor Flash Communication Server MX over RTMP.
- **Flash Output window.** This is probably the best tool to help you debug applications—Flash Communication Server MX or otherwise. This window is used in conjunction with the trace action.
- **Flash Interactive Debugger.** This lets you place watches and monitor the values of complex ActionScript objects and Remote `SharedObjects`.

HTML Container Files and Web Server

Communication applications that use Flash Communication Server MX and Flash can be delivered in two ways:

- **Delivered as a stand-alone executable file sent by email or published onto CD-ROM.** In this scenario, the Flash Player is build into the executable file with the application.
- **Delivered over the Internet using any typical web server.** In this scenario, the application is delivered as an SWF movie and played within the embedded Flash Player installed on the client.

Flash Communication Server MX does not require a web server (such as Apache or Windows Internet Information Services [IIS]) to operate. The web server provides the transport protocol used to deliver the application. It is your option to use either the web server or the executable file to deliver the application. Web servers are not used in any Flash Communication Server MX communication methods.

ActionScript and the Programming Model

ActionScript is the driving force behind Flash Communication Server MX. The prebuilt ActionScript classes and SSAS objects offer an excellent event-based model. It is a model that lets you quickly develop, test, and deploy communication applications. Flash Communication Server MX is one great big class hierarchy. From the server, to the application, and right down to the user—everything about the server is object-oriented programming (OOP) and good.

Let's take a look at what makes Flash Communication Server MX tick, specifically some of the key elements that make up the server:

- Persistent connection
- Flash Communication ActionScript objects
- SSAS
- Streaming
- Remote `SharedObjects`
- Information objects
- Messaging
- The Flash Communication Server MX component framework

Let's look at these elements in detail.

Persistent Connection

RTMP was developed by Macromedia specifically for Flash Communication Server MX applications. It's a persistent communication method that's responsible for transporting AMF packets between client and server. AMF is the same format used in Flash Remoting. The key difference is that RTMP has no disconnection, which gives the developer an opportunity to push data to the client whenever required.

RTMP can operate over any port on your system, including port 80, usually reserved for HTTP-based web servers. As a default, Flash Communication Server MX is set to communicate using ports 1935 (public access) and 1111 (administrator access). Flash Communication Server MX and HTTP *can* interoperate on port 80 using a tunneling technique, but it is strongly recommended that a different interface be used to operate Flash Communication Server MX on port 80.

It takes only two lines of ActionScript to connect to Flash Communication Server MX. One creates an instance of the NetConnection class, and one connects the instance to the server:

```
var my_nc:NetConnection = new NetConnection();
my_nc.connect("rtmp://localhost/myApp/myInstance");
```

You can make this code as dynamic and complex as you need to. Note that in ActionScript 2.0, Macromedia reengineered the NetConnection object into an ActionScript 2.0 class. This upgrade permits a progressive download used strictly to play FLV files without Flash Communication Server MX.

Flash Communication ActionScript Objects

When Flash Communication Server MX was first introduced, it made available a series of new programmable ActionScript objects within the Flash MX authoring environment. These ActionScript objects enabled you to access and control camera and microphone devices, let you persist data on a user's computer, and let you stream pre-recorded video; best of all, these new objects let you code a connection between the Flash Player and Flash Communication Server MX.

Flash MX Professional 2004 has upgraded versions of the original Flash communication ActionScript objects. They have been re-written as ActionScript 2.0 classes with significant performance improvements. These specific ActionScript communication objects include:

- **NetConnection.** This object controls the persistent connection between Flash Player 7 and the Flash Communication Server. It is a multi-direction communication channel.

- **NetStream.** This object manages live and pre-recorded video and audio streams. It manages publishing live streams from the Flash Player to Flash Communication Server MX. It also handles messaging over the stream to and from Flash Communication Server MX and other Flash Players.

- **SharedObject.** This object manages persistent and temporary ActionScript objects on the Flash Communication Server. The ActionScript object doubles its duty by also handling local SharedObjects.

- **Camera.** This object controls the video digitizing engine in Flash Player 7. Quality and video source are managed by referencing this object.

- **Microphone.** This object, like the Camera object, controls the audio digitizing engine in Flash Player 7. Quality and microphone source are managed by referencing this object.

SSAS

SSAS is the scripting language of Flash Communication Server MX. It offers the developer the opportunity to call methods and properties and to handle specific events related to communication applications.

SSAS, like Flash ActionScript, is a derivative of the ECMA Script-262 specification. It also is an invocation of ServerSide JavaScript (SSJS) used in Netscape's Enterprise server.

SSAS contains most of the core Flash ActionScript objects. It contains no movie-oriented objects. SSAS can be developed within Flash using the Integrated ActionScript window. Like ActionScript 2.0, SSAS is case-sensitive. All scripting is done inside or loaded into the file main.asc.

The main.asc file is the class for the application. An application runs from an instance of the main.asc file. When SSAS is modified, each instance of the application must be reloaded for the change to take effect.

Application instances are completely independent of each other. They cannot share data or streams between them without a crossover proxy connection. This operation ensures the security of communication within the instance.

There are five key SSAS objects available to developers. They are: `Application`, `Client`, `NetConnection`, `Stream`, and `SharedObject`.

`Application` and `Client` objects are unique to SSAS. The SSAS objects, `NetConnection`, `Stream`, and `SharedObject`, share similar qualities to the Flash ActionScript counterpart, with some variation on invocation.

The `Application` SSAS object is built on four key system events. These events are invoked at four different times. The first is when the application is started (instantiated). The second is when a connection is requested (client is instantiated). The third is when the client disconnects (instance is destroyed). The last is when the application is stopped or shut down (application instance is destroyed). These events are the foundation for all Flash Communication Server MX-to-client communications.

A simple example of an application event developed using SSAS is as follows:

```
application.onConnect = function(my_client, args) {
        application.acceptConnection(my_client)
        trace(args);
        /* Some SSAS Statements */
}
```

The `Client` SSAS object is used to manage the communication between a single client and Flash Communication Server MX. The object is uniquely instanced each time a client makes a connection request. It is destroyed when the client is disconnected or rejected by the server. New functions defined within the `Client` object instance can be called by the remote client with a procedure called messaging. This process is used to call server functionality from the client, or client functionality from the server. The `Client` object also stores information about the connection, including bytes sent and received and connection speed.

The `NetConnection` SSAS object is similar to the Flash ActionScript object. In SSAS, it is used to proxy, or chain, servers together to redistribute data or streams. This process increases the hardware and licensing capacity of Flash Communication Server MX.

The `SharedObject` and `Stream` SSAS objects are very similar to their Flash ActionScript counterpart. A SSAS `SharedObject` makes reference to a persistent or temporary Remote `SharedObject` on the local server or on another server through a proxy connection. The `Stream` SSAS object is like the Flash ActionScript object, `NetStream`. Although there are some key differences to the way methods are used, the object is fundamentally the same as its Flash ActionScript counterpart.

SSAS can also interact with databases using Flash Remoting. The syntax for Flash Remoting in SSAS is exactly the same as you would use in Flash ActionScript. For more information on Flash Remoting, search for "Flash Remoting" at www.macromedia.com.

Streaming

Flash Communication Server MX has become known as a powerful streaming engine. With the Flash Player having such a large install base, it becomes a great option for companies to stream live and pre-recorded video and audio.

To stream a prerecorded video or MP3 from Flash Communication Server MX, you need only place the FLV or MP3 file on the server, and then place these ActionScript 2.0 statements in your Actions panel:

```
var my_ns:NetStream = new NetStream(NetConnection_nc);
my_ns.play("myStream");

/* Attach the stream to a video object */
my_video.attachVideo(my_ns);
```

The first statement creates an instance object of the NetStream class and the second commands the instance to start playing a prerecorded video stream called myStream.flv. The NetStream class has been reengineered from the ActionScript 1.0 NetStream object. It is 100 percent backward-compatible with Flash Player 6; however, when used with Flash Player 7, it supports progressive HTTP download for the FLV format.

Remote *SharedObjects*

You can use the local SharedObject to store persistent ActionScript objects and data on a user's hard disk. The RSO programming model lets you store the same ActionScript objects on a remote server. If that wasn't exciting enough, these ActionScript objects can be shared between other remote Flash Players.

The basic ActionScript to connect with an RSO is also no more than these two statements:

```
var my_so:SharedObject = SharedObject.getRemote("clientSO", my_nc.uri,
true);
my_so.connect(my_nc);
```

The first statement instances the SharedObject class into a local variable. This is a key statement that identifies what RSO to connect to and where it is. The statement also identifies the persistence of the RSO. The second statement establishes the connection to the (already connected) NetConnection.

Writing data to a Remote SharedObject is simple. SharedObjects store your ActionScript 2.0 objects as a *slot* within the data property. Here's a sample statement that stores an array in a Remote SharedObject:

```
my_so.data["slotName"] = easy_array;
```

Reading data from a Remote SharedObject is equally as simple:

```
var myLocal_array:array = my_so.data["easy_array"];
trace("the value of element 0 is: " + myLocal_array[0]);
```

Figure 15.4 shows the structure of the Remote SharedObject. Notice how it stores the easy_array and product_array as slots within the data property. See Figure 15.5.

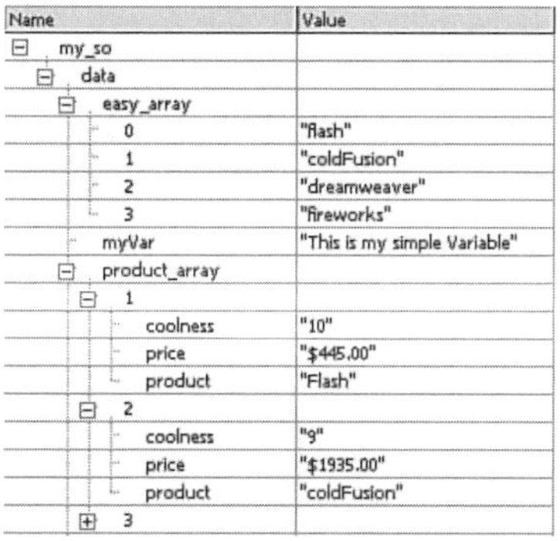

Name	Value
⊟ my_so	
⊟ data	
⊟ easy_array	
0	"flash"
1	"coldFusion"
2	"dreamweaver"
3	"fireworks"
myVar	"This is my simple Variable"
⊟ product_array	
⊟ 1	
coolness	"10"
price	"$445.00"
product	"Flash"
⊟ 2	
coolness	"9"
price	"$1935.00"
product	"coldFusion"
⊞ 3	

FIGURE 15.4   Slots can contain ActionScript objects such as Arrays and Arrays of Objects.

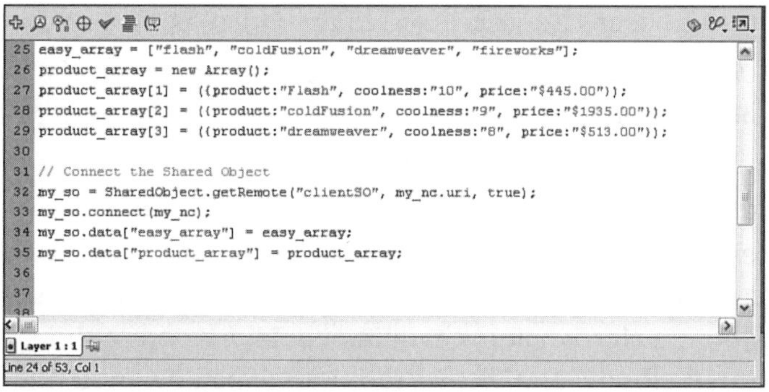

```
25 easy_array = ["flash", "coldFusion", "dreamweaver", "fireworks"];
26 product_array = new Array();
27 product_array[1] = ({product:"Flash", coolness:"10", price:"$445.00"});
28 product_array[2] = ({product:"coldFusion", coolness:"9", price:"$1935.00"});
29 product_array[3] = ({product:"dreamweaver", coolness:"8", price:"$513.00"});
30
31 // Connect the Shared Object
32 my_so = SharedObject.getRemote("clientSO", my_nc.uri, true);
33 my_so.connect(my_nc);
34 my_so.data["easy_array"] = easy_array;
35 my_so.data["product_array"] = product_array;
36
37
38
```

Layer 1 : 1

Line 24 of 53, Col 1

FIGURE 15.5   The SharedObject structure seen in Figure 15.4 is created with this ActionScript.

The real power of RSO is the synchronization engine. Flash Communication Server MX monitors every slot in the `SharedObject` and pushes messages to every client connected to the RSO. It will even inform the client changing the data if the change was successful.

For example, if any value in `easy_array` (see Figure 15.5) is changed or removed, Flash Communication Server MX sends a message that informs all clients to update their reference to the array. The structure development of slots is important to ensure that a conservative approach to data transfer is achieved.

Information Objects

Information objects contain messages for ActionScript that detail status changes or errors occurring with specific object instances. They are as follows:

- **NetConnection.** Information objects inform the player of the connection status and any errors with the connection or messages traveling over the connection. For example, when an information object is returned with a connection error, you could script a reconnect attempt or do something in the UI.

- **NetStream.** This informs the client on the status of streaming objects being played from Flash Communication Server MX or published to Flash Communication Server MX. This is an important object to monitor to ensure the user can see the video as it should be.

- **Camera and Microphone.** These objects inform the player if the user has muted (denied access to) the device. The user can do this by using the Flash Player context menu.

- **SharedObjects.** These have two types of information objects. The status object returns information about the connection and message status of the object. The sync object contains detailed information about a slot when it changes. The sync object should always be monitored closely, and ActionScript statements handle the sync notifications.

Information objects are ActionScript objects with a collection of no more than four properties. Important properties include code and description. Most objects are returned to the onStatus event of the specific instance.

The synchronization objects used in RSOs are returned as an Array of Objects. A single information object can contain change notifications about multiple slots. This is usually the case when a client reconnects to the object and an initial resync takes place.

Messaging

Messaging is another key function of Flash Communication Server MX. Because Flash Player can share a stream or RSO, ActionScript can also send messages to invoke special *handlers* listening on the stream. Because the Flash player and Flash Communication Server MX share an intimate connection, either end can call a remote function and have an ActionScript object returned. There are two methods of messaging within Flash Communication Server MX: a broadcast send or a private, asynchronous call.

Broadcast Send

A broadcast send lets a Flash Player or the Flash Communication Server MX call a function handler on other Flash Players or Flash Communication Server MX. It is a one-way blast to every client that is listening.

Broadcasting messages are sent over a NetStream instance or a Remote SharedObject, each using the send() method. In the case of NetStream, only Flash Communication Server MX or the publishing Player can send a message. Only clients that are subscribed to (playing) the stream can receive the message.

A simple broadcast send might look like this in Flash ActionScript 2.0:

```
publish_ns.publish("someLiveStream", "record");
publish_ns.send("remoteFunction", "A message or AS object");
```

The NetStream handler on Flash Players subscribing to the stream would look like this:

```
play_ns.play("someLiveStream");

play_ns.remoteFunction = function(args) {
     // Some ActionScript statement…
}
```

Asynchronous Call

Asynchronous call is a private messaging channel between Flash Communication Server MX and the client. It operates very much like Flash Remoting. It is asynchronous because it will respond back to the caller; however, it won't happen instantaneously, as when calling a local function. Network congestion and transport slow the operation from returning objects back to the caller.

There are two key differences between this method and the broadcast send: asynchronous is two-way messaging and it is private between the client and the server.

A simple asynchronous call from the Flash Player to the server would look like this:

```
my_nc.call("serverFunction", new resultObject, "A message or object");
```

The call sends the objects returned in the call back to a new instance of the resultObject. This is a custom constructor with an onResult event handler. The onResult event handler will be called when the server responds, like so:

```
resultObject = function() {
        this.onResult= function(retObject) {
                /* ActionScript Statement handling the callback */
        }
}
```

The server handler extends the Client SSAS object. This way, each time a new connection is received, a Client instance is automatically created with this event handler:

```
Client.prototype.serverFunction = function(args) {
        /* Some SSAS statements */
        return "hello from the server, your IP is: " + this.ip;
}
```

An asynchronous call occurs between the NetConnection instance (on the client) and the Client instance (on Flash Communication Server MX).

Flash Communication Server MX Component Framework

Macromedia did not leave Flash Communication Server MX developers alone without giving them a collection of visual UI components specifically for use with Flash Communication Server MX. The UI component set includes basic components for connecting the Flash player to Flash Communication Server MX. It also contains a simple chat component, a video conferencing component, a synchronized presentation component, and a video playback. Figure 15.6 shows the full Library of prebuilt communication components available.

FIGURE 15.6   The Flash UI components offer a quick way to get up and running with Flash Communication Server MX.

The most interesting part of these components, from an ActionScript perspective, is that they deploy an ActionScript framework both in SSAS and in Flash ActionScript. This is very useful for both extending the prebuilt components and building your own.

OOP Nature of Flash Communication Server MX

Flash Communication Server MX will prove to be a very familiar development environment to you. The server itself takes an object-oriented approach. As noted earlier, Flash Communication Server MX applications are a class. The SSAS (main.asc) defines the application methods, properties, and events.

When using a Flash Communication Server MX application, the application class is instantiated. Each instance of the application is a unique entity on the server. An instance runs completely separate from other instances of the same application.

Here is some ActionScript that invokes an application instance called `myInstance`:

```
my_nc:NetConnection = new NetConnection();
my_nc.connect("rtmp://notReal.macromedia.com/myApp/myInstance");
```

Client Object

Application instances handle client connection requests. Each connection is an instance of the `Client` object. The `Client` object also supports a series of prebuilt methods, properties, and events. The `Client` object monitors everything about a specific client. When the instance is created, some properties that are recorded include IP address, client agent, read/write permissions, and bandwidth information. As the client starts communicating with the server, additional statistics on communication events are also recorded. Information types include byte counts, message counts, streaming info, and tunneling information.

You can extend the `Client` object class with additional functionality, properties, or listeners. `Client` instances are linked with the `NetConnection` instance declared in the Flash Player. Messages can be sent between the `NetConnection` instance (on the Flash Player) and the `Client` instance (on Flash Communication Server MX).

The same connect statement also invokes a `Client` object instance on the server. It is handled by the `application.onConnect` event.

Remote *SharedObject*

The Remote `SharedObject` supplies Flash Communication Server MX applications with a method to share, store, and synchronize information.

We know that to create a `SharedObject` in Flash after the `NetConnection` has been established, you use the following ActionScript code:

```
var my_so:SharedObject = SharedObject.getRemote("clientSO", my_nc.uri,
true);
my_so.connect(my_nc);
```

This function will create a persistent `SharedObject` if one doesn't already exist.

If there were a text input instance on the Stage called my_txt, you could send the value of that text object to the RSO with a simple event like this:

```
my_txt.onChanged = function() {
      my_so.data["my_txt"] = my_txt.text;
}
```

This would create a slot called my_txt in the data property of the RSO.

Now every Flash Player connected to that SharedObject would have access to that value. What if you changed the value? The event would rewrite it to the RSO with no problem. However, by using the onSync event of the RSO, you can inform all Flash Players that the slot has been updated. Each Flash Player would then update the text objects on their Stage.

In the following step sequence, you discover the Remote SharedObject synchronization event. As you will discover, onSync is a very powerful feature of Flash Communication Server MX applications. Figure 15.7 shows the completed application running twice.

NOTE

Before you begin this exercise, make sure you have installed the Flash Communication Server MX authoring components for Flash MX Professional 2004. You can download the free installer at www.macromedia.com.

FIGURE 15.7   Two stand-alone Flash Players running the application twice. One application can speak to another.

1. Create the application folder. In Windows Explorer, create a folder in the flashcom\application folder (described earlier in this chapter) called FCS-AS2.

2. In Flash, create a new Flash document, and save it as RSOTest.fla in the folder you just created.

3. On the Flash Stage, place one input text box above one dynamic text box. In the Properties panel of the input text box, set the instance name to my_txt and the dynamic text box to your_txt. (Remember that you can access the Properties panel for Flash symbols by selecting the object on the Stage.)

4. Connect the Flash Player to the Flash Communication Server MX instance of the application FCS-AS2. Open the Actions Panel (F9) and enter the following ActionScript code:

```
var my_nc:NetConnection = new NetConnection();
 connectionLight_mc.connect(my_nc);
my_nc.connect("rtmp://localhost/FCS-AS2/myInstance");
```

5. Connect the Remote SharedObject by using the following code:

```
var my_so:SharedObject.getRemote("clientSO", my_nc.uri, true);
 my_so.connect(my_nc);
```

6. Overwrite the onChanged event for the input text object, which is my_text. Store the changed data into the SharedObject.

```
my_txt.onChanged = function() {
     my_so.data["my_txt"] = my_txt.text;
};
```

7. Overwrite the onSync handler for the SharedObject instance. When this event is called, it receives an information object, which is an Array of Objects describing what the change is. This object *does not* contain the data that was changed; it contains at least two properties: code and name. The code property has five possible values: success, change, reject, clear, and delete. To keep it simple, we will monitor only for a value of change. The name property will contain the slot that was affected.

```
my_so.onSync = function(infoObj) {
     for (item in infoObj) {
  var code:String = infoObj[item].code;
  var name:String = infoObj[item].name;
             trace("Code: " +code);
             //
             switch (code) {
                  case "success":
                  trace("your change was made successfully");
                  break;
                  case "change":
                  your_txt.text = my_so.data[name];
                  break;
             default :
```

```
            }
        }
};
```

8. The information object is an Array of Objects so that Flash Communication Server MX can send multiple sync notifications at once. For example, after testing this application, shut down the SWF files and load them again. You will notice the last value of the slot appears in the bottom text box.

9. For this demonstration, understand that if a Flash Player makes a change, it will receive a `code` value of `success`. If the Flash Player did not make the change, it will receive a value of `change`.

10. Save your application, and publish your movie.

11. Open two instances of the file RSOTest.swf and enter text into the input boxes (on top). Notice that when you type, the changes are reflected on the other Flash Player. To further test this example, try opening more then two instances of the RSOTest.swf movie.

Editions and Licensing

Flash Communication Server MX is available in three different editions. Each edition offers no limitation in basic functionality; however, the Professional Edition offers some additional features for deploying multiple high-volume applications on a single server.

Editions are defined specifically by their bandwidth and simultaneous connection ceilings (or limits). We discuss each in turn.

The Developer Edition

The Developer Edition is a great way to get started with communication applications. It's a free download from www.macromedia.com. Here are the highlights and limitations of this edition:

- Used for learning Flash Communication Server MX
- Used for authoring communication applications
- Has no functionality limits
- Can be "chained together" to increase ceilings

- Should not be used to deploy real-world communication applications
- Cannot accept Capacity Packs

The Personal Edition

The Personal Edition has the following benefits and limitations:

- Can be used with medium-volume applications
- Can be used with limited-bandwidth users
- Can be used with streaming audio and sound (you will run out of bandwidth in streaming solutions without optimizing your media)
- Up to five additional Personal or Professional Edition licenses can be added to increase capacity
- Can be "chained together" to increase ceilings
- Does not accept Capacity Packs

The Professional Edition

The Professional Edition can be used with or by the following:

- High-volume applications
- Applications using a large number of simultaneous users
- Applications using a large streaming requirement
- Application Service Providers (ASP) who plan to offer services to developers
- Up to five additional Personal or Professional Edition licenses to increase capacity
- Chaining to increase ceilings

Unlimited Capacity Packs

Capacity Packs let you temporarily upgrade a Professional Edition to remove all bandwidth and user ceilings. They are available for a 90-day period from the point of install. These are great for short-term events such as corporate sales events, general meetings, or live entertainment events.

Supported Server Environments

Flash Communication Server MX can be installed on any Windows server software (Windows Advanced Server is preferred) or Linux Red Hat 7.3 or 8.0. Using Flash Remoting, Flash Communication Server MX can interact with J2EE servers, such as Macromedia ColdFusion MX, IBM WebSphere, WebObjects, Apache, or Windows servers running .NET.

In the following step sequence, you will use asynchronous messaging combined with broadcast messaging over a stream to record an activity log of a client. The log will be recorded as a Flash video file and then played back. There will be no video in the step sequence, only the messages recorded into the stream. When the recorded log file is played, message handlers are called and they will display the information on the Flash Stage.

Specific topics you will discover in this step sequence include the following:

- Calling functions remotely on the Flash Player from Flash Communication Server MX
- Publishing a stream
- Broadcasting messages over a NetStream
- Playing a prerecorded stream
- Handling messages within a stream
- Playing an MP3 file

SSAS

SSAS has one important responsibility. It calls a remote function on all the Flash Players every two seconds. This call sends an ActionScript object containing all statistics for each client. Figure 15.8 shows a detailed list of all statistics available on each connection. Every two seconds, this object contains new information. This is the information that will be recorded into the Flash video stream. The subsequent step sequence in this chapter will create the SSAS required for this application.

Name	Value
⊟ Client_getStats	
audio_queue_bytes	0
audio_queue_msgs	0
bw_in	0
bw_out	0
bytes_in	78
bytes_out	3411
data_queue_bytes	0
data_queue_msgs	0
dropped_audio_bytes	0
dropped_audio_msgs	0
dropped_video_bytes	0
dropped_video_msgs	0
msg_dropped	0
msg_in	2
msg_out	3
ping_rtt	0
so_queue_bytes	0
so_queue_msgs	0
tunnel_bytes_in	0
tunnel_bytes_out	0
tunnel_idle_requests	0
tunnel_idle_responses	0
tunnel_requests	0
tunnel_responses	0
video_queue_bytes	0
video_queue_msgs	0

FIGURE 15.8   The full listing of statistics available for each connection.

1. In Flash, create a new ActionScript communications file by selecting Select > New. Immediately save this file as **main.asc** in the FCS-AS2 folder, which you created in the first step sequence in this chapter.

2. Create a function that calls the Flash Player. This function will be called by a `setInterval` function when the application starts. The `for` statement loops around the `application.clients` property. This property contains an array of the client instances on the server. On each iteration of the loop, the current client is loaded into a local variable, and is used to return the stats and call the client.

```
doCallClient = function() {
        trace("calling all Clients:::::" + application.clients.length);
        for (index=0; index < application.clients.length; index++) {
            var currentClient = application.clients[index];
            var stats = currentClient.getStats();
            currentClient.call("handleServerCall",
new retObject, stats);
                }
            }
        }
```

Strong Data Typing

You cannot use strong data typing with SSAS variables as you did in Flash ActionScript 2.0.
For example, the following SSAS to set a string variable does not work: `var myVar: String = "something";`. Remember that SSAS is not ActionScript 2.0-compliant. The correct statement in SSAS would be: `var myVar = "something";`.

The `call` statement calls the `handleServerCall` function that will be scripted in ActionScript. That function will return an object back to SSAS and will be handled by a new return object (`retObject`). The ActionScript object, `stats`, will be sent to the client. This object contains all the statistics about the client.

3. Create a return object that handles a call back from the client. The `onResult` function handles the call back, and the `onStatus` function handles any errors.

```
retObject = function () {
    this.onResult = function(result) {
        trace("FlashPlayer> "+result);
    };
    this.onStatus = function(infoObj) {
        trace("error> "+infoObj.description);
        trace("error> "+infoObj.code);
    };
};
```

4. Create the `application.onAppStart` event. This event runs only once per instance of the application. Here it will set an interval to call the function, `doCallClient`, every 2000ms (two seconds).

```
application.onAppStart = function() {
    callClient = setInterval(doCallClient,2000);
}
```

5. Save the main.asc file.

The Flash UI is divided into two sections. The top section controls the publish stream, and the bottom section controls the playback stream, as shown in Figure 15.9.

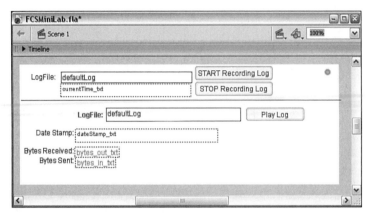

FIGURE 15.9   Use this as a guide to construct our sample application.

In the following step sequence you will create the Flash UI for the exercise. You will use components from the Flash UI Component library installed with Flash MX Professional 2004.

1. Open Flash MX 2004 Professional and create a new Flash Document by selecting File > New > Flash Document. Immediately save the document as FCSMiniLab.fla in the folder FCS-AS2 you created earlier in this chapter. On the Flash Stage, create the upper section of the interface with the elements listed in Table 15.1.

TABLE 15.1   Add These UI Components and Objects to the Flash Stage

FLASH STAGE SYMBOL	PROPERTIES
Two button components	Name(1): startLog_button Label(1): START Recording Log Name(2): stopLog_button Label(2): STOP Recording Log
One connectionLight component	Name: connectionLight_mc
One dynamic text box	Name: currentTime_txt
One input text box	Name: pubName_txt

2. Create the lower section of the interface with the objects in Table 15.2.

TABLE 15.2 Add These UI Components and Objects to the Flash Stage

Flash Stage Symbol	Properties
One button component	Name: `play_button` Label: Play Log
One connectionLight component	Name: `connectionLight_mc`
Three dynamic text boxes	Name: `dateStamp_txt` Name: `bytes_in_txt` Name: `bytes_out_txt`
One input text box	Name: `playName_txt`

3. Create the text labels as shown in Figure 15.9.

The Flash ActionScript connects the Flash Player to Flash Communication Server MX automatically. You will know a connection is successful when the connection light component turns green. In the following step sequence, you will create ActionScript to handle the server calls, publish and record a live stream, and subscribe to the live (and prerecorded) data stream. At the end, ActionScript will start an MP3 stream so that you can monitor data transfer with the server.

1. Connect the Flash Player and instance to the application as `myInstance`:

```
var my_nc:NetConnection = new NetConnection();
connectionLight_mc.connect(my_nc);
my_nc.connect("rtmp://localhost/FCS-AS2/myInstance");
```

2. Start publishing and recording the stream:

```
function doPublishLog() {
  trace("recording Log");
  logOut_ns = new NetStream(my_nc);
  logOut_ns.publish(pubName_txt.text, "record");
}
```

3. Handle the calls from the server. This function will be called every two seconds from Flash Communication Server MX. The `dataObject` it receives will contain the statistics of the connection. In this function, the current date/time will be accessed. The `send` function will send a message over the stream `logout_ns`. The message will contain two arguments, the date and the entire status object received from the server.

```
my_nc.handleServerCall = function(dataObject) {
    trace("received");
    var currentDateTime:Date = new Date();
    logOut_ns.send("onMessage", currentDateTime, dataObject);
    currentTime_txt.text = currentDateTime;
    return "Thanks!";
};
```

When the function completes, it will return a string, thanking the server.

4. Handle the event, startLog_button.onRelease. When the user clicks the startLog button, the event will begin publishing the stream by calling the doPublishLog function.

```
startLog_button.onRelease = function() {
    doPublishLog();
};
```

5. The event stopLog_button.onRelease will stop publishing the stream and close the NetStream connection:

```
stopLog_button.onRelease = function() {
    trace("closing Log");
    logOut_ns.publish(false);
    logOut_ns.close();
};
```

6. The playbutton.onRelease handler is the most complex handler in this step sequence. When the user clicks the button, the event will instance the NetStream object to the variable play_ns. The play statement uses the input from playName_txt as the stream name. The last function within this event defines the onMessage event handler. This custom function defined within the play_ns instance will be called when a stream sends a message. This is the function called to display the log information:

```
play_button.onRelease = function() {
    trace("playing Stream: "+playName_txt.text);
    play_ns = new NetStream(my_nc);
    play_ns.play(playName_txt.text);
    play_ns.onMessage = function(dateStamp, message) {
        trace(dateStamp);
```

```
dateStamp_txt.text = dateStamp;
bytes_in_txt.text = message.bytes_in;
bytes_out_txt.text = message.bytes_out;
for (var i:String in message) {
        trace(i);
}
    };
};
```

7. Play an MP3 stream. Playing an MP3 stream will push data through the stream so that you can see the bytes in and out increase as the stream plays. Add the following ActionScript to the bottom of the Actions panel. It will attach an audio stream to the root timeline.

```
var MP3_ns:NetStream = new NetStream(my_nc);
MP3_ns.setBufferTime(2);
MP3_ns.play("mp3:bRodeo");
this.attachAudio(MP3_ns);
```

8. Copy an MP3 file into the streams folder of the application. Create a folder within the FCS-AS2 folder called streams. Within that folder, create another folder called myInstance and place the MP3 file inside. The name of your MP3 file must be entered into the play statement without the .mp3 extension. In the preceding code, there is a reference to an MP3 file called bRodeo.mp3; notice the omission of the extension .mp3.

9. Save your movie as **MXMiniLab.fla** in the FCS-AS2 folder.

Testing your application can be done very easily, as shown in the following step sequence:

1. With Flash Communication Server MX running, test your movie by selecting Control > Test movie. The light will turn green after the connection has been established.

2. Click the Start Recording Log button. Notice that the time appears below the input text box. Click the Play Log button. The time and date of the date stamp field should be synchronized. This means that you are playing the live stream.

Figure 15.10 shows the result of Step 2 and the three streams in the Communication App Inspector.

3. Now let's play the recorded stream. Click the Stop Recording Log button, and then click the Play button again. Notice that the time and dates are different and that the bytes received/sent are ramping up. The messages that were sent in the live stream are encoded into the FLV stream.

4. Have a look in the streams\myInstance folder into which you placed the MP3 file. There will now be a FLV file and its index (IDX) counterpart. You can save and replay this file anytime you like.

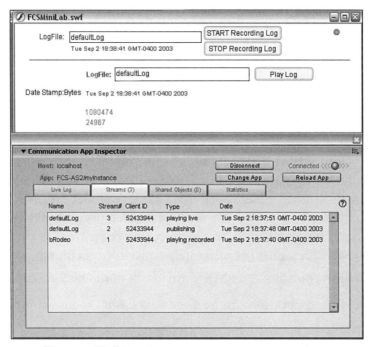

FIGURE 15.10   The completed application, with the Communication App Inspector showing the three streams playing.

Flash Communication Server MX Resources

If you would like to learn more about building Flash communication applications, here are some resources:

- *Macromedia Flash Communication Server MX*, authored by Kevin Towes and published by Macromedia Press
- *Fast Track to Macromedia Flash Communication Server MX,* a formal training curriculum offered exclusively by New Toronto Group (www.NewYYZ.com)
- Macromedia Developer Center (DEVNET) at www.macromedia.com/devnet/mx/flashcom/

Summary

Flash Communication Server MX can supply persistent communications between multiple Flash Players and other Flash Communication Server MX servers. It has a lot of uses, many of which haven't been realized yet. Flash Communication Server MX supports live and prerecorded data, video, and MP3 streaming. It adds some incredible functionality to traditional Flash applications, and it offers some excellent business, education, and entertainment opportunities for the future.

SECTION III
DESIGNING, IMPLEMENTING, AND DEBUGGING THE APPLICATION

CHAPTER 16

PULLING IT ALL TOGETHER

Getting ready to build an application can be a very frustrating task; however, if you approach it with a solid methodology, the frustration can be greatly simplified. In Chapter 8, "Object-Oriented Design," a standard way to approach an object-oriented application was introduced. In this chapter, we will use that process to plan, design, and implement a complete application. Just as was introduced in Chapter 8, it all begins by understanding the business problem which we intend to solve. This begins by identifying the problem domain.

Identifying the Problem Domain

The first step in designing an application is determining the needs of the application. This starts by identifying the boundaries or domain of the problem the application will solve. The better the domain of the problem is understood, the more accurate the class design will be. A frequently encountered problem is when developers dive into coding an application before they fully understand what needs to be done. This, invariably, leads to more time being spent modifying and refactoring the application. To properly understand the domain, we need to begin by understanding the business requirements.

> **NOTE**
>
> As was discussed in Chapter 8, refactoring is the process of revising parts of the plans, designs, or code to address new needs not earlier known. As we will see throughout this chapter, it is inherently cheaper/faster/easier to refactor the application while still in the planning and design phases than it is after the code has been written.

Business Requirements of the Application

XYZ Subscriptions is a magazine subscription wholesaler that has been in business since 1990. When they first opened, they used a Visual Basic Application tied to an MSSQL server to enable their call center representatives to take orders over the phone. In the late 1990s, seeking to reduce costs of deploying updates and fixes to the system, they decided to invest in an HTML/ColdFusion, browser-based intranet. They did this so that the software would be distributed and there would be no need to have a desktop support person constantly installing updates on all the PCs.

For each magazine, there are one or more subscription offers available. Each offer consists of a magazine for a particular duration. Subscriptions with a longer duration will have greater discounts over the single issue price (the price a reader would pay at the news stand).

In addition to facilitating customers signing up for a subscription, a few other features have been requested:

- A Data Entry Representative (DER) needs to be able to enter information about new magazines XYZ Subscriptions will be selling.
- A Subscription Manager (SM) needs to be able to create new subscription offers, associating a magazine, a number of issues, and a price.
- A Phone Center Manager (PCM) needs to be able to monitor and review transactions of each call center representative to determine the effectiveness of the rep's performance. The performance will be judged based on the number of calls a rep handles per day, as well as how successfully each call is handled.

With these loose requirements in mind, a use case diagram and domain model can begin to be assembled to begin determining how to best solve the challenges.

Before a solution can be defined, we need to understand what problem is being solved. In the case of XYZ Subscriptions, they have an existing application. The fact that they are looking to replace it indicates the existing application does not meet their needs.

Understanding the Failing of the Current System

With the upgrade of their system from a VB-based, client/server application to a browser-based intranet system, XYZ Subscriptions was able to save significantly on the cost of keeping the most current software installed on all the employees' machines. However, along with this savings came a new liability: the productivity of the Call Center Rep (CCRs) has dropped significantly with the browser-based system compared to their productivity with the client/server application.

On further analysis, it seems the loss in productivity is largely due to the page-based nature of the application. The reps type in a bit of information, submit it to the server, and wait for a new page to be sent down to them. While the wait times for the pages are not large, the fact that they are forced to stop all entry and wait until the next screen loads has cut into their productivity.

With the client/server application, as some data was being sent to the server, reps were still free to continue entering data into the interface. With that original system, the average call time for a CCR entering a new subscription was 150 seconds. With the browser-based system, the average call now takes 210 seconds.

While an extra 60 seconds may not seem significant, the average number of calls handled by a CCR has dropped from 20 an hour to 14 an hour. While each CCR is handling fewer calls, the overall call volume to XYZ Subscriptions has not diminished. Therefore, XYZ Subscriptions has had to incur the additional expense of bringing in more CCRs and training them.

Further exacerbating the situation is the fact that the executives of XYZ Subscriptions have a business plan to increase the business (and therefore the number of calls) by an additional 20 percent. The fear is that the extra costs needed to hire and train additional CCRs, combined with the marketing efforts that will drive the increase in business, might outweigh the added revenue.

Enhancing Productivity of the Application

The chief technical officer of XYZ Subscriptions has been reading about Rich Internet Applications (RIAs) and believes they may be able to solve the problems of XYZ Subscriptions. By migrating the existing browser-based application to an RIA, he believes that the delays seen by the page-based nature of the Hypertext Markup Language (HTML) solution can be mitigated. They will no longer need to wait for a page to load. The client and server can exchange data seamlessly, without interrupting the CCR's ability to continue entering details about the transaction for a customer.

The intention is to return to the productivity the CCRs had with the client/server application, yet not add back the costs associated with the distribution of that software.

Challenges of a Call Center

The call center application needs to be multi-faceted. The requirements previously stated define a system with four distinct types of users, each of which is likely to require a different set of interfaces. However, there are likely to be some commonalities across the interfaces. For example, consider the following requirements:

- If a caller asks the CCR a question about a particular magazine, the CCR needs to be able to look up details of the magazine to relate the information to the customer.
- The DER will also need an interface to look up and review the details of a magazine so that he or she can determine if it was entered correctly and make modifications if it was not.
- The SM will also need an interface to review magazines, which can be useful as he or she assembles offers.

So, while these three users of the system will each have different ways to reach the magazine lookup screen, they will all access the same screen. Equally, both the CCR and the Call Center Manager (CCM) will need to be able to look up customer records. The CCR will need this to add new subscriptions to existing customers, while the CCM will do this as part of the auditing process. Should they find that several customers cancel their subscriptions after talking to a particular CCR, they may need to look deeper into the CCR's overall performance.

While the two screens described—the Magazine lookup screen and the Customer lookup screen—are not the only places where different users will access the same screens, they certainly give the impression that this will be best built as a single unified application, as opposed to four discrete applications.

Defining the Solution

As part of the process described back in Chapter 8, an iterative approach to development is desirable. As the first pass, we'll examine the way the users interact with the system. A use case diagram will be the basis for the discussion.

Use Case Diagram

By diagramming the interactions between the different types of users with the system, as in Figure 16.1, we can begin to understand how each of the users will use the system and where any crossover will occur.

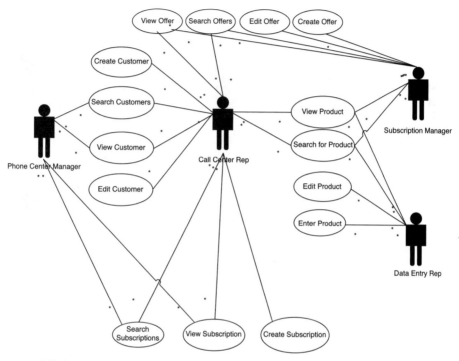

FIGURE 16.1   A use case diagram visually shows how the users interact with the system.

Figure 16.1 lists 15 different interactions between the users and the system. Of the 15, we can clearly see that eight of the interactions will be performed by more than one type of user. As the requirements get further refined, a document will be created describing each of the use cases in greater detail, as seen in Chapter 8.

Domain Model

Before going into too much detail on each of the use cases, we can start to identify the major domains of the system. These domains will later be used to help define the classes. Figure 16.2 shows the use cases being divided up into their respective domains.

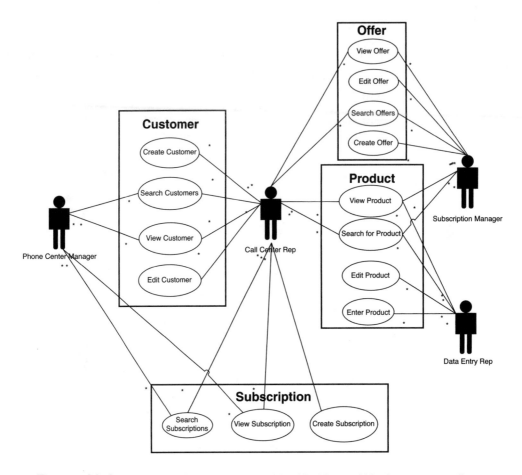

FIGURE 16.2   The individual domains are identified from within the use case diagram.

As we get deeper into defining the solution, classes will be designed to reflect each of the domains in the system, and the properties, methods, and interactions between the domains will be documented.

Designing the System

The iterative approach described earlier recommends designing and implementing individual pieces of the application. The domain model in Figure 16.2 shows four clear domains to be implemented: Product, Offer, Subscription, and Customer. First, we'll explore the Product domain.

Product Domain

Following this best practice, we will start by detailing the use case surrounding the product domain identified earlier.

Product Domain Use Cases

Use Case: Enter product

Actors: DER

Preconditions: Actor has been authenticated to the system, and identified as a member of the Data Entry group. They will begin this process on the Data entry screen.

Primary Flow:

1. Actor chooses to enter a product.
2. A screen is presented to the actor with the following fields:
   - Name
   - Description
   - Publisher
   - Single issue price
3. Actor fills out screen, and clicks button to insert product.
4. Validation routines are run over inputs, assuring that name, publisher, description, and single issue price are not blank, and that single issue price is a number.
5. Once validated, data is sent to server to be inserted.
6. After successful insertion by server, server will return a message to the client indicating successful insertion.
7. User is returned to the Data entry screen, where they have the option to enter another product. If he or she answers yes, the user starts again with Step 2. Otherwise, he or she is returned to the main Data entry screen.

NOTE

The step numbers in the following list (and in similar subsequent lists) map to specific step numbers in the main step sequence for each use case.

Alternative Flow:

4a. If any of the fields fail validation routines, a message box will alert the actor of the problems.

4b. When the user closes the message box, focus will be given to the first field that failed the validation routines.

6a. If server returns a message other than that the data was successfully inserted, the user will be notified that there was a problem inserting the data and will be prompted with a link to mail the issue to the applications administrator.

Use Case: Search for a product

Actors: DER, CCR, and SM

Preconditions: Actor has been authenticated to the system, and identified as a member of one of the groups listed as actors.

Primary Flow:

1. Actor chooses to find a product.

2. A screen is presented to the actor with the following fields:

   - Name
   - Description
   - Publisher
   - Single issue price

3. Actor fills out screen, and clicks button to search for a product.

4. Matching products are presented to user.

5. User chooses a product from the list.

6. Based on role, user is either presented with a screen to edit the product or presented with a screen to view the product.

Alternative Flow:

4a. If there are no matching products, users are redirected to Step 2, with a message indicating that no products have matched. If there is only one matching product, user skips Step 5 and proceeds directly to Step 6.

Use Case: View/edit a product

Actors: DER, CCR, SM

Preconditions: Actor has been authenticated to the system and identified as a member of one of the groups listed above as actors. Actor has chosen a product following the "Search for Product" use case.

Primary Flow:

1. A search screen is presented to the actor with the following fields:
   - Name
   - Description
   - Publisher
   - Single issue price
2. Based on user role, the fields are either dynamic text (CCR) or input text (DER and SM) fields. For a CCR, this is the end of the use case.
3. Actor makes appropriate edits to the text fields.
4. Actor chooses to submit updates to the server.
5. Data is validated, as per "Enter Product" use case, Step 4.
6. Once validated, data is sent to server to be inserted.
7. After successful update by server, server will return a message to the client indicating successful insertion.
8. User is asked if he or she wishes to edit another product. If he or she answers yes, the process starts again with "Search for a Product" use case. Otherwise, he or she is returned to the main screen for users of their role.

Alternative Flows:

5a. If any of the fields fail validation routines, a message box will alert the actor of the problems.

5b. When user closes the message box, focus will be given to the first field that failed the validation routines.

7a. If server returns a message other than that the data was successfully inserted, the user will be notified that there was a problem inserting the data and prompted with a link to mail the issue to the applications administrator.

Product Sequence Diagram

After the use cases surrounding the products are understood, a sequence diagram can begin to be built for the product object, as seen in Figure 16.3.

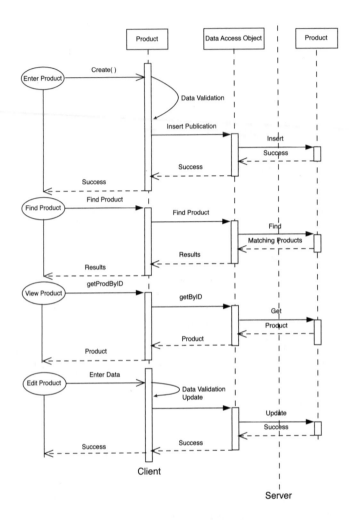

FIGURE 16.3 The sequence diagram of the product helps determine what messages it will need to exchange with other objects.

With a sequence diagram, it can begin to be understood how the Product object will interact with other objects. As can be seen from Figure 16.3, the only entity the product needs to interact with is a DataAccess object. It is responsible for facilitating communication between our client (the Flash Player) and the server-side object, which ultimately will interact with the database.

Product Class Diagram

With the use cases and sequence diagrams in place, a first iteration of the Product class diagram can be derived, capturing the properties identified through the use cases and the methods identified through the sequence diagram. Figure 16.4 shows an initial view of the Product class diagram.

Product
–Name : string –Publisher : string –SingleIssuePrice : float –Description : string
+Create() : Boolean +Update() : Boolean +Get() : Product +Find()

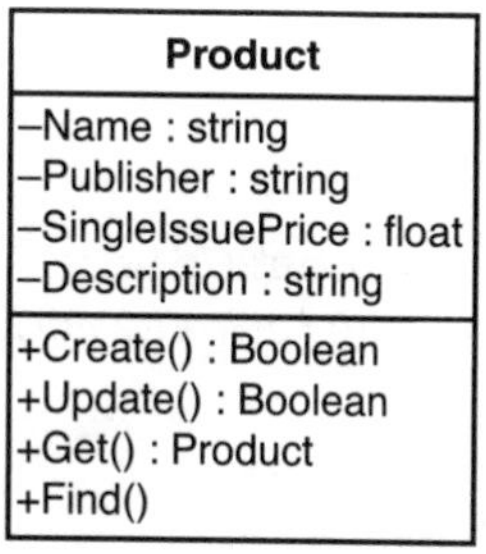

FIGURE 16.4   The class diagram for a product indicates the properties and methods necessary for a Product.

As can be seen in the class diagram, the Product class needs methods to create a product (this will be handled with the product constructor), a method to validate a product, one to update, one to find a product, and lastly, one to retrieve a product. The Product class will also have a static property, dataAccessObject, which will be an instance of the DataAccess class, which was created in Chapter 12, "XML and Flash."

> **NOTE**
>
> The code relating to this class is created in the next section, "First Build of Code."

First Build of Code

After the class diagram is created, we can begin to build our first class file. Listing 16.1 shows the first cut at the Product class.

LISTING 16.1   First Draft of a *Product* Class

```
class Product{
      // instance properties
      private var name:String;
      private var publisher:String;
      private var singleIssuePrice:Number;
      private var description:String;
      private var prodID:Number;

      //static properties
      private static var dataAccessObject:DataAccess = new
DataAccess("http://localhost:8500/oopas2/components/product.cfc?wsdl");

      //consturctor
      function
Product(name:String,publisher:String,price:Number,description:String){
            setValues(name,publisher,price,description);
      }

      //data access functions
      public function insert(resultsMethod:Function,
statusMethod:Function):Boolean{{
            if(this.validateData()){
            trace("calling DAO - Create");

Product.dataAccessObject.accessRemote("create",this.serializeValues());
                  return true;
            } else {
                  trace("Data invalid");
                  return false;
            }
      }
      //validation
      public function validateData():Boolean{
            var isValid:Boolean = true;
            if(!validateString(this.getName())){
                  return false;
            } else if (!validateString(this.getPublisher())){
                  return false;
            } else if (!validateNumber(this.getSingleIssuePrice())){
                  return false;
            } else {
                  return true;
            }
      }
```

```
       private function validateString(string:String):Boolean{

              if(string.length == 0){
                     return false;
              } else {
                     for(var i:Number=0;i<string.length;i++){
                            if(string.charAt(i) != " "){
                                   return true;
                                   break;
                            }
                     }
              }
       }
       private function validateNumber(number:Number):Boolean{
              if (isNaN(number)){
                     return false;
              } else {
                     return true;
              }
       }
       }
       // setter functions
       public function
setValues(name:String,publisher:String,price:Number,description:String){
              setName(name);
              setPublisher(publisher);
              setSingleIssuePrice(price);
              setDescription(description);
       }

       public function setName(name:String):Void{
              this.name = name;
       }
       public function setPublisher(publisher:String):Void{
              this.publisher= publisher;
       }
       public function setSingleIssuePrice(price:Number):Void{
              this.singleIssuePrice= price;
       }
       public function setDescription(description:String):Void{
              this.description = description;
       }
       // getter functions
       public function serializeValues():Object{
              var prod = new Object();
              prod.name = this.getName();
              prod.publisher = this.getPublisher();
```

continues

LISTING 16.1   Continued

```
                    prod.singleIssuePrice = this.getSingleIssuePrice();
                    prod.description = this.getDescription();
                    return prod;
}
        public function getName():String{
                return this.name;
        }
        public function getPublisher():String{
                return this.publisher;
        }
        public function getSingleIssuePrice():Number{
                return this.singleIssuePrice;
        }
        public function getDescription():String{
                return this.description;
        }
}
```

> **NOTE**
>
> Attempting to test this code as written will generate errors. This is due to the fact that the `DataAccess` class isn't defined yet (it's defined in Listing 16.4) or that it's not being tested in the proper context. Please see the note after Listing 16.4 for information about properly testing this class.

This class begins in a fairly straightforward manner. The class file is broken into seven sections, with a comment block between them indicating what type of code will go into each section. The first section declares all instance variables and their data types, as was discussed in Chapter 3, "We're All Described by Our Properties." The instance variables are all set to be `private` so that they can be accessed only by the getter and setter methods.

This is followed by the static properties section. Static properties were covered in detail in Chapter 3 as well. For the `Product` class, the `dataAccessObject` property is set to be static, as we don't want a separate `dataAccessObject` for each instance of the class; instead, we want all products to use the same object for accessing remote data.

Following the static properties is the constructor method. As was discussed in Chapter 2, "All the World Is an Object," the constructor defines how new instances of a class are created.

Following the constructor are the data access methods. These are methods which are responsible for sending and retrieving data to be used by the class.

The data access section is followed by data validation routines, and finally the getter and setter methods of the class.

For this class, there are only two validation rules that need to be obeyed. The first is that some fields need to be non-empty strings. The second is that some need to be numbers. To enforce the first rule, a method called `validateString()` is created to ensure the length of a string is not zero and that it contains something other than just spaces.

This is done by first testing the length property of the string. If the length is 0, the method returns `false`, indicating it is not a valid string. If the length test is passed, each character of the string is looped over, comparing it to a space. If any of the characters are not spaces, it breaks out of the loop, and returns `true`, indicating it is valid. If the string contains nothing but spaces, it will return `false`.

The `validateNumber()` method is much simpler, as it checks whether the data passed in is a valid number, using the `isNaN()` function. If the data is not a number, the method returns `false`; otherwise, it returns `true`.

The `validateData` method calls the appropriate validation routine on each of the properties of the object. We can start to surmise that by the time we are done, the `validateString` and `validateNumber` methods will be moved to an external class which will handle all generic validations for this class as well as others. For now, as this is the only class built, it is not necessary to further abstract it.

There are a few other non-standard methods added to this class, one in the getter and one in the setter sections. In the setter section, the method `setValues()` is defined as a single method to set all the properties. Internally, `setValues()` uses the standard setter methods. The benefit of abstracting the setters to a single method is that there are potentially multiple methods which may attempt to set data (although currently the constructor is the only one in use, it's easy to imagine that `Product` data may come from a database, and need to be set into an object in our application). The other new method is `serializeValues()` which returns an object containing all the properties of a `Product` but none of the methods. This object can be used both to insert a new `Product` into the database as well as to update an existing one. It can even be used to create a copy of a `Product` for use elsewhere in the system, without having to worry about other system entities changing the product.

As defined in Listing 16.1, aside from having the entire infrastructure (properties, validation, getters, and setters), the only use case realized is the Create Product use case. To create a new product, data will be passed to its constructor, which will pass it to the setValues() method, which in turn uses the setter methods to populate the properties. To persist this data to the database, the insert() method will be called. Insert() uses the validateData() method to determine if the data for the product is valid. If so, it passes that data on to the accessRemote() method of the dataAccessObject, and passes it the name of the method on the server responsible for inserting product data and the serialized version of the product.

So far, the class is now built to handle creating an object. Adding a method to update is the next logical step. Listing 16.2 shows one possible approach to the update() method. This method will use a few methods written earlier, such as setValues() and validateData(), to populate the properties and check for their validity. After validation, the serialized data is passed to the update method on the server to enable the data to be persisted.

The refactored method is seen in Listing 16.2.

LISTING 16.2   The *Product* Class Has Been Refactored to Enable Data to be Updated and Inserted

```
    public function update (name:String, publisher:String,
price:Number, description:String){
        setValues(name,publisher,price,description);
        if(this.validateData()){

Product.dataAccessObject.accessRemote("update",this.serializeValues());
        }
    }
```

The final two methods we need to add are data retrieval methods. One will retrieve an array of matching products (aptly named search) and one will retrieve a single product named getById. Listing 16.3 shows these two methods.

LISTING 16.3   To Enable Retrieval of *Products* from the Server, *search()* and *getByID()* Are Added

```
public function search(propertyObj:Object, resultsMethod:Function,
➥statusMethod:Function):Void{
    dataAccessObject.accessRemote("retrieveByProp", propertyObj,
    ➥resultsMethod, statusMethod);
}
```

```
public static function getById(ID:Number, resultsMethod:Function,
➥statusMethod:Function):Void{
    dataAccessObject.accessRemote("retrieveByID",ID, resultsMethod,
    ➥statusMethod);
}
```

The Product class relied heavily on an external class, which is called DataAccess. This class was created back in Chapter 12. Its purpose is to act as a centralized place where all communications between the client and the server will be encapsulated. By setting this as a static property of the Product class, we are able to create a single instance of DAO to be used by all instances of the class. The structure of the DataAccess class is shown in Listing 16.4, as a reminder of the class we wrote in Chapter 12.

LISTING 16.4   The *DataAccess* Class

```
class DataAccess{

    private var webService;
    public var callBack:Object = new Object();

    public function DataAccess(address:String){

        this.webService = new mx.services.WebService(address);
        this.webService.WSDLURL = address;
    }

    public function accessRemote(methodName:String, object:Object,
    ➥resultFunction:Function, statusFunction:Function){

        this.callBack = this.webService[methodName](object);
        this.callBack.resultFunction = resultFunction;
        this.callBack.statusFunction = statusFunction;

        this.callBack.onResult = function(result){
            resultFunction(result);
        }
        this.callBack.onFault = function(status){
            statusFunction(status);
        }
    }
}
```

NOTE

If you insert this code as-is in a new ActionScript file and run the syntax checker, you will see an error from the `DataAccess` class saying the following:

`"DataAccess.as: Line 9: There is no method with the name 'mx'.this.webService`
`= new mx.services.WebService(address);"`

The reason for this is that the `DataAccess` class requires the underlying Web Services classes be loaded into a movie clip before they can be used. To effectively test the syntax of this code, create a new movie clip in the same directory as the `DataAccess` and `Product` class files. Next, the Web Services classes must be added to the movie. This can be done by dragging a `WebServicesConnector` onto the Stage or by opening the `Classes` library (Window > Other Panels > Common Libraries > Classes) and dragging `WebServiceClasses` to the Stage. After the classes are available, we can test our new class by opening the Actions panel, adding `var myProd:Product = new Product();`, and testing the movie.

To begin testing, we'll open a new Flash movie, drag four `TextInput` components onto the Stage, and drag four static text boxes next to them to act as labels. Give an instance name to each of the `TextInput` boxes, so that from top to bottom they are named `name`, `pub`, `price`, and `desc`. Below these add a Button component and give it an instance name of `submit_pb`. The button will be used to trigger the validate and insert methods of the `Product` class. Figure 16.5 shows the Stage with the various elements positioned on it.

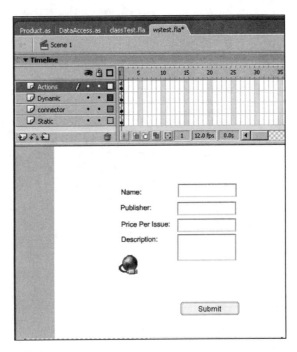

FIGURE 16.5   A simple create product form consists of `textInput` components, four static text labels, and a button.

In our Actions panel, as shown in Listing 16.5, an event handler is assigned to handle a user clicking `submit_pb`. This handler will create a new instance of the `Product` class from the data the user has input. Next, the `insert` method of the `Product` class will be invoked. Insert will first validate the data, and if valid, the `dataAccessObject` will be used to insert this new object into the database. If the validation fails, the newly created object is deleted. Listing 16.5 shows the code which should be entered on the first frame of the timeline.

LISTING 16.5   Building a Simple Movie Clip to Test the *DataAccess* and *Product* Classes

```
var listener:Object = new Object();
listener.click = function(){
    var prod:Product = new Product(name_txt.text, pub_txt.text,
price_txt.text, desc_txt.text);
    if(prod.insert()){
        trace("inserting...");
    } else {
        //show error message
        trace("invalid data");
        delete prod;
    }
}
this.submit_pb.addEventListener("click", listener);
```

Once completed, event handlers will be added to handle successful results or status (error) messages returning from the Web Services call.

The *Offer* Class

With the `Product` and `DataAccess` classes built, we can move onto the next class, `Offer`. An offer consists of a product, a number of issues for that product, and a price. When the system is completed, it is an offer to which a customer will be subscribed.

There can be several different offers for each product (for example, an offer can be made for 12 issues of a product at one price, and another offer can be for 24 issues of that same product at a different price). Walking through the use cases of an offer will help clarify how an offer is used.

Use Cases

Use Case: Create offer

Actors: SM

Preconditions: Actor has been authenticated to the system and identified as a member of the Subscription Manager group.

Primary Flow:

1. Actor chooses to enter an offer.

2. A screen is presented to the actor with the following fields:
   - Menu with all products
   - Number of issues
   - Price
   - Check box indicating whether the offer is active

3. Actor fills out screen, and clicks button to insert offer.

4. Validation routines are run over inputs, assuring that price and number of issues are numeric, and greater than zero.

5. Once validated, data is sent to server to be inserted.

6. After successful insertion by server, server will return a message to the client indicating successful insertion.

7. User is asked if he/she wishes to create another offer. If he or she answers yes, he or she starts again with Step 2. Otherwise, he or she is returned to the Subscription Manager screen.

Alternative Flows:

4a. If any of the fields fail the validation routines, a message box will alert the actor of the problems.

4b. When a user closes the message box, focus will be given to the first field that failed the validation routines.

6a. If server returns a message other than that the data was successfully inserted, the user will be notified that there was a problem inserting the data and prompted with a link to mail the issue to the applications administrator.

Use Case: Search for offer

Actors: CCRs and SM

Preconditions: Actor has been authenticated to the system, and identified as a member of one of the groups listed as actors.

Primary Flow:

1. Actor chooses to find an offer.
2. A search screen is presented to the actor with the following fields:
   - Menu of products
   - Number of issues
   - Price
3. Actor fills out screen and clicks button to search for an offer.
4. Matching offers are presented to user.
5. User chooses an offer from the list.
6. Based on role, user is either presented with a screen to edit the offer (SM) or presented with a screen to view the offer (CCR).

Alternative Flows:

4a. If there are no matching offers, users are redirected to Step 2, with a message indicating that no offers have matched. If there is only one matching offer, user skips Step 5, and proceeds directly to Step 6.

Use Case: View and/or edit an offer

Actors: CCRs and SM

Preconditions: Actor has been authenticated to the system and identified as a member of one of the groups listed as actors. Actor has chosen an offer following the "Search for Offer" use case.

Primary Flow:

1. A screen is presented to the actor with the following fields:
   - Products
   - Number of issues
   - Price
   - Status (is offer active or not)
2. Based on user's role, the fields are either dynamic text (CCR) or input (SM) fields, as shown in Table 16.1. For a CCR, this is the end of the use case.

TABLE 16.1   Based on the Actor's Role, Fields Shown for the View and/or Edit Offer Use Case Will Vary

	CCR	SM
Products	Dynamic text	Menu
Number of issues	Dynamic text	Input text
Price	Dynamic text	Input text
Status	Dynamic text	Check box

3. Actor makes appropriate edits to the fields.

4. Actor chooses to submit updates to the server.

5. Data is validated, as per "Enter Offer" use case, Step 4.

6. Once validated, data is sent to server to be inserted.

7. After successful update by server, server will return a message to the client indicating successful insertion.

8. User is asked if he or she wishes to edit another offer. If he or she answers yes, he or she starts again with the "Search for an Offer" use case. Otherwise, he or she is returned to the main screen for users of their role.

Alternative Flows:

5a. If any of the fields fail validation routines, a message box will alert the actor of the problems.

5b. When the user closes the message box, focus will be given to the first field that failed the validation routines.

7a. If server returns a message other than that the data was successfully inserted, the user will be notified that there was a problem inserting the data and prompted with a link to mail the issue to the applications administrator.

Sequence Diagram

With the Offer's use understood, a sequence diagram can be created showing interactions with the Offer class. Unlike the Product class, which only interacted with the DataAccess class, the Offer class needs to interact with the Product class as well as the DataAccess class. Figure 16.6 shows the sequence diagram for the Offer class.

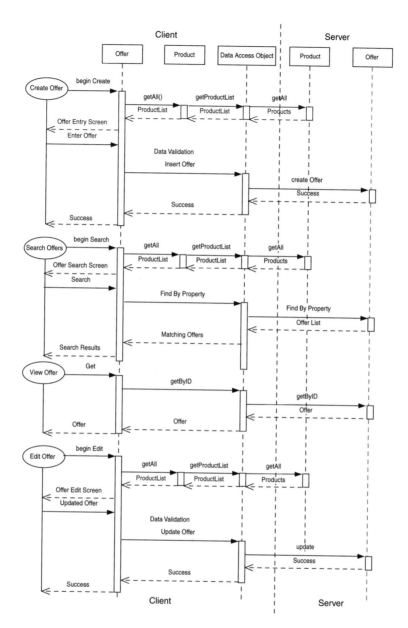

FIGURE 16.6   The sequence diagram of the Offer class shows that it interacts with the Product class as well as the DataAccessObject class.

Class Diagram

Glancing at the sequence diagram, the public methods necessary for an `Offer` become apparent. In fact, we will find that the methods for an offer closely mirror those of the `Product`: `insert()`, `update()`, `search()`, `getByID()`, and `validate()`. These are enumerated into the class diagram, seen in Figure 16.7.

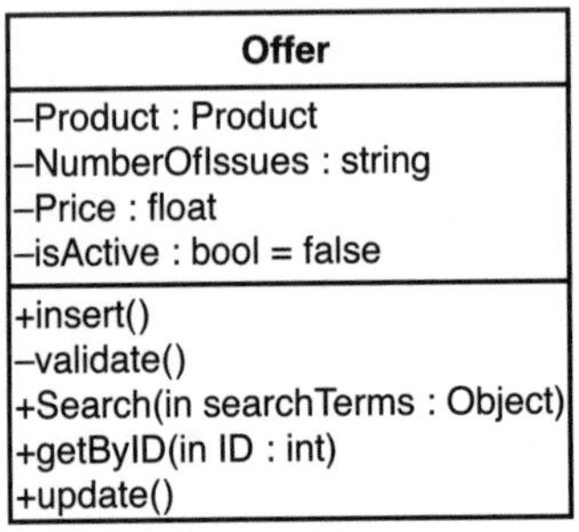

Offer
–Product : Product
–NumberOfIssues : string
–Price : float
–isActive : bool = false
+insert()
–validate()
+Search(in searchTerms : Object)
+getByID(in ID : int)
+update()

FIGURE 16.7   The `Offer` class diagram shows the properties and methods of an `Offer`.

With the class diagram as a blueprint, a first iteration of the code making up the `Offer` class can be created.

Much like we did with the `Product` class, we'll start with the infrastructure (properties, constructor, data access, validation, getters, and setters) for the `Offer` class. This is shown in Listing 16.6.

LISTING 16.6   The Core Infrastructure of the *Offer* Class is Assembled

```
class Offer{
    private var offerID:Number;
    private var product:Product;
    private var numIssues:Number;
    private var price:Number;
    private var isActive:Boolean = false;

    //static properties
    private static var dataAccessObject:DataAccess = new
    ➡DataAccess("http://www.tapper.net/oopas2/components/
    ➡product.cfc?wsdl");

    //constructor
    public function Offer(product:Product, numIssues:Number,
    ➡price:Number,isActive:Boolean){
        this.setValues(product,numIssues,price,isActive);
    }
```

```
    // data access
    //data access functions
    public function insert(resultsMethod:Function,
➡statusMethod:Function):Boolean{
        if(this.validateData()){
            Offer.dataAccessObject.accessRemote("create",
➡this.serializeValues(),resultsMethod, statusMethod);
            return true;
        } else {
            return false;
        }
    }
    public function update (product:Product, numIssues:Number,
➡price:Number,isActive:Boolean, resultsMethod:Function,
➡statusMethod:Function):Boolean{
        this.setValues(product,numIssues,price,isActive);
        if(this.validateData()){
            Offer.dataAccessObject.accessRemote("update",
this.serializeValues(),resultsMethod, statusMethod);
            return true;
        } else {
            return false;
        }
    }
    public function search(propertyObj:Object,
➡resultsMethod:Function, statusMethod:Function):Void{
        Offer.dataAccessObject.accessRemote("retrieveByProp",
        ➡propertyObj, resultsMethod, statusMethod);
    }

    public static function getById(ID:Number,
➡resultsMethod:Function, statusMethod:Function):Void{
        Offer.dataAccessObject.accessRemote("retrieveByID",ID,
        ➡resultsMethod, statusMethod);
    }

    // validation
    public function validateData():Boolean{
            if(!validateNonZeroNumber(this.getNumIssues())){
                return false;
            } else if (!validateNonZeroNumber(this.getPrice())){
                return false;
            } else {
                return true;
            }
        }
```

continues

LISTING 16.6   Continued

```
        private function validateNonZeroNumber(number:Number):Boolean{
                if (isNaN(number) || Number(number) <= 0){
                        return false;
                } else {
                        return true;
                }
        }

// setters
public function setValues(product:Product, numIssues:Number,
➡price:Number,isActive:Boolean):Void{
        this.setProduct(product);
        this.setNumIssues(numIssues);
        this.setPrice(price);
        this.setActive(isActive);
}


public function setProduct(product:Product):Void{
        this.product = product;
}
public function setNumIssues(numIssues:Number):Void{
        this.numIssues = numIssues;
}
public function setPrice(price):Void{
        this.price = price;
}
public function setActive(isActive:Boolean):Void{
        this.isActive = isActive;
}

// getters
public function serializeValues():Object{
        var tmpObject = new Object();
        tmpObject.productID = this.getProduct.getID();
        tmpObject.numIssues = this.getNumIssues();
        tmpObject.price = this.getPrice();
        tmpObject.active = this.getActive();
        return tmpObject;
}
public function getProduct():Product{
        return this.product;
}
public function getNumIssues():Number{
        return this.numIssues;
```

```
    }
    public function getPrice():Number{
        return this.price;
    }
    public function getActive():Boolean{
        return this.isActive;
    }
}
```

The core services of this class closely mirror that of the `Product` class. The specific properties of an offer are declared first, along with their datatypes. One thing to note here is that the `Offer` class will use an instance of the `Product` class as a property called `product`.

Next, the static properties are listed. These are nearly identical to those of the `Product` class, with the exception of the arguments passed into the constructor of the `DataAccess` class. If other classes continue to follow these conventions, it may be better to create a superclass that implements our data access methods. As was discussed in Chapter 5, "The Meek Shall Inherit the Earth," it often makes sense to create a superclass when more than one class has similar methods and properties and those classes can all be effectively described as something else. So far, we could safely describe both `products` and `offers` as persistable objects.

After all the instance and static properties are declared, the constructor method is shown, which simply takes in arguments and passes them to the set values method for the class.

The constructor is followed by the data access methods. These closely mirror the data access methods from the `Product` class.

Next, the validation methods are defined. The `Offer` class uses only a single validation method, `validateNonZeroNumber`, which is similar to the `validateNumber` method from the `Product` class. With this defined, it's starting to become apparent that it would make more sense to add a superclass to both the `Product` class and the `Offer` class, which also contains the validation routines for each. We'll investigate this shortly.

The final section of the `Offer` class contains the getter and setter functions. Just like the `Product` class, there is one `setValues()` method that takes all the properties and uses the setter methods, and there is one `serializeValues()` method that uses all the getter methods to return a flat snapshot of the object. With the data access properties and methods as well as validation routines, we have started to identify certain redundancies between the Product and Offer classes. To simplify the construction and maintenance of the application, we will refactor both, and move the common methods to a superclass of each, which we will call PersistableObject. Our first attempt at the PersistableObject class is shown in Listing 16.7.

LISTING 16.7   The *PersistableObject* Class Will Act as a Superclass to Any Classes Needing Data Access and Validation Behaviors

```
class PersistableObject{
        // static properties
        private static var dataAccessObject:DataAccess;
        private var validateData:Function;
        private var serializeValues:Function;

        //empty constructor
        function PersistableObject(){}

        // data access methods
        public function insert(resultsMethod:Function,
statusMethod:Function):Boolean{
                if(this.validateData()){

PersistableObject.dataAccessObject.accessRemote("create",this.serialize
Values(),resultsMethod, statusMethod);
                        return true;
                } else {
                        trace("Data invalid");
                        return false;
                }
        }

        public function search(propertyObj:Object,
resultsMethod:Function, statusMethod:Function):Void{

PersistableObject.dataAccessObject.accessRemote("retrieveByProp",
propertyObj, resultsMethod, statusMethod);
                }

        public static function getById(ID:Number, resultsMethod:Function,
statusMethod:Function):Void{

PersistableObject.dataAccessObject.accessRemote("retrieveByID",ID,
resultsMethod, statusMethod);
                }
```

```
// validation methods
private function validateString(string:String):Boolean{
        if(string.length == 0){
                return false;
        } else {
                        for(var i:Number=0;i<string.length;i++){
                        if(string.charAt(i) != " "){
                                return true;
                                break;
                        }
                }
        }
}
private function validateNumber(number:Number):Boolean{
        if (isNaN(number)){
                return false;
        } else {
                return true;
        }
}
private function validateNonZeroNumber(number:Number):Boolean{
        if (!validateNumber(number) || number <= 0){
                return false;
        } else {
                return true;
        }
    }
}
```

The `PersistableObject` class simply defines our static properties, validation routines, and the common data access methods (`insert()`, `getByID()`, and `search()`). One thing to note is that anything specific to the `Product` or `Offer` classes is not defined within the `PersistableObject` class, but instead is left to be implemented at the specific class level.

For this reason the `update()` method is not implemented here; as it currently stands, the `update()` method takes specific arguments for each class. With a bit more reworking, we could create a separate method for updating the objects data within each class, and then have an `update()` method in the `PersistableObject` class as well, but for simplicity sake, we will keep that one data access method to be implemented within each subclass.

The `validateData()` method of the `Offer` and `Product` classes is not implemented in `PersistableObject`, as they specifically determine how the individual properties of those classes will be validated.

However, the methods `validateData()` uses are implemented within the superclass. The `validateNonZeroNumber()` method has also been modified to make use of the `validateNumber()` method to determine if the argument is indeed a number, before checking to see if it is greater than zero. Next, we need to tell the `Product` and `Offer` classes that they are to inherit from `PersistableObject`, and any code moved to the superclass will be removed from these two classes. The modified versions of the `Product` and `Offer` classes can be seen in Listing 16.8.

LISTING 16.8   *Product* and *Offer* Classes Are Modified to Extend the *PersistableObject* Class

```
class Product extends PersistableObject{
        // instance properties
        private var name:String;
        private var publisher:String;
        private var singleIssuePrice:Number;
        private var description:String;
        private var prodID:Number;

        //static properties
        private static var dataAccessObject:DataAccess = new
DataAccess("http://www.tapper.net/oopas2/components/product.cfc?wsdl");

        //consturctor
        function
Product(name:String,publisher:String,price:Number,description:String){
                setValues(name,publisher,price,description);
        }

        //data access functions

                public function update (name:String, publisher:String,
price:Number, description:String, resultsMethod:Function,
statusMethod:Function){
                        setValues(name,publisher,price,description);
                        if(this.validateData()){

Product.dataAccessObject.accessRemote("update",this.serializeValues());
                        }
                }
```

```
        //validation
        public function validateData():Boolean{
              var isValid:Boolean = true;
              if(!validateString(this.getName())){
                    return false;
              } else if (!validateString(this.getPublisher())){
                    return false;
              } else if (!validateNumber(this.getSingleIssuePrice())){
                    return false;
              } else {
                    return true;
              }
        }


        // setter functions
        public function
setValues(name:String,publisher:String,price:Number,description:String){
              setName(name);
              setPublisher(publisher);
              setSingleIssuePrice(price);
              setDescription(description);
        }

        public function setName(name:String):Void{
              this.name = name;
        }
        public function setPublisher(publisher:String):Void{
              this.publisher= publisher;
        }
        public function setSingleIssuePrice(price:Number):Void{
              this.singleIssuePrice= price;
        }
        public function setDescription(description:String):Void{
              this.description = description;
        }
        // getter functions
        public function serializeValues():Object{
              var tmpObject = new Object();
              tmpObject.name = this.getName();
              tmpObject.publisher = this.getPublisher();
              tmpObject.singleIssuePrice = this.getSingleIssuePrice();
              tmpObject.description = this.getDescription();
              return tmpObject;
        }

        public function getName():String{
```

continues

LISTING 16.8   Continued

```
                return this.name;
        }
        public function getPublisher():String{
                return this.publisher;
        }
        public function getSingleIssuePrice():Number{
                return this.singleIssuePrice;
        }
        public function getDescription():String{
                return this.description;
        }
        public function getID():Number{
                return this.prodID;
        }
}
class Offer extends PersistableObject{
        private var offerID:Number;
        private var product:Product;
        private var numIssues:Number;
        private var price:Number;
        private var isActive:Boolean = false;

        //static properties
        private static var dataAccessObject:DataAccess = new
DataAccess("http://www.tapper.net/oopas2/components/product.cfc?wsdl");

        public function
Offer(product:Product,numIssues:Number,price:Number,isActive:Boolean){
                this.setValues(product,numIssues,price,isActive);
        }

        //data access functions
        public function update
(product:Product,numIssues:Number,price:Number,isActive:Boolean,
resultsMethod:Function, statusMethod:Function):Boolean{
                this.setValues(product,numIssues,price,isActive);
                if(this.validateData()){
                        Offer.dataAccessObject.accessRemote("update",
this.serializeValues(), resultsMethod, statusMethod);
                        return true;
                } else {
                        return false;
                }
        }
```

```
    // validation
public function validateData():Boolean{
        if(!validateNonZeroNumber(this.getNumIssues())){
             return false;
        } else if (!validateNonZeroNumber(this.getPrice())){
             return false;
      } else {
          return true;
      }
}


    // setters
    public function
setValues(product:Product,numIssues:Number,price:Number,isActive:Boolean
):Void{
        this.setProduct(product);
        this.setNumIssues(numIssues);
        this.setPrice(price);
        this.setActive(isActive);
    }

    public function setProduct(product:Product):Void{
        this.product = product;
    }
    public function setNumIssues(numIssues:Number):Void{
        this.numIssues = numIssues;
    }
    public function setPrice(price):Void{
        this.price = price;
    }
    public function setActive(isActive:Boolean):Void{
        this.isActive = isActive;
    }

    // getters
    public function serializeValues():Object{
        var tmpObject = new Object();
        tmpObject.productID = this.getProduct.getID();
        tmpObject.numIssues = this.getNumIssues();
        tmpObject.price = this.getPrice();
        tmpObject.active = this.getActive();
        return tmpObject;
    }
    public function getProduct():Product{
        return this.product;
```

continues

LISTING 16.8   Continued

```
    }
    public function getNumIssues():Number{
            return this.numIssues;
    }
    public function getPrice():Number{
            return this.price;
    }
    public function getActive():Boolean{
            return this.isActive;
    }
}
```

With the `Products` and `Offers` ready, we should next consider the customer.

Customer

A customer is a person who buys subscriptions from the company. They are a key aspect of the system, as without customers, the company would cease to exist. The following use cases will help understand how users of the system interact with a customer.

Use Case

Use Case: Search for a customer

Actors: CCR and PCM

Preconditions: Actor has been authenticated to the system and identified as a member of one of the groups listed as actors.

Primary Flow:

1. Actor receives a phone call from a customer.

2. A screen is presented to the actor with the following fields:

   - First name

   - Last name

   - Street address

   - City

   - Combo box with all U.S. states

   - Zip code

   - Phone number (divided into two fields, area code and phone number)

3. As actor fills out screen, each time he or she clicks away from the Last name or Phone number fields, those fields will be passed to the search engine.

4. Matching customers are presented to actor.

5. Actor chooses a customer from the list.

6. Based on role, actor is either presented with a screen to view the customer (CCR) or is presented with a menu allowing him or her to either edit customer or add subscription. They will be redirected to appropriate use case based on this choice.

Alternative Flows:

4a. If there are no matching customers, actors can complete the form, click the Insert Customer button, and continue with the "Insert Customer" use case.

Use Case: Insert customer

Actors: CCR

Preconditions:

- Actor has been authenticated to the system and identified as a member of the Subscription Manager group.
- New customer has called call center with the intention of subscribing to a magazine.
- Actor has searched for a record matching a customer and found no matches.

Primary Flow:

1. Actor fills out screen and clicks button to insert customer.

2. Validation routines are run over inputs, assuring that firstname, lastname, streetAddress, city, and zip are non-empty strings, that area code is a three-digit number, and that phone number is a seven-digit number.

3. Once validated, data is sent to server to be inserted.

4. After successful insertion by server, server will return a message to the client indicating successful insertion.

5. Actor will then proceed to the "Add Subscription" use case.

Alternative Flows:

    2a. If any of the fields fail validation routines, a message box will alert the actor of the problems.

    2b. When actor closes the message box, focus will be given to the first field that failed the validation routines.

    4a. If server returns a message other than that the data was successfully inserted, the actor will be notified that there was a problem inserting the data and prompted with a link to mail the issue to the applications administrator.

Use Case: Edit customer

Actors: CCR

Preconditions:

- Actor has been authenticated to the system, and identified as a member of the applicable group(s).
- Customer has called call center and been identified by the actor.
- Actor has searched for a record matching a customer and chosen to edit the customer.

Primary Flow:

1. Actor is presented with a prefilled screen with the following fields:
   - First name
   - Last name
   - Street address
   - City
   - Combo box with all U.S. states
   - Zip code
   - Phone number (divided into two fields, area code and phone number)
2. Actor edits data on the screen and clicks button to update customer.
3. Validation routines are run over inputs, assuring that firstname, lastname, streetaddress, city, and zip are non-empty strings, that area code is a three-digit number, and that phone number is a seven-digit number.
4. Once validated, data is sent to server to be inserted.
5. After successful insertion by server, server will return a message to the client indicating successful insertion.
6. Actor will be presented with menu of options for that customer.

Alternative Flows:

3a. If any of the fields fail validation routines, a message box will alert the actor of the problems.

3b. When actor closes the message box, focus will be given to the first field that failed validation routines.

5a. If server returns a message other than that the data was successfully inserted, the actor will be notified that there was a problem inserting the data and prompted with a link to mail the issue to the applications administrator.

Sequence Diagram

From these use cases, it can clearly be seen that the Customer class is central to the application. Further details about this class can be derived by examining its interactions through the use of a sequence diagram, as seen in Figure 16.8.

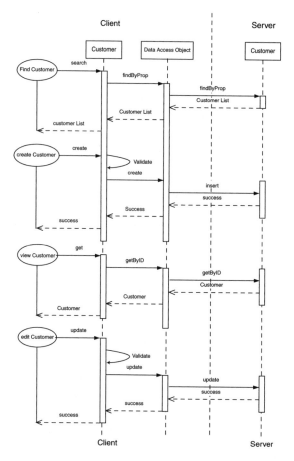

FIGURE 16.8   The sequence diagram for the Customer class shows interactions between users of the system and customers.

Class Diagram

Much like the previous classes, the core interactions with the Customer class involve methods to create, update, validate, find, and view customers. These methods and the necessary properties are enumerated in the class diagram shown in Figure 16.9.

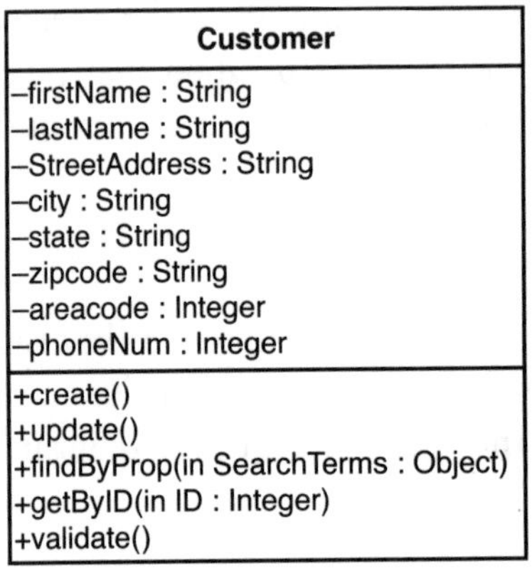

Customer
–firstName : String –lastName : String –StreetAddress : String –city : String –state : String –zipcode : String –areacode : Integer –phoneNum : Integer
+create() +update() +findByProp(in SearchTerms : Object) +getByID(in ID : Integer) +validate()

FIGURE 16.9   The properties and methods of the Customer class are enumerated in the class diagram.

Learning from our experiences with the Product and Offer classes, we will implement Customer as a subclass of PersistableObject. This will provide the core infrastructure for validation and data access, leaving us the rest of the infrastructure to define, such as properties, constructor, getters, and setters. The first iteration of the Customer class is shown in Listing 16.9

LISTING 16.9   The *Customer* Class Is Built as a Subclass of *PersistableObject*

```
class Customer extends PersistableObject{
    // instance properties
    private var firstName:String;
    private var lastName:String;
    private var areaCode:Number;
    private var phoneNum:Number;
    private var street1:String;
    private var city:String;
    private var state:String;
    private var zipCode:String;

    //static properties
    private static var dataAccessObject:DataAccess = new
    DataAccess("http://localhost:8500/oopas2/components/Customer.cfc?
    wsdl");
```

```
    //constructor
    public function Customer(firstName:String, lastName:String,
areaCode:Number, phoneNum:Number, street1:String, city:String,
state:String, zipCode:String){
        this.setValues(firstName, lastName, areaCode, phoneNum,
street1, city, state,zipCode);
    }

//data access functions
    public function update(firstName:String, lastName:String,
areaCode:Number, phoneNum:Number, street1:String, city:String,
state:String, zipCode:String, resultsMethod:Function,
statusMethod:Function):Boolean{

this.setValues(firstName,lastName,areaCode,phoneNum,street1,city,state,
zipCode);
        if(this.validateData()){

Customer.dataAccessObject.accessRemote("update",this.serializeValues(),
resultsMethod, statusMethod);
            return true;
        } else {
            return false;
        }
    }

    //validation
    public function validateData():Boolean{
        if(!validateString(this.getFirstName())){
            return false;
        } else if (!validateString(this.getLastName())){
            return false;
        } else if (!validateNumberForLength(this.getAreaCode(),3)){
            return false;
        } else if (!validateNumberForLength(this.getPhoneNum(),7)){
            return false;
        } else if (!validateString(this.getStreet1())){
            return false;
        } else if (!validateString(this.getCity())){
            return false;
        } else if (!validateString(this.getState())){
            return false;
        } else if (!validateString(this.getZipCode())){
            return false;
        } else {
            return true;
```

continues

LISTING 16.9   Continued

```
            }
        }

        // setter functions
    public function setValues(firstName:String, lastName:String,
areaCode:Number, phoneNum:Number, street1:String, city:String,
state:String, zipCode:String):Void{
            this.setFirstName(firstName);
            this.setLastName(lastName);
            this.setAreaCode(areaCode);
            this.setPhoneNum(phoneNum);
            this.setStreet1(street1);
            this.setCity(city);
            this.setState(state);
            this.setZipCode(zipCode);
    }

    public function setFirstName(firstName:String):Void{
        this.firstName = firstName;
    }
    public function setLastName(lastName:String):Void{
        this.lastName = lastName;
    }
    public function setAreaCode(areaCode:Number):Void{
        this.areaCode = areaCode;
    }
    public function setPhoneNum(phoneNum:Number):Void{
        this.phoneNum = phoneNum;
    }
    public function setStreet1(street1:String):Void{
        this.street1 = street1;
    }
    public function setCity(city:String):Void{
        this.city = city;
    }
    public function setState(state:String):Void{
        this.state = state;
    }
    public function setZipCode(zipCode:String):Void{
        this.zipCode = zipCode;
    }

    // getter functions

    public function serializeValues():Object{
```

```
            var tmpObject = new Object();
            tmpObject.firstName = this.getFirstName();
            tmpObject.lastName = this.getLastName();
            tmpObject.areaCode = this.getAreaCode();
            tmpObject.phoneNum = this.getPhoneNum();
            tmpObject.street1 = this.getStreet1();
            tmpObject.city = this.getCity();
            tmpObject.state = this.getState();
            tmpObject.zipCode = this.getZipCode();
            return tmpObject;
    }
    public function getFirstName():String{
            return this.firstName;
    }
    public function getLastName():String{
            return this.lastName;
    }
    public function getAreaCode():Number{
            return this.areaCode;
    }
    public function getPhoneNum():Number{
            return this.phoneNum;
    }
    public function getStreet1():String{
            return this.street1;
    }
    public function getCity():String{
            return this.city;
    }
    public function getState():String{
            return this.state;
    }
    public function getZipCode():String{
            return this.zipCode;
    }
}
```

Structurally, this class is just like the ones defined earlier. It begins by declaring the class Customer as a subclass of PersistableObject, which defines the validation and data access details. This is followed by the declarations of the instance properties and the datatypes of each property. The properties and their types are defined exactly as they were designed in the class diagram in Figure 16.9. Next, the specific dataAccessObject property for this class is created as a static property, with the URL for the server-side Customer object passed as an argument.

After all the properties are defined, the constructor is declared. Much like the constructors of the previous classes, the arguments are passed to a `setValues()` method to reduce duplication of effort across the constructor and update methods.

The `update()` method definition follows. Like the classes previously defined, the `update()` method will validate the data before passing it on to the `accessRemote()` method of the `dataAccessObject`. Next, the data validation method is defined. For this class, we needed a new validation rule to handle validating phone numbers and area codes. According to the use cases, not only do those fields need to be numeric, but also they are required to have a certain number of characters. To facilitate this, we will add a new method to the `PersistableObject` class, named `validateNumberForLength()`. This method is shown in Listing 16.10. The `Customer` class is completed with the definitions for the getter and setter methods for the class.

LISTING 16.10   The *PersistableObject* Class Is Enhanced with the Addition of a *validateNumberForLength()* Method

```
class PersistableObject{
     // static properties
     private static var dataAccessObject:DataAccess;
     private var validateData:Function;
     private var serializeValues:Function;

     //empty constructor
     function PersistableObject(){}

     // data access methods
     public function insert(resultsMethod:Function,
statusMethod:Function):Boolean{
          if(this.validateData()){

PersistableObject.dataAccessObject.accessRemote("create",this.serialize
Values(),resultsMethod, statusMethod);
               return true;
          } else {
               trace("Data invalid");
               return false;
          }
     }

     public function search(propertyObj:Object, resultsMethod:Function,
statusMethod:Function):Void{

PersistableObject.dataAccessObject.accessRemote("retrieveByProp",
propertyObj, resultsMethod, statusMethod);
          }
```

```
    public static function getById(ID:Number, resultsMethod:Function,
statusMethod:Function):Void{

PersistableObject.dataAccessObject.accessRemote("retrieveByID",ID,
resultsMethod, statusMethod);
        }

    // validation methods
    private function validateString(string:String):Boolean{
        if(string.length == 0){
            return false;
        } else {
            for(var i:Number=0;i<string.length;i++){
                if(string.charAt(i) != " "){
                    return true;
                    break;
                }
            }
        }
    }
    private function validateNumber(number:Number):Boolean{
        if (isNaN(number)){
            return false;
        } else {
            return true;
        }
    }
    private function validateNonZeroNumber(number:Number):Boolean{
        if (!validateNumber(number) || number <= 0){
            return false;
        } else {
            return true;
        }
    }
    private function validateNumberForLength(number:Number,
length:Number):Boolean{
        if (!validateNumber(number)){
            return false;
        } else if (String(number).length != length){
            return false;
        } else {
            return true;
        }
    }
}
```

The new method, `validateNumberForLength()`, begins by using the `validateNumber()` method to check whether the specified value is indeed a number. If that test is passed, the value's length is checked by casting it as a `String` and using the `length` property of the `String` class. If the length matches, the method returns `true`; otherwise, it fails and returns `false`.

The *Employee* Class

We now need to create a class to represent the users of the system. We need to detail only a single use case. It describes how an employee is authenticated to the system.

Use Case

Use Case: Log in

Actors: CCR, PCM, SM, and DER

Preconditions: None

Primary Flow:

1. Actor launches application.
2. A screen is presented to the actor with the following fields:
   - User name
   - Password
3. When fields are filled, actor clicks the Submit" button.
4. Server attempts to authenticate actor.
5. If authenticated, user is redirected to the primary page for the Users group.

Alternative Flows:

4a. If username and password do not match username and password on the server, user is redirected to login screen and presented with a message that he or she did not enter a valid username and password.

Sequence Diagram

The only use case identified here for the `Employee` class deals with how they are authenticated to the system. Let's look at the sequence diagram (Figure 16.10) showing how that login routine works within the system.

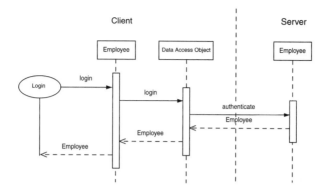

FIGURE 16.10   The sequence diagram for the `Employee` class shows interactions between employees and the system.

Class Diagram

The login routine diagrammed here is pretty straightforward. It passes the login data to the data access object, which in turn passes it on to the server-side method. While not specifically required for the application, a few more properties and methods will be added when we create the class diagram, as we know that employees are at their core, people, and therefore have some inherent properties, such as name, address, and phone number. These are detailed along with the login specific properties and methods in Figure 16.11.

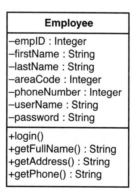

FIGURE 16.11   The initial version of the `Employee` class is very simple, yet its similarity to the `Customer` class may hint at a better solution.

Comparing the Employee class diagram to that of the Customer class shows some similarities. Both have names, addresses, and phone numbers, and both have methods for retrieving them. This might seem a good place for a Person superclass, which implements the common properties and methods of both Employee and Customer. However, there is a key difference between the two: customers are a PersistableObject, meaning that the system will be responsible for creating and updating instances of Customer. Employees, however, are not a PesistableObject; the means to add, update, and delete employees exists in a separate HR application, which has no bearing on the application being designed here. The only overlap between the two applications is that the application designed here will use the Web Services the HR application has exposed for authenticating users and retrieving their information. That web service exposes methods to allow for neither creating nor updating employees.

Without improperly forcing the Employee class to subclass PersistableObject, it won't be possible to have both the Employee and Customer classes inherit from a common superclass; ActionScript 2.0 does not allow multiple inheritance. The only remaining way to enforce the commonalities between these classes will be to create an *interface* that both classes can implement.

NOTE

For details on interfaces, see Chapter 6, "Understanding Interfaces in ActionScript 2.0."

Because a class cannot inherit from more than one superclass in ActionScript 2.0, we will instead implement an interface to ensure that common methods such as getFullName, getPhone, and getAddress exist for all people, whether they are part of the Employee or Customer class. With this interface in place, the existing Customer class needs to be refactored to implement the interface, and the newly created Employee class also needs to be set to implement it.

Figure 16.12 shows the modified class diagrams for the Employee and Customer classes, including a newly defined interface, Person.

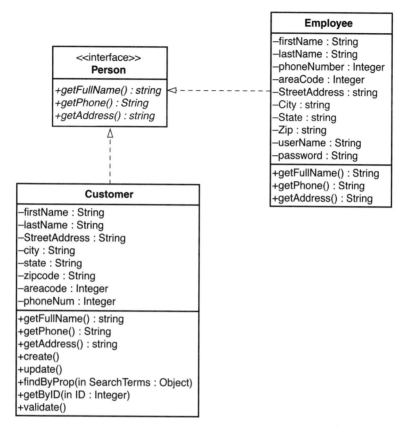

FIGURE 16.12   An interface `Person` is created to enforce that both `Employees` and `Customers` have common methods.

Listing 16.11 shows the new `Person` interface, the `Employee` class, and the modifications to the `Customer` class. For the `Customer`, the changes are shown in bold.

LISTING 16.11   The *Employee* Class, with *Person* Defined

```
interface Person{
    public function getFullName():String;
    public function getPhone():String;
    public function getAddress():String;
}
class Employee implements Person{
        private var empId:Number;
        private var firstName:String;
        private var lastName:String;
        private var areaCode:Number;
```

continues

LISTING 16.11   Continued

```
        private var phoneNum:Number;
        private var street:String;
        private var city:String;
        private var state:String;
        private var zipCode:String;
        private var userName:String;
        private var password:String;

        private static var dataAccessObject:DataAccess = new
DataAccess("http://localhost:8500/oopas2/components/Employee.cfc?wsdl");

        public function Employee(firstName:String, lastName:String,
areaCode:Number, phoneNum:Number, street1:String, city:String,
state:String, zipCode:String){
                this.setValues(firstName, lastName, areaCode, phoneNum,
street1, city, state,zipCode);
        }
        // data access
        public function login(userName:String, password:String,
resultsMethod:Function, statusMethod:Function):Void{

Employee.dataAccessObject.accessRemote("login", [userName,password],
resultsMethod, statusMethod);
        }

        //interface functions

        public function getFullName():String{
                return this.getFirstName() + " " + this.getLastName();
        }
        public function getAddress():String{
                var theAddress = this.getStreet + newline + this.getCity()
+ " " + this.getState() + ", " + this.getZipCode();
        return theAddress;
        }
        public function getPhone():String{
                return "(" + this.getAreaCode() +") " +this.getPhoneNum()
;
        }

        // setter functions
        public function setValues(firstName:String, lastName:String,
areaCode:Number, phoneNum:Number, street1:String, city:String,
state:String, zipCode:String):Void{
                this.setFirstName(firstName);
```

```
        this.setLastName(lastName);
        this.setAreaCode(areaCode);
        this.setPhoneNum(phoneNum);
        this.setStreet(street);
        this.setCity(city);
        this.setState(state);
        this.setZipCode(zipCode);
}

public function setFirstName(firstName:String):Void{
        this.firstName = firstName;
}
public function setLastName(lastName:String):Void{
        this.lastName = lastName;
}
public function setAreaCode(areaCode:Number):Void{
        this.areaCode = areaCode;
}
public function setPhoneNum(phoneNum:Number):Void{
        this.phoneNum = phoneNum;
}
public function setStreet(street1:String):Void{
        this.street = street1;
}
public function setCity(city:String):Void{
        this.city = city;
}
public function setState(state:String):Void{
        this.state = state;
}
public function setZipCode(zipCode:String):Void{
        this.zipCode = zipCode;
}

// getter functions

public function serializeValues():Object{
        var tmpObject = new Object();
        tmpObject.firstName = this.getFirstName();
        tmpObject.lastName = this.getLastName();
        tmpObject.areaCode = this.getAreaCode();
        tmpObject.phoneNum = this.getPhoneNum();
        tmpObject.street = this.getStreet();
        tmpObject.city = this.getCity();
        tmpObject.state = this.getState();
        tmpObject.zipCode = this.getZipCode();
```

continues

LISTING 16.11   Continued

```
            return tmpObject;
      }
      public function getFirstName():String{
            return this.firstName;
      }
      public function getLastName():String{
            return this.lastName;
      }
      public function getAreaCode():Number{
            return this.areaCode;
      }
      public function getPhoneNum():Number{
            return this.phoneNum;
      }
      public function getStreet():String{
            return this.street;
      }
      public function getCity():String{
            return this.city;
      }
      public function getState():String{
            return this.state;
      }
      public function getZipCode():String{
            return this.zipCode;
      }

}
class Customer extends PersistableObject implements Person{
      // instance properties
      private var firstName:String;
      private var lastName:String;
      private var areaCode:Number;
      private var phoneNum:Number;
      private var street1:String;
      private var city:String;
      private var state:String;
      private var zipCode:String;

      //static properties
      private static var dataAccessObject:DataAccess = new
      DataAccess("http://localhost:8500/oopas2/components/Customer.cfc?
      wsdl");

      //constructor
```

```
    public function Customer(firstName:String, lastName:String,
    areaCode:Number, phoneNum:Number, street1:String, city:String,
    state:String, zipCode:String){
            this.setValues(firstName, lastName, areaCode, phoneNum,
street1, city, state,zipCode);
    }

    //interface functions

        public function getFullName():String{
                return this.getFirstName() + " " +
this.getLastName();
        }
        public function getAddress():String{
                var theAddress = this.getStreet1 + newline +
this.getCity() + " " + this.getState() + ", " + this.getZipCode();
                return theAddress;
        }
        public function getPhone():String{
                return "(" + this.getAreaCode() +") "
+this.getPhoneNum() ;
        }

//data access functions
    public function update(firstName:String, lastName:String,
areaCode:Number, phoneNum:Number, street1:String, city:String,
state:String, zipCode:String, resultsMethod:Function,
statusMethod:Function):Boolean{

this.setValues(firstName,lastName,areaCode,phoneNum,street1,city,state,
zipCode);
        if(this.validateData()){

Customer.dataAccessObject.accessRemote("update",this.serializeValues(),
resultsMethod, statusMethod);
                return true;
        } else {
                return false;
        }
    }

    //validation
    public function validateData():Boolean{
        if(!validateString(this.getFirstName())){
                return false;
        } else if (!validateString(this.getLastName())){
```

LISTING 16.11 Continued

```
                  return false;
              } else if
(!validateNumberForLength(this.getAreaCode(),3)){
                  return false;
              } else if
(!validateNumberForLength(this.getPhoneNum(),7)){
                  return false;
              } else if (!validateString(this.getStreet1())){
                  return false;
              } else if (!validateString(this.getCity())){
                  return false;
              } else if (!validateString(this.getState())){
                  return false;
              } else if (!validateString(this.getZipCode())){
                  return false;
              } else {
                  return true;
                  }
              }

              // setter functions
public function setValues(firstName:String, lastName:String,
areaCode:Number, phoneNum:Number, street1:String, city:String,
state:String, zipCode:String):Void{
              this.setFirstName(firstName);
              this.setLastName(lastName);
              this.setAreaCode(areaCode);
              this.setPhoneNum(phoneNum);
              this.setStreet1(street1);
              this.setCity(city);
              this.setState(state);
              this.setZipCode(zipCode);
      }

      public function setFirstName(firstName:String):Void{
          this.firstName = firstName;
      }
      public function setLastName(lastName:String):Void{
          this.lastName = lastName;
      }
      public function setAreaCode(areaCode:Number):Void{
          this.areaCode = areaCode;
      }
      public function setPhoneNum(phoneNum:Number):Void{
```

```
        this.phoneNum = phoneNum;
}
public function setStreet1(street1:String):Void{
        this.street1 = street1;
}
public function setCity(city:String):Void{
        this.city = city;
}
public function setState(state:String):Void{
        this.state = state;
}
public function setZipCode(zipCode:String):Void{
        this.zipCode = zipCode;
}

// getter functions

public function serializeValues():Object{
        var tmpObject = new Object();
        tmpObject.firstName = this.getFirstName();
        tmpObject.lastName = this.getLastName();
        tmpObject.areaCode = this.getAreaCode();
        tmpObject.phoneNum = this.getPhoneNum();
        tmpObject.street1 = this.getStreet1();
        tmpObject.city = this.getCity();
        tmpObject.state = this.getState();
        tmpObject.zipCode = this.getZipCode();
        return tmpObject;
}
public function getFirstName():String{
        return this.firstName;
}
public function getLastName():String{
        return this.lastName;
}
public function getAreaCode():Number{
        return this.areaCode;
}
public function getPhoneNum():Number{
        return this.phoneNum;
}
public function getStreet1():String{
        return this.street1;
}
public function getCity():String{
        return this.city;
```

continues

LISTING 16.11   Continued

```
}
public function getState():String{
      return this.state;
}
public function getZipCode():String{
      return this.zipCode;
}
}
```

First, we see the newly defined `Person` interface, which requires that all implementing classes have methods to retrieve the person's name—one to retrieve the address and one to retrieve the phone number. Next, the refactored portions of the `Customer` class are shown, including the class definition, which now includes the command to implement the `Person` interface. Also shown are the specific methods required by the interface and their specific implementation for `Customers`.

The interface definition is followed by the newly created `Employee` class. Notice that the `Employee` class definition specifies that it will implement the `Person` interface. The class definition is very similar to the classes previously defined, except `Employee` does not extend `PersistableObject` class and has no validation rules. The only data access method defined is the `login()` method, which passes a username and password to the `login()` method on the server. The getter and setter methods are straightforward and closely mirror the structure of the previously defined classes.

The `Employee` class is followed by the modified `Customer` class. In Listing 16.11, the changes from the previous definitions of this class are set in bold.

With the addition of the ability to authenticate users, all that remains to be defined is the `Subscription` class. We discuss that next.

The *Subscription* Class

When a customer signs up for one of the offers, a subscription is created for that customer.

Use Case

Use Case: Create subscription

Actors: CCR

Preconditions:

- Actor has been authenticated to the system and identified as a member of a group listed previously.

- Customer has called, indicating he or she wishes to subscribe to a magazine.

- Customer record has either been found or created.

Primary Flow:

1. Actor is presented with screen containing a menu of all products.

2. Actor chooses a product from the menu and is shown a second menu, containing all active offers for that product.

3. Actor clicks button indicating that the chosen offer is the one to which the customer wishes to subscribe.

4. Actor is presented with a verification screen, showing the customer and the address on file for that customer. Actor will check if the address is both the shipping address and the billing address for the customer.

5. Actor confirms the subscription details, telling the customer that he or she will be billed at their billing address soon and that the subscription will begin shortly.

Alternative Flows

1a. Actor can choose to see details of currently selected product.

2a. Actor can choose to see details of currently selected offer.

5a. Actor can enter a separate billing address or change the customer's shipping address.

Use Case: Search and view subscription

Actors: CCR and PCM

Preconditions:

- Actor has been authenticated to the system and identified as a member of a group listed.

Primary Flow:

1. Actor requests to search subscriptions.

2. Actor is presented with an interface representing the various aspects on which he or she can search:

   - Text input for customer name
   - Menu populated with products
   - Menu populated with offers (which shows offers only for the currently selected product in the product menu)

3. Actor clicks button to initiate a search.

4. Matching results are shown to the actor.

5. Actor can choose a single subscription from the matching results.

6. All details of chosen subscription are shown to actor.

Alternative Flows:

4a. If no subscriptions match the search criteria, actor is informed that there are no results.

Sequence Diagram

Subscriptions are potentially the most difficult of the system entities to understand because they interact with nearly every other entity we have designed. Looking to the sequence diagrams in Figure 16.13 shows the interactions necessary to implement the use cases.

Class Diagram

As we begin to define the class diagram for the Subscription class, we find a few shortcomings in the other classes which will need to be addressed. There are many reasons for this, among them, a subscription will need an end date; we also need a way to determine how frequently issues are sent so that the number of issues for an offer can be computed to a certain length of time. To facilitate this, a new property of Product is added, called issuesPerYear. To make use of this from the Offer class, a new method named getDuration() is added. It will return the number of months for which the issues will be sent for a particular offer. (Considering that different publications are published on different schedules, 12 issues of a weekly will last only three months, while 12 issues of a monthly will last a year.)

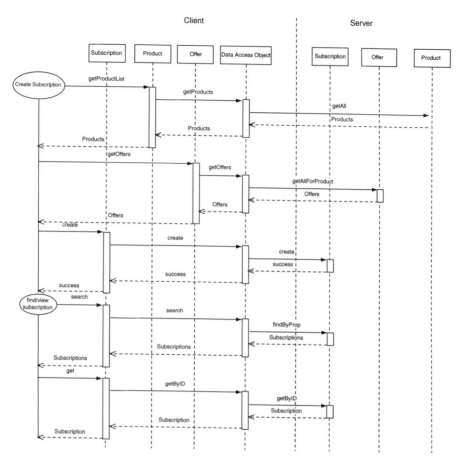

FIGURE 16.13   The sequence diagram for the `Subscription` class shows that it requires interactions with the `Offers` and `Products` classes.

A second change that impacts several classes is the need for a subscription to have both a billing and shipping address. With this information, XYZ Subscriptions can send the bills for a given subscription to an address that is different than the shipping address. There are different possible approaches to this.

One approach would be to store an array of addresses for each customer and then store the array index for those values in the subscription. While this approach is valid, the fact remains that the existing data structure (from the legacy application) for a customer has only a single address record. To have a minimal impact on the existing database, but yet retain the maximum flexibility for the new system, an `Address` class will be created. The class will store all the address fields (street, city, state, and zip). Then, any classes needing to make use of an address will have one of their properties assigned an instance of the `Address` class.

To implement the Address class, we will need to go back and refactor the Customer and Employee classes (both of which made use of addresses) as well as the Person interface, which initially required the getAddress() methods to return a string. Instead, the getAddress() methods of classes implementing that interface will return an instance of the Address class. Lastly, the properties shippingAddress and billingAddress will be added to the Subscription class, and each will hold an instance of the Address class. With the knowledge of the changes that need to be made, we refactor the classes and derive the class diagram, shown in Figure 16.14.

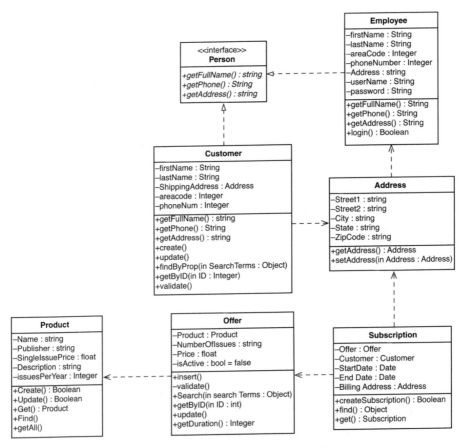

FIGURE 16.14   In creating the class diagram for the Subscription class, nearly every other class has been refactored.

After the structure of the `Subscription` class is understood, as well as the other changes, we can make an attempt at implementing them. Listing 16.12 shows the new and refactored classes.

LISTING 16.12   The Definition of the *Subscription* Class Necessitates Refactoring Many Other Classes

```
class Subscription extends PersistableObject{

    private var offer:Offer;
    private var customer:Customer;
    private var startDate:Date;
    private var endDate:Date;
    private var billingAddress:Address;
    private var shippingAddress:Address;

    private static var dataAccessObject = new
    DataAccess("http://localhost:8500/oopas2/components/Subscription.
    cfc?wsdl");

    public function Subscription(offer:Offer, customer:Customer,
startDate:Date, billingAddress:Address, shippingAddress:Address){
            setOffer(offer);
            setCustomer(customer);
            setStartDate(startDate);
            setBillingAddress(billingAddress);
            setShippingAddress(shippingAddress);
            setEndDate(this.computeEndDate());
    }

    private function computeEndDate():Date{
            var year:Number = this.startDate.getFullYear();

            var endMonth:Number = this.startDate.getMonth() +
this.offer.getDuration();

            if (endMonth > 11){
                    var yearsOver = Math.floor(endMonth/12);
                    year += yearsOver;
                    endMonth -= (yearsOver*12);
            }
            return new Date(year,endMonth,startDate.getDate());
    }

    //setter functions
    public function setOffer(offer:Offer){
            this.offer = offer;
    }
```

continues

LISTING 16.12   Continued

```
        public function setCustomer(customer:Customer){
                this.customer = customer;
        }
        public function setBillingAddress(billingAddress:Address){
                this.billingAddress = billingAddress;
        }
        public function setShippingAddress(shippingAddress:Address){
                this.shippingAddress = shippingAddress;
        }
        public function setStartDate(startDate:Date){
                this.startDate = startDate;
        }
        public function setEndDate(endDate:Date){
                this.endDate = endDate;
        }
        //setter functions
        public function getOffer():Offer{
                return this.offer;
        }
        public function getCustomer():Customer{
                return this.customer;
        }
        public function getStartDate():Date{
                return this.startDate;
        }
        public function getEndDate():Date{
                return this.endDate;
        }
}

class Product extends PersistableObject{
        // instance proprerties
        private var name:String;
        private var publisher:String;
        private var singleIssuePrice:Number;
        private var description:String;
        private var prodID:Number;
        private var issuesPerYear:Number;

        //static properties
        private static var dataAccessObject:DataAccess = new
DataAccess("http:/localhost:8500/oopas2/components/product.cfc?wsdl");

        //consturctor
```

```
        function Product(name:String, publisher:String ,price:Number,
description:String, issuesPerYear:Number){
                setValues(name,publisher,price,description,issuesPerYear);
        }


        //data access functions

                public function update (name:String, publisher:String,
price:Number, description:String, issuesPerYear:Number,
resultsMethod:Function, statusMethod:Function){

setValues(name,publisher,price,description,issuesPerYear);
                        if(this.validateData()){

Product.dataAccessObject.accessRemote("update",this.serializeValues());
                        }
                }

        //validation
        public function validateData():Boolean{
                var isValid:Boolean = true;
                if(!validateString(this.getName())){
                        return false;
                } else if (!validateString(this.getPublisher())){
                        return false;
                } else if (!validateNumber(this.getSingleIssuePrice())){
                        return false;
                } else if
(!validateNonZeroNumber(this.getIssuesPerYear())){
                        return false;
                } else {
                        return true;
                }
        }


        // setter functions
        public function
setValues(name:String,publisher:String,price:Number,description:String,
issuesPerYear:Number){
                setName(name);
                setPublisher(publisher);
                setSingleIssuePrice(price);
                setDescription(description);
                setIssuesPerYear(issuesPerYear);
        }
```

continues

LISTING 16.12   Continued

```
public function setName(name:String):Void{
       this.name = name;
}
public function setPublisher(publisher:String):Void{
       this.publisher= publisher;
}
public function setSingleIssuePrice(price:Number):Void{
       this.singleIssuePrice= price;
}
public function setDescription(description:String):Void{
       this.description = description;
}
public function setIssuesPerYear(issuesPerYear:Number):Void{
       this.issuesPerYear = issuesPerYear;
}
// getter functions
public function serializeValues():Object{
       var tmpObject  = new Object();
       tmpObject.name = this.getName();
       tmpObject.publisher = this.getPublisher();
       tmpObject.singleIssuePrice = this.getSingleIssuePrice();
       tmpObject.description = this.getDescription();
       tmpObject.issuesPerYear = this.getIssuesPerYear();
       return tmpObject;
}

public function getName():String{
       return this.name;
}
public function getPublisher():String{
       return this.publisher;
}
public function getSingleIssuePrice():Number{
       return this.singleIssuePrice;
}
public function getDescription():String{
       return this.description;
}
public function getID():Number{
       return this.prodID;
}
public function getIssuesPerYear():Number{
       return this.issuesPerYear;
}
}
```

```
}class Address extends PersistableObject{
      private var street1:String;
      private var street2:String;
      private var city:String;
      private var state:String;
      private var zipCode:String;

      public function
Address(street1:String,city:String,state:String,zipCode:String,street2:
String){
             this.setStreet1(street1);
             this.setStreet2(street2);
             this.setCity(city);
             this.setState(state);
             this.setZipCode(zipCode);
      }

      // validation
      public function validateData():Boolean{
             if (!validateString(this.getStreet1())){
                   return false;
             } else if (!validateString(this.getCity())){
                   return false;
             } else if (!validateString(this.getState())){
                   return false;
             } else if (!validateString(this.getZipCode())){
                   return false;
             } else {
                   return true;
             }
      }

      // setter functions

      public function setStreet1(street1:String):Void{
             this.street1 = street1;
      }
      public function setStreet2(street2:String):Void{
             this.street2 = street2;
      }
      public function setCity(city:String):Void{
             this.city = city;
      }
      public function setState(state:String):Void{
             this.state = state;
      }
```

continues

LISTING 16.12   Continued

```
        public function setZipCode(zipCode:String):Void{
              this.zipCode = zipCode;
        }

        // getter functions
        public function serializeValues():Object{
              var tmpObject = new Object();
              tmpObject.street1 = this.getStreet1();
              tmpObject.street2 = this.getStreet2();
              tmpObject.city = this.getCity();
              tmpObject.state = this.getState();
              tmpObject.zipCode = this.getZipCode();
              return tmpObject;
        }
        public function getStreet1():String{
              return this.street1;
        }
        public function getStreet2():String{
              return this.street2;
        }
        public function getCity():String{
              return this.city;
        }
        public function getState():String{
              return this.state;
        }
        public function getZipCode():String{
              return this.zipCode;
        }
}

interface Person{
      public function getFullName():String;
      public function getPhone():String;
      public function getAddress():Address;
}

class Customer extends PersistableObject implements Person{
      // instance properties
      private var firstName:String;
      private var lastName:String;
      private var areaCode:Number;
      private var phoneNum:Number;
      private var address:Address;
```

```
        //static properties
        private static var dataAccessObject:DataAccess = new
        DataAccess("http://localhost:8500/oopas2/components/Customer.cfc?
        wsdl");

        //constructor
        public function Customer(firstName:String, lastName:String,
areaCode:Number, phoneNum:Number, address:Address){
                this.setValues(firstName, lastName, areaCode, phoneNum,
address);
        }

        //interface functions

            public function getFullName():String{
                    return this.getFirstName() + " " +
this.getLastName();
                }
            public function getAddress():Address{
                    return this.address;
            }
            public function getPhone():String{
                    return "(" + this.getAreaCode() +") "
+this.getPhoneNum() ;
                }

//data access functions
        public function update(firstName:String, lastName:String,
areaCode:Number, phoneNum:Number, address:Address,
resultsMethod:Function, statusMethod:Function):Boolean{

this.setValues(firstName,lastName,areaCode,phoneNum,address);
            if(this.validateData()){

Customer.dataAccessObject.accessRemote("update",this.serializeValues(),
resultsMethod, statusMethod);
                    return true;
            } else {
                    return false;
            }
        }

        //validation
        public function validateData():Boolean{
            if(!validateString(this.getFirstName())){
                    return false;
```

continues

LISTING 16.12   Continued

```
        } else if (!validateString(this.getLastName())){
            return false;
        } else if
(!validateNumberForLength(this.getAreaCode(),3)){
            return false;
        } else if
(!validateNumberForLength(this.getPhoneNum(),7)){
            return false;
        } else if (!this.getAddress().validateData()){
            return false;
        } else {
            return true;
            }
        }

        // setter functions
    public function setValues(firstName:String, lastName:String,
areaCode:Number, phoneNum:Number, address:Address):Void{
            this.setFirstName(firstName);
            this.setLastName(lastName);
            this.setAreaCode(areaCode);
            this.setPhoneNum(phoneNum);
            this.setAddress(address);
    }

    public function setFirstName(firstName:String):Void{
            this.firstName = firstName;
    }
    public function setLastName(lastName:String):Void{
            this.lastName = lastName;
    }
    public function setAreaCode(areaCode:Number):Void{
            this.areaCode = areaCode;
    }
    public function setPhoneNum(phoneNum:Number):Void{
            this.phoneNum = phoneNum;
    }
    public function setAddress(address:Address):Void{
            this.address = address;
    }

    // getter functions

    public function serializeValues():Object{
            var tmpObject = new Object();
```

```
            tmpObject.firstName = this.getFirstName();
            tmpObject.lastName = this.getLastName();
            tmpObject.areaCode = this.getAreaCode();
            tmpObject.phoneNum = this.getPhoneNum();
            tmpObject.address = this.getAddress().serializeValues();
            return tmpObject;
        }
      public function getFirstName():String{
            return this.firstName;
        }
      public function getLastName():String{
            return this.lastName;
        }
      public function getAreaCode():Number{
            return this.areaCode;
        }
      public function getPhoneNum():Number{
            return this.phoneNum;
        }

}


class Employee implements Person{
      private var empId:Number;
      private var firstName:String;
      private var lastName:String;
      private var areaCode:Number;
      private var phoneNum:Number;
      private var address:Address;
      private var userName:String;
      private var password:String;

      private static var dataAccessObject:DataAccess = new
DataAccess("http://localhost:8500/oopas2/components/Employee.cfc?wsdl");

      public function Employee(firstName:String, lastName:String,
areaCode:Number, phoneNum:Number, address:Address){
            this.setValues(firstName, lastName, areaCode, phoneNum,
address);
        }
      // data access
      public function login(userName:String, password:String,
      resultsMethod:Function, statusMethod:Function):Void{
         Employee.dataAccessObject.accessRemote("login",[userName,
password],resultsMethod, statusMethod);
        }
```

continues

LISTING 16.12   Continued

```
//interface functions

public function getFullName():String{
      return this.getFirstName() + " " + this.getLastName();
}
public function getAddress():Address{
      return this.getAddress();
}
public function getPhone():String{
      return "(" + this.getAreaCode() +") " +this.getPhoneNum() ;
}


// setter functions
public function setValues(firstName:String, lastName:String,
areaCode:Number, phoneNum:Number, address:Address):Void{
          this.setFirstName(firstName);
          this.setLastName(lastName);
          this.setAreaCode(areaCode);
          this.setPhoneNum(phoneNum);
          this.setAddress(address);
}

public function setFirstName(firstName:String):Void{
          this.firstName = firstName;
}
public function setLastName(lastName:String):Void{
          this.lastName = lastName;
}
public function setAreaCode(areaCode:Number):Void{
          this.areaCode = areaCode;
}
public function setPhoneNum(phoneNum:Number):Void{
          this.phoneNum = phoneNum;
}
public function setAddress(address:Address):Void{
          this.address = address;
}

// getter functions
public function serializeValues():Object{
          var tmpObject = new Object();
          tmpObject.firstName = this.getFirstName();
          tmpObject.lastName = this.getLastName();
          tmpObject.areaCode = this.getAreaCode();
```

```
            tmpObject.phoneNum = this.getPhoneNum();
            tmpObject.address = this.getAddress().serializeValues();
            return tmpObject;
        }
    public function getFirstName():String{
            return this.firstName;
        }
    public function getLastName():String{
            return this.lastName;
        }
    public function getAreaCode():Number{
            return this.areaCode;
        }
    public function getPhoneNum():Number{
            return this.phoneNum;
        }

}
```

As can be seen, nearly every class already defined has been refactored to implement subscriptions properly. Remember, as discussed back in Chapter 9, "Building and Using UI Components," refactoring is a natural process within object-oriented design. You shouldn't fear it; you should embrace it. It's much quicker and cheaper to make these changes now rather than later.

Listing 16.12 begins with the Subscription class. Like the rest, we begin by defining the properties, which match those shown in the class diagram. Next, in the constructor, all the properties, except for endDate, are passed in. The reason for the exception is that endDate is a computed field, based on the number of issues for an offer and the number of times a year a product is published. Therefore, in the final line of the Constructor, the endDate is set, like so:

```
setEndDate(this.computeEndDate());
```

This is the final line of the constructor, so it can be known that the rest of the properties have already been properly set.

The constructor is followed by the definition of the computeEndDate() method. This method begins by determining the current year. Next, the duration of the subscription (derived by calling the getDuration method of the Offer instance) is added to the current month to begin computing the end month of the subscription. If the resulting sum is greater than 11 (remember that in ActionScript, December is seen as month 11 because months are a zero-indexed array), the number of years until the subscription expires is computed by dividing the sum of the months by 12 and rounding down. The number of years is added to the current year. Then, the number of years multiplied by 12 is subtracted from the end month to determine the correct ending month. Finally, the method returns a new instance of the Date class, using the computed year and month. The remaining methods are simple getter and setters.

After the end of the Subscription class definition, Listing 16.12 next shows the newly created method of the refactored Offer class. This method simply determines the number of issues per month a product will ship by dividing the number of issues per year by 12. Without this method, the subscription would not be able to determine an end date.

Next, the refactored Product class is shown. All the refactoring surrounds the declaration, getting and setting of the issuesPerYear property.

This definition is followed by a newly created Address class. This class is set as a subclass of PersistableObject, not because it will make use of a DataAccessObject on its own, but to allow use of the validation methods. There are no surprises to the Address class definition. It has a standard set of properties and a constructor, followed by data validation and the getters and setters. If you review where we started with the Customer class, the data validation, getters, and setters were lifted wholesale from their origins in the Customer class.

The new Address class definition is followed by the revised Person interface. All that has changed here is the return type of the getAddress() method. Rather than returning a string, it now returns an Address object. This, of course, necessitates a reworking of the Customer and Employee classes so that they can properly implement this interface.

The Customer class is addressed next. The properties are revised to show an address property which will be an instance of the Address class. This is done instead of using separate properties for each piece of an address. Then, the constructor is modified, showing the passing in of an Address object, which is then passed on to the setValues method. The update method has also been similarly revised.

Next, the validateData() method is revised. To validate an address, we will invoke the Address classes validateData() method. The setValues() method is modified to also set the address field. Then, a setAddress() method is created to assign new Address objects to instances of Customer. The modifications to the serializeValues() method simply use the Address classes serializeValues() method to embed an Address object into the tmpObject.

The final part of Listing 16.12 is the revised `Employee` class. The only changes to this class are the removal of the address specific properties (street, city, and so on) and the replacing of them with the new `address` property.   This change is reflected in the properties declaration, the constructor, the `update()` method, the validation rules, and the getters and setters.

With all this in place, we're ready to pull it all together into a cohesive application.

Tying It All Together

With the class files for our core entities of the system built, all that remains is to assemble them into a single cohesive application. This will be done by creating a series of movie clips, which will act as the user's view to the application. The individual class files will act as the controllers, while the `DataAccessObject` class will be responsible for the model. The code representing the views for each screen will be located in class files associated with each movie clip. There are several benefits to moving the code from the timelines to independent class files.

Movie Clip Architecture

To begin, we need to understand how the various movie clips will interact with each other. We'll be architecting the movie clips to start with a single movie (main.fla), which will act as the overarching controller, loading and unloading other movies as needed. This first movie will create empty movie clips into which the various components can be loaded. There are three empty movie clips that will be used throughout: Login_mc is a clip that holds the login screen; nav_mc holds clips that have the navigational structure; and body_mc holds the core of each screen.

Building the Classes

To provide some necessary framework for each class file associated with a movie clip, a superclass named `ApplicationView` will be created. The class definition for `ApplicationView` can be seen in Listing 16.13.

LISTING 16.13 *ApplicationView* Acts as the Superclass to All the Classes Acting as a View

```
class ApplicationView extends MovieClip{
      public function ApplicationView(){}

      public function onEnterFrame(){
            postInit();

      }
      public function postInit(){
            this.onEnterFrame = null;
      }
}
```

The value of the `ApplicationView` class might not be obvious at first glance. It is set to inherit from the `MovieClip` class, contains an empty constructor, and two methods: `onEnterFrame()` and `postInit()`. `onEnterFrame()` is an event handler, which is called at the frame rate of a movie. We are using it to work around synchronicity issues with Flash.

When a class is associated with a `MovieClip`, the entire class is parsed before any visual elements are rendered on the Stage. This can lead to issues when the code is trying to address those elements. If they have not yet been rendered, they will not yet exist, and therefore the code in the class will have no effect. By adding an `onEnterFrame()` event, it is possible to instruct the class to execute certain commands after all the elements are rendered.

The one command in the `onEnterFrame()` method is a call to the `postInit()` method. The `postInit()` of `ApplicationView` sets the `onEnterFrame` event handler equal to `null`, effectively telling Flash not to continue to handle that event after the first time. Structurally, this enables us to create a `postInit()` method for each subclass, where any code relating to visual elements can be added with the safe knowledge that those elements already exist. All that needs to be remembered for each subclass is to make a call to `super.postInit()` so that the `onEnterFrame` is set to null.

The Main Movie Clip

If properly designed, main.fla will require no visual elements on the Stage except for an empty movie clip, to which our main.as class file will be attached. That class will contain the code only to implement the applications architecture. In the following sections, we examine each of the movie clips that make up the application. See Listing 16.14.

LISTING 16.14   Main.as Contains the Class File That Determines How Movies Will Be Loaded and Unloaded from the Application

```
class Main extends ApplicationView{
        var currentUser:Employee;
        var body_mc:MovieClip;
        var login_mc:MovieClip;
        var nav_mc:MovieClip;

        function postInit(){
                super.postInit();
                if(currentUser == undefined){
                    this.createEmptyMovieClip("login_mc",
this.getNextHighestDepth());
                    login_mc.loadMovie("login.swf");
                }

this.createEmptyMovieClip("nav_mc",this.getNextHighestDepth());

this.createEmptyMovieClip("body_mc",this.getNextHighestDepth());
        }

        function loadBody(mc:String):Void{
            body_mc.loadMovie(mc);
            body_mc._x = 200;
            body_mc._y = 0;
        }
        function loadNav (mc:String):Void{
            nav_mc.loadMovie(mc+".swf");
        }
}
```

This class begins declaring the local variables, in this case, a variable called currentUser of type Employee; also declared are the three MovieClip objects that will be created through code: body_mc, nav_mc, and login_mc.

This is followed by the postInit() method. As described earlier, our postInit() method will fire after all the code and visual assets are done loading. The first line of the postInit() method is a call to the super.postInit() to ensure that the onEnterFrame event handler is set to null. Next, we check to see if the currentUser property has already been populated; if not, we load the login screen so that the end user can be authenticated to the system. The last part of postInit() creates two more empty MovieClip objects, which will ultimately hold the navigation and body of our application.

Navigation Clips (DataEntry.fla, SubManager.fla, and CustService.fla)

Each section of the application will need a navigation structure. Generally, this will consist of a series of buttons for navigating between screens. Figure 16.15 shows the navigation for the Data entry screens.

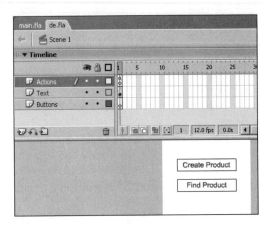

FIGURE 16.15   The screen consists of two buttons.

DataEntry.fla is the first of three navigation screens that will be used in the application. Each consists of a movie clip in the Library for each button. Each clip contains a text field, indicating what the link does, as well as a button. The buttons are all named `the_btn`. The buttons are placed on the Stage and converted into a single movie clip instance named `nav`. The class files are associated with the `nav` clip.

Listing 16.15 shows the class file associated with the `nav` movie in dataEntry.fla. The class files associated with these clips simply contain an `onRelease` handler for each button. Listing 16.15 shows the ActionScript for DE.fla. The other two navigation files closely follow this model.

LISTING 16.15   ActionScript for DE.fla

```
class DataEntryNav extends ApplicationView{
        var create_mc:MovieClip;
        var find_mc:MovieClip;

        function postInit(){
                super.postInit();
                create_mc.the_btn.onRelease = createProduct;
                find_mc.the_btn.onRelease = findProduct;
        }
```

```
function createProduct(){
    _parent._parent._parent._parent.loadBody
    ➥("createProduct.swf");
}
function findProduct(){

    _parent._parent._parent._parent.loadBody("findProduct.swf");
}
}
```

This class contains no real surprises. First, the visual elements create_mc and find_mc are declared as properties. Next, the postInit() method is defined. Just like the previous one, this postInit() also begins with a call to super.postInit(). The remainder of the postInit() method associates methods of this class with onRelease events of visual objects. The button within create_mc will trigger the createProduct() method, while the button in find_mc will trigger the findProduct() method. Last, the createProduct() and findProduct() methods are defined. These simply invoke the loadBody() method of main.

The only tricky part to these two methods is understanding why the proper path to the loadBody() method is _parent._parent._parent._parent. To understand this path, it helps to add the command trace(this) as the first line of either onRelease() handler. When that trace command is added and dataEntry.swf is loaded through main.swf, the trace statement will show level0.main.nav_mc.nav.create_mc.the_btn. This shows us that the onRelease event handler is fired in the scope of the button that was clicked and released. Table 16.2 shows the paths from the_btn.

TABLE 16.2   The Relative Paths from the *onRelease* Event Handler

PATH	DESTINATION
_parent	create_mc
_parent._parent	nav
_parent._parent._parent	nav_mc
_parent._parent._parent._parent	main

With the data entry navigation structure in place, the next logical step is to create the pieces that will comprise the body for the data entry screens.

The Create Product Screen

As we determined in the use cases earlier, Data Entry employees have two main interactions with the system: creating products and finding products. We are next going to define the Create product screen, as shown in Figure 16.16.

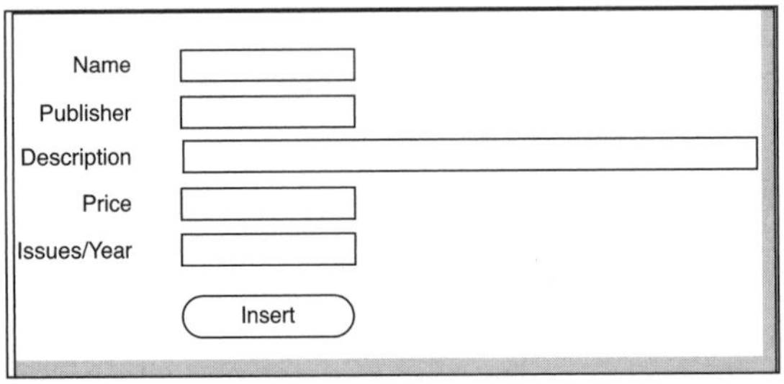

FIGURE 16.16   The screen for product creation.

To facilitate creating a product, a Data entry screen for products is implemented. This screen is fairly straightforward, in that it contains five input text fields and an Insert button, as shown in Figure 16.16. Listing 16.16 shows the class file attached to this movie clip.

LISTING 16.16   The Class Associated with Product Creation

```
class CreateProduct extends ApplicationView {
        var insert_pb:mx.controls.Button;
        var name_txt:TextField;
        var pub_txt:TextField;
        var price_txt:TextField;
        var desc_txt:TextField;
        var issues_txt:TextField;

        function postInit():Void {
                super.postInit();
                insert_pb.addEventListener("click", addProd);
        }
        function createResult(res){
                trace("results");
                for(var i in res){
                        trace(i+":"+res[i]);
                }
        }
```

```
function createStatus(res){
        trace("status");
        for(var i in res){
                trace(i+":"+res[i]);
        }
}
function addProd() {

        var prod:Product = new Product(_parent.name_txt.text,
_parent.pub_txt.text, Number(_parent.price_txt.text),
_parent.desc_txt.text, Number(_parent.issues_txt.text));
        prod.insert(createResult,createStatus);
}

}
```

The code for the screen is not complicated. First, the properties are declared. These consist of a push button and five text fields. Next the postInit() method is defined, which assigns the addProd() method of the class as the handler for clicks on the push button. This is followed by the definition for the createResults() and createStatus() methods. These methods are designed to handle either results or statuses returning from the Web Services call. All these do for now is trace the results or status, but when the system is fully fleshed out, they can follow the use cases for their behaviors. Last, the addProd() method is defined. This method assembles a new Product from the user's input and calls the insert() method to send it to the server. Earlier, in the definition for the Product class, the insert method was defined to first validate the data, and when successfully validated, to pass the product data to its DataAccessObject to be persisted on the server.

The Find Product Screen

The other action that a data entry employee can take is to find a product already in the database. Figure 16.17 shows the interface that a user can use to find a product.

The search interface for products has a similar look to the Product creation screen, with the addition of a DataGrid below the fields in which search results can be displayed. Other than the grid, this movie has the same five text fields and a button (see Figure 16.17), much like the previous screen.

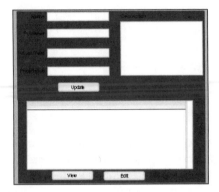

FIGURE 16.17   The product search interface.

Listing 16.17 shows the class file associated with this clip.

LISTING 16.17   The *FindProduct* Class Is Associated to the Movie Clip in findProduct.fla

```
class FindProduct extends ApplicationView{
        var details_mc:MovieClip;
        var name_txt:TextField
        var pub_txt:TextField;
        var desc_txt:TextField;
        var price_txt:TextField;
        var find_pb:mx.controls.Button;
        var products_dg:mx.controls.DataGrid;
        var view_pb:mx.controls.Button;
        var edit_pb:mx.controls.Button;

        function postInit():Void{
                super.postInit();
                find_pb.addEventListener("click",findProd);
                view_pb.addEventListener("click",showDetails);
                edit_pb.addEventListener("click",showDetails);
                this.showHidden(false);
                details_mc._visible = false;
        }

        function findProd(){
                var propObj:Object = new Object();
                if(name_txt.text.length){
                        propObj.name = name_txt.text;
                }
                if(pub_txt.text.length){
                        propObj.publisher = pub_txt.text;
                }
```

```
            if(desc_txt.text.length){
                    propObj.description = desc_txt.text;
            }
            if(price_txt.text.length){
                    propObj.singleIssuePrice = Number(price_txt.text);
            }
            Product.search(propObj,this.searchResult,this.error);

    }

    function showDetails(obj){
            var selectedButton = obj.target.label;
            if (selectedButton == "View"){
                    var isEditable:Boolean = false;
            } else {
                    var isEditable:Boolean = true;
            }

            var activeProd:Object =
_parent.products_dg.getItemAt(_parent.products_dg.selectedIndex);
            _parent.details_mc._visible = true;
            _parent.details_mc.showDetails (activeProd,isEditable);
    }

    function searchResult(theData){
            products_dg.dataProvider=theData;
            this.showHidden(true);
    }

    function error(status){
            trace(status.description);
    }

    function showHidden(bool:Boolean):Void{
            products_dg._visible = bool;
            edit_pb._visible = bool;
            view_pb._visible = bool;
    }
}
```

This class, like the other View classes, begins by declaring the class as a subclass of ApplicationView. Next, the visual elements on the Stage are declared
as properties of the class. These properties include one MovieClip (which will
have its own class file), four TextFields, three Buttons, and a DataGrid.
Next, the postInit() method assigns event handlers to each component. Also
in postInit() is code to hide the visual elements that are not yet in use.

The postInit() method is followed by the event handlers. The first event handler method is findProd(). This method is invoked when the Find button is clicked. It checks each text field and any that are not blank are added to an object, which is sent to the server as a search strategy. When the search() method is invoked against the Product class, the method searchResult() is specified as the handler for any successful results, while the method error() is used to handle any errors.

Next, the event handler method showDetails() is defined. This method will be invoked when either the edit or view buttons are clicked. To properly determine which button has been clicked, we specify an argument to the method, obj. As we discussed in Chapter 9, the arguments to any component event handlers contain an object. One of the properties of that object is an object named target. The target object has a property label that contains the label of the button that was clicked.

Because we have two different buttons, each using this same method, we start with a conditional statement, determining which button was clicked. This condition will determine whether the details screen is loaded in a read-only or read/write fashion. The variable isEditable is created as a Boolean value to hold either true or false, determining whether the details screen will be editable. Next, the method determines which item from the DataGrid was selected and sets the selected item into a variable named activeProd. Last, the method tells the details_mc movie clip to be visible and populates it using that clip's showDetails() method. The showDetails() method can be seen in the class file for the details_mc clip.

The last few methods are fairly simple. The searchReults() method is a callback, which is invoked when data is returned from the server-side search. This simply takes the data from the server and populates the DataGrid with that data. Next, the error() method acts as an event handler for any errors returned by the server-side search. In this case, we are simply tracing the error message, but before the application is launched, a more robust error handling strategy would be implemented. Last, the showHidden() method is defined. This method is responsible for hiding or showing the DataGrid and its associated buttons. It takes a single Boolean argument and uses that to set the _visible property of the DataGrid and Buttons.

Next, we explore details_mc and the class associated with it, ProductDetails. This can be seen in Listing 16.18.

LISTING 16.18 *ProductDetails* Is The Class Associated with the *details_mc* Clip in the findProduct
Movie

```
class ProductDetail extends ApplicationView{
      var name:mx.controls.TextInput;
      var pub:mx.controls.TextInput;
      var issues:mx.controls.TextInput;
      var price:mx.controls.TextInput;
      var desc:mx.controls.TextArea;
      var update:mx.controls.Button;
      var prod:Product;

      function postInit(){
            super.postInit();
            update.addEventListener("click",updateProd);
      }
      function showDetails(activeProduct:Object, editable:Boolean){
            this.prod = Product(activeProduct);
            name.text = activeProduct.name;
            pub.text = activeProduct.publisher;
            issues.text = activeProduct.issues;
            price.text = activeProduct.price;
            desc.text = activeProduct.desc
            this.isEditable(editable);
      }
      function isEditable(bool:Boolean){
            name.editable = bool;
            pub.editable = bool;
            issues.editable = bool;
            price.editable = bool;
            desc.editable = bool;
            if(bool){
                  update.label = "Update";
            } else {
                  update.label = "Return";
            }
      }
      function updateProd(){
            trace(name.text);
            prod.update(name.text, pub.text, price.text, desc.text,
issues.text, updateResult, updateStatus);



      }
      function updateResult(){
this._parent._parent.products_dg.replaceItemAt(this._parent._parent.
products_dg.selectedIndex,prod);
```

continues

LISTING 16.17   Continued

```
            this._parent._visible=false;
    }

    function updateStatus(status){
            trace(status.description);
    }
}
```

This class follows the same structure as the `View` classes we have already defined. It begins by extending the `ApplicationView` class. Next, each visual object is declared as properties. In this class, we have four `TextInput` components (we are using TextInputs rather than TextFields for the ease of their editable property), one `TextArea`, and one `Button`. One more property is also defined, `prod`, which will hold the active product.

Next, the `postInit()` method is defined. Other than the call to `super.postInit()`, this method assigns the click handler for the Button. This method is followed by the definition for the `showDetails()` method. In Listing 16.16, we used `prodDetails_mc.showDetails()` to pass the selected product from the `DataGrid` to the details clip. This is the method that received that message. It takes two arguments, `activeProd` and `editable`. First, we cast `activeProd` into a member of the `Product` class and store that in the class property `prod`. Next, the properties of the `activeProd` are used to populate the `TextInput` fields. Finally, the `editable` property is passed on to the `isEditable()` method.

The `isEditable()` method is defined next. This method takes a single argument, `bool`, which will contain a true or false value, and uses that to set the `editable` property of the four `TextInput` and one `TextArea` components. A conditional statement also is used to set the label on the `Button` to either `Update` or `Return`. Regardless of what the label property of the button says, the event handler remains the same.

Next, the `updateProd()` method is defined. This method acts as the event handler for the button. When invoked, it checks the label of the button that was pressed (just like the `showDetails()` method from the `FindProduct` class did). If the label reads `Update`, the method calls the `update()` method of the `prod` object and passes the new values from the `TextInput` components. It also passes a result and status method. If the label is not `Update`, the details screen is simply hidden again, returning the user to the search screen.

The final two methods of the class act as the result and status handler for the update() web service call. If the call returns without error, the updateResult() method will update the DataGrid on the search screen with the updated data and hide the details screen. If there are errors, the updateStatus() method will trace the error message.

The Create Offer Screen

Following the use cases, the next logical screens to work on are the screens relating to an offer. Figure 16.18 shows an Offer creation interface. This interface consists of a combo box that will be populated with products; two TextInput components to allow input for the number of issues and the price; a check box, indicating whether the offer is yet active; and an insert button.

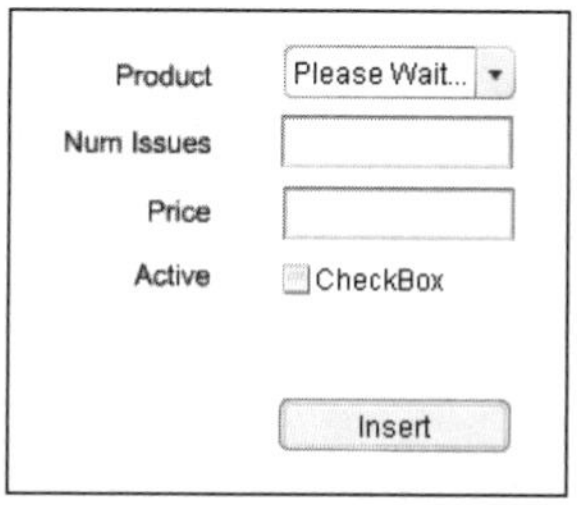

FIGURE 16.18   The Offer creation interface.

These elements are combined into a movie clip, which will be associated with a class file containing all the logic for this screen. This class, CreateOffer, can be seen in Listing 16.19.

LISTING 16.19   The *CreateOffer* class Is Associated with the Movie Clip in the Create Offer Interface

```
class CreateOffer extends ApplicationView{
        var prod_cb:mx.controls.ComboBox;
        var numIssues:mx.controls.TextInput;
        var price:mx.controls.TextInput;
        var active:mx.controls.CheckBox;
        var insert_pb:mx.controls.Button;
        var productDAO:DataAccess;
        var prodArray:Array = new Array();

        function postInit(){
            super.postInit();
            insert_pb.addEventListener("click",makeOffer);
```

continues

LISTING **16.19**   Continued

```
                    productDAO = new  DataAccess("http://localhost:8500/
                    ➥oopas2/components/product.cfc?wsdl");

productDAO.accessRemote("getAll",null,getAllResult,commError);
            }

        function getAllResult(res){
                var num:Number = res.length;
                trace(this);
                trace(_parent);
                trace(_parent._parent);
                prod_cb.removeAll();
                for (var i:Number=0;i<num;i++){
                        // build product array
                        prodArray[i] = new Product(res[i].NAME,
➥res[i].PUBLISHER, res[i].SINGLEISSUEPRICE, res[i].DESCRIPTION,
➥res[i].ISSUESPERYEAR)
                        // add product to combo box
_parent.prod_cb.addItem(res[i].NAME,res[i].PRODUCTID);
                    }
            }
        function makeOffer(){
                var offer:Offer = new Offer(
➥_parent.prodArray[_parent.prod_cb.selectedIndex],
➥_parent.numIssues.text, _parent.price.text, _parent.active.selected);
                offer.insert(makeOfferResult, commError);

            }

        function makeOfferResult(res){
                trace("offer inserted");
            }

        function commError(status){
                trace(status.description);
            }
}
```

By now, the structure of the `View` classes should be very familiar. `CreateOffer` begins in the same way, declaring the classes properties, both those that are visual objects and those that are data properties. The properties representing visual objects in this class are a `ComboBox`, two `TextInput`s, a `CheckBox`, and a `Button`. Two other properties are also declared: `prodArray`, which will hold an array of products, and `productDAO`, which will be an instance of the `DataAccess` class.

Next, the `postInit()` method is declared. An event handler is declared for the push button here. Also implemented in this method is the creation of a `DataAccess` instance. As we are not already working with an instance of the `Product` class, we need some way to be able to retrieve all the products from the server, so a new `DataAccess` instance is added to this class as a property named `productDAO`. In the `postInit()` method, `productDAO` is initialized with the URL of the `Product` web service, and the `accessRemote()` method is used to retrieve all products. Results are routed to a callback method named `getAllResult()`, while any errors are routed through a method named `commError()`.

The next method is `getAllResult()`, which acts as the callback for results from the call to the server to retrieve all products. This method begins by clearing everything from the products combo box. Next, it loops over the results and makes an instance of the `Product` class for each item in the results. These instances are stored in the `prodArray` property. Still in the loop, each product is added to the combo box, using the item's name as the label and the entire object as the underlying data.

The `makeOffer()` method is defined next. This method is the callback for the click event on the button. When clicked, it creates a new `Offer` object from the user's input in the components, and it uses the `insert()` method of the `Offer` class to persist the new offer to the server.

Next, the `makeOfferResult()` method is defined to act as a call back for the server-side call to insert an offer. For now, the new `offerID` returned to the callback is traced; however, before going to production, this information would be displayed to the user in a more friendly fashion.

Finally, the `commError()` method is defined to handle any communications errors between the screen and the server.

The Remaining Screens

Following the model we have used for the movie clips so far (createProduct.fla, findProduct.fla, and createOffer.fla), we can easily implement the remaining use cases detailed earlier. Each screen starts with a visual layout that is converted to a movie clip, and then a class is associated with that clip.

Each class needs to begin by extending the `ApplicationView` class. Next, we need to declare all the visual objects contained in the movie clip, as well as any other properties the clip will need. Next, a `postInit()` method needs to be defined, which will associate any event handlers with visual objects, as well as establish any commands that we want to run as soon as the visual objects are set on the Stage. It is important to remember that the first line of the `postInit()` method should be `super.postInit()` so that the `onEnterFrame()` event handler only executes once. If we forget to add this, the `postInit()` method will fire at the frame rate of the movie (usually 12 times a second), which could have undesirable effects.

The final steps for each `View` class is to build any specific methods needed by the class. Table 16.3 shows the remaining classes to be built and the properties and methods of each class.

TABLE 16.3   Remaining Classes

CLASS	PROPERTIES	METHODS
FindOffer	prodArray:Array	findProd()
	prod_cb:mx.controls.ComboBox	searchResult()
	numIssues:mx.controls.TextInput	getAllOfferResult()
	price:mx.controls.TextInput	getProdResult()
	active:mx.controls.CheckBox	
	insert_pb:mx.controls.Button	commError()
	productDAO:DataAccess	showHidden()
	products_dg:mx.controls.DataGrid	showProdDetails()
	view_pb:mx.controls.Button	
	edit_pb:mx.controls.Button	
	details_mc:MovieClip	
	activeOffer:Offer	
OfferDetails	prod_cb:mx.controls.ComboBox	showDetails()
	numIssues:mx.controls.TextInput	isEditable()
	price:mx.controls.TextInput	updateOffer()
	active:mx.controls.CheckBox	
	desc:mx.controls.TextArea	
	update:mx.controls.Button	
CustomerSearch	firstName:TextField	findCustomer()
	lastName:TextField	findCustResult()
	street:TextField	insertCustomer()
	city:TextField	insertCustResult()
	state:mx.controls.ComboBox	showDetails()

	zipcode:TextField	addSub()
	areaCode:TextField	commError()
	phoneNum:TextField	
	stateArray:Array	
	search:mx.controls.Button	
	custResults:mx.controls.DataGrid	
	edit:mx.controls.Button	
	view:mx.controls.Button	
	addSub:mx.controls.Button	
Login	user:mx.controls.TextInput	authenticate()
	pass:mx.controls.TextInput	authenticateResult()
	login_pb:mx.controls.Button	commError
CreateSubscription	activeCustomer:Customer	createSub()
	prodArray:Array	getProd()
	prod_cb:mx.controls.ComboBox	getProdResult()
	offerArray:Array;	getOffer()
	offer_cb:mx.controls.ComboBox	getOfferResult()
	street:TextField	showVerification()
	city:TextField	commit()
	state:mx.controls.ComboBox	cancel()
	stateArray:Array	
	zipCode:TextField	
	cancel:mx.controls.Button	
	submit:mx.controls.Button	
FindSubscription	customer:mx.controls.TextInput	search()
	prod_cb:mx.controls.ComboBox	searchResult()
	offer_cb:mx.controls.ComboBox	getProd()
	prodArray:Array	getProdResult()
	offerArray:Array	getOffer()
	search_pb:mx.controls.Button	getOfferResult()
	view_pb:mx.controls.Button	viewSub()

The complete code for the classes in Table 16.3, as well as the other classes from this chapter, can be found on the book's website at www.oopas2.com.

Adapting to Changes

In addition to meeting the needs of XYZ Subscriptions, this newly designed and implemented system has the flexibility to adapt to future changes. In this final section, we look at a few potential requests that may be made of the system and discuss how these can be implemented.

System Auditing

With minimal impact on the system, you can add a new role of user to allow for monitoring and auditing of CCRs. With this addition, XYZ Subscriptions can determine how effective various CCRs are and help those who are less effective become better at their jobs. One fundamental way in which effectiveness can be measured for the CCRs is by measuring the average time needed from beginning of a call until completion of the customer's transaction.

To implement this auditing, a new class will need to be added. The new class, `Transaction`, will associate an employee (an instance of the `Employee` class) with a subscription. Also included in a transaction will be a date/time stamp and a number indicating the length (in seconds) of the call. No change will need to be made to the user interface for creating a subscription. What will need to change is the ActionScript 2.0 code on the Subscription creation screen. Rather than directly creating a subscription, the code will instead delegate to the new `Transaction` class and allow the subscription to be created as part of the process of capturing the transaction.

The last change required to implement the auditing will be a new user interface. This new interface call allows auditors to find, view, and report on transactions within the system. The core infrastructure this system will use is already in place, so implementing this change should not be a painful task.

Public Website

Another change that may be requested of the system is the ability to add a public web interface to allow customers to order their own subscriptions over the Web without needing to call the call center. This enhancement will be simple to implement. You need only add a new role to the system that will represent a public website customer. Next, the `Customer` class will need to be modified to allow for a customer to choose a username and password so that he or she can be authenticated to the system. Last, the Create customer and Create subscription screens will need to be made available to the public website.

Summary

Throughout this chapter, the design and implementation of a call center application have been discussed in depth. By following the principles of object-oriented design, as they have been presented throughout the book, the process to plan, design, implement, and maintain our call center application was greatly simplified. Those who traditionally bypass the planning and design stages to rush into coding might find the process described earlier to be very design heavy. However, experience has shown that the extra time spent planning and designing the application will be saved many times over in the implementation and maintenance of it.

Key among the object-oriented design principles followed in planning, designing, and implementing this application was the iterative process. By breaking the application into many small parts, we were able to start with the simplest pieces of the application and build those out. Then we were able to build upon what was already built. When necessary, we would refactor the previously built classes to adapt to the requirements for other classes. This approach allows us to rapidly design the application and to catch items that need to change and to do so early in the process, when change is the easiest and cheapest.

After all the core classes for the system were designed, they were pulled together into Flash movies, where the visual aspects were drawn on the Stage; the code lived in class files associated with the movie clips.

In Chapter 17, "Debugging and Tuning the Application," we will examine how to debug and enhance performance of this application.

CHAPTER 17

DEBUGGING AND TUNING THE APPLICATION

Debugging and tuning an application has always been one of the most frustrating aspects of Flash development. Thankfully, ActionScript 2.0 now displays detailed error messages explaining exactly what is wrong, which goes a long way to helping debug applications. If we as developers remember to type all of our Objects and Functions, Flash will also perform type checking which will display many more error messages than in earlier versions of Flash. Just by using ActionScript 2.0, debugging an application becomes much easier because much more detailed error messages are displayed to the developer.

In this unit, we will explore how to improve on the debugging capabilities of ActionScript. We will examine the usefulness of the `trace` statement which is still one of the most important tools in Flash debugging. However, one of the most frustrating aspects of using the `trace` statement is the fact that it can be difficult to view complex data structures. For example, if we view an Array of Objects using the native trace function in Flash, we often just see `[Object Object]` and Flash does not display the data structure, as shown in Figure 17.1.

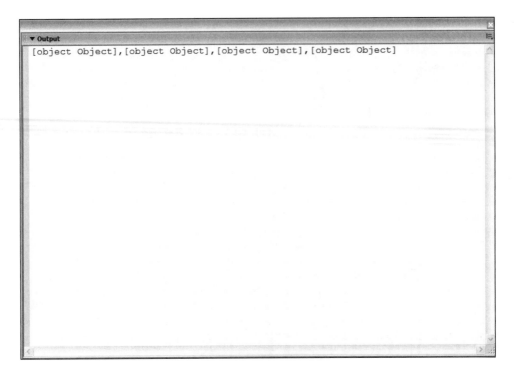

FIGURE 17.1   Viewing a complex data structure, an Array of Objects with the trace function.

To remedy this, we will greatly improve the trace functionality and build a class that will dump out complex data structures and display these to the Flash developer because that functionality is not native to Macromedia Flash MX 2004. This class will be invaluable in debugging any application that uses complex data. In addition, ActionScript 2.0 offers new exception-handling capabilities that make finding specific errors in our code much easier. We will explore the exception handling and the new ActionScript 2.0 commands `try`, `catch`, `finally`, and `throw`.

Using DataTyping

In order for error handling to work in ActionScript 2.0, it is essential that we specify the data type (or the class) of all Objects, including visual Objects, at the beginning of the class file or at the top of the timeline code:

```
var myArray :Array = new Array();
var myObject :Object = new Object();
var myColor :Color = new Color();
var myCombo :mx.control.ComboBox;
var myMovieClip :MovieClip;
```

It is also important to specify what type of data a function returns:

```
function getArray () :Array {
    return myArray;
}
```

Specifying a data type causes ActionScript 2.0 to perform type checking and display detailed error messages to the developer which greatly helps with debugging.

If a function does not return any data, we should type that function as Void:

```
function setArray (passedArray :Array) :Void {
    this.myArray = passedArray;
}
```

> **NOTE**
>
> ActionScript 2.0 will allow you to declare an Object or Function without specifying a data type. However, before compiling your code, in order to receive the most verbose error messages possible, it is a best practice to make sure that all Objects and Functions have a data type specified. This will go a long way to making the debugging process easier.

Using the *Trace* Function

The trace function is invaluable in debugging Flash applications, and it can be extremely useful for debugging applications that have a heavy server-side component. The trace function can display all types of data to the user.

When the trace statement is used with a variable or even with a simple Array, Flash will display the contents of the variable or the simple Array. Consider the following code, as displayed in Figure 17.2:

```
var magTypesArray :Array = new Array();
magTypesArray[0] = "News"
magTypesArray[1] = "Technology";
trace (magTypesArray);
```

FIGURE 17.2   Using the `trace` statement with a simple Array.

This is not the most descriptive message we could receive, but it is usable. It would be nice if it told us at what index each item was or even just that this particular Object was an Array.

The `trace` statement will also display the path of a movie clip Object, or an Object that inherits from the movie clip class. Consider a combo box on the Stage with an instance name of `myCombo`. Figure 17.3 shows what happens when a `trace` function is performed on the instance name.

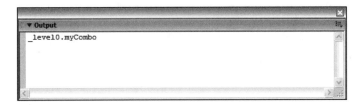

FIGURE 17.3   Using the `trace` function with a movie clip or component.

The `trace` function will also display all properties of Objects that are an instance of the `LoadVars` class. The `trace` function will even display the property names and the ampersands which is exactly how the information is stored in the `LoadVars` Object. The data needs to be retrieved from the server using ampersands. An example `LoadVars` Object is shown in the following code:

```
var myVariables :LoadVars = new LoadVars();
myVariables.employeeName = "Jeff";
myVariables.employeeAddress = "NY";
myVariables.employeeID = 1;

trace (myVariables);
```

Figure 17.4 shows the result of the preceding code.

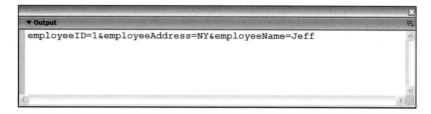

FIGURE 17.4 Using the `trace` Action with a `loadVars` Object.

Consider the following XML:

```
<?xml version="1.0" encoding="UTF-8"?>
<employees>
<employee name="James">
<description>Author</description>
</employee>
<employee name="Robin">
<description>Author</description>
</employee>
<employee name="Jeff">
<description>Author</description>
</employee>
</employees>
```

The `trace` function will also dump out the contents of any ActionScript XML Object once the XML has been loaded in. This allows us to immediately see the XML data structure, as shown in the following code:

```
var myXml :XML = new XML();
myXml.load ("http://localhost/myTrips.xml");
myXml.onLoad = function () :Void
{
trace (myXML);
}
```

The preceding code results in the following in Figure 17.5.

FIGURE 17.5   Using the `trace` statement to display the contents of an XML Object.

One limitation of the `trace` function is that it does not display useful information when an Object from the `Object` class is traced. Consider the following code:

```
var newsWeek :Object = new Object();
newsWeek.idNo =  1;
newsWeek.productName = "Newsweek";
newsWeek.productType = "News";
newsWeek.productDescription = "America's source for current events and
the latest in what's happening";
trace (newsWeek);
```

Figure 17.6 shows what is displayed, which is not the most useful information.

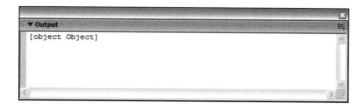

FIGURE 17.6   [Object Object] appears whenever an Object is traced,
which can making debugging data structures difficult.

In order to debug the application and be sure that all of the data is present, we
need to see all the properties of the Object instance. The [Object Object]
displayed in the figure is of very little use to us, and does not assist in
debugging.

The [Object Object] output gets even worse when we deal with complex
data structures. If we have many Objects inside an Array, we will simply get the
[Object Object] output and wonder what properties are actually contained
in the Object. Consider the following code:

```
var newsWeek :Object = new Object();
newsWeek.idNo =   1;
newsWeek.productName = "Newsweek";
newsWeek.productType = "News";
newsWeek.productDescription = "America's source for current events and
the latest in what's happening";

var time :Object = new Object();
time.idNo =   2;
time.productName = "Time";
time.productType = "News";
time.productDescription = "Simply the best on indepth analysis of
today's current events";

var magArray :Array = new Array;
magArray[0]  = newsWeek;
magArray[1]  = time;
trace(magArray)
```

When we use the `trace` function with the Array of Objects, the following screen in Figure 17.7 is displayed, which is not too useful for the developer:

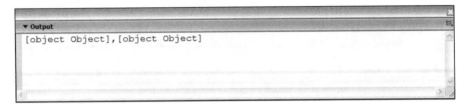

FIGURE 17.7   Using the `trace` command with an Array of Objects.

The `trace` command will display some data structures, such as Arrays, XML Objects, `LoadVars` Objects, and variables but it does not display the contents of Object instances. If we have an Array inside of an Object, or an XML Object inside of an Object, or any combination of factors, the `trace` command will simply display the ubiquitous `[Object Object]`, which is of very little use to developers. Therefore, to debug the application, we need to build a better way to dump complex data structures. In the next section, we will build a class that will be used strictly for debugging and that will dump out complex data structures.

Building a *Dump* Class

At this point, Macromedia Flash MX 2004 does not have a simple way to display complex data structures to the developer in ActionScript itself, especially if we build our application like the call center application, using custom classes. If we return an Array of Objects or an Array embedded within an Object or any complex data structures, it can be very difficult to ascertain what is inside by simply using `trace` statements within our code.

We are going to build a class that will "dump" out any complex data structure that we pass to it. Whether we have an Array of Objects, an Object with Arrays inside, or an Object with Objects inside, the `Dump` class will display the contents to the developer.

The Dump class will focus on dealing with complex hierarchical data structures that would likely be returned from Web Services, Flash Remoting, Extensible Markup Language (XML), or other server-side solutions. Examples of these data structures include arrays, Objects within arrays, arrays within Objects, and so on.

Building and Structuring the *Dump* Class

In this section, we build a custom Dump class that will display complex data structures to the developer, to facilitate debugging of the application. First we will define the class, then interrogate the data structure that is passed to it and apply the appropriate ActionScript to display the structure to the developer. Finally, we will utilize the programming principle of recursion in case an Object is within an Object or an Array is within an Array, to produce clear, concise code.

1. To build the Dump class, define the Dump class and the constructor in an ActionScript (AS) file with the name of Dump:

```
class Dump {

    function Dump() {}
}
```

The class will contain one static method, dumpThis. This method will be static because this class is a debugging tool and there is no reason to waste client resources with the instantiation of another Object each time we want to display the contents of a data structure. It also requires less code for the developer. If we define dumpThis as a static method, we can call it simply by referencing the name of the class:

```
Dump.dumpThis();
```

The dumpThis method will take any data structure passed to it and display the contents to the developer. The dumpThis method will interpret the data passed to it—for example, decide whether the data structure is an Object or an Array. The class will then loop over an Object, Array, or whatever data structure we pass to it and display the contents to the developer.

We will write the dumpThis method so that it is able to accept *any* data structure—for example, an Array of Objects, an Array of Arrays, an Object of Arrays, and so on. Add the static method dumpThis to your Dump class so the code appears as shown here:

```
class Dump {

    function Dump() {}

static  function dumpThis () {
}}
```

2. Build the dumpThis method. We will need to interrogate the data structure that the developer has passed to the Dump class. To do this we will use the instanceof operator. The instanceof operator programmatically determines the class that an Object we are passing in belongs to:

```
function dumpThis (theObject :Object) {
if (theObject instanceof Array) {
    trace ("Array:");
}
```

If theObject is an instance of the Array class, the if statement will return true. Remember that every class in ActionScript descends from the Object class so we can pass in the parameter as an Object. As we know, all Objects in Flash inherit from the Object class. However, we can still use Object as a condition and instanceof will only return true if the Object passed in actually belongs to the Object class and does not just inherit from it. This is perfect for our dumpThis method because we need to determine if the Object is an instance of the Array class or the Object class so we can call the appropriate looping convention, either a for loop to loop through an Array or a for-in loop to loop through an Object.

3. Add the following ActionScript so that the dumpThis method will accept an Object as a parameter. Remember that all functions in ActionScript 2.0 should be typed. This function will not actually return anything, so be sure to type the function as Void. Instead of returning the output, we will utilize the trace function within the method. Your dumpThis method should now look like this:

```
static function dumpThis (theObject:Object):Void {}
```

Remember that all classes inherit from the Object class so if we type the parameter itself to an Object, we can pass in any class, including an Array. Function parameters do not differentiate like `instanceof` does.

4. Add the conditional logic that will test to see if the Object passed in is an instance of the `Array` class. Add the code to the method and ensure that your `dumpThis` method looks like this:

```
Static function dumpThis (theObject:Object):Void {
        if (theObject instanceof Array) {
           //code to loop through an Array
      }
}
```

5. Add the conditional logic that will test to see if the Object passed in is an instance of the `Object` class. Add the following code to the `dumpThis` method and be sure the complete `dumpThis` method looks as shown:

```
static function dumpThis (theObject:Object):Void {
        if (theObject instanceof Array) {
           //code to loop through an Array
      }
                else if (theObject instanceof Object) {
                   //code to loop through an Object
}
}
```

6. The `trace` function will trace out movie clips, strings, `loadVars` Objects, and XML Objects as well as other data types. Let's use the trace function to trace the passed data structure if it is neither an Array or an Object and the following `else` statement to the `dumpThis` method using the `else` operator:

```
static function dumpThis (theObject:Object):Void {
        if (theObject instanceof Array) {
           //code to loop through an Array
        }
                else if (theObject instanceof Object) {
                   //code to loop through an Object
          }
          else {
           trace (theObject);
          }
}
```

7. Write the ActionScript that will actually dump out the contents of an Array passed in. The easiest way to loop through an Array is to use a for-in loop. We are going to loop through the Array that is passed to the dumpThis method by creating a variable that is equal to the length of the Array and then using that variable as the iterant for the loop. We can use methods and properties of the Array class because we have already used conditional logic to determine that the Object passed in is in fact an instance of the Array class.

It is a good idea to utilize recursion here and call dumpThis again in case it encounters another instance of the Array or Object class. If this happens, it will simply call the dumpThis method again and dump out the Object or Array it encounters. By utilizing recursion, we can handle any complex data structure that the developer will pass to the method, and all we have to do is call the dumpThis method again.

> **NOTE**
>
> Generally, the use of recursion can lead to slower execution of ActionScript but, in this case, it doesn't matter too much since we will only be using the Dump class for debugging.

8. Add the following ActionScript, which dumps out the contents of an Array to the dumpThis method within the conditional logic that tests for an Array:

```
class Dump {

    function Dump() {}

        static function dumpThis (theObject:Object):Void {
            if (theObject instanceof Array){
                trace ("Array:");
                var len = theObject.length;
                for (var i=0;i<len;i++) {
                trace ("[" + i + "]");
                dumpThis(theObject[i]);
        }
        }
        else if (theObject instanceof Object) {
            //code to loop through Object
            }
```

```
                              else {
                                      trace (theObject);
                        }

              }
}
```

9. Write the ActionScript that will dump out the contents of an Object if an Object is passed in to the dumpThis method. The easiest way to loop through all of the properties of an Object is to use a for-in loop. The *for-in* loop lets us loop over all the properties of any Object. The syntax is as follows:

```
for (var prop in Object) {
trace (prop)
}
```

This ActionScript returns the names of all the properties in the Object. We cannot access a property value using dot notation if the property name is dynamic. To access the value of named properties inside the loop, we need to use the bracket notation, which evaluates the value of the property name.

If the Object that is passed in to dumpThis is in fact an instance of the Object class, we need to recursively call the dumpObject method, and we will use an else if conditional statement to test. If the parameter is in instance of the Object class, we will call the dumpThis method again, and if not we will simply trace the contents of the property. Add the following code to ensure that the dumpThis method looks as shown here:

```
class Dump {

    function Dump() {};
        static function dumpThis (theObject:Object):Void {
            if (theObject instanceof Array){
                trace ("Array:");
                var len = theObject.length;
                for (var i=0;i<len;i++) {
                trace ("[" + i + "]");
                dumpThis(theObject[i]);
            }
            }
            else if (theObject instanceof Object) {
```

```
//code to loop through Object
trace ("Object:");
for (var prop in theObject){
    if (theObject[prop] instanceof Object) {
        dumpThis(theObject[prop]);
    }else {
        trace (prop+"."+theObject[prop]);
    }
}
} else {
    trace (theObject);
}
}
}
```

10. There is one other type of data structure we need to account for in the dumpThis method, and that is an associative Array. An *associative Array* is in fact an instance of the Array class but acts just like an Object as shown here:

```
var myPublishers = new Array();
myPublishers["publisher1"] = "Pearson";
myPublishers["publisher2"] = "MM Press";
myPublishers["publisher3"] = "New Riders";
```

Associative Arrays have no numerical iterant, and it is not possible to use Array methods or properties on them. This means that our dumpThis method will not be able to handle an associative Array because it will attempt to use a for-in loop to loop through an associative Array as shown here, and this will not work because the associative Array does not have an iterant:

```
static function dumpThis (theObject:Object):Void {
    if (theObject instanceof Array){
        trace ("Array:");
        var len = theObject.length;
        for (var i=0;i<len;i++) {
        trace ("[" + i + "]");
        dumpThis(theObject[i]);
    }
    }
}
```

In order to loop through an associative Array, we need to use a for-in loop. However, in our dumpThis method, we need to test and see if the Array has an iterant. To do this we can use the following conditional logic after we have confirmed that theObject passed in is in fact an instance of the Array class:

```
if (theObject instanceof Array){
if (theObject[0] != null){
    //code to loop through Array
}
}
```

If this returns true, we know we are dealing with a regular Array and can perform the usual for-in loop. However, if theObject[0] is in fact null, this means we are dealing with an associative Array and we must use a for-in loop. Add the code to the Dump class and be sure the final Dump class appears as shown here:

```
class Dump {

    function Dump() {};
        static function dumpThis (theObject:Object):Void {
            if (theObject instanceof Array){
                if (theObject[0] != null) {
                trace ("Array:");
                var len = theObject.length;
                for (var i=0;i<len;i++) {
                trace ("[" + i + "]");
                dumpThis(theObject[i]);
                }
            }else{
                trace("Associative Array:");
                for (var j in theObject) {
                        trace (j+"."+theObject[j]);
                    }

            }
            }
            else if (theObject instanceof Object) {
                //code to loop through Object
                trace ("Object:");
                for (var prop in theObject){
                    if (theObject[prop] instanceof Object) {
                        dumpThis(theObject[prop]);
                    }else {
```

```
                            trace (prop+"."+theObject[prop]);
                    }
                }
            } else {
                trace (theObject);
            }
        }
    }
}
```

The Final Dump Class

We can now view debug complex data structures using the Dump class that we built. This class will allow us to see the data coming back from Remoting, or a web service, or an Array that we build in XML. Once we understand how the data is structured, we can see how it can be utilized in ActionScript 2.0.

1. Create an Array and display the contents to the user. We will use all types of data structures in the Array to ensure that our Dump class works properly. We will use an Array of Objects, a simple string, and an associative Array. Add the following code to build a simple Array of Objects:

```
var newsWeek :Object = new Object();
newsWeek.idNo =  1;
newsWeek.productName = "Newsweek";
newsWeek.productType = "News";
newsWeek.productDescription = "American's source for current events and
the latest in what's happening";

var time :Object = new Object();
time.idNo =  2;
time.productName = "Time";
time.productType = "News";
time.productDescription = "Simply the best on in-depth analysis of
today's current events";

var myPublishers = new Array();
myPublishers["publisher1"] = "vPearson";
myPublishers["publisher2"] = "MM Press";
myPublishers["publisher3"] = "New Riders";

var magArray :Array = new Array;
magArray[0] = newsWeek;
magArray[1] = time;
```

```
magArray[2] = "PC World";
magArray[3] = myPublishers;
```

2. In order to call the Dump class, we simply have to reference the name of the class and the dumpThis method. We can pass any type of complex data structure to the dumpThis method. Add the following code after the magArray has been created.

```
Dump.dumpThis (magArray);
```

This will display a detailed description of the data structure that was passed to the dumpThis Object method. Figure 17.8 shows the results of this code being added.

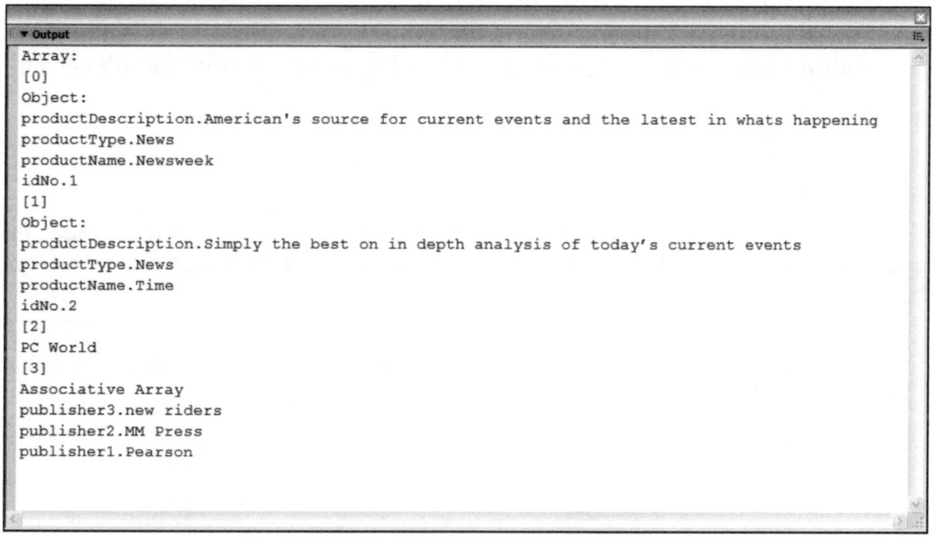

```
▼ Output
Array:
[0]
Object:
productDescription.American's source for current events and the latest in whats happening
productType.News
productName.Newsweek
idNo.1
[1]
Object:
productDescription.Simply the best on in depth analysis of today's current events
productType.News
productName.Time
idNo.2
[2]
PC World
[3]
Associative Array
publisher3.new riders
publisher2.MM Press
publisher1.Pearson
```

FIGURE 17.8   Viewing an Array of Objects with the Dump class.

Exception Handling

An *exception* is an event that occurs during the execution of a program that disrupts the normal flow of instructions. Many kinds of errors can cause exceptions—problems ranging from serious hardware errors, such as a hard disk crash, to simple programming errors, such as trying to access an out-of-bounds Array element. The exception handling and debugging in Macromedia Flash MX 2004 has been greatly improved from previous versions of Flash. With the robust exception handling now available, ActionScript joins the ranks of other languages such as C#, Java, and even JavaScript in its handling of errors that occur at execution.

Robust error handling allows the creation and debugging of complicated applications, such as the call center application created in the previous chapter. In previous versions of ActionScript, there were many *silent errors*, where the Flash Player would fail at execution but no message would be generated to the developer.

In this part of the chapter, you will learn how to avoid this by establishing good coding practices by separating error handling from regular code. ActionScript 2.0 provides three new operators that take care of all exception handling, and *only* exception handling is done with these operators. They are `try`, `catch`, and `finally`. You still have to manually build in all exception handling using the `try/catch/finally` keywords; if not, the player will fail silently.

WARNING

Note that exception handling will not work in the Flash 6 Player; it is only supported in the Flash 7 Player. If you publish for the 6 Player, all `try/catch/throw/finally` statements will be commented out and functionality will be lost.

NOTE

Exception handling is available in either ActionScript 1 or 2, but you must target the Flash 7 Player.

Errors usually prevent the program from continuing while with exceptions, the program can continue although it may be crippled. Exception handling allows us to write our own code to replace the default behavior of the Flash Player. In most cases, of course, the player does nothing when encountering an exception.

Exception handling also allows the developer to control the error information that end users end up seeing; we can easily write custom error messages that will handle situations specific to the call center application. If we write our exception handlers effectively, it will allow the Flash Player to easily recover from exceptions (for example, not loading data properly) and move on to the next task while interrupting the flow of the application as little as possible. We could also easily send the diagnostic information to a database so it can be stored and viewed later. The `try`, `throw`, and `catch` keywords allow us to separate all of our runtime exception handling from our regular code.

Using the *Try*, *Throw*, *Catch*, and *Finally* Keywords

Generally, as we have seen, when the Flash Player encounters an exception nothing at all is displayed to the end user in the Player. For example, consider the following code:

```
var myXML: XML = new XML();
myXml.load ("http://localhost/xml/magazines.xml");
myXMl.onLoad = function ()
{
//code to process XML
}
```

This code will work perfectly if the server is running and the XML file is located in the appropriate directory. However, if the server happens to be down nothing will be displayed to the user in the Flash Player. The developer will see an Unable to load URL message in the development environment. This can make debugging a nightmare—the user may not have Internet access, the server could be down, the directory path could be wrong, or there could be all kinds of issues affecting this at runtime. Without runtime exception handling, neither the end user or the developer would know anything went wrong.

Of course, the application would not function properly, but it would be ideal if the developer could write some code that would allow the application to continue its flow, despite the error. For example, we would want to tell the user that an error has occurred possibly by populating an alert or a text box with a message. It might be possible to load the data from a shared Object instead of the server; we may want to tell the user to check his or her Internet connection. All of this is easily achieved using the new exception handling built into Flash MX 2004. The general structure of exception handling is as follows:

```
try
{
//this is the code that performs an action that could fail
//this code MUST have conditional logic that tests for a failure
//this code MUST have a throw statement that returns an error
}

catch (error)
{
//this code is only called if an error is thrown. Within this code we
could load data from a shared Object, we could display a message to
the user, we could save information to a database.
```

```
}

finally
{
//this code is called every time whether there is an error or not. It
is called after all other code has been executed. For example, onLoad
of an XML Object will be called before this code is executed. It is
useful for cleaning up.
}
```

Of course, it would be possible to handle the error using regular conditional logic but ActionScript 2.0 allows a more robust and flexible way through exception handling. We surround the code with try, catch, and/or finally statements. In this situation, the XML, for whatever reason, may not load properly. With the try keyword and conditional logic, ActionScript will display an error using the throw keyword:

```
try
{
myXml.load ("http://localhost/xml/magazines.xml");
if (//check to see if XML loaded)
{
throw "XML was not loaded";
}
}
```

The throw statement will return any type of Object in Flash from a Boolean to a custom class, as shown here:

```
throw false;
throw new XmlErrorClass();
```

The best way to display an error is to use the new Error class or use a custom class that extends the error class. The class in Macromedia Flash MX 2004 allows error messages to be displayed. It contains a toString method as well as two properties, message and name. For example, in the following code:

```
var myError :Error = new Error("XML could not be loaded"");
```

the message property of the error Object would be "XML cannot be loaded" and the name property would be Error, which is the default value. See Table 17.1.

TABLE 17.1 Properties and Methods of the `Error` Class

NAME	METHOD/PROPERTY	FUNCTION
`toString`	Method	Converts an error message into a string. By default, returns the string `Error`.
`Message`	Property	Contains the error message, which the developer can specify.
`Name`	Property	A string that contains the name of the error Object.

The following code would try to load in the XML file and throw an error if it was unable to do so:

```
var myXml: XML = new XML();
try {
myXml.load ("http://localhost/xml/magazines.xml"); //attempt to load
the XML
if (//code to check if XML loaded)
        {
            throw new Error ("Could not load XML");
        }
}
```

A best practice is to create custom classes for each type of error that could be thrown. For example, in the previous case, it may be useful to create a custom class that indicates whether or not XML has been successfully loaded, in order to better manage types of exceptions.

```
class XmlLoadError extends Error
{
    var message :String;

    function XmlLoadError ()
    {
        this.message = "XML could not be loaded";
    }

    public function getError()
    {
        return this.message;
    }
}
```

The exception handling would now look like this:

```
var myXml: XML = new XML();
try {
myXml.load ("http://localhost/xml/magazines.xml"); //attempt to load
the XML
if (//code to check if XML loaded) //XML could not be loaded
        {
                var magazineLoadError :XmlLoadError = new XmlLoadError();
                throw XmlLoadError.getError();
        }
}
```

Our exception handling is not complete yet. In fact, if you compile the previous-ly listed code, Flash will generate an error. A try statement must be followed by either a finally statement or a catch statement. Once the throw keyword has been executed (for example, an exception has been caught), control is automati-cally passed to the catch statement. It is important to note that the rest of the code in the try block will not be executed so it's important to surround only related code with try statements. Again, the catch statement is only called if an exception is thrown. Each try block can only have one catch block.

> **NOTE**
>
> You can have as many try blocks as you like nested within each other, but each try block can only have one catch block.

The error message from the appropriate try block is passed to the catch state-ment as a parameter. The catch statement is where we would notify the user that an error occurred, possibly by populating a text box or alert component. In the catch statement, we may load in XML from a shared Object, or ask the user to check his or her Internet connection.

We can also define a finally handler. The finally handler will always exe-cute whether or not an error is actually thrown, so that limits its use for actual-ly catching errors or performing alternative actions. However, the finally handler can be very useful for performing cleanup actions such as deleting Objects because it is executed after the catch and try statements.

In the following step sequence, we use the try/catch/finally statements for simple form validation.

1. Create a simple form with two text area components: a push button and a label component. Use the component inspector so the label of the push button is `submit` and the text of the label component is `user`. Arrange the components so.they look like Figure 17.9.

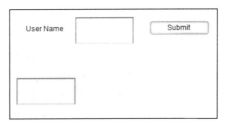

FIGURE 17.9   UI of a simple Flash form.

2. Assign the top text area component an instance name of `user_txt`. Assign the bottom text area component an instance name of `message`. Assign the push button an instance name of `submit _pb`.

3. Add a `click` listener to the push button by adding the following code:

```
var clickObj :Object = new Object;
clickObj.click = function (){

    }

submit_pb.addEventListener ("click", clickObj);
```

4. Within the `click` method of the `clickObj` Object, add the following try/catch statement to test for form validation. Ensure that the code appears as shown here:

```
var clickObj :Object = new Object;

clickObj.click = function (){

try
{
    if (user_txt.length < 1 )
{
        throw new Error ("User field must be populated");
}
}

catch (e)
{
```

```
        message.text = e;
}
}
```

```
submit_pb.addEventListener ("click", clickObj);
```

5. Test the movie. Note that if you leave the user field blank, the error message will appear in the message text area component. If the user field is populated, no error occurs.

6. Within the `click` method of the `clickObj` Object, add a `finally` statement that will trace the contents of the message field. This will display the error message; because it displays the error message, it means that the `finally` statement has been executed after the `catch` statement. This makes `finally` extremely useful for performing actions that must be done each time whether or not an error occurs. Be sure the `click` method appears:

```
var clickObj :Object = new Object;
clickObj.click = function () {

try
{
if (user_txt.length < 1 )
{
throw new Error ("User field must be populated");
}
}

catch (e)
{
message.text = e;
}
finally {
    trace (message.text);
}
}
```

```
submit_pb.addEventListener ("click", clickObj);
```

Using Error Handling in Functions

We could surround a group of functions with a `try` statement and if any one of those functions generated an exception, we could handle it in the `catch` statement. In the example shown next, if the user left any of the fields blank, ActionScript would display the appropriate error message to the user:

```
function checkUser()
{
    if (user.length <1 )
{
      throw new Error ("User field must be populated");
}
}

function checkAddress () {
    if (address.length <1 ) {
      throw new Error ("Address field must be populated");
}
}

function checkState () {
    if (state.length < 1) {
      throw new Error ("State field must be populated");
}
}


try
{
checkUser();
checkAddress();

checkState();

}

catch (e)
{
message.text = e;
}
```

This is an example of *bubbling up*. If a function does not handle an exception that is thrown by using a catch statement, the function stops executing and the same check is performed on the next outer function. The function calls are *unwound* until a catch handler is found. If no catch handler is ever found, then the entire script stops executing. In this case, a catch handler is found on the main timeline.

Summary

Every language offers tools for debugging, but historically this is one area that ActionScript has fallen short in. ActionScript 2.0 offers much improved exception handling that allows us to easily handle runtime errors and to separate the error handling from the rest of the application.

One of the most important ways that the error handling has been improved is through the use of data typing. By typing all our variables, Objects, and functions in ActionScript, the compiler is able to generate much more detailed error messages. It also enables the compiler to check for any type mismatches and to easily report these to the developer. Because of the improved, verbose error messages in ActionScript, it is now possible to go line by line through any error messages and make the appropriate changes. This was difficult at best in previous versions.

One of the most important parts of debugging an application is actually viewing the data structures used in the application. The trace function is one way of doing this. trace will allow developers to view Arrays, Strings, Numbers, LoadVars Objects, XML Objects, and the path of a movie clip Object. However, trace will not display all the properties of regular Objects. Rather, the developer will simply see the message [Object Object] in the output window. In addition, the trace function will not display an associative Array which can also be common in building data structures. This is a huge limitation in terms of debugging because it is extremely common to use Arrays of Objects, Objects of Arrays, and other data structures with Object or associative Array properties.

To remedy this issue, we built a custom Dump class that will be able to handle any possible data structure that the developer can pass to it. This class uses one static method dumpThis that the developer can pass any data structure to. This method tests the Object passed in, remembering of course that all Objects descend from the Object class. The dumpThis method determines if the Object is an Array, an Object, or an associative Array, and performs the appropriate looping. A for-i loop is used to loop over a standard Array, while a for-in loop is used to loop through an associative Array or an Object.

We also explored the new try, catch, and finally operators available in ActionScript 2.0. These allow us to easily catch runtime errors that we may not have control of during the application development phase. For example, a runtime error could be that XML was not loaded properly because a server is down or simply that a user did not fill out a form properly. By using the try, catch, and finally operators, in conjunction with conditional logic, we can separate the runtime error handling from the rest of our code. Any code that might possibly fail is surrounded by a try statement. If in fact an error does occur at runtime, control is immediately passed to the catch block where we can place the specific code to handle the error. In addition, ActionScript 2.0 has a new Error class that allows us to return, or *throw*, different types of error messages. The finally statement is executed in every case, whether or not an error occurs, and is extremely useful for cleaning up because it is executed after the catch statement if an error occurs. Armed with the new tools that ActionScript 2.0 has provided us, many hours previously spent debugging an application can now be put to better use.

INDEX

Symbols

+ operator, 57

A

access modifiers, 95

accessibility, compoents, 163

accessing external resources, 208

accessRemote(), 265, 356

Action Message Format (AMF), 308

ActionScript, 4-5
  basic syntax, 7
    ActionScript editor, 10
    case sensitivity, 7
    code hinting, 8-9
    datatypes, 9-10
    typing variables, 8
  classes, 11
    class keyword, 12-13
    dynamic attributes, 16
    extends keyword, 15
    getters/setters, 17, 19-21
    linking to visual classes, 16
    public and private attributes, 13-14
    referencing ActionScript files, 12
    static attributes, 15
  components, 162-163
    accessibility, 163
    building applications, 174-180
    Component Inspector, 164
    Schema tab, 167
    SWC files, 163-164
    usability, 163
    visual data binding, 166-170
  connector components, 277-278
  datatypes for methods, 76-77
  developing Flash Communication Server
    MX applications in Flash, 312
  Flash, 333-335
  Flash Communication Server MX, 313
  functions versus methods, 72-74
  improvements to, 4
  publishing Flash Player 6 applications, 5-6
  role of methods, 70-71
  SSAS, 312
  user-defined functions to methods, 74-76

ActionScript editor, 4, 10

ActionScript Messaging Format (AMF),
  248, 272

ActionScript objects, Flash Communication
  Server MX, 315